The Best of
MARY McGRORY

A Half-Century of Washington Commentary

Edited by Phil Gailey

Andrews McMeel
Publishing, LLC
Kansas City

The Best of MARY McGRORY:
A Half-Century of Washington Commentary

06 07 08 09 10 FFG 10 9 8 7 6 5 4 3 2 1

Library of Congress Cataloging-in-Publication Data

McGrory, Mary, 1918-2004
    The best of Mary McGrory: a half-century of Washington
    commentary/edited by Phil Gailey.
        p. cm.
    ISBN-13: 978-0-7407-6071-6
    ISBN-10: 0-7407-6071-8
     I. Gailey, Phil. II. Title.

    PN4874.M483975A25 20006
    814'.54—dc22

                                  2006047616

www.andrewsmcmeel.com

Book Design by Diane Marsh

Contents

Contents

Contents

Contents

Contents

Contents

Mary McGrory, B. 1918
A *Star* Columnist

by Maureen Dowd

first realized that writing a column could be a good gig when I saw all the cute guys clustered around Mary McGrory's desk in the back of the *Washington Star* newsroom, hard-boiled political reporters acting as adoring as Las Vegas chorus boys.

But while my status changed over the decades, as I slowly clambered up from *Star* clerk to *Times* columnist, Mary's status never changed. Maria Gloria, as she signed her handwritten notes in her beloved Italian—she was the last person who loved the U.S. Mail—was always the same bella figura: She Who Must Be Obeyed.

I tried to learn from her. Not about cooking. Her Jell-O Surprise was frightening and her meatloaf worse. And it was impossible to write as she did. It was a truth universally acknowledged, as her idol Jane Austen wrote, that nobody could write with the sense and sensibility, the luminous prose and legendary reporting, of Mary McGrory.

But I emulated her other talents:

Her uncanny ability, even in remote parts of New Hampshire or Ireland, to find some sucker to carry her bags or drive her car.

The way she nobly resisted the passing fad called technology, often writing in longhand when her laptop—or "fiendish little gadget," as she called it—gave her fits.

The way she acted helpless like a barracuda.

From Joe McCarthy to Henry Kissinger to Robert McNamara to Linda Tripp, every public figure learned to beware when Mary started asking confused and innocent-sounding questions, like some Capitol Hill Columbo.

Mary became a star at the *Star* with her courageous coverage of the Army-McCarthy hearings in 1954. It was my dad, Mike Dowd, a D.C. police inspector who was in charge of Senate security for twenty years, who helped Mary get her big break by giving her a front-row seat for the spectacle. "He wanted to help out a nice Irish girl," my brother, a Senate page at the time, remembered.

Mary always got her way—one way or another. When her editor at the *Washington Post*—where she moved after the *Star* folded—told her he did not have an extra pass for her to get into the Clarence Thomas hearings, Mary was displeased. Shortly thereafter, the editor was watching the hearings on TV and suddenly saw Mary being escorted to a front-row seat by the committee chairman, Joe Biden.

Mary loved the *Star* and Rome and rogues and children and losers and underdogs and Jack Kennedy. "He walked like a panther," she told me.

She did not love, as her nephew Brian McGrory, the *Boston Globe* columnist, said, pomposity or self-involvement or bullies or Richard Nixon. She was very proud of being on his enemies' list. She hated blowhards. Once she wanted to get away from John Volpe, who had been in the Nixon cabinet, when he was droning on at her during a party at the Shoreham Hotel. "Hey," she interrupted him finally, "you were the secretary of transportation. Where are the elevators?" And away she went.

Mary treated the powerful and the powerless the same, with what her *Post* editor Bill Hamilton called an exasperated "Good help is hard to get" manner.

When I was a cub reporter at the *Star*, she invited me to one of her A-list Sunday brunches. Only twenty-five, I thought, sashaying up to her apartment in my best outfit, and I have already entered the sanctum sanctorum of Washington politics.

When Mary pointed me toward the blender and told me to make a daiquiri for Teddy Kennedy, I realized I was not there as a guest. At least I was in good company. George Stephanopoulos, a Dick Gephardt staff member, occasionally passed canapés at later parties. Mary's servants had an excellent record of upward mobility.

She also shanghaied me to come swim with the kids from St. Ann's Infant and Maternity Home in Ethel Kennedy's pool at Hickory Hill in McLean, Virginia, on Wednesday afternoons. At the time, I was working in a different suburb in a different state, Rockville, Maryland, and I didn't know how to swim.

But Mary didn't let me weasel out of it. Mangling, intentionally perhaps, my editor's name, she instructed him to give me Wednesday afternoons off. "Yes, Mary," he replied, humbly, gratefully.

Over the years, she would continue to call me with other offers I couldn't refuse. She wanted me to come to Ireland in May 1998. We would cover the peace referendum and have a fun girls' bonding trip, she said. There was no chance to bond, of course. On the train from Dublin to Belfast, after staying up all night on the plane, Mary interviewed everyone at the station, everyone on the train, including the lame woman whom she got to carry her bags, the cabdriver on the way to the hotel, the waitress at the hotel coffee shop, the room-service waiter carrying our tea, and the priest at Sunday Mass.

Another time, in the Clinton years, she telephoned and said in a chirpy voice, "Let's go see Yasser Arafat at the White House and then go shopping!"

Mary continued to call me after she had a stroke in March 2003. You could understand a bit here or there—"casserole" or "Cheney." It broke my heart to hear the words coming out so jumbled, from lips that never uttered a less than perfect sentence.

Once, in a private diary of the *Star*'s final days in 1981, Mary had written, "I do not want anyone to think I have collapsed under calamity."

She never did. She approached life and sickness and death with the same Yankee pluck she developed at Girls' Latin School in Boston. I will continue to emulate Mary and follow the invaluable advice she once gave her nephew Brian at a stuffy Washington party: "Always approach the shrimp bowl like you own it." ■

The Lives They Lived
An end-of-year tradition from the New York Times Magazine
Copyright © 2004 by Maureen Dowd. Reprinted by permission.
—December 26, 2004

Introduction

by Phil Gailey

Over the years I cheerfully carried Mary McGrory's bags on the campaign trail, did sweat labor in her small flower garden, served as bartender at her parties, helped out with the abused kids at St. Ann's Infant and Maternity Home, where she was a volunteer for four decades, and did just about anything else she asked of me. I was never any good at saying no to Mary, which may be why she asked me, in person and in her will, to put together this book.

More than one publishing house pleaded with Mary during her long newspaper career to collect some of her columns between hard covers. Her answer was always the same: She was too busy; a promotion tour would be out of the question—"I faint at the sight of a camera." And besides, she didn't think her columns were all that good, certainly not worth the price of a book.

In a 1978 letter to Edwin Barber of W. W. Norton & Co., Mary expressed her "gravest misgivings about being collected." She explained: "My feeling is I would be exposed as not quite a fraud, but as someone slightly overappreciated. I have always thought that while my copy may look okay beside offerings from people dictating from gas stations during riots on deadline, it would look quite thin on its own—inside hard covers with a price on the jacket. I think it has a sameness, even monotony, and the formula—which I can't quite define, but seems to involve throwing a lot of information around between smart remarks about what it might mean—would show through."

Devoted readers can appreciate her modesty, if not her self-assessment. Toward the end of her life, Mary came around to the idea that maybe her work was worth collecting in a book after all. I kept urging her to get started on the project and even offered to help. "You do it when I'm gone," she would say.

"Why me?" I kept asking. Mary said she trusted me and knew that I wouldn't give short shrift to those columns, her personal favorites, that she feared were underappreciated by her colleagues—elegantly written essays on her struggles as a gardener; on dogs, squirrels, and other critters; on Jane Austen; on the post office; on her ineptitude when it came to operating a laptop computer ("a fiendish gadget"), a Cuisinart, or just about any other device that represented a technological advance, however small; and on a variety of other subjects some would deem beneath a writer of her stature and talent.

Her reputation as a journalist was built on her exquisite commentaries on the Army-McCarthy hearings, the assassination of President Kennedy, the Vietnam War, Watergate, Iran-Contra, the intern sex scandal that almost brought down Bill Clinton's presidency, and other big-bang Washington stories. She was proud of those pieces, but said she got her greatest response from readers when she wrote about the little struggles of everyday life.

Naturally, I included what some will consider a disproportionate number of those columns in this collection, and some of you may fault me for this. But Mary made it my call.

During a newspaper career that spanned almost fifty years, first at the *Washington Star* and then at the *Washington Post*, Mary wrote, by my rough estimate, seven to eight thousand columns. From those I had to choose one hundred or so for this book. Had I just picked columns at random, I would have had a book of great newspaper writing. Going through her columns was like sorting through treasure chests, having to choose among gold, emeralds, and diamonds.

Mary was the first woman to win the Pulitzer Prize for commentary, in 1974 for her columns on Watergate, although she considered her highest honor to be seeing her name on Richard Nixon's "enemies" list. In my opinion, she should have won two other Pulitzers earlier in her career—one for her sidebars on the Army-McCarthy hearings and another for her commentaries on President John F. Kennedy's assassination and funeral. More than four decades later, her Kennedy columns still stand as an example of the finest writing ever to grace the pages of an American newspaper. She wrote:

Of John Fitzgerald Kennedy's funeral it can be said
he would have liked it.

It had that decorum and dash that were in his special style. It was both splendid and spontaneous. It was full of children and princes, of gardeners and governors.

Everyone measured up to New Frontier standards.

This collection, which I think reflects the wit, poetry, and passion she brought to her work, starts with one of Mary's commentaries on the 1954 Army-McCarthy hearings, which brought her to prominence at a time when women did not have an easy path in journalism, and ends with the last column she wrote, "Blossoms and Bombs," which ran in the *Post* on March 16, 2003. Mary hated war as much as she loved springtime in Washington, and in that column, written just before President Bush launched a U.S. military invasion of Iraq, she juxtaposed the drumbeat for war with the budding signs of spring.

She wrote:

The hounds of spring are on winter's traces and so, of course, are the dogs of war. Who will win the race?

The signs of spring are everywhere. Snowdrops bloom where snow was banked just yesterday. City workers have turned in their shovels for flats of pansies to plant around our trees.

The sounds of war grow louder every day.

Shortly after finishing the column, on the eve of the St. Patrick's Day party she hosted each year at her Macomb Street apartment, Mary suffered a stroke that left her unable to read, write, or speak more than one or two coherent sentences at a time. "Worse than death," she managed to say during one attempt at conversation. And for a woman whose life and love were words, I'm sure it was. It was an awkward and heartbreaking time for friends who wanted to stay in touch, by phone or with visits. Mary kept trying to speak and became frustrated when she realized people were unable to understand her. Thirteen months after her stroke, on April 21, 2004, Mary died of a ruptured appendix. She was eighty-five.

In its front-page obituary, the *Washington Post* called Mary "a major figure in twentieth-century American journalism, a writer of lasting influence, exquisite technique, liberal convictions, a contempt for phonies and a love of orphans and delphiniums."

Unlike most Washington columnists, Mary practiced shoe-leather reporting. She was constantly on the move, from congressional hearings and White House briefings to the campaign trail, from courtrooms to news conferences. "I can't do it any other way," she said. "I have to see, I have to hear. I'm primitive, I guess. I don't want anyone else doing my listening or watching for me."

Mary was asked to write a piece for the *Washington Post* newsroom staff directory, on the best preparation for newspaper writing. Study Latin and read poetry, she advised.

She wrote:

> Latin helped me to learn English. In our English class, we diagrammed sentences, another useful exercise. I also advocate poetry reading for clues in distillation. The only thing I know for sure about writing—other than it is difficult—is that in dealing with subjects of heavy emotion, the only way is to write short sentences. I learned that the hardest way, during the six hours I spent trying to write the story of John Kennedy's funeral. Once I chopped my long, soggy sentences in half, it moved.

Mary never forgot her roots. She was Boston Irish, the daughter of Mary Catherine and Edward Patrick McGrory. Mary often spoke of the sacrifice her father made for his family. He was a high school Latin scholar and had a scholarship to go to college. But his father died, and he had to go to work. He never complained. A postal clerk in south Boston for forty years, he was Mary's hero. "He taught my brother and me to recite poetry and to treasure words—and to enjoy the small things of life, like walking and talking and nice dogs and fresh raspberries and blueberries and things like that," she once said.

She graduated from Girls' Latin School in Boston, which had rigorous academic standards that Mary compared to the Marine Corps. "It was basically impossible," she said. "Nothing was good enough." By the time she graduated from Boston's Emmanuel College, Mary had an itch to work for a newspaper. But in those days, a woman's place in newspapers was either writing book reviews or features for the women's section. Mary's first job was as an assistant to the book editor of the *Boston Herald Traveler*. Before long she was writing book reviews that caught the attention of editors in New York and Washington. In 1947, she landed a job as the second book reviewer at the *Evening Star*, at the time

Washington's dominant newspaper. She also wrote occasional dog stories that caused her editors to take notice.

Mary got her big break in 1954 when the *Star*'s executive editor, Newbold Noyes Jr., who had a keen eye for talent, dispatched her to Capitol Hill to help cover the Army-McCarthy hearings, the sensation of the time. He gave her this advice: "Write it like a letter to your favorite aunt."

Her reports sparkled with color and insight and little details that captured the scene or the moment. Army Secretary Robert Stevens, by contrast with Senator Joseph McCarthy, the red-baiting demagogue, looked "about as dangerous as an Eagle Scout leading his first patrol." Roy Cohn, McCarthy's chief counsel, "looks like a boy who has had a letter sent home from school about him, and has come back with his elders to get things straightened out."

Suddenly, Mary was the talk of Washington at a time when women could not even be a member of the National Press Club. By 1958, *Time* magazine called her the "Queen of the Corps." It wrote: "Her technique is all her own. Pert and comely, she sits quietly in meetings and hearing rooms, watching gestures, listening to sounds, painting mental pictures. She writes swiftly and well, turns out some of the most perceptive, pungent copy in Washington."

James "Scotty" Reston of the *New York Times*, who said Mary had a "poet's gift of analogy," tried to hire her away from the *Star*, although, the story goes, he suggested she might have to work the Washington bureau's switchboard part-time. The *Washington Post* pursued Mary for more than twenty years, but she said no thanks. The *Star*, even as its future grew dimmer by the year, was her home and family, and leaving it, even for more money and a bigger platform, was unthinkable.

Mary's devotion to the *Star* was one of the great love stories in American journalism. As a *Star* alumnus, I am often asked what was so special about the place, and I tell people the *Star* was to newspapers what television's 4077 MASH unit was to army hospitals in the Korean War, although the *Star* was for real. It attracted the best reporters and editors. It was tolerant of booze, song, and eccentric characters like slot editor Earl "Tiger Ass" Heap. Hawkeye Pierce would have been at home there, and Klinger, too.

Mary described the *Star* as a "lovely . . . place to work, a garden of eccentrics, wits, and strong wills, where copy boys read the *Iliad* in the original Greek and others were not allowed to take themselves seriously."

The spirit of the *Star* newsroom spilled over into Mary's living room, where she hosted some of the liveliest and most eclectic parties in Washington. She called her group of party regulars the Lower Macomb Street Choral Society, and they kept the joint jumping with Irish ballads, clog dancing, and gospel music. As chairwoman, she ruled the society with an iron hand. The regulars were mostly old friends, newspaper colleagues, congressional aides, and a couple of Salvation Army colonels who sang like angels. She threw into the mix ambassadors, White House aides, and members of Congress. All were expected to perform for their supper, usually Mary's homemade lasagne. If you couldn't sing, play an instrument, dance, read poetry, or tell a good story, you might wind up in the kitchen helping with the dishes or serving after-dinner brandy.

In early 1982, Mary hosted a christening party for our three-month-old son, Daniel O'Neal Gailey, and it was the most unforgettable evening I ever had in Washington. At one point, House Speaker Tip O'Neill cradled the guest of honor in his arms and sang "If You're Irish, Come into the Parlor," accompanied by Reagan aide Michael Deaver on the piano. Later in the evening, my father-in-law, a farmer and school lunch-room cook from Tiger, Georgia, sat in the center of Mary's living room explaining to O'Neill, Deaver, and several U.S. senators how the school lunch program worked at his end of the chow line. It's hard to imagine such a scene at a Washington dinner party, but not at Mary's place, where egos, pretensions, and job titles had to be checked at the door.

Mary, who came to regret that she never married, had another special family—the abused and neglected children at St. Ann's. They were starved for the kind of love and attention they received in Mary's caring arms. The kids had trouble pronouncing her last name until one little girl started calling her "Mary Gloria." Mary melted, of course, and the name stuck. She knew each child's name and history. She read to them and took them to McDonald's. She threw a big Christmas party for the kids, and, in the summer, hauled them to Hickory Hill, Ethel Kennedy's place, for swimming parties. And on those rare occasions when she was on good terms with the president of the United States, she even arranged special White House tours for the children.

When the *Star* folded in 1981, Mary moved her column to the *Post* without missing a beat. But her heart was not part of the deal. It forever belonged to the *Star*. At her funeral, front-row seats at the Shrine of the Most Blessed Sacrament were reserved for old *Star* colleagues, and Mary had asked me to talk about why the *Star* was such a special place in my eulogy.

At the *Post*, Mary went through culture shock. She thought *Post* people took themselves too seriously and suggested they might benefit from celebrating Pulitzer Prizes with a little ale instead of the ceremonial cake. She contrasted the *Post* and the *Star* with two great cities: "The *Star*, disheveled, disorganized, welcoming, mellow, and forgiving was Rome. The *Post*, structured, disdainful, elegant, and demanding, was Paris."

Over the years, however, and especially after her stroke, Mary found that the *Post* was more like Rome than Paris. The Graham family was there for her until the end, as were her colleagues at the *Post*, and especially Tina Toll, her devoted assistant.

One of the most predictable things about Mary was her vacation plans. Every year, in late August or early September, she would spend a week or so in Antrim, New Hampshire, a small village in the Monadnock Mountains, and then she was off to Italy for two weeks, usually to the Plaza Hotel in Rome, where she was treated like royalty. A few years ago, my wife Joyce and I met Mary in Rome for the best vacation we have ever had. Of course, traveling with Mary meant accommodating what one *Post* colleague called her "queenly expectations of deference" in all things. You were expected to make sure she didn't leave her jacket in the backseat of a cab or her purse under the table at a restaurant.

On our first day in Rome that year, Mary managed to lose her American Express card, her passport, and her prescription medicine for high blood pressure. We called American Express to cancel her credit card, and her doctor in Washington phoned a pharmacy in Rome to take care of a prescription refill. The U.S. Embassy worked overtime to replace Mary's passport in less than forty-eight hours. No one minded. After all, you haven't seen Rome unless you were fortunate enough to have seen it with Mary, who spoke the language and loved the people.

Although Washington was her home for more than five decades, Mary chose to be buried in Antrim, in a tree-shaded cemetery on the edge of town. On her modest grave stone is this simple inscription, which she wrote herself: *Mary McGrory—Newspaper Woman and Volunteer.*

That's all she ever wanted to be, and she was the best at both. ■

1

Army-McCarthy
Hearings

Welch Defends One Friend and
Finds He's Made Many—June 10, 1954

Mary McGrory came to prominence as a journalist writing sidebars from the Army-McCarthy hearings. In this column, which ran in the Washington Star *on June 10, 1954, she captures the hearings' most memorable moment, when Joseph Welch, the army counsel, asked a question that drove a stake through the heart of Senator Joseph McCarthy communist witch-hunt.*

M r. Welch came to Washington to defend the army. But he had his finest hour defending a friend.

In lighter moments, Mr. Welch has often said he was here "just to ask a few questions."

And yesterday, he asked one that went to the heart of the matter, even if it no more bore on the issues in the case than the charges which provoked it.

He asked it of Senator McCarthy, in tones of shock and outrage, twice. The question was: "Have you no sense of decency, Senator?"

Senator McCarthy did not answer Mr. Welch. He went rumbling along in his allegations against a member of Mr. Welch's Boston law firm.

The young man's former membership in an organization which the attorney general has sought to brand subversive was known to Mr. Welch. He explained this was the factor that decided him against allowing the young man's participation in the case.

It was a precaution, however, that was taken in vain. Senator

McCarthy, sitting one seat away from Mr. Welch, and gaining momentum with every word, accused Mr. Welch of trying to "foist" the young man on the committee.

During six stormy weeks of the hearings, Mr. Welch has borne Senator McCarthy's personal attacks on him with equanimity and grace, sometimes merely acknowledging them with an interested nod.

But the senator's attack on Mr. Welch's friend brought an end to this silent toleration of McCarthyism. It also brought forth a display of eloquence and indignation that rocked the caucus room.

"Until this moment, Senator," said Mr. Welch, "I think I never really gauged your cruelty or your recklessness."

Acting Chairman Mundt intervened twice during the hearing's most dramatic moments, to say that Mr. Welch had not recommended the young man in question to the committee.

He might as well have saved his breath.

Senator McCarthy roared on. He tried to equate his allegations about Mr. Welch's friend with what he called Mr. Welch's "baiting" of the young chief counsel of the McCarthy Committee, Roy Cohn, who was then on the witness stand.

Mr. Welch and Mr. Cohn had had some barbed exchanges about Mr. Cohn's nightclub activities, but Mr. Welch turned to him with hand outstretched.

"I did you no personal injury, I think, Mr. Cohn?" he asked.

And Mr. Cohn shook his head and said, "No, sir."

Mr. Welch returned to the defense of his absent friend. "Let us not assassinate this lad, further, Senator. You have done enough. Have you no sense of decency, sir, at long last? Have you left no sense of decency?"

Mr. Welch ended by saying he had no further questions of Mr. Cohn. After a moment's silence, the caucus room broke out into its applause—an "audible manifestation" forbidden by the rules. But Mr. Mundt banged his gavel only for a recess.

Mr. Welch, his face working, made his way quickly to the door. A woman there patted his arm and then burst into tears.

Mr. Welch walked down the hall.

The caucus room's greatest wit, he is also its greatest walker. The first day of the hearing—before he and Senator McCarthy had taken each other's measure—he had been observed strolling down the hall, in typical toes-out fashion, with his hands in his pockets, bemusedly observing the would-be spectators crowded behind the velvet ropes in the rotunda.

On another happier day, to the ill-contained wrath of Senator McCarthy, he took another walk. That time, with a troop of reporters and photographers at his heels, he went down the broad staircase to make a telephone call to find out Mr. Stevens's sentiments about cutting off the hearings.

But yesterday, Mr. Welch walked alone. The corporal who carries his briefcase and guides him through the labyrinthine ways of the Capitol and the Pentagon, followed him a little apart. A little group of photographers and reporters stood at a distance.

Finally, with an obvious effort, Mr. Welch, looking for once, every minute of his sixty-three years, went back into the caucus room.

He took his seat, two places away from Senator McCarthy at the end of the committee table. He appeared a sickened and shaken man as he leaned his head on his hand. He listened to Special Counsel Jenkins's jovial direct examination of the senator, who whacked large maps and charts with two pointers. He heard, with no change in his stricken expression, the junior senator from Wisconsin say in his self-styled "hog-caller's voice," that communism had made more converts than Christianity. ■

Kennedys

What We Shall Remember—November 23, 1963

He brought gaiety, glamour, and grace to the American political scene in a measure never known before. That lightsome tread, that debonair touch, that shock of chestnut hair, that beguiling grin, that shattering understatement—these are what we shall remember.

He walked like a prince and he talked like a scholar. His humor brightened the life of the Republic. While striving for his great office, he had often concealed his amusement at the incongruities of life, lest he be thought not only youthful but frivolous as well. When safely ensconced, he saw no reason to hide his wit. It glinted at every press conference. It informed his private utterance. Shown his latest nephew in August, he commented, "He looks like a fine baby—we'll know more later."

One day he strolled onto the porch outside his office and found an old friend admiring the garden. The lawn was a source of unreasoning pride and constant concern to him; the flowers, while he was uncertain of their names, pleased him. He indicated the tangle of petunias and ageratum, and said dryly, "This may go down as the real achievement of this administration."

His public statements were always temperate, always measured. He derided his enemies—he teased his friends. He could be grave, but not for long.

When the ugliness of yesterday has been forgotten, we shall remember him smiling. ∎

A Reporter Recalls the Dash, Glamour, Glitter, Charm—November 23, 1963

He was just home from the Pacific when I first saw him in 1946. He was thin as a match and still yellow from malaria.

But he was blithe and determined and wherever he went he was surrounded by young men who felt with him that the Irish had something more to give to American political life than a last hurrah.

The hard-eyed pros didn't like him much. "Harvard Irish," they scoffed. The backers of the other four contenders for a seat in the House said sourly he would buy his way in with his father's millions.

But his followers, who from the first regarded him as one of themselves—and yet above them—said, "He's class," or, because the word can be either a noun or an adjective in Boston, "He's got class."

He was twenty-nine then, but with his hollow cheeks and tousled hair, he looked years younger. He thought a hat would help as an earnest of maturity, but he never could remember to bring one. One of his aides usually had to give him his own before they rushed into a meeting.

Handsome, graceful, surefooted, he moves around the tenements of Everett and Charlestown, dazzling the housewives with his wide smile, impressing the men with his grasp of the facts, leaving one and all wondering why, with all he had, he should want public office.

Solemn and statistical on the platform, he was, on the ground, casual and gay. "See you soon," he said once, ending an interview. "I have to go down to the firehouse and press a few palms."

He won the House seat and soon challenged Henry Cabot Lodge for his place in the Senate. Always a man for the direct confrontation, he was delighted to have a debate with the incumbent. He came on, composed as a prince of the blood, chestnut thatch carefully brushed, facts straight, voice steady.

"Look at him," breathed the proud Irishman next to me in the excited audience. "He's a thoroughbred."

When he decided to go for the presidency, he went about it with the patience that was so at variance with his restlessness of body and spirit.

The most rational of men, he was intolerant of a lack of political realism. The grinding primaries irritated and tired him.

Once he voiced a melancholy doubt. He had come back late from a fruitless early foray into California where Governor Pat Brown was being both obdurate and coy. He stood on the edge of an airfield, his imperially slim figure outlined in the landing lights and the lights of the aircraft.

"My days are in the yellow leaf," he quoted somberly.

"Why does Hubert do it?" he asked late one night in the corridor of a hotel in Oregon in February 1960. He was referring to Senator Humphrey's bid for the presidency. "He can't make it. I like campaigning, but this is just a waste of time."

In West Virginia, I remember him standing on street-corner platforms before hungry, unemployed miners. "I need your help," said this darling of fortune to those desperate men. They gave it to him.

The morning after his election, I greeted him on the lawn of his father's house in Hyannis Port. He was carrying Caroline piggyback.

Later that same day, I saw him display the only emotion he ever revealed in public. He was claiming the victory. He made a little speech—"not much longer, Jackie," he said to his pregnant wife. His closest aides were clustered around the foot of the platform. Tears stood in his eyes.

When he came to the White House, suddenly everyone saw what the New Frontier was going to mean.

It meant a poet at the inauguration; it meant swooping around Washington, dropping in on delighted and flustered old friends; it meant going to the airport in zero weather without an overcoat; it meant a rocking chair and having the Hickory Hill seminar at the White House when Bobby and Ethel were out of town; it meant fun at presidential press conferences.

It meant dash, glamour, glitter, charm. It meant a new era of enlightenment and verve; it meant authors and actors and poets and Shakespeare in the East Room.

When he made his first trip to Europe in May 1961, he arrived at Orly and was firmly taken in hand by the lordly president of the Republic. Making his way across the field, he spotted the familiar faces of the White House press corps. He waved to us, a low surreptitious, underhanded wave which somehow conveyed his whole situation.

He loved being president. He wanted to bring moderation, balance, flexibility—his own qualities—to it. He told me he thought his cabinet was a more harmonious group than Roosevelt's, a source of pride to him.

The only time I ever heard him brag was about the White House garden.

I saw him last at his last press conference. He was invited to castigate Congress. But this most rational man refused. It was not his style. Instead, he quoted from a poet:

"But westward, look, the land is bright." To the end, he was hoping that reason would prevail. ■

They Were Waiting at the Airport—November 24, 1963

I t was his last airport arrival.

The field was garishly lit, as it had always been, by landing lights and television light. A misty quarter moon was rising over Andrews Air Force Base.

There was a crowd, as always. At the fence were gathered several hundred people, uniformed men of the air force and their families. There was even a camera or two.

There were high officials of the New Frontier. Undersecretary of State Averell Harriman, face gaunt and drawn, stood at the head of a disconsolate line. With him were new Postmaster General Gronouski, HEW Secretary Celebrezze, Undersecretary of Commerce Franklin D. Roosevelt Jr., Supreme Court Justice Arthur Goldberg and his wife.

The leaders of the Senate were there, Majority Leader Mansfield, and his weeping wife, Majority Whip Humphrey of Minnesota, who told of how the president, just before he left for Texas, had told an aide he feared for the life of President Betancourt of Venezuela.

Senator Aiken, Republican of Vermont, who used to counsel a young senator from Massachusetts from the office across the hall on farm legislation, was there and Senator Inouye from Hawaii, and Senator Pell from Rhode Island were with them. Minority Leader Dirksen was trying to tell, above the usual airport racket, of a White House meeting scheduled for seven fifteen.

Off to the side stood aides of Lyndon B. Johnson of Texas, who had been sworn in as president on the plane that was bringing the tragic party home.

Secretary of Defense McNamara was by himself, looking off into the distance. McGeorge Bundy, the president's foreign policy adviser, was carrying a dispatch case under his arm.

Theodore C. Sorensen, the president's young special counsel, looking white-faced and stricken, was unseeing and unhearing in the nightmarish light and noise.

The dean of the diplomatic corps. Ambassador Sevilla-Sacasa of Nicaragua, by habit took his place at the head of a little cluster of diplomats who were milling about uncertainly. There was one tall African, stately in his native robes.

A few minutes after six, an honor guard of six young enlisted men marched smartly forward. A gray navy hearse backed up to face the waiting crowd. A cargo lift, a large rolling platform with a high yellow frame, was rolled into position.

At a few minutes after six, United States Air Force One, all white and blue, landed amid a deafening roar. The back door was flung open. But this time there was no familiar graceful figure, fingering a button of his jacket, waiting to smile, waiting to wave.

Instead the light fell on the gleam of a bronze casket.

And around it, sharply outlined in the yellow frame of the cargo lift, stood the old guard of the dead president.

The light played on the bald head of David Powers, the president's pal, and his first political mentor, who eighteen years ago towed him around the three-decker flats of Everett and Charlestown, when a slender young navy veteran was starting on the glory road.

On the other side of the bronze casket stood Lawrence F. O'Brien, since 1961 the president's congressional liaison man, but in the old days his chief organizer and vote-counter.

Behind him was P. Kenneth O'Donnell, who would have died for him, and who had watched over him every step of the long campaign trail that led to the White House. At the foot of the coffin, white gloves sharp against her black suit, was Evelyn Lincoln, his secretary from the years in the House.

The men picked up their inexpressible burden and placed it on the top of the platform, and it was lowered into the hearse.

Then in the frame stood his wife, Jacqueline, in a rose-colored suit with black facings. By her side was his favorite brother, Robert, the attorney general, who had somehow gotten onto the plane although he never left Washington. He was holding Mrs. Kennedy by the hand.

She was lifted down from the platform and opened the door of the gray hearse and climbed in the back. Bobby followed her.

Several minutes later, the new president walked slowly down the ramp with his wife.

With tears on their faces, the leaderless men of the New Frontier went up to greet him. ■

A Young Widow Brings Meaning to Tragic Chaos
—November 25, 1963

Only one person has managed to pierce the black pall of horror and unreality that has gripped the nation since last Friday.

It is Jacqueline Kennedy, the president's widow.

Mrs. Kennedy has borne herself with the valor of a queen in a Greek tragedy.

Shock alone might have explained her dry-eyed composure. But Mrs. Kennedy has moved with more than the mechanical compliance that sometimes overtakes people in appalling circumstances.

Everything she has done seems to be a conscious effort to give to his death the grandeur that the savagery in Dallas was calculated to rob it of.

It has been as though she were trying to show the world that courtesy and courage did not die in Dallas last Friday, nor the tradition that was personified by her husband, struck down in brutal irrelevance.

She agreed to his burial in Arlington National Cemetery rather than in Boston, so that he would belong to the nation and his death would not in the end have the stamp of a local tragedy.

She has overwhelmed White House aides with her meticulous attention to the melancholy arrangements that have had to be made. She designed herself the memorial cards for his requiem mass. She suggested that she should receive the foreign dignitaries who had come from so far away to pay him last honor.

From the moment she arrived back in Washington, erect and composed, wearing the blood-stained clothes of the infamous day in Dallas, she has imparted meaning and order to the chaos around her.

She has not wanted anything to be lost on the world.

She brought her two children to the Capitol yesterday.

If she wanted them to see, however imperfectly what their father meant, she also dramatized to the world and the evil people in it that a young father had been slain as well as a president.

It was, with the irony that has marked this entire episode, approximately the moment when her husband's suspected killer was being murdered in a Dallas police station.

She took six-year-old Caroline by the hand and led her to the flag-covered bier, knelt and kissed it and returned to her place.

She again came to the Rotunda with her brother-in-law, the attorney general, at nine o'clock in the evening. She looked intently into every face she saw in that throng. She walked down Capitol Hill and stopped to talk to a group of nuns.

The crowd was, as a matter of fact, rewarding her heroism with a heroism of its own. They waited hour after hour in the cold evening. They complained only when interlopers crossed the many intersections between them and the Rotunda.

The line stretched for many blocks and remained long after the rudest calculation proved there was no hope of entry. They waited with good humor and camaraderie. Seven blocks from the Capitol dome stood a young man with a guitar. One of the seven children of a man in his neighborhood carried the guitar case.

Once reminded that the president's favorite song had been "Bill Bailey, Won't You Please Come Home," they sang it through. Then they did "Swing Low, Sweet Chariot."

A young mother, coping with five-year-old twin boys, said she would wait all night to go in.

A bespectacled Negro said simply, "It's the last, least thing I could do for him."

A woman who had just had a foot operation stood clutching a tree on the sidewalk. "I hope I can make it," she gasped, "I wouldn't do this for anyone but President Kennedy."

There were students from Syracuse, a couple from New York, a boy from Toronto, and everywhere the crowd was punctuated with the black and white habits of sisters, out long after their bedtime, poignantly recalling a recent Kennedy quip that while bishops and monsignors were always Republicans, sisters were inevitably Democratic.

Inside, four young sailors performed a last act that was perfectly in the Kennedy style. One by one, they halted before the exact center of the casket, squared their white caps and executed their best salutes for their fallen commander in chief.

It is just what this young woman, hitherto celebrated for her beauty and elegance, has been doing in her own way in these black days. ■

The Funeral Had That Special Kennedy Touch
—November 26, 1963

Of John Fitzgerald Kennedy's funeral it can be said he would have liked it.

It had that decorum and dash that were in his special style. It was both splendid and spontaneous. It was full of children and princes, of gardeners and governors.

Everyone measured up to New Frontier standards.

A million people lined every inch of his last journey. Enough heads of state filed into St. Matthew's Cathedral to change the shape of the world.

The weather was superb, as crisp and clear as one of his own instructions. His wife's gallantry became a legend. His two children behaved like Kennedys. His three-year-old son saluted his coffin. His six-year-old daughter comforted her mother. Looking up and seeing tears, she reached over and gave her mother's hand a consoling squeeze.

The procession from the White House would have delighted him. It was a marvelous eye-filling jumble of the mighty and the obscure, all walking behind his wife and his two brothers.

There was no cadence or order, but the presence of General de Gaulle alone in the ragged line of march was enough to give it grandeur. He stalked splendidly up Connecticut Avenue, more or less beside Queen Frederika of Greece and King Baudouin of Belgium.

The sounds of the day were smashingly appropriate. The tolling of the bells gave way to the skirling of the Black Watch Pipers whose lament blended with the organ music inside the cathedral.

At the graveside there was the thunder of jets overhead, a twenty-one-gun salute, taps, and finally the strains of the navy hymn "Eternal Father Strong to Save."

He would have seen every politician he ever knew, two ex-presidents, Truman and Eisenhower, and a foe or two. Govenor Wallace of Alabama had trouble finding a place to sit in the cathedral.

His old friend, Cardinal Cushing of Boston, who married him, baptized his children, and prayed over him in the icy air of his inaugural, said a low mass. At the final prayers, after the last blessing, he suddenly added, "Dear Jack."

There was no eulogy. Instead, Bishop Philip M. Hannan mounted the pulpit and read passages from the president's speeches and evoked him so vividly that tears splashed on the red carpets and the benches of the cathedral. Nobody cried out, nobody broke down.

And the bishop read a passage the president had often noted in the Scriptures: "There is a time to be born and a time to die." He made no reference to the fact that no one had thought last Friday was a time for John Fitzgerald Kennedy to die—a martyr's death—in Dallas. The president himself had spent no time in trying to express the inexpressible. Excess was alien to his nature.

The funeral cortege stretched for miles. An old campaigner would have loved the crowd. Children sat on the curbstones. Old ladies wrapped their furs around them.

The site of the grave, at the top of one slope, commands all of Washington. Prince Philip used his sword as a walking stick to negotiate the incline.

His brother, Robert, his face a study in desolation, stood beside the president's widow. The children of the fabulous family were all around.

Jacqueline Kennedy received the flag from his coffin, bent over, and with a torch lit a flame that is to burn forever on his grave—against the day that anyone might forget that her husband had been a president and a martyr.

It was a day of such endless fitness, with so much pathos and panoply, so much grief nobly borne that it may extinguish that unseemly hour in Dallas, where all that was alien to him—savagery, violence, irrationality— struck down the thirty-fifth president of the United States. ∎

A Gifted Man Is Gone—June 9, 1968

When John Kennedy was murdered, people were kind and gentle to each other for four days. The consolation was that the country would be shocked into virtue. Squares, streets, airports, and schools were named after him. The worst has happened, we said, things will be better.

In April, Martin Luther King was shot, and people said to each other, this is so bad, we can start over. People will try harder, things will work out.

But now Bobby Kennedy has been killed, and there is nothing to say. Once again, the country is being revived by the sight of a Kennedy wife behaving with perfect nobility. But we have been through it before. We know that, in the long run, it does not help.

We are living in an era when the lunatics, not the leaders, are writing the history. We face the prospect that the rest of the election will be held under armed guard. The candidates will be escorted to television stations in closed cars. Robert Kennedy thought he should be among the people; he has paid the price.

It is not good enough to say that he had been courting death, one way or another, since his brother died, or that his rendezvous with a gunman under the smoggy sky of Los Angeles— where wandering souls tell themselves that it is somebody else's fault that they are not rich and famous like the Kennedys—was inevitable.. It is not good enough.

He was too young to die, for one thing. The circumstances of his death make it difficult to mourn him. He is lost in the general horror of who will be next.

He was a gifted person. He intensified life for those who knew him and for those who did not. He was decent and pious. He was good to widows and orphans. He visited the sick and comforted the dying. He was courageous and cautious. He saw life in his own terms, convinced of what was right for others, if not for himself.

He deserved pity because he had a broken heart. He had found his greatest fulfillment in being his brother's keeper. Little mattered after that. He was thought to be consumed with ambition. During the winter and spring after Dallas, he sat for long hours in his Justice Department office, staring out the window.

13

When a friend in that period suggested he might have a future, he burst into tears.

He had a capacity for giving total devotion and inspiring it. He gathered around him, as attorney general, a team of brainy and brave young men who could have run the country and who virtually saved it when the racial violence first began in the south.

He had been brought up to compete and win. Persuaded he had to restore the family to presidential power, he invaded New York and entered the Senate race against Kenneth Keating, and with the help of Lyndon Johnson, his enemy, he won.

He became the champion of the poor, the blacks, the Indians. Although possessed of advantages, he felt himself as one with the disadvantaged. He had been dispossessed of his treasure, his brother.

It was painful to him to discover during the campaign he entered late and haplessly— having taken too much contrary advice—that he was not his brother. Jack had been Anglo-Saxon in temperament, detached, amused, intellectual. Bobby was a Celt—"unassimilated," Robert Lowell once called him—warm-hearted, vindictive, humorous, moody, intuitive. He loved and hated, and was, in his turn, loved and hated. He could never be unkind to anyone who had been kind to his brother, or kind to anyone who had been unkind. He was intense; he cared. He was a natural organizer.

He tried pathetically to be like his brother, to read the same books, cultivate the same people, and consult the same advisers. He was torn between what he felt and what he thought. He opposed the war with his whole soul, but feared to oppose Lyndon Johnson. He was weighed down by dynastic considerations. Did he have the right to risk the family's political future?

He suffered over the decision. Once a friend called him in his New York apartment, during another canvass of his circle. Kennedy said, "There is a ship going down the river. I wish I were on it."

At the end, he was a forlorn figure, caught between the past and the future, motorcading between miles of people who rushed to touch him and reassure him. His tragedy was not only that he had not achieved his full potential, but that uncertainties and pressures had prevented him from seeing what it was. Like his brother, he deserved better from his country. ■

The Eternal Jackie—May 22, 1994

She was a First Lady like no other. She was improbably beautiful, she rode to hounds, did exactly as she pleased, and knew just what she wanted.

Jacqueline Kennedy Onassis wanted babies and fine arts in the White House. She would pose with the occasional poster child but not with county chairmen. She was a perfectionist who pored over histories and other old tomes to find out exactly how the White House was supposed to be and then set about restoring it. She had the State Dining Room painted nine times before she got the right shade of white.

The country was not sure what to make of her. She was half of the handsomest couple ever sent to the White House. Whether to dismiss her as a Newport irrelevant or a clothes horse occupied much speculation until she went with the president to Europe in June 1961 and created a sensation. In Paris, the French, contemplating the wide-set eyes, luxuriant black hair, and delicate nose, forgot to be superior and sniffy. By the end of the second day, Kennedy was presenting himself as "the man who brought Jackie Kennedy to Paris."

In Vienna, they lined the streets murmuring *"suess"* (sweet) in such volume that it sounded like a giant, enveloping hiss. She stood next to Khrushchev's bulky wife, Nina, on a balcony—a referendum on the cold war, and the West won in a walk. The president had a rough time with Khrushchev, but Jackie came home to glory—and to new respect from her Irish in-laws, having proved herself world class.

Jackie Kennedy was not into issues like Eleanor Roosevelt was. In her rare public statements, she stressed the importance of raising one's children well. She didn't hold press conferences, didn't give interviews. People told her she had to, but she knew better. Her silence added to her glamour. She kept her children out of camera range and gave elegant parties. Grown men cried if not invited. Poets and musicians came to dinner. There was waltzing in the foyer.

In Dallas, the First Lady became a queen. Her bearing during the traumatic weekend when the young president lay in state in the Rotunda and the country sobbed was an above-and-beyond demonstration of noblesse oblige, worthy, many said at the time, of royalty. The thirty-four-year-old socialite understood that she had a shattered country on her hands and that she had to hold it together. She made her tragic rounds with dignity and grace. She planned her husband's funeral to the last trumpet and piper. She researched the hanging of crepe on the White House. She oversaw the funeral invitation list to St. Matthew's Cathedral. She saw to the eternal flame. She walked down the aisle holding daughter Caroline's hand. The child felt the sobs and reached over and patted her mother's arm. Outside, three-year-old John saluted the casket. She had taught her children love and manners.

When it was over, after she had seen off the last head of state, she did something else. She put her own spin on the Kennedy years. Reticence set aside, she summoned Teddy White, the romantic chronicler of presidential campaigns, to Hyannis Port and told him what it was all about. It had been Camelot, she told him. And for a generation, while tales of presidential philandering filtered out of congressional committees and revisionism broke through the vale of tears, Camelot was the theme.

She was mobbed, revered, pestered by paparazzi, and reckoned a saint by some who had originally judged her a snob. She lived in New York, supported cultural causes, tutored a Harlem high school student, enjoyed her children and her job, as a book editor.

The tranquility came to a screeching halt in October 1968, when she married Aristotle Onassis, an obscenely rich and somewhat primitive Greek shipping magnate. People were shocked, furious that she should step down from her stained-glass window. She never explained, never apologized. She was again, her friends said, about the business at hand. Bobby Kennedy's death had made her see her vulnerability, her need for protection and financial security.

Onassis died as they were planning a divorce. Onassis's family settled a fortune on her. Her life seemed peaceful. She attended gatherings of the clan. She observed the scene with the attention and wit of another daughter of New York, Edith Wharton. She watched as the governor of New York came down the path at Hickory Hill at the wedding of Kerry Kennedy and Andrew Cuomo. "Somehow," she said. "I think the Cuomos will hold their own as in-laws."

Her suffering during her last illness seemed gratuitous, totally inappropriate for someone who had had much trouble. She was cheerful through it all, they say. She saw friends and family and adored grandchildren who called her "Grand Jackie." She conversed as long as she could. Once again, Jacqueline Kennedy Onassis was showing us how to behave. We shall miss her exquisite tutelage. ▪

Jacqueline Kennedy Onassis Kept Her Thoughts High—May 24, 1994

Jacqueline Kennedy Onassis's death, all agree, was not appropriate—"She was too young to die," said brother-in-law and eulogist Senator Edward Kennedy. Her funeral was, however, perhaps because she planned it. For the hour or so that it was broadcast over CBS, daytime radio was a better place.

One felicity succeeded another. All the readings were perfectly chosen and read with emotion by her children and her friends. Daughter Caroline read Edna St. Vincent Millay's "Memory of Cape Cod." The music, which ranged from austere Gregorian chant to the satin river of Jessye Norman singing "Panis Angelicus," bordered on the sublime. Somehow the whole affair, packed with old New Frontiersmen, members of the clan, and show-biz celebrities, was both elegant and intimate.

She had become a Kennedy again with the decision to have her buried in Arlington National Cemetery. Her being committed there with her first husband and their two babies suggests that her marriage to tycoon Aristotle Onassis is being erased. This is considered a good idea by both idolaters and friends, who regarded that marriage as an aberration unworthy of a lady who looked and acted like someone who had stepped out of the pages of a medieval chronicle.

The place in the family of the last man in her life, Maurice Tempelsman, a diamond merchant, was defined for the curious. He walked between Caroline and John behind the coffin.

Another statement added to the eternal interest in the Kennedy tribe. Among the pallbearers was William Kennedy Smith, the young doctor of the sensational Palm Beach rape case. Jackie was a great one for nonverbal communication.

Tempelsman read a poem that was one of Jacqueline Kennedy Onassis's little surprises. Called "Ithaka," it is the work of an obscure nineteenth-century Greek poet, C. P. Kavifis, and it could well be the story of Mrs. Onassis's philosophy and life: "Keep your thoughts high," and

May there be many summer mornings when,
with pleasure, what joy,
you enter harbors you're seeing for the first time.

Mrs. Onassis saw many harbors in her day and navigated most of them with great flair. Few traveled more. But son-in-law Edwin Schlossberg spoke of the patriot, not the jet-setter. He referred to the "nation whom she served and sustained"—and every mind flashed back to Nov. 22, 1963, and her distinguished service.

Her fortitude and her flair—rarely combined—is what is remembered. And her success as a single mother. The onetime debutante of the year lived to become the valiant woman of the Bible.

As ever, her wishes were being debated. What would she think of the fact that son John went Rollerblading with his girlfriend while his mother was being waked in her Fifth Avenue apartment? She might have thought that grief takes many forms.

On the streets of New York, for instance, it has taken the form of quiet and civility—except, of course, among barbarian photographers who mobbed the family.

In the baroque Jesuit church of St. Ignatius Loyola, the preoccupation was with "this Christian woman," as the Reverend Walter Modrys called her in his homily. He spoke of her "difficult dying." Of all the things that happened to her, the voracious cancer that killed her seems the cruelest.

"She had her share of tears," said Modrys. He suggested that the scriptural passage, "My father's house hath many dwelling places," was apt for one who had lived in so many mansions—and redecorated them all.

The congregation was sad and restrained, overwhelmed with regret, not the raw grief that choked them when her husband was killed thirty-one years ago. They mourned a shame, not a tragedy.

It was a private funeral, admission by invitation, but Hillary Rodham Clinton's presence at the front of the church signaled that it was not for long. Mrs. Clinton, a fan of another unconventional First Lady, had come to accompany Jackie back to Washington and her place in history.

The singing of "America the Beautiful" ended the services. By the time the motorcade headed out of the city, past lines of somber citizens, gently waving and saluting, the airwaves had been returned to their usual proprietors. Rush Limbaugh was yapping about wives of "Democrat-liberal presidents" who have to tolerate dissolute behavior by their husbands.

It just went to show how much we needed Jacqueline Kennedy Onassis in a world that grows more crass and gross by the day. ∎

John Kennedy Measured by What He Was, Not What He Did—July 22, 1999

To understand the round-the-clock coverage of John Kennedy's death, the unending talk about it and the makeshift memorials, it helps to remember what the country felt about his parents. His father, John Fitzgerald Kennedy, handsome and dashing, came out of Boston insisting on being our first Catholic president—and was assassinated in November 1963. His beautiful mother, Jacqueline Bouvier, once dismissed as a social butterfly, stepped forward and held the country together. She arranged a funeral that was majestic and moved through it like a queen. She saw to every detail, from the kilted Scottish pipers to the eternal flame.

When it was over she summoned the most famous political scribe of his time, Theodore White, and put a name on her husband's time in office, Camelot. The country has been emotionally involved with the Kennedys ever since. They are numerous, good-looking, and always up to something. They have provided an endless pageant of smiles, tears, and scandals.

When John Kennedy's single-engine plane, with him at the controls, fell off the radar at the Martha's Vineyard airport, the nation once again went to its post by the television to keep vigil with the Kennedys.

In the five days that followed, the dread and dismay were laced with indignation. This was not supposed to happen. This was entirely gratuitous. The crown prince had been exempt from "the curse of the Kennedys"—a phrase coined by Uncle Teddy during the Chappaquiddick crisis. Had not Jackie Kennedy sequestered her children from the turbulence at the Kennedy compound in Hyannis Port, as Bobby Kennedy's fatherless sons wrestled with various demons? She took John and Caroline over the water to Martha's Vineyard.

John had not followed in his father's footsteps. He was his mother's son. She brought him up not to be a Kennedy, but to be himself. He shared her detachment about politics. When asked a while back, in the light of his father's posthumously revealed promiscuity, about how Jack Kennedy would have tolerated today's press scrutiny, John Kennedy said coolly he thought his father might have chosen to go into another line of work.

John Kennedy died like his father, violently and too soon. His blond wife, Carolyn Bessette, and his sister-in-law, Lauren Bessette, died with him. At thirty-eight, he left more unfulfilled promise than performance. He was strikingly handsome and unexpectedly nice for one of his looks and station. He was courteous to all, even the paparazzi who dogged him from the age of three, when he broke the nation's heart by saluting his father's coffin. The tabs called him "The Hunk" and *People* magazine said he was the sexiest man alive. If the grief seems disproportionate to his life, it is easily explained. He was measured by who he was, not what he did.

His mother vetoed his first choice of a career, the theater. He went into the law, but not for long. He founded a magazine he called *George*. It was to be a glossy, trendy monthly that treated politics as entertainment.

He courted publicity for *George*, sometimes doing odd things: He posed nude for an illustration to accompany a critique of his Kennedy cousins' behavior. More recently, he visited Mike Tyson, the convicted rapist, in prison; he invited pornographer Larry Flynt to the White House correspondents' dinner.

Like his mother, he never explained his actions. He was a free spirit. His father, despite his private excesses, was decorous in his public life, having a politician's perpetual concern about what the neighbors will think. Jack Kennedy was witty, sometimes in the mordant Irish way; his son was whimsical. Politics does not allow for whimsy.

John's love life was of aching, international interest. He courted a string of gorgeous girls, and then married willowy, fashionable Carolyn Bessette at a secret wedding on an island off Georgia. He was terribly proud of his coup against the press. He released one picture. It was of him kissing his bride's hand. It was drop-dead romantic.

The country spent the weekend soaking up every detail, watching hour after hour of Jack's funeral, Bobby's funeral, touch football, prayers at Arlington. The context was pure, incredible Kennedy.

The clan had gathered at Hyannis Port to celebrate the wedding of Rory Kennedy. A huge tent had been set up on Ethel's lawn. It was the one mercy of the grim weekend. The Kennedys, who derive such solace from each other, were together. The wedding was postponed early Saturday. The family mourned.

Washington talked of nothing else. Arguments broke out over "the curse of the Kennedys"—was it really the rashness of its members? "Where was God in all this?" one man demanded to know at a subdued Saturday night party. At the White House, the president was in constant touch with the Coast Guard.

All agreed on one point: It was a shame. ■

3

Nixon-Watergate

Walking on Eggs—January 6, 1974

Vice President Gerald R. Ford has been practicing his skiing in the Colorado mountains. Better he should have been taking a course in walking on eggs. No public man has a more delicate path to tread in 1974.

Ford must appear to be loyal, grateful, and respectful toward his sinking patron, the president, while maintaining the esteem of his countrymen, who, after the briefest encounter, like him better than any other politician on the Scene—at least according to the Harris Poll.

Other Republicans, startled by Ford's astonishing first-foot strength, are saying that the votes are more against Nixon than for Ford. Ford is a blind date who has been proposed to. He has to be awfully careful lest further acquaintance lead to second thoughts.

Ford has done the White House a few small favors lately. Before he was confirmed, he went before the National Realtors Association and suggested that if the Silent Majority thought that some solution short of impeachment or resignation were possible, it should take pen in hand.

He also sternly counseled disbarment of William Dobrovir, the Nader lawyer who played a White House tape at a Georgetown cocktail party. He has yet to be asked if he would apply the same standard to his predecessor, Spiro Agnew, who is fighting disbarment proceedings in Maryland.

What will happen if the president, or General Alexander Haig, the chief of staff who believes in the existence of a "sinister outside force," calls Ford down to the White House and hands him a savage script aimed at one of the president's traditional enemies—of the kind that Agnew unquestioningly read aloud from the stump from time to time.

Agnew as attack dog simply had to be pointed in the right direction.

Did Ford work out an agreement, at the time of his appointment, that gave him the chance to turn down White House speeches? If he did, he can continue on his course of mild censure of presidential persecutors. If not, he will have to fight out every case.

So far, on the explosive question of impeachment, he takes the White House line on material suitable for the House Judiciary Committee. He said a month ago he thought the committee has the "obligation to fit the allegation within the framework of the language in the Constitution," which fits in with White House strategy to fight committee subpoenas for documents sheet by sheet, with the president apparently deciding which papers relate to "impeachable" offenses. Ford, awkwardly, once said an impeachable offense is what a majority of the House decides it is.

What Ford will absolutely not do, it seems fair to say, is to attack the last target left to the president. The day he was sworn in, as waves of applause rolled over him, he looked back over his left shoulder and up at the press gallery. The friendliest of salutes and smiles were exchanged. He likes the press and vice versa.

Nor is he likely to belabor the Ervin Committee, which is presumably going to be back on television at the end of the month. Agnew charged them. Ford is a man of Congress, not given to snarling at fellow clubmembers.

Vice presidents have dissipated their constituencies at the command of their principal. Hubert Humphrey blew up his liberal support when Lyndon Johnson sent him out to defend the war. It cost Humphrey his chance at the White House.

Ford, now that he has become the most popular politician in the country, will surely be asked by the president to show his gratitude and stiffen the House Republicans against impeachment.

Ford would probably prefer to stay out of sight until the whole thing blows over. But he cannot. He will be asked about every development, and he promised at his confirmation hearings to have frequent press conferences. He also promised to be a unifying and healing influence in the country.

How can you champion the cause of a discredited president without losing the regard of a disillusioned country? If Gerald Ford can manage it, he will deserve the good will he currently enjoys. ■

Situation Comedy—February 3, 1974

The town needed a laugh, heaven knows, but who would have thought that the president, of all people, would provide us with forty-five minutes of low comedy in, of all things, his State of the Union message?

Basically, it was situation comedy. Here was a president facing impeachment, waiting for the multiple indictments of his closest aides, fighting off a court summons from one of the "two finest public servants" he has ever known, hanging onto his great office by his fingernails.

The heavily made-up man on the podium spoke of himself as a miracle worker.

He has cleaned the air and made peace. He has reduced subsidies. He will bid the waters of recession recede, and they will obey. He will heal the sick with a health plan that will not require new taxes.

The only possible reason for turning him out of office, as he told it, would be that he is too good for us.

The Republican members of the Congress, who know that his persistence spells their ruin, went along with the gag, clapping wildly at every opportunity. They heard him as patiently and encouragingly as one would listen to a man who has been declared bankrupt telling of his plans for a new killing on the market or the purchase of the state of Florida.

The great joke of the evening, however, was the president's straight-faced declaration of his promise to protect the privacy of the individual citizen.

Here is the man who authorized the larcenous plumbers, taped his every unsuspecting visitor until discovered, who shocked even J. Edgar Hoover with his spy schemes, whose staff bugged each other. Here he is announcing "a major initiative to define the nature and extent of the basic rights of privacy and to erect new safeguards to insure those rights are respected."

It was as if Dracula had suddenly proposed to establish a blood bank.

The chairman of the Joint Chiefs of Staff, Admiral Thomas Moorer, looked unconcernedly off into space during the passage. He has lately been revealed as the receiver of documents stolen from the office of his commander in chief. Perhaps he thought it had nothing to do with him, since the president was inveighing against "electronic surveillance" and the admiral had used human agents for his espionage.

24

The new attorney general, William O. Saxbe, who authorized three new wiretaps in his first week in office and hopes others will require less fuss, applauded lustily.

The secretary of state, Henry Kissinger, who was into wiretapping himself, had the grace to look faintly amused.

In the postscript to the speech, the president's new-found concern for the privacy of individuals was revealed in its full dimension. Obviously, his own will be protected first.

He called for an end to investigations of what he always refers to as "the so-called Watergate affair"—the Republicans again interrupted him with possibly heartfelt applause. He recognized patronizingly that the House Judiciary Committee has a "special responsibility," and he declared that he would cooperate in "any way I consider consistent with my responsibilities"—by which it was generally understood they can go fish.

The sound of hissing was heard in the chamber, a historic first, and it came from people who by this time had wearied of the travesty.

The Republicans gave him a standing ovation. If it wasn't his swan song, it was theirs. If he survives to give another January Fantasy they don't expect to be around to hear it. That was the reality that was carefully blotted out in the chamber. So the Republicans chatted, smiled, and clapped for what every last one of them hopes will be Richard Nixon's last State of the Union. ■

A Committee Votes—July 18, 1974

The words that heralded the fatal roll calls were pedestrian. At seven P.M., Chairman Peter Rodino said: "The question is on the Sarbanes substitute."

The question was really on Richard Nixon's fitness to continue in office. It was answered in an atmosphere of deepest melancholy.

The silence that fell on the room was broken only by the call of the roll and the click of cameras as photographers, huddled over the clerk, snapping the tally as the names were called.

The "ayes" of the Democrats were whispered rather than spoken. Barbara Jordan, the handsome and eloquent black congresswoman from Texas, had her eyes fixed on the table. Representative Ray

Thornton, one of the three southern Democrats on the committee, also was looking down.

James Mann of South Carolina, the Democrat, who looks like a founding father and had spoken like one during the debate, sighed his "aye." He was the architect of the first article of impeachment. He had moved between the Republican reluctants and the southern Democrats carrying drafts and redrafts of the charges against the president.

Edward Hutchinson of Michigan, the ranking Republican, recorded his "no" resoundingly. It was all he could do for Richard Nixon. He is ailing, he took no part in the fight. He could only register from time to time his disapproval of its existence.

Two weeks ago in a Republican caucus, he asked Tom Railsback of Illinois, in tones of horror, "Do you mean to say you would vote to impeach a Republican president?"

Railsback, who has been equally horrified at the prospect, responded, "I would vote to impeach any president who I thought was subverting my government."

It fell to Railsback to cast the first Republican vote against the president. Hamilton Fish of New York, M. Caldwell Butler of Virginia, William Cohen of Maine, predictably, softly gave their verdict.

Only Harold Froehlich of Wisconsin was a surprise. The stillness in the room was rippled with gasps, when through tight lips he blurted his "aye."

He had tried to get out of it. During the hurly-burly of the third day's struggle while Nixon's friends were taunting their opponents for proof, Froehlich had threatened to reconsider his dread resolve. A few minor changes he wanted were made in the article. His escape was cut off.

All twenty-seven of them were taking a leap in the dark. For the southern Democrats and the Republicans it was an act of conscience and courage that could bring them honor, but oblivion.

In the end, they returned to the mood in which they began, speaking of the Constitution and their pain. As the afternoon wore on, Hutchinson began visiting the Nixon loyalists, moving among them as if in a hospital ward, patting shoulders, pressing arms. They had done their best. But even Charles Sandman, of New Jersey, a gifted heckler, admitted by sundown there was nothing more to be said.

They began their good-byes. William Hungate, the Missouri Democrat who provided comic relief, apologized if his humor offended anyone, then quoted from the piercing inscription on the Omaha Beach memorial: "They endured all, they suffered all that mankind might know freedom and inherit justice."

And then they decided to bring out what Cohen had called in the rhetorical phase of the proceedings, "the sword in the temple."

Mann, who had become the leader of that mission to the temple, spoke with his usual gravity as the members dispersed.

"You don't like to be cornered, but when you are, and your conscience is with you, you are comfortable."

"You don't feel exhilarated," he added as he went off to another drafting session. "You don't feel happy." ∎

Dr. Ford's Attempt at Healing Merely Left Wounds
—September 7, 1974

His first time out as a healer, Gerald Ford has won only charges of malpractice from a large segment of the community.

The pardon he gave Richard Nixon has cured nothing but the illusions about himself.

It was preventive medicine, he explained at his second White House press conference. The patient was the country, which to his practiced eye looked to be heading for a severe attack of "turmoil and division."

Actually, the country had been feeling fine. It thought it had finally come out of a long siege of Nixonitis. When Ford prescribed pardon, the country promptly went into shock and revulsion and began exhibiting its old symptoms of rage and frustration.

As for the immediate recipient of the pardon, which he accepted, he said, for the good of the country, it has not helped either his phlebitis or his gloom. Richard Nixon's doctor, who is more in the news than Dr. Ford, announced that Nixon is suffering from a second blood clot and refuses to go to the hospital for fear he "would never come out alive."

As a matter of fact, he was reluctant to take the medicine. His son-in-law David Eisenhower informed us last week that he had said he would not swallow it if it had any tincture of Vietnam amnesty, in it. He would have, despite his depression and ill health, undergone the rigors of a trial rather than open wide.

Finally, when a huge dose of tapes was offered, he decided he would accept.

Nixon's ill health, Ford did not consider of paramount concern, he said, since he was really ministering to the country.

One arm of the body politic, the Republican National Committee, seemed to be suffering ill effects of the Ford healing. The members gathered at the Mayflower and when the doctor came they gave him a hand but no huzzas.

He did not refer to the case at all. He spoke of Henry Kissinger, George Bush, new party chairman Mary Louise Smith, and Nelson Rockefeller. Together, he said they will elect an "inflation-proof Congress."

Thanks to his treatment, some of the party candidates seem to be suffering from a depression as acute as Richard Nixon's.

Although they could not discuss the cure, the Republicans took a hand at healing, too. Richard Nixon was commended in a resolution for his "achievements." They joined with "President Ford in praying that Mr. Nixon, who brought peace to millions, find it for himself, that he be restored to good health, and that God bless and comfort him and his loyal and loving wife and family."

Mrs. Smith asked herself rhetorically what the Republicans could be doing wrong. She concluded they were being "outorganized or outsold."

Ford, at his press conference, did come around to agreeing that pardons are, generally administered to guilty people. He said he could see where the acceptance of one "can be construed by many if not all, as an admission of guilt."

He had not brought in outside experts, as he had promised to do in deciding to "heal the wounds throughout the United States" because he had to search his soul by himself.

He had come to realize that the pardon medicine did not go down very well. He is sure the country will feel better soon. He may keep around for a while the elixir of tapes which he had planned to administer massively to Richard Nixon.

He was absolutely emphatic there were no secret reasons for giving the pardon to the country—no deals, no hidden motives.

His wife may have given the best explanation Thursday night at the reception for the Israeli prime minister.

"We are very fond of the Nixons," she told reporters.

The country had been giving strong indications of contrary sentiments, and had been asking for justice rather than mercy in its hope of complete recovery from Watergate.

Now it is telling Gerald Ford, "Physician, heal thyself." ■

Watergate Finale: Time to Cast Stones Is at Hand
—December 30, 1974

The last outpost of Watergate, that once mighty Roman Empire of a scandal, is about to be abandoned.

The little village of the conspiracy trial is in its final hours.

Nothing like it was ever seen. The five defendants at five separate tables, each with its own neighborhood character: John Mitchell's winter palace, John Ehrlichman's bunker, H. R. Haldeman's command post, Robert Mardian's bristling blockhouse, and Kenneth Parkinson's house on the hill, far from the town bullies.

The bland, blond, overheated courtroom presented society in miniature. There was the artists' colony in the front row, the press corps behind and across the aisle the dependents' enclave and a shifting population of tourists. As a final, homey touch, a supermarket cart stood in the corner, ready to wheel tapes from the prosecutors to the tape machine.

The founding father of Watergate, Richard Nixon, never came. But he had provided the tapes, and they were enough. The tapes were like a mighty river running through the trial. The prosecutors sometimes used buckets, sometimes dippers, but Richard Nixon, the pardoned exile, was in every drop.

Judge John J. Sirica was the town cop, directing traffic, brusquely urging people to move along. Legal loiterers were picked up promptly. Legal arguments got short shrift.

"I do what I think is right at the time." He would say to some fancy Dan lawyer trying to argue him out of a ticket, "you know what I mean?"

After sixty-one days, they knew what he meant, and they knew he didn't want the ghost of Richard Nixon hanging around his courtroom.

James F. Neal, the chief prosecutor, was the sheriff. He knew every move the defendants made, their comings and goings by night and by

29

day. He did not want to prosecute Richard Nixon, although it was hard for him not to.

He must have been tempted, but he is sage. The pardon hung over the early days of the trial like a miasma. Powerful personalities, dynamite evidence was needed to dispel it.

It was easy to prove that Nixon was the "maestro" of the conspiracy orchestra, as Ehrlichman's lawyer called him in his otherwise empty final argument. But Neal relentlessly pounded the point that the five defendants were all over twenty-one, that four of them were lawyers and that one of them had been attorney general of the United States.

Except for Parkinson, who was unfailingly polite, and Haldeman, who was unfailingly forgetful, the defendants came on like Chinese wrestlers, bellowing and making hideous faces as if to frighten the prosecutors to death. Mardian had, in fact, behaved so boorishly that his young attorney, Thomas Green, felt constrained to apologize for his conduct on the stand.

Parkinson alone behaved as if the charges against him had been brought by rational men. His squeaky-voiced defender, Jacob Stein, was able to pull out a handkerchief in his final argument and weep with some plausibility that his client was a good man led astray.

Neal said in his rebuttal that the other defendants were, in their curious behavior in the courtroom, simply following the instructions—to stonewall, to forget—that the former president had given them almost two years ago in the Oval office.

But the governing body, the village elders of the last Watergate outpost, is the jury. It's what they think of Richard Nixon's pardon, what they think of the five men who served him that matters. They will ratify or refute Neal's climactic contention that "the only salvation, for us all and for the retention of our form of government, is the faith of the people that their high officials will be fair, honorable, and lawful, that the officials of the land will not play ignoble roles—they may strike hard blows but must strike fair ones."

In a low, hoarse voice, Neal spoke the epitaph of Watergate and his own. Prosecutors do not enjoy throwing stones, he said, "but to keep society going must be cast—people must be called to account." ■

For a Lot of People, It Has Changed Everything
—January 2, 1975

Guilty, guilty, guilty, guilty.

The word stabbed the still, close air of the courtroom fifteen times, spoken mildly, noncommitally by the gray-haired clerk, James Capitanio, no one's first choice for the voice of doom.

John Mitchell, guilty; H. R. Haldeman, guilty; John Ehrlichman, guilty; Robert Mardian, guilty. Was it the only word in the English language? Finally, another was heard. "Not guilty," twice for Kenneth Parkinson, whom the jury believed when he said he had fallen among evil companions.

Parkinson's right hand, which had been twitching uncontrollably, went quiet. His lawyer, Jacob Stein, reached up to clap him on the back. Mitchell, his face still flushed from the jolt he had taken, looked over and mouthed the words "good boy" at the lucky man.

Only Mardian seemed surprised. When "guilty" hit him, he flung his head to one side like an angry horse about to bolt.

Mardian's cover-up career had been the briefest of the five. But he had been surly and contemptuous on the stand, and he may have been judged as much for that as for participation in the panic that followed June 17, 1972.

The verdict in the second Watergate trial, the real one, came unexpectedly on a quiet, sunny New Year's Day afternoon at 4:25. The judge, who had, to the open-mouthed amazement of a British correspondent, gone downstairs an hour earlier to pose with the whole cast, minus the defendants, for what was billed on the pressroom blackboard as a "class foto," was sitting in his chambers with seven reporters he had invited in for a chat and reminiscence. He was midway in a recital of a forty-year-old arson case when the marshal appeared at the door.

He broke off, apologized and said casually, "There's another note from the jury."

It was indeed a note, the long-awaited, long-deferred judgment of Watergate. The jury, which had not been in any hurry for sixty-four days, had abruptly packed it up.

The defendants, their defenders, a handful of holiday spectators, and the reporters trooped into the large blank room where since October 1 they have sat together and listened to the history of the

Nixon administration and its efforts to "keep the lid on" the greatest political scandal in the country's history.

Haldeman knew what was coming. His oblong face was set. He folded his arms on the table, braced himself for it. Mitchell's dread took the form of an unprecedented animation. He chatted with his second lawyer, Plato Cacheris. The usually pleasant face of his chief attorney, William G. Hundley, was stiff with melancholy. Ehrlichman's back, which was to the room, seemed relaxed. Only Mardian looked genuinely expectant.

The room was so quiet the only sound was the whirring of the air-conditioning. The judge who presided at both trials took his place. The jury, led by its foreman, John Hoffar, came in, appearing serene and relieved. Hoffar's election had sent the last days' one quiver of hope through the demoralized ranks of the defense. A former park police-man, the only white male and the only registered Republican of the twelve, he was figured for an Archie Bunker.

His pale face never registered the slightest interest, his pale blue eyes had played coldly on the witnesses. The dramatic, sometimes hilarious summing-up of Chief Prosecutor James F. Neal had roused him from torpor, but his general demeanor had cried for the caption, "Everybody does it."

But Hoffar, the foreman, was changed. His eyes glinted, he smiled a bit. He had become purposeful. He was carrying judgment under his arm in a large manila envelope.

He stood up. Yes, he was the foreman. Yes, the jury had reached a verdict. The envelope, followed by a hundred eyes, was handed over. In his diffident tones, Capitanio instructed the best and the brightest of the Nixon administration to rise. Then he tonelessly began his reading. The "guilties" and the gasping began.

Andrew Hall, Ehrlichman's second lawyer—his chief advocate, William Frates, had flown back to Florida—asked for a poll of the jury. Some of the yeses were barely audible, others in voices that suggested they should be asked again.

David Bress, Mardian's ailing counsel, who had been absent for most of the trial, noted the stricken condition of his client—who was indeed slumped down as if he had had been shot in the stomach—and asked for another poll. The judge brusquely denied it.

The judge thanked the jury. and Mrs. Mardian formed a Bronx cheer. Mrs. Ehrlichman, sitting beside her, was composed.

The heavy scene dissolved. A little congratulatory group formed around Parkinson. John Mitchell reached for his pipe. On his way out, he collided with a junior attorney. Mitchell apologized profusely and put a solicitous hand on the youth's shoulder. Mrs. Ehrlichman made her way to her husband. They stood with an arm around each other, their backs to the room.

But Mardian would not leave the seat which he had taken as a free man. He held his bald head in his hands, he bent it almost to the level of the table. Bress leaned over and tried to console him. Mrs. Mardian, fresh from an encounter with Neal and Assistant Prosecutor Richard Ben-Veniste—she is said to have told them both she would "get" them—was summoned. She put a supporting hand under her husband's elbow. With some of the gentility he had displayed on the stand, he flung it off. She tried again and got him to his feet. He seemed barely able to walk to the door.

Outside the court, a storm of Shakespearean fury had suddenly blown up. Haldeman went out in the rain to say he was the only man who could judge his innocence. Ehrlichman sent word he would talk to the reporters. He came into the littered pressroom—the poker chips and the cards for the long waiting game were whisked out of sight against his arrival—and while the rain lashed the windows and the wind howled, he waxed philosophical, judicious, dispassionate, and compassionate. A friend to all men, including Richard Nixon, he declared himself innocent.

"As far as the verdict is concerned," he said, "it changes nothing."

For a lot of people, though, it has changed everything. A judgment that seemed inevitable had finally been rendered. ■

Saying Good-bye to a Political Adversary
—May 1, 1994

Richard Nixon and I shared a hymn book at Martin Luther King's funeral in Atlanta in April 1968—various entourages got folded into each other in the small space of the Ebenezer Baptist Church. Four years later, I was on his enemies list.

Those were the twin poles of his nature, politeness and paranoia.

In the church, he was his mother's genteel son, making sure I was ready when he turned the pages. He sang the old hymns—"Softly and Tenderly," "I Walked in the Garden"—in his pleasant baritone. It was the one moment of harmony in a long association rising from the fact that he was a politician and I write about politics.

The news that I had made his enemies list was greeted with hilarity and even elation at the *Washington Star*, my old paper. We were in straits, and attention was welcome. Art Buchwald, not listed and jealous, took me to lunch at Sans Souci, a restaurant that is no more, near the White House. I got a standing ovation.

When I heard last Friday that Nixon was dead, I felt an unexpected pang, the feeling of a sudden void. I had expected him, combative as he was, to give death more of a scrap.

The Niagara of praise that thundered forth surprised me somewhat. It probably would have stunned him, too—with delight.

The Vietnam War was treated as an inherited misfortune. The four years filled with pain and poison when he prolonged the war were referred to mostly in terms of the opening to China— a move no politician dared to make for twenty-five years, largely because of Nixonian criticism. Watergate, the tapes, and the taps merited only mention. The ruthless campaigning, one commentator suggested, was learned by an innocent from Dwight Eisenhower and John Kennedy.

In the floodtide of rampant revisionism, columnist Russell Baker begged for a respite. He lamented the absence of an H. L. Mencken, who wrote of the newly departed William Jennings Bryan with undiminished virulence. "He hated the press with a fury that deserved the fury of at least one press giant who could hate him back with a grandeur to match his own," Russell Baker wrote.

The rigid enforcement of the rule of the ancients, *"De mortuis nil nisi bonum"*—speak only good of the dead—may have been inspired by, of all people, the North Vietnamese. With restraint that no Christian could surpass, their government issued a statement saying, "May he rest in peace."

The turnout at Nixon's wake in Yorba Linda, California, was more illuminating. The old crowd-counter would have gloated over forty-two thousand people, some of whom waited in the rain for hours. It was his Silent Majority, his wartime allies coming through for him again. They called him "a great president" and "a great man." Some wept. He could not have asked for more.

In his long, bumpy political career, Nixon had a constituency that went well beyond the conservative Republicans he claimed to represent. He was no natural politician—a Calvinist from pleasure-seeking California; an introvert in an extrovert's game. Men, particularly, identified with him: his awkwardness, his wistful passion for sports. His resentments, they understood. They, too, felt at a disadvantage, with their functional equivalent of rich fathers who sent their sons to Harvard while poor boys worked their way through Whittier.

His recreation was theirs. He installed a bowling alley in the White House. If he had a mean streak, they saw it as toughness that was used on their behalf.

Anyone could feel sorry for Nixon the child, about whom he told us so much. He grew up in a bleak house where he had to compete for his mother's attention with a brother who was dying. Henry Kissinger said he was insufficiently loved to be a great president. It is hard to think how he could have been better loved. His wife, Pat, inventor of the adoring upward gaze on the platform, stood by her man. His daughters doted on him.

At the funeral, Julie Nixon Eisenhower's sweet face spoke her devotion. She was drinking in every word of tribute to her father. Considerable men rallied to him. Sardonic Bob Dole broke down during his eulogy.

I wondered, watching his funeral, with every honor—half the Congress and the diplomatic corps, all the living presidents, including the incumbent, a war protester—and flags and bugles and twenty-one-gun salutes, if children would be puzzled. They missed his presidency and the postdisgrace climb back to respectability as the sage who brought communist countries in from the cold. Seeing the glory of his farewell, they might wonder why this remarkable man was driven out of office.

Maybe we should tell them that Richard Nixon learned too early the importance of being earnest, that he was smart but got something big wrong: He thought politics was war and that everything is justified.

And what we can learn from this week is how much Americans want to love their presidents—and they will, in life as well as in death, if they are given half a chance. ∎

Twenty Years Later, Watergate Still Offers Lessons to Learn—July 26, 1994

It was a wallow, no two ways about it. For Watergate junkies, it was a wonderful way to begin the week. The people who twenty years ago caused, carried out, reported, or prosecuted the still-unbelievable activities of the stunning scandal gathered at the National Press Club and stepped up to their necks into the familiar waters.

The morning was like old times. There was talk of tapes and mad treason, of midnight rides and lost evidence, of hatred and history and flashes of old hostility between John Dean and James McCord, and wonderful retellings of near-misses by Sam Dash, the Senate Watergate Committee counsel, who began his sentences with the chilling, thrilling phrase, "But for. . ."

Why Watergate? Why, twenty years later, when all the culprits but one have paid for their sins, and the exception is lying in his grave in Yorba Linda, California?

Because, says the British correspondent Fred Emery, author of *Watergate*, a hefty new recap, "you have to retell the story for every generation." Emery covered the mess for *The Times* of London, and his editor, William Reese-Mogg, was an admirer of Richard Nixon and basically didn't want the story in the paper. Emery's book is now a documentary jointly produced by the Discovery Channel and the BBC.

It was always necessary to repeat, because Nixon fought a shameless rearguard action for rehabilitation, and won a decisive victory by dying. His fans rushed forward to make the familiar claim that he was a genius abroad and a closet progressive at home, not to be judged by one aberration. At Nixon's funeral in California, President Clinton contributed to the moral confusion in his eulogy by bidding people to view the "entire life and career" of his predecessor—which was no help at all to those who remembered Nixon's entry into politics as much like his exit.

Clinton would have enjoyed the forum more than anyone. Beside the dark doings and constitutional assaults, Whitewater is a Mark Twain prank and Clinton looks like Huckleberry Finn.

Nixon's surge toward sainthood was, in any case, stopped in its tracks by the recent publication of H. R. Haldeman's diaries, an unsparing account of Nixon's anti-Semitism, his breathtaking banalities, and his constitutional inability to take responsibility for anything.

The first panel of what moderator Daniel Schorr called "a class reunion" was composed of Nixon nemeses, the five people who had the most to do with his downfall. First was Daniel Ellsberg, peddler of the Pentagon papers, who started the whole thing by pushing Nixon's Vietnam button. The ransacking of Ellsberg's psychiatrist's office by the White House plumbers was a complicating factor in facing up to Watergate and making a clean breast of it. Overlapping personnel, like Howard Hunt and G. Gordon Liddy, the hand-on-the-candle hitman, were involved.

Beside Ellsberg was James McCord—an ex-spook who was being closely watched from the audience by ex-CIA chief Richard Helms. He shattered the Watergate stonewall by writing a letter to Judge John Sirica. McCord, in his high, hoarse voice, said he has "straightened out everything with my Lord"—although plainly not with John Dean, the White House counsel who declined to be Nixon's fall guy and sang to the prosecutors. McCord accused him of having a "slippery" memory.

Dean, the long-ago blond glamour boy of Watergate hearings, is now a mergers and acquisitions man in California. He has lost some hair but not his composure. He smiled at McCord's attack.

The most impassioned words were spoken by Alexander Butterfield, the White House staff member who told the biggest secret of all: that Nixon bugged himself. Butterfield, now white-haired and distinguished, feelingly demolished the "overzealous subordinates" argument.

"Haldeman and Richard Nixon were the co-conspirators; nothing happened that Richard Nixon did not OK. . . . I would stake my life on it."

At another point, Butterfield railed at Nixon for watching young White House helpers go off to jail. "He should have said, 'My guys don't go to jail.'"

Nixon's "loyalty was only to himself," said former White House counsel Leonard Garment, who came the closest to defending Nixon, although in a world-weary, take-it-or-leave-it, Washington way. He detailed Nixon's "substantial contributions," made the "everybody does it" argument, and marveled at Nixon's failure to burn the tapes.

Did he think it was "reprehensible" that Nixon kept the Vietnam War going for four-and-a-half years—as documented by Haldeman—to safeguard his re-election?

"Tragic," he said, carefully missing the point, and reeled off other contemporary calamities, proving that once a staff man, always a staff man. ■

Colson's View of Nixon as Peacemaker Rings False
—January 2, 1996

A line from a *New York Times* op-ed piece by Charles Colson leapt off the page.

"What drew me to Nixon in the first place was . . . his passionate desire for world peace."

Excuse me, is an asterisk called for? Never would I second-guess Howell Raines, the editorial page editor of the *Times*, but what about innocents born since Watergate—which was, after all, more than twenty years ago? The study of history in our schools today is a bit sketchy. And our universities turn out graduates who have majored in public relations and minored in film. Such disciplines provide few weapons in the search for truth.

It perhaps figures that a whopper like Oliver Stone's great splat would generate other whoppers, like Colson's about Nixon. This was a man whose "passionate desire for world peace" led him to prolong an ugly war for four more years, who began his administration with the "secret" bombing of Cambodia, a country he later invaded, and who presided over military operations that brought death to thousands of Americans and uncounted Asians. He tore his country apart and poisoned political discourse for a generation.

Of course Colson has a right to write what he wants about Nixon or anyone else. But to have him lecture us on the evils of "deconstructionism" in history is a bit much: After all, despite a rather noisy repentance, he has declined to detail his sins in the White House. Howard Hunt, the spooky plumber Colson hired to burgle Daniel Ellsberg's psychiatrist's files, is dismissed in half a sentence in his memoirs.

Colson deplores Oliver Stone's "radical subjectivism" and tsk-tsks that he "would sacrifice truth for the sake of ideology." This from the man whose most famous contribution to the political discourse of the '60s was, "I would walk over my grandmother if necessary to re-elect Richard Nixon."

He does not say in his *Times* screed that he is a different man today because he was "born again." He chastely states, "What was done in Watergate was bad enough, and I have taken responsibility for my part in it." For the benefit of those who can't imagine what this could be, it should be stated that Colson pleaded guilty more than two decades ago to obstructing justice. He now runs a prison ministry. Do any inmates feel that being preached to by Colson constitutes "cruel and unusual punishment"? Some might find it so.

We still grapple with the truth about the Vietnam War. Some of those most prominently involved in it continue to thrash about as if there were some mystery about its origins and causes.

Actually, the war was a reflection of three presidents: John Kennedy, the cold warrior who thought he could paste the Russians on the cheap in a toy country; Lyndon Johnson, who thought he could succeed where Kennedy had failed; and Richard Nixon, whose "they-can't-do-this-to-me" combativeness, combined with his paranoia, self-pity, and mania for secrecy, made him and Vietnam a toxic mix.

Kennedy's secretary of defense, Robert McNamara, was last seen wandering around Hanoi, conferring with the small generals who had confounded his projections and cost-benefit analyses—not to mention "strategic hamlets," pacification, Rolling Thunder, and winning hearts and minds. He asked the *Washington Post*'s Keith Richburg, "How did it come about?"

McNamara's quest has all the credibility of O. J. Simpson's search for his ex-wife's killer. He should read William Prochnau's excellent new book, *Once Upon a Distant War*, and see himself as he was: the lead advocate of this doomed and wretched war, with his slide-rule mind, his snapping-turtle certainties, and his obtuseness.

Ostensibly a vivid and meticulous reconstruction of a little band of tiger journalists—young, rebellious, and driven—the book is on another level the story of a government bent on deceiving itself.

Kennedy wanted to intervene in Vietnam, but invisibly; he wanted to escalate, but unobserved. The defining metaphor is presented by Prochnau: In 1962, a U.S. carrier in plain sight of the whole world steamed up the river to the heart of the teeming city. The military denied it was there.

The U.S. military was charged with the mission of telling the U.S. correspondents that everything was under control, that the Vietnamese units were fighting bravely and taking over the defense of their own country. The correspondents—David Halberstam of the *New York Times*, Neil Sheehan of United Press International, Malcolm Browne and Peter Arnett of the Associated Press, Horst Fass, a German combat photographer, and lordly Charlie Mohr of *Time*—would have none of it. They would grab a cab and go to the front and see the truth.

By 1968, only Richard Nixon would have sought to revive and prolong the unspeakable war. Only Chuck Colson would have the gall to present the sick and destructive impulse as "a passionate desire to bring peace to the world." ■

Nixon's "Sick Little World" Uncovered at Archives
—February 27, 1997

It was eerie. Clear as a bell, I heard my name on the big earphones the National Archives had loaned me.

The voice was unmistakable, too. It was Richard Nixon's.

He and his "zero-defect" right-hand man, H. R. Haldeman, were talking about me and other offending scribblers in the Washington press corps. It was hard to hear exactly what was said; there was a kind of buzz and the sound of hammering that could have been someone drumming on a desk.

Nixon was particularly hard to get. He had a strong voice and was too close to his microphone. I managed to make out that I was part of what Haldeman called "our tax project"— which I instantly assumed was a euphemism for having me audited. Then Nixon said, chuckling, "Gives them something to worry about." He forgave himself with a characteristic flourish, "It's routine."

I had always wondered about the audit I underwent in 1971—the tape I was listening to was made on September 18 of that year. I was pleased to see my paranoia confirmed. It was Nixon, not the luck of the draw, that sent me trembling to the Washington office of the Internal Revenue Service with a shopping bag of receipts. Nixon was right: It gave me sleepless nights.

I knew he didn't like me. I was on both of his famous enemies' lists.

The official reason: "syndicated columnist of New Left" and "daily hate-Nixon articles." Actually, I wrote only four times a week for my dear, dead paper, the *Washington Star*, but it plainly seemed more to Nixon.

I had spent most of my adult life with this joyless Californian. He was eternally coming and going. He was finished; he was back. He was always changing his persona, but it was always the same. He was mawkish, snide, savage; full of rage and grievance. I found him a pre-posterous politician—awkward, angry, aggrieved. He gave politics a bad name. "A world-class whiner," my colleague Dan Balz called him.

Henry Kissinger said Nixon needed love. I thought he needed a sense of humor—and a rest from the seething, plotting, and vengeful-ness that consumed him.

I wanted to listen to his tapes so I could find out why the dislike was so mutual. It's not so easy. In the first place, Archives II, where they are housed (in a large, antiseptic gray-and-white complex in College Park, Maryland), is a twenty-dollar cab ride from downtown Washington. When you get there, it's like what I imagine it is to visit a relative in jail. First you have to fill out an application card and get any papers you are carrying stamped. Then you have to put all your worldly belongings into a locker. You must give up your pencils and pens. They provide you with extremely hard pencils, which write faintly.

You consult a log and a summary of the contents of the tapes and write out a request in triplicate for what you want. You take them out one at a time.

Luckily, I had an interpreter-guide with me: a blond, deep-voiced newsroom troubleshooter named Barbara Saffir. She is a genius with machines and bureaucrats. She has merely to look at my computer for it to stop persecuting me; and she knows the ropes at the archives, having sped out there often recently for various "openings" of such incomparable Nixon offerings as his orders to "get the Jews" and to find an IRS commissioner who would give him tax returns he requested without a lot of guff.

Barbara and I spent the morning stalking references to me. Some were unintelligible; others were obscure. We found out that any slighting mention of me was well received.

Henry Kissinger, for instance, spoke heavily of possibly having lunch with Eugene McCarthy. He prided himself on contacts to peaceniks. He tried to keep them well-conned as he kept the Vietnam War going for four years. It was not easy, Kissinger said: "If I have lunch with him [McCarthy], he'll leak to Mary McGrory."

All along the way are arresting glimpses of a fortress under siege, of a court gathered around a doomed monarch who is ready to listen to any kind of nonsense that tells him that all is well even as the ground is trembling under his feet.

It is June 15, 1973, and Nixon press secretary Ron Ziegler is making points by referring to "Mary McGrory and her sick little world."

He branches out to "spin" Nixon about the Ervin hearings, which have just heard CREEP [Committee to Re-Elect the President] aide Jeb Magruder confirm the story of the Watergate break-in on national television. It was the beginning of the end.

"The Ervin Committee is a little burlesque show in the slummy part of town, a lynch mob. All that remains to be done is to cut down the body." "Not yours, Mr. President," adds the courtier, floundering in his metaphor.

Nixon resigned on August 9, 1974. The tapes provided the evidence that did him in.

The years do not diminish the weirdness of his presidency or the tragedy that such a man ever led the country. I just wish the archives would make transcripts of the tapes so it would be easier to remind ourselves to be careful what kind of people we send to the White House. ∎

Do We Have to Pay Again for Nixon's Excesses?
—April 13, 1997

He's back. We know it's him because he's asking for something, this time for $26 million.

Of course, Richard Nixon never really went away. From the grave he has kept in close touch through his tapes. He never lets us down. This is a soap opera that never ends. The latest episodes show the raving anti-Semite, the godfather in the White House.

Nixon has managed to call into doubt one of the enduring givens of Watergate, that he never knew about the break-in before it happened. The new tapes have him pounding the table in exasperation because the sissies around him never pulled off the break-in at the

Brookings Institution, which he ordered three times. "Blow the safe," he commanded.

He comes to us now through his family's request for $26 million for his presidential papers. Other presidents have donated their files and built their presidential libraries from money they raised themselves. We should not be surprised: We have always paid a heavy price for having Nixon around.

He imposed heavy fines on us at every stage of his career. First we had to sympathize with him for his uncherished childhood. No pony, no love. At the "Checkers" phase, he bade us be sorry that his wife didn't have a mink. When he was in the White House, we had to commiserate with him about the "vicious" press coverage he got. And when he finally left the great office he had disgraced, we were supposed to join his rage over the faithless congressional allies who faded in the impeachment fight.

When Nixon retired, his fans tried to picture him as a dear old sage whose banalities about politics were unique and acute. He himself ground out unreadable books full of cold war clichés, and reporters made pilgrimages to New Jersey to report on his state. It was never clear whether we were supposed to feel guilty for having turned him out of office or failing to appreciate his accomplishments.

He did some good things, on the domestic front. He instituted the Environmental Protection Agency; he sponsored a welfare bill that was infinitely better than the cruel version signed by Bill Clinton.

What I found most reprehensible about Nixon was his unconscionable prolonging of the Vietnam War. It so happens that this week those bitter years, with their rage, rancor, and deaths, were relived at a daylong observance of 1972 peace candidate George McGovern's seventy-fifth birthday. Old allies and friends gathered at the National Archives to discuss old wounds. People that Richard Nixon totally disapproved of—Hunter Thompson, Arthur Schlesinger Jr., me, Frank Mankiewicz, McGovern's campaign manager—recalled Nixon's conversation with Charles Colson after the shooting of George Wallace in May 1972: Get someone to Milwaukee to break into the assassin's apartment and plant McGovern literature.

The archivist of the United States was on hand for the reunion, John Carlin, to whose care the Nixon tapes have been consigned. During his first week in office, Julie Nixon Eisenhower came to see him about

43

resolving the situation of her father's papers. An appeals court had ruled that the government had seized the president's property—which provided evidence in several criminal trials—and owed him compensation. Julie Eisenhower told the archivist that, as the wife of a historian, she was eager to have the records open and available to the public.

Carlin knows nothing about the negotiations that resulted in the $26 million offer. We get stuck with the bill for building the library at Yorba Linda, California, and for carting out all the tapes that are housed in special facilities at an archives annex in College Park, Maryland.

Carlin says of the true value of the papers, "I have heard that they could bring as much as $250 million, which is why some people think it is a bargain."

If the government finds the Nixon family figure an offer it can refuse, the matter will go to court. A trial is scheduled for June.

What is wrong with having Richard Nixon being posthumously tried? It's time. If it's a jury trial, it's a cinch you can't find twelve residents of the District of Columbia who think that Nixon is worth $26 million or that his family needs the money, $10 million of which will go to lawyers.

The one thing we can be sure of is that Nixon will not go away. Some people are determined to bring him back. Lately they have been writing to me demanding that I compare Clinton to him. His followers seethe over the fact that while huggy, kissy Clinton sails on, their dark-browed hero with his switchblade smile was devoured by similar campaign excesses. They overlook the fact that Clinton so far has not been linked to any impeachable conduct. Nixon's troubles began with a break-in and advanced to obstruction of justice, both of which are criminal offenses. Must we pay again? ■

4

War

An Obscene Spectacle in Vietnam—April 1, 1975

If any doubt remained about our inability to do anything right in Vietnam, this past weekend brutally resolved it.

If any further proof were needed that all we can do for that stricken country is to leave it alone, the sight of the final air and sea rescue missions provided it.

Americans watched on their television sets the obscene spectacle of South Vietnam's best troops trampling women and children to claw their way on to the last plane out of Da Nang.

The sealift was halted when similar scenes were reenacted on the last boat for Cam Ranh Bay.

So much for "our brave little ally," as President Ford called it. So much, incidentally, for President Thieu's promise that Da Nang would be "defended to the death."

The president interrupted his golfing vacation at Palm Springs to have his press secretary term the fall of Da Nang "an immense human tragedy."

And in a miracle of timing, the day after it went down, the president chose to announce that the architect of these horrors, Henry A. Kissinger, had graciously consented to continue to serve as secretary of state.

Five years ago, at San Clemente, in one of his more sententious moments, Kissinger said, "History teaches us that people do not forgive their leaders for producing disasters."

But the way he and the other officials of the administration are choosing to handle this particular disaster is to pretend it is not happening or, if it is, that it is someone else's fault.

The immense human tragedy of Vietnam is that it has never been treated in terms of the people involved. It has always been regarded as a domestic political problem. Four presidents have sworn to end it. They just didn't want it to happen in their time.

When it became apparent that Congress would not cough up the additional $300 million in emergency aid, Ford changed his tack by asking for just three more years of support for the Thieu regime. That would, of course, take him safely by the next election. Nobody could accuse him of "losing" Vietnam.

His reaction to the disintegration of the South Vietnamese army has been that of his predecessors. Throw more time at it, throw more money and some miracle will occur to prevent what Richard M. Nixon called on the occasion of the incursion into Cambodia, "the first defeat in (America's) proud 190-year history."

Recently, Ford summoned to the White House General William C. Westmoreland, who presided over the bloody and inconclusive phase of our troop involvement in Vietnam. The general came out and said what the military has always said, "Bomb Hanoi."

His next move was to dispatch the Army Chief of Staff, General Frederick C. Weyand to Saigon. If Weyand comes back as every other American general has done for the past ten years, he will tell us that with a little more money and a little more time the Vietnamese can "hack it."

Unlike Johnson and Nixon, Ford has no peace movement to blame for the current catastrophe. "The effete corps of impudent snobs" as Spiro T. Agnew once called it, has spread to include 78 percent of the American people. So Ford is preparing to unload the debacle on the Congress.

But as long as the fighting continues. as long as the killing goes on, the policy cannot be officially labeled a "failure."

That is probably why President Thieu is not following the example of President Lon Nol, who is packing for parts unknown.

Thieu understands the realities of the situation. He realizes that, while the South Vietnamese soldiers are not willing to stand and fight for his government, the Ford administration is.

He understands that the man in the White House, whoever he is, will put up with anything—repression, wholesale jailings of political dissidents, massive corruption, a one-man election—anything that will put off the evil day when the fact must be faced that it is over in Vietnam.

If Ford really wanted to end the suffering of the Vietnamese people, he would have sent quietly an American mayor or governor to Saigon to hand Thieu a plane ticket and encourage the formation of a coalition government that is called for in the Paris Accords, and that could negotiate terms.

But that would be an admission that it has all gone wrong. By sending a general, by sending ships and planes, Ford maintains at least for himself the illusion that something can be done. Henry Kissinger, by clinging to his office as those soldiers clung to the wings of the outgoing planes, is telling us that if South Vietnam is falling apart, the Ford administration is standing together in hypocrisy.

Only the North Vietnamese can end the war. ■

Ford Stance Reveals His Unreal View—April 4, 1975

Gerald Ford tramped in from the golf course, assessed the damage, and said it was greatly exaggerated.

Vietnam is in agony. America is sick with shame and humiliation. The golfer says we can salvage the situation.

It was a time for greatness—or at least for delicacy, contrition, and common sense. Ford gave us confusion, sophistry, and politics.

We must look on the bright side, he urged.

He has ordered the immediate evacuation of two thousand Vietnamese orphans. How can anyone think we are helpless when we can do that? We are a resourceful and compassionate people. We swoop down from the skies, scoop up the helpless, and carry them to safety.

The babies will help us to forget what we did to their country.

He may even bring out some older people. There is a law that permits that. The president was vague, but the hint may be enough to send more terrified Vietnamese to the airports or set them to storming those few remaining American installations that are still operating. We cannot evacuate an entire population, but we can salve our consciences and show the world we do not abandon an ally.

Gerald Ford looks at those refugees and he sees a people "willing to fight for their freedom." Soldiers walked over their grandmothers for places on planes and ships that were sent to rescue civilians. Gerald Ford has interpreted their panic as resolve to live to fight another day.

The orphans will be used, apparently, to pry more money out of Congress for "humanitarian aid."

The refugees, Ford was trying to tell us, in his muddled way, illustrate the rightness of our intervention.

They will be used, it is clear, as an argument for more military aid. Their "will to fight"—expressed in pell-mell retreat—will be cited as a reason to continue the policies that brought about the present horror.

As Ford tells it, Henry Kissinger promised to save the South Vietnamese in the Paris Accords. That "commitment," which is written in invisible ink, must be honored, lest the world think that the United States is losing its nerve.

What a majority of Americans thought they heard four presidents saying was that we would help the South Vietnamese to resist a Communist takeover. Some $150 billion dollars and fifty-five thousand American lives were spent in that effort. It has failed, but Gerald Ford says it's not over yet.

And were those lives spent in vain? he was asked. He stumbled into the subjunctive. They would not have been if Congress had kept Henry Kissinger's promise.

President Ford bears no ill will toward President Thieu for pulling out his troops without consultations. He would not dream of urging him to resign. Besides, Thieu's departure would have no effect on our "humanitarian" efforts.

What he would like to do, although he could not say so, was to turn the clock back to the days of his patron, Richard Nixon, who, when he was not actually bombing, was threatening to do so.

A shortsighted Congress has robbed this commander in chief of those deterrents. Nor has he any prisoners of war to justify more strenuous efforts to prove America's resolve and optimism.

He is left only with the orphans and the refugees.

The most that can be said about the press conference was that Ford believed what he said. Even without the coaching of Henry Kissinger, he would have taken the same line. Ford has never entertained the idea that our exercise in "nation-building" was wrong. He is a militarist who believes utterly in the wisdom of the Pentagon, the power of weaponry, and the invincibility of America.

To say what could have been said was utterly beyond him. To say that we had been blind and arrogant, to voice sorrow and promise humility is not in his nature. To admit defeat, to admit we had blundered and destroyed a nation in the process, is not the way of a congressman from Grand Rapids. Even if Henry Kissinger had urged him to express remorse or to summon the United Nations to heal the wounds we have inflicted, Gerald Ford could not have done it.

The sky is fallen in Vietnam. Gerald Ford is telling us it is blue. Henry Kissinger said our response to the calamity would show what kind of people we are. All it has shown us so far is what kind of leader Gerald Ford is. His press conference reminded us that he was chosen by Richard Nixon, who told us he was bringing "a generation of peace." ■

Guts Needed to Abstain on Vietnam—April 7, 1975

As it required in the beginning, the Vietnam War requires at its end the courage of America to do nothing.

To do nothing goes against the grain of America. The informing principle of our participation has been that it is better to do anything than to do nothing.

Gerald Ford, the fourth president of the United States who does not wish to be the first president to admit defeat, is again telling us that America's honor is at stake in a wretched civil war which would have ended the same way a long time ago without our intervention.

Congress had its chance to be brave ten years ago when Lyndon Johnson leaned on it for the Tonkin Gulf Resolution. Only two senators, two Democrats who have since died, Ernest Gruening of Alaska and Wayne Morse of Oregon, had the courage to say no.

Gerald Ford is preparing to give them another chance, this war has always moved presidents to set Americans against Americans. President Johnson called his critics "nervous Nellies." They graduated to traitors in Richard Nixon's day. Now with the peace movement a majority, Gerald Ford has chosen Congress as his scapegoat and is threatening reprisal if they fail to support the Thieu government.

Lyndon Johnson exhorted the country to support our brave boys and not question why they were there. Richard Nixon represented himself as obsessed with the plight of our prisoners of war. Now the

49

Vietnamese war orphans, the most touching victims, are brought before our eyes. Whenever a mindless policy is endangered, its casualties are presented as a reason for continuing it.

Why did it take a Communist offensive to unlock the orphanage doors and cut the red tape and make it official policy to bring them here? The children have long been homeless in Saigon. Thousands of Americans have been yearning and pleading to take them in. The flamboyant pilot, Ed Daley, broke the rules and brought the first batch here. The first official flight ended in a crash, another unbearable reminder that whatever we undertake in that country seems doomed.

President Ford has learned nothing from Vietnam. He has also learned nothing from John F. Kennedy, who said "Victory has a thousand fathers; defeat is an orphan." Kennedy claimed that orphan. He was president, he was responsible for the Bay of Pigs, which was less tragic and terrible, but a defeat which he and the country survived.

What Gerald Ford should be looking for, instead of excuses to persist, is the words to explain to the American people what has happened. He should be searching for those grave and somber terms to define failure so its lessons might be learned.

Instead, Ford is busy fashioning the "nightmare of recriminations" that Richard Nixon told us he would avert by prolonging the war. He says while denying he is pointing a finger at anyone, that the tragedy "could have been avoided" if Congress had not perfidiously turned its back on "solemn commitments." He is being assisted in the poisoning of the air by the secretary of state who sees in congressional resistance a wanton move to "destroy our allies."

What chapter 2, article 7 of the Paris Accords says is the following:

"The two South Vietnamese parties shall be permitted to make periodic replacements of armaments, munitions, and war material which have been destroyed, damaged, worn out or used up after the cease-fire on the basis of piece for piece, of the same characteristics and properties."

Many years ago, a presidential aide said sadly, "Vietnam is an illness in the White House walls."

The illness was best diagnosed in a book called *Men, Stress, and Vietnam* by a Washington psychiatrist named Peter Bourne, who was a member of a Walter Reed research team which spent a year in Vietnam during 1965 to 1966.

Bourne says, "The overwhelming desire for the success of policies to which a strong emotional attachment has been made also leads to an attempt to alter those facts over which one has control, making them consistent with the outcome that is desired. It is as though there is an expectation at a magical level that events over which one has no control will then also fall into the desired pattern. . . . Emphasis is placed on humanitarian acts of reconstruction while they remain trivial next to the enormity of the destruction . . ."

Those words were written five years ago. They are still true. And General Frederick C. Weyand has come back, as has every general before him, telling us that with a little help from their friends, the South Vietnamese can overcome. ■

Bush's Telegenic Halftime War—January 22, 1991

So far, President Bush has given the country the war it said it wanted in the polls: a war almost free of casualties, or at least many that we can see.

Moreover, Operation Desert Storm is a telegenic combination of air show arms bazaar, with marvelous weapons for every contingency being uncovered precisely when needed. "Pinpoint bombing," derided through the Vietnam War years as a joke, now could be viewed on television: A missile found the chimney of the building it wanted to off and suavely slipped down its length.

Wall Street fell in love. Ignorant civilians became instantly knowledgeable about technological miracles like the F-4G Wild Weasel plane, which zapped enemy radar, and the aptly named Patriot missile, which bloodlessly felled the Scuds, several of which were duds. For eventualities, there is the Warthog, a plane that knocks tanks silly. Things are going so well, the firepower is so awesome, that Saddam's infantry could collapse before the first shot is fired on the ground, particularly if his foot soldiers are as languid as his air force.

For the war-watchers there were harrowing moments. Who will soon forget the sight of NBC's Martin Fletcher broadcasting through his gas mask, while the sirens wailed through the windows? Television correspondents are the new folk heroes—daring, dedicated, well groomed. The air warriors themselves are implausibly good looking, ridiculously well trained, cheerful, and modest. They come back from their missions giving the thumbs-up, they exchange high-fives with their delighted crews. The volunteer army is cool, no question about it.

The Pentagon is smiling. It controls the news as it controls the skies over the desert. The airwaves ring with its praises. Hosannas are heard for Ronald Reagan. He was right, crow his fans, who have been crestfallen of late. Your trillion-dollar defense budget is worth every penny. Senator Sam Nunn (D-GA) invited the military-industrial complex to take a bow. Sure, they spent a little too much and took a little too long. But look what they produced.

Who can fault a war that lets you play basketball and the professional football championship games—and gives war bulletins between plays? Sometimes the war is less messy. Americans haven't felt so good since the 1980 Winter Olympics.

How wonderful a war it is whose greatest political problem is keeping our friends, the fighters in the region, from getting into it on our side? Israel is being called "magnificent" for not striking back under attack.

History has seldom provided a more cooperative enemy than Iraqi President Saddam Hussein. He gives retroactive reasons for taking arms against him. He helps validate accounts of super-careful, civilian-sparing bombing by not showing any damage or corpses to the world. He kicks out those who might have reported it.

He launches Scud missiles against Israel, giving the world chilling glimpses of women and children struggling into gas masks, which, with their googly eyes and their long snouts, make people look like horses. Pictures of humble homes ruined, stories of Soviet immigrants—after hellish years of waiting—being welcomed to their new country with explosions and flying glass have created maximum sympathy for Israel. Our president calls their prime minister three times in one day. A new honeymoon period between the two countries is inaugurated. The Palestinians, who are at the heart of all the trouble, have kicked away all support by leading the cheers for Iraq.

Saddam, who released hostages in December, is back in his monster mode. He parades captured allied fliers on television. They hang their heads. Their faces are bruised, they speak reluctantly, haltingly. Some of them condemn their country's aggression. This may play well among Arabs. It ignites and unites Americans. Seeing their compatriots abused makes Americans fighting mad.

Bush is at a zenith of popularity. Democrats think he will not just win the war in the next few weeks, but the 1992 election, as well.

Says Senator Howard M. Metzenbaum (D-OH), a leader in the fight against the war, "These are rough times." Presidential opponents seem like spoilsports in the stands of the great television show of the century. This is not Vietnam, with mud, blood, and haunted-eyed grunts. This is the new, crisp order of warfare.

Nobody is thinking much about the future, about the poisoned peace that will follow the hostilities. The region may be changed unalterably. So could this country. The military budget will again receive respectful treatment. The wonder weapons will have to be replaced.

The United States did not go into this enterprise as Athens, exactly, but it will almost surely come out as Sparta—armed to the teeth and spoiling to fight. ■

McNamara's Truths Are Too Little, Too Late
—April 13, 1995

Now he tells us. Twenty-five years after it could help or comfort or enlighten, former secretary of defense Robert McNamara has written his memoirs, *In Retrospect*, in which he says the Vietnam War was wrong, dead wrong, flat wrong—just as millions of people knew without benefit of briefings, cables, charts, graphs, projections, and memos. The motives and intentions were good, but Lyndon Johnson's war cabinet was deaf, dumb, and blind when it came to reason, common sense, and common humanity. The domino theory prevailed.

Maybe McNamara feels better for having gotten all this off his chest. But what about the rest of us? He says grandly that he wrote to prevent recurrence of such folly and to arrest the corroding effects of cynicism about government. But it's too late for all that. One question looms: Where has he been?

The ultimate SecDef, with his shiny, patent-leather hair and his gleaming, rimless glasses, spewing out statistics like a slot machine, apparently feels he has atoned for failures freely confessed. But his explanation is a mystery.

During Johnson's presidency, McNamara felt that speaking out was out of the question: "I believe that would have been a violation of my responsibility to the president and my oath to uphold the Constitution."

McNamara rationalized then and thinks now that he had no higher responsibility. Thousands of young Americans were being sent to a war that he knew, despite contrary assurances to Congress and the country, could not be won. We could have sought a settlement, he writes, in 1963, 1964, or 1965. It went on, as we all know, until 1973.

Inexplicably, the end of the Johnson presidency did not mean an end to McNamara's obligation to Johnson. He felt no duty to tell people it was all insane: Rolling Thunder, Search and Destroy, Operation Phoenix, Operation Daisy Cutter—the whole obscene repertory of death and pain that poisoned the political life of the country for a generation, divided friends and families, and made us brutes and fools before the rest of the world.

Did it occur to McNamara as he watched Richard Nixon prolong the war that he had an obligation to tell what he knew about the false premises and "totally incorrect appraisals" that ended in fifty-eight thousand American deaths and God only knows how many Vietnamese?

McNamara never knew—or understood, given his self-confessed obtuseness, that Nixon and Kissinger made a totally cynical decision to continue the war lest the inevitable defeat damage Nixon's chances for reelection in 1972. But even if McNamara did not have the benefit of H. R. Haldeman's memoirs, in which Kissinger tells Haldeman it would not be safe to finish it off until the end of the campaign, McNamara might have noticed that while Vietnam was "winding down," twenty thousand more GIs were being killed.

That was a moment for him to write what he has written now. He was one of the highest-ranking officials of the Johnson administration; he could have made a difference. He might have spared us the invasion of Cambodia, Kent State, the presidential pitting of hard-hat against student, the Vietnam Veterans Against the War encampment on the Mall, the fight over the flag, the shredding of the bonds of civility.

Maybe he would simply have been reviled by Nixon's bullies. But he could have tried. That is what's unpardonable, not to have tried. He could have lent the authority of documents to the undocumented certainties of the dissenters.

Says former senator Eugene McCarthy, presidential candidate of the antiwar insurgency: "Once people are dying, the rules change. It isn't like price supports. He could have been helpful at almost any time."

McCarthy is preparing for a trip to Kent State for a memorial service for the four students killed on the campus in the wake of the Cambodian-invasion protest. He thinks the best time for McNamara to have gone public would have been in 1969 or 1970. McNamara could have offered Nixon political support to end the war.

But McNamara, who had an answer for everything, except why it was acceptable to send young men to die in an unjust cause, has a tremendous capacity for self-absorption.

During Vietnam, he gave hints of opposition—just enough to keep liberals bemused. When White House press secretary Bill Moyers quit his job, McNamara attended a Georgetown farewell party and raised a glass "to the doves; we need more of them." It caused a thrilled stir, nothing more. The war went on.

Maybe McNamara deserves credit for telling us how bad it was on the inside, how adamant and arrogant officials were, how off in their judgments and appraisals, how oblivious to tempering events. But that is not the point. The reviews of this book can be written only at the Vietnam Wall, with its fifty-eight thousand names. ∎

Bob Kerrey's Burden—May 3, 2001

Bob Kerrey a baby-killer? Laughing, literate Bob Kerrey, who in the Senate was best friends with sage Pat Moynihan? Who quoted Emily Dickinson and Robert Frost, who kept a scrapbook of clippings about life's absurdities? Always quizzical, he ran for the presidency in 1992, in a way that suggested he thought politics was a joke—he spent a lot of time in his van watching old movies.

There was nothing to suggest that the Medal of Honor winner was hauling around a burden of "guilt and shame" from Vietnam that only Nathaniel Hawthorne or Graham Greene could do justice to. There was only an expression of pain in his eyes to suggest a damaged soul.

Yes, it's that Bob Kerrey who has reignited the rage and passion of the Vietnam years with his story of a black night in the Mekong Delta thirty-two years ago. He has upset both hawks and doves, those who thought they could have won the war if the left had let them, and those who remain outraged to this day that we fought a war for no reason we could cite, using methods that sickened and shamed us all.

The left finds in the Kerrey story an appalling instance of what was wrong with Vietnam. *New York Times* columnist William Safire sees another lamentable outburst of the "self-flagellation" that Henry Kissinger, the histrionic secretary of state, ascribed to those who wanted to end the war before it was safe for Richard Nixon to do so.

Kerrey's mission in Thanh Phong on February 25, 1969, when he was a green and gung ho navy SEAL, was to "take out" a Viet Cong leader thought to be holding meetings in the village. The SEALS never found him.

According to Kerrey's account, his seven-member team took fire and returned it. That was no big deal, but when he found out that he and his men had killed fourteen unarmed women and children, he was horrified. He kept his secret for thirty-two years and revealed it only when the *New York Times Sunday Magazine* scheduled publication.

Five members of his unit backed up his story. But a sixth, Gerhard Klann, says Kerrey had the women and children rounded up and gave an order to shoot them at close range. Last Thursday, Kerrey, looking haunted and haggard, faced a Manhattan press conference and the jackals had at him for a painful hour. Tuesday night, Dan Rather reviewed the situation on *60 Minutes*, which was even more excruciating.

Kerrey's erstwhile Vietnam caucus comrades rallied to him, claiming that people who hadn't been there should not judge him—an understandable but not completely tenable position. They appeared together on ABC Sunday morning. Senator John Kerry of Massachusetts, who had been a skipper on the Mekong River, said that the Phoenix program, under whose auspices the operation was carried out, was an assassination program.

This was hotly denied at the time at the highest level, but William Colby, while director of the CIA, finally conceded at a congressional hearing that some twenty-one thousand Vietnamese, presumably of the VC infrastructure, had been killed.

Republican voices are calling for an investigation of Bob Kerrey. More who loved the war, although not well enough to go or send their sons to it, will probably be clamoring for "the truth." By all means, put Kerrey in the dock. But let's not forget the perpetrators. Let's call Robert McNamara, the ultimate secretary of defense, who wrote a book twenty-five years after his long service as one of its principal cheerleaders, saying he knew as early as 1963 it could not be won. And we should hear from Henry Kissinger, who bamboozled the press—he still does—into thinking he was ending the war when he kept it going for four years. It isn't as if we need them to tell us what went on. We knew at the time.

On April 23, 1971, John Kerry, then a navy lieutenant and the leader of Vietnam Veterans Against the War, testified before the Senate Foreign Relations Committee about what our soldiers were doing in Vietnam.

"I would like to say that several months ago in Detroit we had an investigation at which over 150 honorably discharged veterans testified to war crimes committed in Southeast Asia. . . . They told stories that at times they had personally raped, cut off ears, cut off heads, taped wires from portable telephones to human genitals and turned up the power, cut off limbs, blown up bodies, randomly shot at civilians, razed villages in fashion reminiscent of Genghis Khan, shot cattle and dogs for fun, poisoned feedstocks, and generally ravaged the countryside of South Vietnam in addition to the normal ravage of war and the normal and very particular ravaging which is done by the applied bombing power of this country."

Bob Kerrey, who lost a leg and his peace of mind in Vietnam, should not be asked to answer for all this. ■

Talk of War Darkens a Sunny Piazza in Italy
—October 13, 2002

War seemed unthinkable in the Piazza della Signoria in Florence, when I was there lately. There was too much else going on, mostly happy stuff, and the variety and vivacity of the crowd might have diverted even George Bush and Dick Cheney from their absorption in missiles and rockets and cakewalks in Baghdad.

Italians, who are with us on the war against terrorism, are two-thirds opposed to Bush's war against Iraq, even though Prime Minister Silvio Berlusconi is trying to give Britain's Tony Blair a run for his money as George Bush's best friend in Europe.

But for his people, one war at a time is enough. They agree with Bush's description of Saddam Hussein as "a homicidal dictator who is addicted to weapons of mass destruction." But they don't think he is suicidal.

Our little party lingered for hours in the famous square—waiters do not bring checks except by invitation. Life was at the bubble all around us. There was an ambulance parked in the entrance, surrounded by anxious tour mates of a woman who had collapsed on one of Florence's ornate trash bins. A police car was inching its way through the crush.

Hard by was a jazz combo warming up. In the center, a classical trio was at the ready, and a soprano with a rich voice was singing "Ave Maria"; she was accompanied by a harpist who was wearing a dinner dress. A man dressed in white tails, with flour on his face, was entertaining tourists with impersonations of Mark Twain and Charlie Chaplin. We counted three brides as they headed for photo ops before the most famous city hall in the world, with a reproduction of Michelangelo's imperturbable *David* at its side. Much applause from waiters and loungers occurred.

Under the blue sky, the only discordant notes were to be found in the newspapers. Thunderbolts emanated from Washington. The president and the secretary of defense seemed beside themselves with rage at Germany. The news that the country that had plunged the world into two murderous conflicts in the last century had finally kicked the habit and gone dove could have caused celebration. But Gerhard Schroder had campaigned against Bush's "adventure" in Iraq, and he won.

Rumsfeld was so steamed that he wouldn't shake hands with his Teutonic counterpart at an international conference; the president has yet to congratulate Schroder on his election, and one of the White House warlords, Richard Perle, told a German publication that Schroder should resign.

In the midst of it all, while Uncle Sam was bent on showing the world how cooperative and multilateral he is, a decree was issued in the name of the first woman national security adviser, Condoleezza Rice—remember how we longed for a woman at the top in Vietnam councils? It was a rugged document, proclaiming the policy of preemptive war. It smacked much more of Julius Caesar than of George Washington.

We could see that Bush was breaking all institutions in sight, like kindling over his knee. He threatened the United Nations with irrelevance; he made the European Union, the Democratic Party, the

House, and the Senate lie down and roll over.

The Italians were baffled. *"E pazzo?"* (Is he crazy?) they would ask politely. The van driver who drove us back to our hotel along the Arno, the Villa La Massa, took both hands off the steering wheel to inquire passionately of his nervous American passengers, "Why you want the war?" He did not blame America, only Bush.

Filippo drove us every day to the Ponte Vecchio, where we had one of those delightful encounters for which Italy is famous. We met what we considered the flower of Florence, a beautiful golden retriever who was a professional panhandler. She sat on a pink mat with a basket in her mouth. When a passerby dropped a coin in her basket, she offered, on command from her master—a rather villainous-looking man sitting on a nearby curbstone—a paw, her left one, because the basket tilted a little to the right.

The dog was like the Italians around her, cheerful and good at her job. She posed willingly for pictures and bestowed kisses and smiles on an emotional Englishwoman, who seemed torn between caressing Doris and thrashing her master for animal exploitation. Doris seemed to like him and rested her chin on his knee during her infrequent breaks.

My friend Phil has a theory that the Lord, having made teenagers, felt constrained to make amends and so created the golden retriever. Doris certainly made up for lots of green hair and nose rings.

War could bring death to the fun in the piazzas on sunny afternoons. Filippo and Doris could lose their jobs. The Italian economy would suffer, and so would we if we couldn't go to the country where kindness to strangers is a religion, you can't turn your head without seeing something beautiful, and you can't get a bad meal if you try. ∎

Mistaken Patriots—October 17, 2002

Are Democrats making a major effort to reduce voter turnout in the coming election? Or are they just trying to fight free of the trap they diligently fashioned for themselves on the subject of war with Iraq?

By their conduct on the issue in the recent congressional debate, they seemed eager to show there was no difference between them and the Republicans—a strategy that guarantees voters will ask themselves, when it comes to digging out on a cold November morning, "Why bother?"

By way of preparing for the election, Democrats decided to get the war issue "out of the way." By overwhelmingly backing President Bush's desire to blow the bugle without the blessing of the United Nations, they ensured that the commander in chief will be at center stage. The papers throb with accounts of his minions moving troops and launching training exercises as if war had been declared.

Sheepish Democrats continue to show the electorate that when it comes to the fateful business of sending young Americans into battle, they are at one with the Republicans. They turned aside the known skepticism of the uniformed military. They were undeterred by the newly enunciated doctrine of "preventive war," which all previous presidents have rejected. While they declared in their floor speeches that they were uncertain of the danger posed by Saddam Hussein, their votes said they were mindful of the danger to themselves and they were taking no chances.

Candidates around the country were on their own in trying to make judgments about the right thing to do. The debate won't help them much. The votes in both houses of Congress for the new Tonkin Gulf Resolution are still being studied for surprises and contradictions, particularly by liberals, who, according to the *Washington Post*'s Thomas Edsall, are outraged by the absence of strong convictions on the part of their leaders.

Senate Democrats are quick to blame House Democratic leader Dick Gephardt, who has wraparound ambitions—to be either president or House Speaker. They say a coalition of moderates from both parties, who wanted UN approval of any use of force, fell apart when Gephardt emerged as Bush's chief lobbyist on the Hill. Republicans said they didn't want to be "to the left of Gephardt."

The whole slate of Democratic presidential hopefuls lined up for the president's right to make war unilaterally. Of them all, Senator John Kerry had a unique foreign policy perch. A decorated war veteran who also came home and led a brilliant demonstration to end the war, he delivered a sophisticated critique of the botched hunt for Osama bin Laden. But he joined the gang voting for the president—such notable peaceniks as Tom Harkin, Chris Dodd, and Tom Daschle, not to mention Hillary Clinton.

The majority leader hated to do it, but in the end he threw in the towel to show the world the country is "unified" on the issue.

The country is ambivalent. On the one hand it is all for a short, sharp replay of Gulf War I that would be relatively casualty-free. But bring up body bags and they recoil. Polls show that the country would rather have the president protect it from the wolf at the door—layoffs, market collapses, and the like—than from the beast of Baghdad, who might nuke us if he got the right stuff.

Teddy Kennedy made daily speeches against going to war. He and Robert C. Byrd, long-ago rivals, did their best, but Kennedy couldn't even convince his son in the House, Patrick Kennedy of Rhode Island, that he should give peace a chance. Rhode Island did, however, offer the Senate's only Republican profile in courage: Lincoln Chafee, faithful to his father's legendary independence, voted no.

The Democrats hope that with the war issue "settled" they can drag voters' attention back to the economy, which can be criticized without fear of their being called unpatriotic. Bush brushes them off. You don't like my tax cuts? OK, you want to rescind them? No, of course not, the Democrats protest.

Pollster Peter Hart thinks the economy doesn't need much rhetoric. The ravages are all around and brought home in people's reports about their 401(k)s. And people can recall the Clinton boom to be reminded of how different things can be.

At the height of the debate, House Whip Nancy Pelosi implored Democrats to remember that while a show of force in Iraq would surely demonstrate U.S. power, negotiation and diplomacy would show our strength. Her colleagues were not listening.

Democrats know exactly how they feel about prescription drugs and the privatization of Social Security, but when it comes to war and peace, people dying and all that, they really have no comment. They just salute the commander in chief and hope voters mistake them for patriots. ■

I'm Persuaded—February 6, 2003

I don't know how the United Nations felt about Colin Powell's *"J'accuse"* speech against Saddam Hussein. I can only say that he persuaded me, and I was as tough as France to convince.

I'm not exactly a pacifist. Vietnam came close to making me one, but no one of the World War II generation can say war is never justified. I have resisted the push to war against Iraq because I thought George W. Bush was trying to pick a fight for all the wrong reasons—big oil, the far right—against the wrong enemy.

The people who were pushing hardest are not people whose banner I could follow. I find our commander in chief a flighty thinker. The drumbeaters didn't inspire my confidence. All of them, despite their clamorous anticommunism, declined to wear the uniform for Vietnam, and some of them had the nerve, when the fighting was finally over, to write pieces for their neocon journals about how sorry they were to have missed the camaraderie of the foxhole and the firing line.

Richard Perle, a lead tenor in the war chorus, was the right hand of the late Henry Jackson, a hawk of hawks on defense issues. Gene McCarthy once remarked of Jackson, as a presidential candidate, "If he's elected, you will never see the sun—the sky will be black with planes."

Among people I know, nobody was for the war. All of us were clinging tightly to the toga of Colin Powell. We, like the rest of the world, trusted him. We read Bob Woodward's *Bush at War* with admiration and gratitude for our stalwart secretary of state. We wished Powell would oppose the war, because it seemed like such a huge and misdirected overreaction to a bully who got on the nerves of our touchy Texas president.

But resistance of any kind at 1600 Pennsylvania Avenue was a boon to peaceniks. Powell patiently and humbly waited for his chance to convince the president that he couldn't have a shootout with Saddam Hussein and ride off into the sunset of world approval. When the protest crowds came to Washington, full of scorn for the commander in chief and his Cabinet cohorts, they made an exception of Colin Powell.

Powellites had a bad moment when he lost his cool with the French ambassador to the United Nations. The French invited him to a seminar on terrorism, but when he got there he received an antiwar blast from Dominique de Villepin. State Department and White House spinners put it out that the secretary was "livid" and "humiliated," and soon the buzz was that Powell, in his rage, had gone prowar. I was told to remember that Powell was above all "a good soldier" and, once a decision was made, would salute.

Was it appalling that a man of Powell's stature would be small enough to think that because he had lost face, thousands might lose their lives? I knew the issue was bigger than that. But on Iraq, the president has been generous in sharing his personal feelings.

Yet the key to Powell's sterner line came from an unexpected source: the long-suffering chief of what Bush chose to call "the so-called inspectors": Hans Blix. In a progress report on January 21, Blix castigated Hussein for having "no genuine acceptance of the demand to disarm" and for "a failure to demonstrate active cooperation with inspection."

Of course, Bush chose Powell to make the case before the United Nations. He has no one else who so commands the country's respect—or the world's. Powell took his seat in the United Nations and put his shoulder to the wheel. He was to talk for almost an hour and a half. His voice was strong and unwavering. He made his case without histrionics of any kind, with no verbal embellishments.

He aired his tapes of conversations between Iraqi army officers who might well be supposed to be concealing toxic materials or enterprises. He talked of the mobile factories concealed in trains and trucks that move along roads and rails while manufacturing biological agents. I was struck by their ingenuity and the insistence on manufacturing agents that cause diseases such as gangrene, plague, cholera, camelpox, and hemorrhagic fever.

Would Saddam Hussein use them? He already has, against his own people and Iranians. He has produced four tons of deadly VX: "A single drop of VX on the skin will kill in minutes."

The cumulative effect was stunning. I was reminded of the day long ago when John Dean, a White House toady, unloaded on Richard Nixon, and you could see the dismay written on Republican faces that knew impeachment was inevitable.

I wasn't so sure about the al-Qaida connection. But I had heard enough to know that Saddam Hussein, with his stockpiles of nerve gas and death-dealing chemicals, is more of a menace than I had thought. I'm not ready for war yet. But Colin Powell has convinced me that it might be the only way to stop a fiend, and that if we do go, there is reason. ■

To My Very Persuasive Readers—March 6, 2003

Dear Readers:

We have been through a great deal together—the Kennedy assassination, Vietnam, El Salvador, Grenada, Lebanon, and Florida. For the first time I can remember, we are estranged. That is, you have been since I wrote a column on February 6 about Colin Powell's UN indictment of Saddam Hussein. You have declared yourselves to be shocked, appalled, startled, puzzled, and above all disappointed by what you thought was a defection to the hawk side. I'M PERSUADED said the headline, which went a little beyond the story.

But it was my fault. I did not make it clear enough that while I believed what Colin Powell told me about Saddam Hussein's poison collection, I was not convinced that war was the answer. I guess I took it for granted that you would know what I meant. The flow of letters has abated somewhat, but last week I had a call from a woman who identified herself as a longtime reader and asked me sternly, "Don't you think you should explain yourself—this schoolgirl crush on Colin Powell?" I hope it's not too late.

I write about this outrage because the letters tell you, if the demonstrations didn't, that opposition to the war is deep and widespread. I received just two letters commending me for being a turncoat. One was from Germany, from a man who said he was glad to see my position was "evolving." A man from Lowell, Massachusetts, urged me to "break away from the left in this country." I regret to say that several members of Congress who cravenly voted for the war resolution sent word that my column had "liberated" them.

Otherwise, it was all reproach and dismay. "What happened to you?" asked San Diego. "Has the White House threatened you?" "Did they torture you?" Springfield, Virginia, inquired, or had I been "intoxicated" by my paper's prowar editorials? A woman from the District of Columbia made me flinch with just two lines: "How could you? Truly, how could you?"

Burke, Virginia, said: "We were very disappointed to see you so duped by Colin Powell." "George Bush and Richard Perle are gloating," wrote another reader from nearby Virginia. And in fact, I was mentioned, for the first time ever with approval, by Ari Fleischer, who cited me as Exhibit A of the newly convinced.

I have thought well of Colin Powell since I heard him say that the most important lesson to teach the young is that they should do whatever job is assigned and do it well. As a teenager he mopped the floors at a soft-drink bottling factory so well he was promoted to the bottling line. His role in the Iran-Contra scandal as an aide to Caspar Weinberger was not glorious, but I was ready to vote for him for president if he ran in 1996. I was grateful he was Bush's secretary of state, and more so when I read in Bob Woodward's *Bush at War* that he was the buffer between two gung ho Baghdad cakewalkers, Dick Cheney and Donald Rumsfeld. He was not a peacenik, but he was all we anti-invaders had.

But now Powell, apparently convinced by his own speech, has joined the "time is running out" crowd, and the pope and Ted Kennedy are the high-profile holdouts.

One disillusioned local enclosed a letter from a public health physician named David Hilfiker, who has helped the homeless in Washington. From Baghdad, the doctor describes the misery of children who are dying for lack of pure drinking water—sanctions forbid importation of parts for water treatment plants, he says.

What impressed me about Powell's presentation, besides his magisterial presence and impeccable prose, were the poisons he showed and the malice behind them. I did not have the benefit of the informed criticism that followed. The *Washington Post's* Walter Pincus wrote a summation of the weakest link in Powell's speech, the al-Qaida connection. Lately, the coming conflict is presented seamlessly as "a war against Iraq and terrorism."

The last time I experienced large-scale consumer protest was in September 2001, when I wrote that Bush should have returned immediately to the capital after the 9/11 attack. The response was explosive—floods of letters, a $7^{1}/_{2}$-inch pile of e-mails, and furious phone calls that tied up the line for days.

The difference in the tone of the thunder from the left is instructive, I think. The right-wing readers came at me like eagles with claws unsheathed. I was accused of working for Osama bin Laden. I should go "back to Afghanistan." I was castigated for a want of intelligence and patriotism. I was called unprintable names. By contrast, the lefties were reproving. Some thanked me for having, in the past at least, gotten it right and given them comfort.

65

I failed as a writer to take time to make myself clear. And I did something that George Bush never does: I offended my base. You see how sorry I am. I hope now that all is forgiven and that I can come home again.

Yours,

The Unintentional Wanderer ■

Bragging about What We Can Do; Boasting about What We Won't—March 9, 2003

The president's press conference was meant to be a demonstration—as he stands on the brink of unleashing "shock and awe" on Iraq—of how much he hates war. One of many unasked questions was: Does he hate war as much as he hates press conferences?

The president has a profound aversion to being called on to explain himself, and he has conveyed this not only by keeping to three the number of formal press conferences he has held since taking the oath, but also by using body language that conveys his resentment at the process.

He had obviously been counseled to be calm; characteristically, he overdid it, and appeared comatose. Message: I am not a bully.

He kept saying war could still be averted, but never said how. He said he respected the opinions of dissenting nations and then declared we will not be deterred from going it alone.

The strangest thing was his way of recognizing reporters. He was going by a chart that had the names and the order in which he was to call on them. "This is scripted," he said in an aside. What he did was to meld the name of the reporter he was about to recognize into the sentence he was uttering on some great matter. Without any pause or inflection, he made the name part of his declaration. It tended to deprive what he was saying of any seriousness or significance.

Example: "The risk of doing nothing, the risk of hoping that Saddam Hussein changes his mind and becomes a gentle soul, the risk that somehow inaction will make the world safer, is a risk I'm not willing to take for the American people, John King."

The president is aware that while his performance as frontier sheriff fighting terrorism still goes down well, if slightly less well, in the country, it has bombed in the world. Old Europe is miffed, and our closest neighbors, Mexico and Canada, are offended by crude hints of vengeance if they vote in the United Nations against us—against war. We'll be friends again, he said.

He made a point of our solicitude for the Iraqi people, about our elaborate plans to avoid what up until now the military has referred to cheerfully as "collateral damage." High-tech, laser-guided bombing and sharper intelligence will seemingly avoid a repetition of the three thousand casualties in Baghdad in the first Bush war.

All week the brass has been out emphasizing a concern for Iraqi citizens that Saddam Hussein has never shown. A briefer at the Pentagon emphasized the need to be nice if we intended to stay and mold Iraq into a democracy. Supreme commander Tommy Franks injected a note of reality. He was making no promises: War is war, he said in effect.

The Pentagon is torn between bragging about what it can do and boasting about what it won't do as we liberate Iraq. In the middle of the stream of reassurances of our mercy was a jarring reminder of our overwhelming power. The air force unveiled a twenty-thousand-pound bomb without saying where it would be used. The pope sent over a cardinal for an eleventh-hour appeal to the Oval Office. The pope was trying to warn the president of the baleful consequences in the Arab world of invading a Muslim country.

Retired General Anthony Zinni made the same point before a congressional hearing. His nightmare was the prospect of seeing, on a split TV screen, Israelis killing Arabs on the West Bank and Americans killing Arabs in Iraq. He suggested it might stimulate enlistments in al-Qaida.

Bush does not like to hear about the consequences of his obsession and deals harshly with those who discuss them. The most severe punishment was meted out to Larry Lindsey, his erstwhile economic adviser, who put the bill for the war in Iraq at $200 billion. He was fired.

General Eric K. Shinseki, the army's chief of staff, committed the error of truth-telling and was set down hard. When asked, he estimated that it would take two hundred thousand troops to occupy Iraq. Deputy Defense Secretary Paul Wolfowitz landed on him. "Way off the mark," he steamed. Bush said at his press conference, almost airily, that the costs of the war would be taken care of in a supplemental appropriation.

In the Bush circle, zeal is much prized. Machiavelli's advice to courtiers is followed: "Do not question the ends of the prince—just tell him how to best do what he wants to do."

Bush insists that war or peace is all up to Saddam. To the American people he says, remember 9/11, trust me. As he said at his press conference, "When it comes to our security, we really don't need anybody's permission."

In other words, let the shock and awe begin. ■

5

Presidents

Johnson Loves His Job—November 1, 1964

One thing Lyndon B. Johnson has done in his campaign is to blow sky-high the "splendid misery" concept of the presidency.

He loves every minute of the job he always wanted and never expected to get. He speaks of its awesome responsibilities, while plainly relishing every detail of them.

What Andrew Jackson did in fact, he does in his speeches. He opens the iron gates of the White House to every man within the sound of his voice. He has brought the Oval Room and its fateful business into every city hall and auditorium where he has spoken.

His predecessor, John F. Kennedy, was at pains to maintain a distance between himself and the electorate. Johnson can't get close enough to the voters, to display there is no alienating distinction between them.

Kennedy's reserve was so ingrained that his single burst of personal reference in his 1960 campaign was to confide that he was an overseer of Harvard University.

REFERENCES TO FAMILY

Johnson, by contrast, takes his crowds to his daddy's deathbed and to his mother's knee. He even shares with them the notes his wife sends him on the platform begging him to wind up his speeches.

Sometimes it seems as though he were asking not for votes but for reassurances that people enjoy having him in the White House as much as he enjoys being there.

Sometimes it seems he wants not just a cross on the ballot but some personal expression, like "I think you're wonderful" written in.

His campaign has not been an argument with Barry Goldwater. The Arizona senator is a speck on the mile-wide horizon of Lyndon Johnson, a mere page boy who keeps bringing him one delicious issue after another.

Johnson's whole discussion has been with the people, particularly with those he suspects might not be about to go all the way with LBJ.

PRESSURE TREATMENT

He approaches them in the fashion familiar, to dissenting colleagues in his Senate majority leadership days. The country as a whole has been subjected to the famous treatment.

The president has been stepping up the pressure in the last weeks, proceeding on his tested theory that people harassed long and intensely enough will generally give him what he wants, just so he will leave them alone.

It is noteworthy that suitably responsive audiences get off easy. Very often he simply reads to them the remarks laboriously prepared for him by an army of speechwriters, led by Labor Secretary W. Willard Wirtz, who put words in Adlai E. Stevenson's mouth, and Richard Goodwill, who did the same for John Kennedy.

But let Johnson sniff the least apathy, hostility, or sullenness and he goes into high gear.

Last Wednesday in Los Angeles, the smog was low and so was the spirit of the thirty thousand people gathered before him. Some forty-three minutes and two frantic notes from the First Lady later, he had won them over. They had tired feet, but he had stirred their tired blood.

EFFECTIVE PERFORMANCE

It was a vintage Johnson performance, gaudy, intimate, abrasive, and effective. The grammar was indifferent, but the sentences had a beat and an inner rhyme that made them sound like a folk song in a thousand verses.

Federal prose has no greater natural enemy than Lyndon Johnson. He paints vast problems in vivid word pictures that any twelve-year-old can grasp.

Hear him, for instance, on the subject of urban renewal, that subject of so many learned monographs: "The cities have filled up with slums and we see kids, out there playing in the streets when the cars are trying to drive by."

Here is an Old-Frontier rendition of the thermonuclear confrontation of 1962 that Secretary of State Dean Rusk would, hardly recognize: "Mr. Kennedy put his knife right there in his ribs and he held it, Khrushchev put his there and held it; and neither of them shook, trembled, or developed palsy; neither one of them wobbled."

Here is the president's picture of himself bringing peace to labor and management during the General Motors–UAW dispute: "And if you don't do it," he said he told the principals, "I am going to come up there and pull my chair up to that table and talk to you."

THE BUDGET CUTTER

Here he is as the budget cutter: "I come in representing all the people, Uncle Sam, and I take my butcher knife and I slice out 52 percent of it for the government."

And here he is as the prudent leader of the Western world: "Just because we're powerful we can't just mash a button and tell an independent country to go to—because they don't want to—and we don't get very far rattling our rockets or lobbing them into the men's room, or bluffing with our bombs."

If the electorate doesn't know by now a great deal about government, the presidency, and Lyndon Johnson of Texas, it is not his fault.

It is his own unique, fantastic way of convincing the people that the country is in the very best of hands and should be kept there. ■

Johnson "Kidnaps" Lincoln—February 14, 1965

The Republicans, who have lost so much lately, have now lost Lincoln. President Johnson has boldly stolen him away from his own party and claimed him for his own.

This is the year that the first Republican president is an embarrassment to some Republicans and a reproach to others.

The GOP tributes are paltry and almost grudging in nature. The president evidently could not resist showing them how Lincoln's birthday should be celebrated.

The White House, where Lincoln's presence is still strongly felt, is, of course, an incomparable setting. No Republican orator speaking in some drafty banquet hall could have matched the effect of the president who spoke in the East Room where Lincoln lay after his assassination. He called the Republican saint "the better angel of the American nature."

CIVIL RIGHTS CITED

He spoke not of the Civil War, but of civil rights to make his point that the Democrats are the true inheritors of the Lincoln tradition.

Lincoln has never been so honored by any president.

After Johnson was warmly applauded by the hundred-odd Lincoln lovers present at the gathering Friday, he led them into lunch in the state dining room, where they sat under A. P. Healey's portrait of a quizzical Lincoln.

The political abduction was disguised as a treat for scholars, and they were babbling with scholarly joy. After lunch, at Mrs. Johnson's invitation, they all trooped upstairs to see the Lincoln bedroom, to inspect the huge carved wooded bedstead and the framed copy of the Gettysburg Address, which is one of five in Lincoln's own clear handwriting.

Finally, the president bundled the whole company into cars and army buses and took them over to the Lincoln Memorial. He placed a wreath at the foot of Daniel Chester French's great statue and stood in silence on the damp marble for a few minutes while around him tourists buzzed about their incredible luck.

HOMAGE AND CRAFT

The president's observance was a blend of homage and craft that no Republican could decently protest.

The GOP chairman himself could have passed the non-political guest list which included at least four Pulitzer Prize-winning Civil War historians, the chairmen of Civil War Centennial Commissions, three actors who have portrayed Lincoln, scores of Lincoln buffs, and the president of one Lincoln Savings Bank and a Lincoln Life Insurance Co.

The only senator included was a Democrat—Ralph Yarborough of Texas—but he was present in his capacity as a member of the Centennial Commission. Raymond Massey, one of the Lincoln actors, is an ardent Republican, a Goldwater fund-raiser during the campaign. After the heady events of the day he said he was "still a Republican" but would not hesitate to characterize the observance as "inspiring."

The table talk was of "the war" and second volumes and new Lincoln finds. Bruce Catton, the poetic historian of the Civil War, told his neighbors he was about to finish his account of Appomattox, and that when he writes a biography of General Grant, he will be mustered out of the army of Civil War writers. General Grant's grandson General U. S. Grant III, another Republican, told of being carried piggyback by his grandfather and being shown his war trophies.

CONTROVERSIAL FIGURE

The unprecedented democratic observance in honor of one of the founders of the Republican Party was not lost on the scholars.

"But the president did not take Lincoln away," said one of them, "they left him a long time ago."

For in this season of dismay some Republicans have come to look upon their most humane president as a controversial figure. The new southern Republican Party is built on white supremacy. The liberals in the north cannot find phrases to explain how the party of Lincoln was stolen from them in San Francisco, without inflicting fresh wounds on the followers of Goldwater, who won only six states in the election, five of them members of the Old Confederacy.

Lincoln's birthday represented an irresistible opportunity to Mr. Johnson. He seized it in a bold and brilliant stroke that will be much noted and long remembered. ∎

Power Goes with Johnson—August 8, 1965

President Johnson is fond of saying that "power is where power goes." Power these days is following him around like his pet beagle, Him.

He went on Friday to claim his triumph on the voting rights bill before the cabinet, the diplomatic corps, and the whole Congress. He stood between two statues of Lincoln.

Martin Luther King sat in the back row of the first section of folding chairs in the Capitol Rotunda. As a civil rights leader, he has been outdone by the president.

It is a common fate for champions of great causes. The president has preempted the entire field of political action from the prekindergarten (Head Start) to the Old Folks' Home (Medicare).

He is more for immigration than a Greek peasant; more for public schools than Horace Mann; more for flowers than Agaesiz; more for forests than Theodore Roosevelt; more for housing than Franklin Roosevelt; more against poverty than a West Virginia miner; more against crime than a Washington policeman; more, just last week, for D.C. home rule than the Americans for Democratic Action of Joseph L. Rauh Jr., hitherto the most clamorous advocate.

The senators who trailed him on his rounds of the scenes of the childhood of his power—his years as Senate majority leader—must indeed have wondered how in the world they could make a name for themselves. How can they find an issue he has not already made his own? Only poets and professors have not been lashed to his chariot wheels, and the fight isn't over yet.

His old colleagues looked on as he took his old majority leader's seat in the front row, and leaned across the aisle to take the hand of Minority Leader Everett McKinley Dirksen, who alone is fighting the notion that in the Johnson era the Senate has become somehow the House of Lords.

The opposition is, at the moment, routed and silenced. The hawks and the doves have returned to their nests, and a great quiet prevails since the president's last pronouncement on South Vietnam.

Another man might have let it go at that. But President Johnson seized last weekend to deal another blow at the demoralized opposition. He unleashed a ferocious attack on House Minority Leader Gerald Ford of Michigan, whose crime it was to suggest that the president had been influenced by other opinions in making up his mind.

The furor is still on, but when it all settles down, Ford's real sin may have been to expose a Johnson ploy. It is a technique of the president's to appear to listen dubiously to arguments he agrees with on the theory that if he accepts them, he makes the advocates beholden to him.

It now appears he had already decided not to escalate in South Vietnam, but conveyed to some Democratic senators the impression that he was allowing them to dissuade him from extreme measures.

Ford's indiscretion was embarrassing to the master chessplayer. Besides he had been giving himself airs as a national figure, and was piling up points as a patriotic supporter of the administration's position, while suggesting the president could not cope with opposition in his own party.

Ford, having had his head chopped off, understandably did not appear at the signing of the voting rights bill.

The president had effectively answered other criticism in the foreign policy field by two brilliant appointments. Tagged as an enemy of the United Nations, he suddenly reversed himself and started giving the impression he relied on the UN only slightly less than on McGeorge Bundy. He reached up to the Supreme Court and pulled from the bench the supremely suitable person of Arthur Goldberg for ambassador.

He was criticized for letting the Voice of America go undirected for four months. He dragooned one of the ablest and most respected correspondents in the field of communications, NBC's John Chancellor.

A man might be excused for intimations of immortality after such a long streak, and it was perhaps no wonder that this week the president, master of all he surveys, came out against death.

At the signing of the Community Health Services Extension Act, the president declared that people must live longer.

"Now last year," he said in the Rose Garden, "we lost $32 billion just from people dying. What they would have produced if they had lived. We are going to—from heart, cancer, and stroke. We can take one billion of that $32 billion and we can have $31 billion to divide among everything else, if we just spend $1 billion to stop it now. It is going to be stopped." ■

Johnson's Vietnam Dilemma—August 20, 1967

President Johnson stood in the sunlit Rose Garden listening with an attention that went beyond politeness while the theatrically silver-haired chancellor of West Germany, Kurt Kiesinger, responded to his formal welcome.

In the great flow of gutturals, the word "Vietnam," which is the same in both languages, did not occur.

The president had to content himself with the cold comfort of a quotation from Emerson:

"To have a friend, be a friend."

The president has made no new friends lately and lost some old ones. He dropped to a new low in the polls. He cannot fight the war in the slums because he has to fight the war in Vietnam. The hawks have become bolder, the doves more numerous and clamorous.

His allies in Southeast Asia tell his emissaries he is doing the right thing, although they do not dare say so at home. His allies in Europe, including Kiesinger, tell him the same thing in private, but do not care to dwell on the point in public.

Governor George W. Romney's contribution was a maddening reminder that involvement in the first place was "a tragic mistake." Johnson thought so at the time and protested to the Eisenhower administration.

The governor also suggested that the real problem was to "destroy the infrastructure of the Viet Cong." Johnson has dispatched some five hundred thousand Americans to Vietnam to do that very thing.

The hawks tell him to increase the bombing. The doves tell him to stop it.

The hawks say if he does not want to go all out in the air, he should pull out on the ground. The doves say the elections are a farce and hint he should use them as an excuse to wind up the engagement. The hawks say if he doesn't hit more "meaningful targets," they will oppose the new troop increase of forty-five thousand.

The president usually tries to give each side something at the same time. In January 1966, he took the war to the UN, but resumed the bombing.

The new targets were the first unbalanced concession to the hawks. Privately, doves were assured they would have their day after the elections, when the victorious candidates could make good, during a bombing pause, on the pledge which all have taken, to seek negotiation.

Ho Chi Minh has not been heard from. He hears neither threats nor blandishments. He thinks American public opinion will force a conclusion to the war. The president thinks that another round of TNT will bring the North to its knees. Everyone agrees that the bombings have no visible effect on the battle in the South. The pacification program is incoherent.

The candidates are behaving irrationally. They promise not what they will do if elected, but what they will do if not elected. There is much talk of riots, chaos, and coups d'état. The administration says we expect too much of a people having their first exercise in democratic government. General Thieu, the leading contender, says we need more Americans to fight.

The president sees himself as Lincoln, isolated, unpopular, maligned, and misunderstood, but embarked on a proper course and certain of vindication. He is bitter about his critics, who tell him what not to do, but not what to do. The most dedicated doves have yet to say that he should pull out. One and all, they pronounce it "unthinkable."

Yet they complain he is behaving like a timid politician, heeding the imperatives of another era in American politics. No one remains in the administration to urge de-escalation and disengagement, to suggest that a solution, however unsatisfactory, to an unwinnable war would be absorbed by the 1968 election.

But Johnson, his critics say, is mindful of Richard M. Nixon in the wings, ready to cry "appeasement" and "sellout" if anything less than victory is achieved. The Democrats heard they had "lost China" all through the '50s. Johnson will not risk being charged with "being soft on Communism" in Southeast Asia. When the Dominican Republic crisis blew up, he was heard to say he would not have "another Cuba" in this continent.

Supposedly John F. Kennedy, though skeptical, decided to intervene in Vietnam because in the wake of the Bay of Pigs he had to prove he would stand up to the Soviets.

Johnson fears a new wave of McCarthyism if he shows signs of slowing down in Vietnam. The doves say McCarthyism is on the rise because of the suppression of dissent and they are its victims.

So he presses on, with no end in sight, convinced there is no other way out. ∎

The New Lyndon Johnson—November 26, 1967

That genial impostor who insists he is president of the United States turned up at the White House again last week at the signing of the clean air bill.

It was his second appearance, and, as on his now-historic debut at a November 17 press conference, he was in great form. He cuffed the congressmen a little about their manners, quoted Dante on pollution, and growled cheerfully that he would settle for passage of 95 percent of his program.

He said he remembered an old friend who told him when he first came to Washington thirty-five years ago, "Son, you get ready. If you're going to live in this town, you are either going to shove or someone is going to be shoving you."

Everybody laughed and afterward fell to talking about the great new masquerade that is the talk of the town. The tall, gray-haired man who makes jokes and smiles so much is certainly a dead ringer for Lyndon Johnson in looks. His hair is a little longer in the back and he doesn't fool with contact lenses. He wears honest old-fashioned rimless glasses.

But the difference between the new man and the old is the tone. The new man appears to think rather well of people on the whole. The old one seemed to think there was a conspiracy against him. The new man thinks it's all right to disagree with him providing you don't go too far. The old one thought they were no better than traitors.

The old man used to hold press conferences at dawn or midnight, in odd corners, hoping nobody much would turn up. The new man gave twenty-four hours' notice that he would see the reporters in the East Room. He got rave notices for November 17, and his only problem is to convince the public that there are not two men in the White House, but that the real Lyndon Johnson has finally stood up.

Now that the reviews have been so dazzling a lot of people are claiming credit for the startling change that has occurred in a president who was losing friends and alienating people every day.

Things reached the low point over the Veteran's Day weekend, when the president made a round of appearances at military installations. The pictures and the reports made presidential loyalists shudder. There was Lyndon Johnson barking at his critics at a southern army camp. There was Lyndon Johnson shouting peace offers to Hanoi from the flight deck of an aircraft carrier. If he was a president, it was for, by, and to the military.

The talk began around Washington that Lyndon Johnson would have to conduct his re-election campaign on the steps of the Pentagon. The excursion underlined the fact that there is no city in America he can visit without fear of pickets or demonstrations.

Where could he go? What could he do? Finally someone came up with the brilliant idea that the White House is a perfect platform for a president. The East Room cannot be improved upon for a set. The press conference had served Eisenhower and Kennedy superbly. A gadget-minded president was finally induced to use the gadget of the press conference to appear before the people.

Somebody obviously told him to do what he keeps telling the dissenters to do—to count ten before he criticized. And while he came dangerously close to lashing out at wrong-thinkers—the press that will not confine itself to reporting his legislative victories and the progress in Vietnam, the dissenters who cannot get it through their heads that the war is just—he reined himself in every time.

The chances are that he will try this unbelievable mechanism he has just discovered again and again. There has been curious evidence, beginning in 1964 when Henry Cabot Lodge, six thousand miles away in Saigon, triumphed over two panting contenders in the field in the New Hampshire primary, that the public enjoys its candidates more in absence than in the flesh. The trend is advanced somewhat by the odd circumstance that George Romney began to fade in the polls as soon as he began to run, and that he has recently been surpassed by Richard Nixon, who hasn't been seen in months.

But a president cannot hide. The public wants to see him. Johnson has plainly been persuaded that to win the hearts and minds of his countrymen, he better project something other than lowering disapproval. The "nice-guy" experiment has been a smash. And the cream of the jest for the president is that he can use the press, his tormentors, to put it over. ■

Johnson Once Again a Leader—April 9, 1968

Lyndon Johnson, ex-candidate, looked like a president again during the recent racial disturbances here.

He set the tone, used the full power of his office. No single act of official idiocy was registered during the wild aftermath of Martin Luther King's death. From the moment of the first rock thrown through a window, there was no recrimination.

Johnson the war president has been repudiated. But he resurfaced as a civil rights leader and exhibited all the compassion and restraint which has eluded him in his conduct of Vietnam.

He has received an avalanche of criticism from merchants who complain his policy of not shooting the looters cost them millions. But he has also come in for unaccustomed praise for understanding how the Negroes felt and by addressing himself in a powerful message to their shock and outrage.

The president has lately been harping on "law and order." When it began to collapse in Washington, he issued a powerful statement beseeching Negroes not to give "violence its victory."

His representatives in the federal city, Mayor Walter Washington, Public Safety Director Patrick V. Murphy, Rev. Walter Fauntroy, and presidential troubleshooter Cyrus Vance, initiated a policy of full disclosure, a practically unknown feature of Johnson's Washington.

They went before the public with a great deal of information, including the reassurance that the troopers' guns were not loaded. They explained, they exhorted, they pleaded, but they did not scold. Neither did the president.

The fact is that Lyndon Johnson is at his best during a domestic emergency. He likes to cope with trouble. This is a strong strain in the American character, and his action brought interesting reaction from his fellow-citizens in Washington.

The outbreak, which has been expected for the last three years, was treated by many of them not as a tragedy, but as a calamity.

American women relish calamity. It gives them a chance to exercise their latent executive gifts. The response of the suburban matron who went to the outlands to avoid the Negro was one of the most interesting phenomenon of the weekend. She could not do enough for the victims of the riot.

And infected with the official spirit, she did not stop to think what was wrong or whose fault it was or even of how much she disapproves of arson and pillage. She started moving the food and clothing toward the ghetto.

At the Blessed Sacrament Church at Chevy Chase Circle, several months ago, a band of parishioners stomped out of a mass in a fury to protest a sermon on open housing. Last Sunday they collected six tons of canned goods for the ghetto inhabitants.

The two races, both of whom know the other was under extreme provocation, seem to have discovered a basic feeling about each other which under pressure did not go below a certain point. When the National Association for the Advancement of Colored People issues a statement in praise of the police, than it seems that an era has ended.

BRUTALITY'S ABSENCE

If the police of Washington failed to display any police brutality from Thursday night to Sunday, there is in the minds of many a revival of hope that the country may survive.

Lyndon Johnson has contributed to that feeling by his recent actions. He is a liberated man now. He acted in a free manner that would have been impossible or at least improbable before his political retreat. He has demonstrated a riot need not be the end of the world.

Even the occupation, of the military has been benign. The Eighty-second Airborne Band played for the pupils of Spingarn High—some of whom, presumably, had been happily looting a few days ago—and a pair of them were seen speaking soothingly to a pair of old ladies from Cathedral Mansions who had never thought they would live to see the day. ■

Playboy Interview: Carter Goes Too Far
—September 21, 1976

Jimmy Carter has confessed to *Playboy*. He has sinned.

He has never committed adultery, mind you. But he has thought about it, which, he correctly observes, is just as bad in the eyes of the Lord.

Playboy, a magazine which never mentions the word *adultery* and in fact is dedicated to the proposition that all sex is fun, did not ask the candidate if he had ever strayed. Interviewer Robert Scheer merely inquired, after a series of recorded encounters, if the Plains Sunday school teacher had reassured people who are "uneasy about his religious beliefs" and fear he would be "a rigid, unbending president."

Whereupon Jimmy Carter told all. He is no pharisee. He is not proud, not self-righteous. He is human, he is tempted. He has "looked on a lot of women with lust."

Lust, except for office, has not been an issue in the campaign. Abortion is, of course, but the discussion has focused on the consequences rather than the cause. And it, is hard to think that Gerald Ford will demand equal time to give his views on adultery and to tell us whether he has been guilty in thought or deed. Since he prides himself on being specific, we might be in for a spate of names and dates. That is, if he has anything to tell us.

Nor is it likely that adultery will be the subject of the debates, although it can be argued that such an exchange could tell you more about a man than his sentiments on F-14s to Iran, for instance.

Even if you didn't want to be given a guided tour of Jimmy Carter's innermost soul and would rather hear him on taxes than on sex, you would have to say that he is scripturally sound.

Matthew Chapter 5, verses 27 and 28 are the basis:
"Ye have heard that it was said by them of old time,
Thou shall not commit adultery:
"But I say unto you. That whosoever looketh on a
woman to lust after her hath committed adultery with
her already in his heart."

It is difficult theology not just for readers of *Playboy*, who don't think in those terms, but for others who decide that they might as well go ahead since they're in trouble anyway.

But Jimmy doesn't judge those who succumb—"Judge not that ye be not judged" (Matthew 7.1)—or as he puts it, "shack up with somebody out of wedlock."

Those words you won't find in the King James Version of the Bible. And that is where Jimmy may have given offense, even in those who admire his high standards for himself and his granting of blanket amnesty for adulterers. His rendition of the Scriptures—he was obviously striving for the man-to-man tone—just doesn't sound right from a Baptist deacon's lips:

"Christ says, Don't consider yourself better than someone else because one guy screws a whole bunch of women while the other guy is loyal to his wife. The guy who's loyal to his wife ought not to be condescending or proud because of the relative degree of sinfulness."

If he goes on with the discussion, he would be advised to stick to quoting the Bible. His interpretation may be sound, but the language is jarring. Billy Graham doesn't talk that way. and the electorate has been sensitized by the episode in which Nelson Rockefeller made an obscene gesture to hecklers in New York. The campaign seems to be getting out of hand.

The only question to be asked is whether Jimmy Carter's outpouring has helped make people less nervous. Obviously, people who are not accustomed to public confession will be unnerved all over again. And people who stick to the straight and narrow and are so self-conscious in an age of permissiveness probably won't be able to admit they are glad that Jimmy Carter is a faithful husband. And maybe the young, who hailed Betty Ford for saying she wouldn't be shocked if she heard her daughter were having an affair, will think Jimmy Carter is pretty modern after all.

The politicians will snicker and be appalled. They are supposed to make public their medical and financial records. Has Jimmy Carter required them to stand up on the stump and testify about their lusts? The political campaign, it should perhaps be noted, tries the soul of the most faithful husband. There are any number of groupies around who crave to share a "meaningful experience" with the candidate; the hours are long, the opportunities unlimited.

Jimmy Carter says God will forgive them, as God has forgiven him. And he won't hold their trespasses against them. But the office-seekers are worried about whether the voters will forgive them for other things. Democrats would on the whole prefer to talk about their record on full employment rather than the history of their dalliances.

Jimmy Carter went just a little too far, as he often does in trying to make a point that is mainly of interest to himself. That should have been an off-the-record conversation with God, not one taped by *Playboy*. ■

Carter Better Pray Nixon Can't Make It
—January 4, 1977

It's going to be wonderful if Richard Nixon accepts Jimmy Carter's invitation to the inauguration. Carter may get into the tenth paragraph of the stories about the affair, and squeeze out a few seconds on television if he sits close enough to his guest.

The idea of Richard Nixon sitting up there on the stands will really freak out a number of people. He'd be on the steps of the Capitol in the presence of the Congress that was set to impeach him. Who could notice a Georgia peanut farmer in that company? What's an inauguration compared to a resurrection?

Carter apologists say that Carter really had no choice but to invite a former president, even one who was an unindicted coconspirator in the worst presidential scandal in history.

Research, they say, showed that any former president who is receiving the full emoluments of his former office is entitled to be asked.

"But if the Republicans could leave him out of their convention, couldn't Jimmy Carter have left him out of the inaugural?" asked a dismayed Carter transition worker.

Carter's move was explained as an act which reveals his profound faith in redemption.

Carter can begin to pray that Nixon will not feel up to the trip or that some impulse toward seemliness will overtake him as he ponders the invitation.

The hermit of San Clemente must be terribly pleased at this chance to be born again. Last year he made a journey to China, which was supposed to restore him to public esteem—and didn't.

"It borders on a religious concept of forgiveness," explained a Carter defender. "Also he understands that the inclusion of former presidents is the most sacred item of protocol in inaugural tradition. Carter was, just not prepared to change it."

The fact that Nixon was the only chief executive to resign from office in disgrace was not, of course, covered by protocol. And despite the high crimes and misdemeanors voted by the House impeachment committee, the pardon has wiped the slate clean. It supposedly extends forward to his recent conviction, in effect, as a wiretapper. While waiting to hear the amount of damages he must pay to Morton Halperin, Nixon must have been delighted to find a special inaugural invitation in his mailbox.

Carter never could quite find fault with the pardon. He always gave Ford the benefit of the doubt. His running mate, Senator Walter Mondale, took the opposite view.

In a campaign speech about lawlessness in government, Mondale defied his principal and severely criticized the pardon.

"No act," declared Mondale "more perpetuated Nixon's own dangerous doctrine that a president is somehow above the law."

And Jimmy Carter, by treating him like any other president who left at the end of his term, is perpetuating "Nixon's own dangerous doctrine" reverence for the presidency.

It doesn't really sort well with Carter's strenuous efforts to be a common man, and to de-imperialize the presidency. He is putting on a public relations campaign that is aimed at proving that presidents are ordinary mortals, and citizens are being encouraged to write or phone in the suggestions to help him remember. But the invitation says that presidents, even the criminal kind, are a breed apart.

Forgiveness is in the winter air, Gerald Ford was semipublicly importuned by Mrs. Philip Hart on the occasion of her husband's death to grant unconditional amnesty to Vietnam era draft-dodgers, deserters, and thousands of men with less than honorable discharges.

Ford was so embarrassed by the reaction and repeated questions of the press at Vail that he was driven to call for statehood for Puerto Rico, which apparently doesn't want it, just to change the subject.

His wife, Betty, who is so tolerant of other lapses of conventional morality, took it upon herself to speak for Gold Star mothers—an odd office for the mother of three draft-age sons. None of whom were drafted or volunteered for the war—and has plainly been counseling the "never" approach. She had no difficulties she has cared to confide about the Nixon pardon.

Could it be that Carter is making this show of forgiving Richard Nixon and inviting him to upstage him at his own inaugural as a prelude to broadening his pardon of Vietnam offenders?

The argument is made by Nixon champions that he was as much a victim of Vietnam as the men who can't come home. It is true, of course that Nixon began his assault on the Constitution because he wanted to prolong the war—he fell to wiretapping immediately upon the secret bombing of Cambodia. And he blames Daniel Ellsberg for provoking him into a violation of the Fourth Amendment by publishing the Pentagon papers.

It doesn't make much sense, but then neither does Jimmy Carter's invitation to Richard Nixon.

"It will serve him right if Nixon accepts," said an incredulous Democratic senator. ■

Jerry Leaves Jimmy Feeling Pretty Blue
—April 22, 1977

It was a little bit like the princess and the pea.

Jimmy Carter, president, commander in chief, leader of the Western world, was everywhere you looked this week, rearranging the lifestyles of his people, exhorting Americans to abandon their cars, urging them to sacrifice, and not to complain.

But underneath this great show of purpose and power, Jimmy Carter was feeling pretty blue.

Gerald Ford was saying mean things about him, and he had *promised* he wouldn't.

The vice president conveyed the president's sense of shock and outrage at a White House leadership meeting Tuesday. Apparently the president couldn't trust himself to say how much it hurt. Maybe he was afraid he'd cry.

Senate Whip Alan Cranston passed along a report of the sad little scene and sometime later, the vice president, who has been known to bring a light touch to the practice of politics, took to the airwaves to chide the "unseemly" attack from one "who knows how tough the job is."

Unexpected echoes were provided by House Speaker Thomas P. O'Neill, a veteran of Boston's robust politics, but who nonetheless managed a perfectly straight face, when he chided Ford for bad manners.

"I don't think it looks well in the eyes of the world for the president to be criticized by his predecessor," O'Neill said solemnly.

Jimmy Carter believes in free speech for a lot of people who take issue with U.S. policies and principles, and in some cases, his performance. Billy Carter, General Brown, and Andrew Young spring to mind as examples of presidential permissiveness. But Gerald Ford is excluded from the First Amendment by virtue of his former office.

All Ford remarked in Los Angeles was that Carter's economic policies were not that different from his own. Admittedly, this is a rather harsh thing to say in view of Carter's promises.

But it hardly warrants the unfavorable comparison with Richard Nixon which it evoked from a pouting president.

Nixon, it appears, is being helpful. He calls up and offers free advice on how to stand up to the Soviets. This, in Carter's view, makes him an elder statesman, whatever effect it may have on those Americans who thought they were voting, in part, last November to rid themselves of the consul from San Clemente.

Nixon must be charmed at this public testimony to the value of his guidance and the excellence of his deportment.

It came at a particularly apt time. Nixon's lawyer was in the Supreme Court this week fighting for custody of White House tapes that might do damage to his contention that a lifetime of devoted public service was cut short by the cowardice of Congress. Nothing could provide better advance publicity for his series of interviews, also taped, with David Frost.

Nixon may have almost abandoned hope of being considered a good president. But now a Democratic chief executive has called him an ideal ex-president, which is a cut above anything he's heard lately from any member of his own party.

Even happier is Gerald Ford. He has been lonely on the links. His coy hints that he has not put away all thought of being his party's standard-bearer one more time have evinced little but shudders from his fellow Republicans. They somehow do not relish the idea of Ford and Reagan once again tearing the elephant apart.

Now Ford is in business. Nothing distinguishes a man more than criticism from a president. Richard Nixon in 1967 had his face pressed against the window. Lyndon Johnson called him a "chronic campaigner," and he was born again as front-runner.

The Republicans, totally astonished at the evidence that the supremely self-confident president may be basically insecure, are sputtering—and reappraising. Last year, they fielded a known hatchet man, Robert Dole, to get Carter's goat. It never occurred to them that Ford could do the job. They will inevitably urge him forward as chief picador.

Of course, Carter wasn't president when he said last autumn that Gerald Ford was worse than Nixon, but Ford was. That was different. That was a campaign. And delicate-minded though he may be, Jimmy Carter thinks anything goes while the horses are on the track.

He can't stand candidates. Remember what he said about Henry Jackson after the Massachusetts primary? Suggested Jackson beat him with "race." Remember what he said when Hubert Humphrey pulled out of New Jersey? He said he wished Humphrey had stayed in so he could beat him.

Jimmy Carter hates it when people run against him.

It is not Ford, the ex-president who riles him. It's Ford, the future candidate. That automatically makes him vicious and formidable in Carter's eyes.

Nobody on the White House staff is claiming credit for the war on Gerald Ford. In fact, some of them think it is "unseemly" that, after one hundred days, Carter appears so conscious of a battle three years away.

They don't think it looks good for a president who is telling people they've got to be big about things like the gasoline tax. ∎

Washington Ought to Split Up and Get Out of Town
—July 22, 1979

If Washington were a cabinet member, it would have the decency to submit its resignation.

Its First Citizen, Jimmy Carter, just can't stand the capital. It's the city he loves to hate.

Last Sunday, he said. "Whenever you have a chance, say something good about our country."

But whenever he has the chance he says something bad about us.

We're an "island"—actually we're more of a swamp right now—we are "isolated." The rest of the country is stuffed with wise, decent, strong people. Not Washington.

The city may look beautiful, with its white marble, green trees, and wide streets. But Jimmy Carter knows that it is rotten at the core, a man-eater, a dream-killer, infested with pesky press, cowardly Congress, balky bureaucrats.

"What can we do?" as the president asked in his speech.

"First of all," he said, "we must face the truth—then we can change our course."

It's difficult for Washington to change course. With every new man, New Deal, New Frontier, New Foundation, it promises to start a New Life.

But its personality disorders—delusions of grandeur, acute status anxiety, aggravated turf-consciousness, just to mention a few—are so intractable that within months it is back on its barstool, backbiting, rumor-mongering, sniping, cavilling.

It goes to the Kennedy Center once in a while but it doesn't watch the play. It's too busy studying the audience to see who's there. Take it to a party, it frets until it finds its placecard, sulks when seated next to an assistant secretary instead of a senator, and broods that the other table is feeding on delicious morsels of Ham and Jody while it is served SALT.

Many people in Washington go home every night, worry about their lawns and their children and don't even notice when the Carters have gone to Camp David. Their only link with "official Washington" is their income tax bills.

They are the kind of people that Carter likes—or would, if he met them someplace else.

But they are here, so they won't do.

Jimmy Carter is going to get out of town as often as he can.

Maybe the only way to save Washington is to destroy it. Not physically, of course. The British burned it down, and it didn't help.

But Jimmy Carter could break it up and disperse it through the countryside. That way, people wouldn't "turn to the federal government." As he said they were doing. They wouldn't even be able to find it for a while.

First of all. Carter himself would want to relocate in a more "mainstream" community. In a morale-building logistics feat, he could take the White House with him. If by some remote chance, we ever elect a president who actually likes Washington, it could be brought back.

Hackensack, New Jersey? Rockford, Illinois? Toledo, Ohio? Rosedale, Mississippi? Where to for reviving contact with real people? Perhaps he could withdraw to Camp David to think it over and get advice.

Wherever he goes, the White House press corps would headquarter in Indianapolis, a forbidding city, with many war memorials. The natives are not friendly. After a few encounters with voters snapping "I have a cake in the oven" or "I never vote," the nosy newsies would fall on their knees in gratitude for Jody Powell's telephoned briefings.

The vice president would be in a separate city, eliminating morbid curiosity about how close he really is to the president.

Congress would be, as Jimmy Carter said, "twisted and pulled in every direction," and the debate could last years. A shameless few would hold out for Paris, France, on economy grounds—taxpayers would be spared the expense of sending them there during recesses.

Congress might split up, the Senate heading for Newport, and an abandoned mansion nearly as lordly as its new office building. The compulsive commuters in the House might end up on a permanent "district work period."

A natural selection process for other agencies leaps to mind. The high-rollers at the Pentagon belong in Las Vegas. The Nuclear Regulatory Agency could get new quarters cheap at Three Mile Island. The Department of Energy mushes to the new pipeline in Alaska, throwing gas allocation plans to the wolves on the way. HEW sets up in North Carolina, with Welfare assigned to California and Ronald Reagan's watchful eye for cheaters. Agriculture plants corn for synthetic fuels in Central Park. NASA can't come back until it has found every last fragment of Skylab in the South Pacific.

The Supreme Court's new digs would be the Columbia School of Journalism—or, better still, the Law School. The Internal Revenue Service gets reeducated, in New Hampshire, where income tax is outlawed.

The Department of Transportation is based on Amtrak, rolls around the country, repairing tracks as it goes.

The whole project would take a lot of planning, and more money, perhaps, even than the new energy program. It would be worth it, though. Think of having an election with nobody campaigning against Washington. ■

A Farewell without the Ambiguities
—January 18, 1981

Jimmy Carter is leaving Washington as he came, a mysterious and contradictory man.

His last days in the White House are a montage of moving vans and last suppers, melancholy and mordant humor.

"Was Saigon like this?" asked an aide in the last week of the interminable transition. People who used to race around looking for budget figures that could, if adopted, change a million lives, are down to searching for the Spanish phrase for "until we meet again" for use at yet another staff farewell.

Jimmy Carter is going through the twilight zone in fairly good spirits. The one thread that binds him to the vast power he is relinquishing—and Ronald Reagan is about to grasp—is the fate of the hostages.

A new tenderness has appeared at court. Now that the endless jockeying for position is over, the president is receiving unpurposeful affection. Now that it no longer matters—"the barbed wire is down"— the White House and the press are behaving toward each other like human beings.

Jody Powell said on a morning news show that he wishes now that he had brought the president and the commentators together more often—so they could see "what he was all about."

In his last full week in office, he sent out conflicting signals. He gave a farewell address to the nation which bespoke a statesman, speaking of the future in broad and magnanimous terms, shrewdly giving pointers to his successor on issues that subtly recalled his own finest hours.

The same day, he issued a list of recipients of the Medal of Freedom, the highest civilian honor he can bestow. Several names proclaimed the politician settling old scores.

Take the case of Zbigniew Brzezinski, his clamorous and hawkish national security adviser. Once Hamilton Jordan succumbed to pinstripes and circumspection, Brzezinski became the most controversial figure in the White House, one who gave offense, both in policy and taste, to so many Democrats that he had to be benched during the campaign.

He personified Carter's reluctance to make up his mind between conflicting viewpoints. He was also proof of Carter's stubborn refusal to abandon underlings of proven incapacity to rally support for his programs—Frank Moore, his hapless Congressional liaison, was Brzezinski's domestic counterpart.

To Carter's consternation, the civil war over Brzezinski flared into print in his last days of the transition siege.

Hodding Carter III, friend and spokesman of former secretary of state Cyrus Vance, painted Brzezinski as "a second-rate thinker . . . (who) never let consistency get in the way of self-promotion."

The measure of Carter's chagrin was measured in a riposte from Powell, his most faithful squire, who wrote reproachfully of "public carping and petulance on the part of losers in the internal debate."

But Carter had the last word. Brzezinski's Medal of Freedom.

Two other names appeared on the honors list to cause derision and diminish the luster of the farewell address.

One was that of Robert Strauss, who rendered service to the Democratic Party and also to the country as a Mideast and trade negotiator. But he was Carter's campaign chairman, and Republicans chortled that Carter was once again thumbing his nose at Washington.

The other eyebrow-raiser was actor Kirk Douglas. The president's men mumbled explanations all day long. Finally, one of them said sardonically, "Well, Douglas has a good record on human rights—he freed all those slaves in *Spartacus*."

But the Wednesday night speech brought no such ambiguities. Jimmy Carter refrained from rehearsing achievements or rationalizing failures. He gave no hint of his true feeling—which is that the country will be sorry. He merely cited areas of worry about Ronald Reagan, and bade him in acceptably impersonal terms to have a care for special interest groups, nuclear weaponry, the environment, and human rights. To his everlasting credit, Carter made human rights a foreign policy consideration.

It was an uneven effort, but nonetheless proof that the president of the U.S., to use *Dallas* terminology, can be Bobby Ewing, instead of J. R., in dealing with the rest of the world. He knows, from the confirmation hearings, that the Reagan people think human rights is sissy stuff. But nothing he did so became him as trying to advance America's values as well as its interests.

Jimmy Carter goes back to his native South—he referred to it in his farewell as almost another country, and his suspicion that it is may have been the root of all his troubles—leaving the town and the country as puzzled as when he came. To the end, he was the president who never stopped being the defiant outsider. ∎

The Hostage Crisis Dogs Carter to the Last
—January 20, 1981

It was 4:56 on Monday morning and Jimmy Carter was beginning the last thirty-one hours of his presidency.

He came to the pressroom to say the words he had longed to say for fourteen months. The agony and humiliation that had obsessed him and the country was about to end. Nothing in his face—which was drained and splotched—or his voice, which was flat and lifeless—suggested joy, or even relief. His blue eyes were blank with exhaustion.

"You have been up all night with me, and I appreciate it very much," he murmured by way of greeting the hundred or so bedraggled reporters, who had been keeping the watch since ten o'clock on Sunday morning, since the announcement from Tehran that "agreement had been reached."

The room was redolent of sweat, fatigue, and spilled coffee. The floor was littered with cigarette butts, chicken bones, orange rinds, the remains of the Sunday papers. The president began his statement.

"We have now reached agreement with Iran. It will result, I believe, in the release of our American hostages."

SUPERLATIVES MISSING

Where were the superlatives, which came so easily to southern lips at less cosmic moments? Reporters were ready for tears and cheers. But Carter spoke rapidly and matter-of-factly at the moment of redemption.

"What are your personal feelings?" asked a cheated scribe.

Carter flashed a ghost of his smile.

"I will have more to say when the hostages clear Iranian airspace." he said without expression. He abruptly left the room.

So ended the crisis.

But nothing in his manner indicated cause for rejoicing. It was, he knew, a wrong righted, not a triumph. If it had not cost him the presidency, the long captivity had cost him the regard of the country. If he had made too much of it, in the beginning, when it served him well, he had, in the end, paid dearly.

The resolution had come too late for him. And he probably sensed it had come too late for him to go out with a touch of glory—a last flight as leader of the Western world to greet the hostages in Germany.

The press was on his side. He had saved the hostages' lives. Except for the rescue mission, he had resisted pressure for force. Nobody is sure if his successor across the street would have been as forbearing.

Nobody, knowing how much he minded losing, could begrudge him a brief escape from the California lushness of the Reagan inaugural, from the sound of the cheers of the crowd who watch the exits and entrances of the president-elect across the street in Blair House, the limousines and minks of the victors.

And there was, of course, the irony of it all. Jimmy Carter, one of our least theatrical chief executives, was presiding over a drama that the most fantasy-struck officials of the extravaganza, with their fireworks and festivities, could not match.

Reagan was, as he often did in his movies, playing second lead. He had the parties; Carter still held the power.

All through the night, reporters plagued the faces of his disciples for clues. Hamilton Jordan said it was "bankers and lawyers." Press Secretary Jody Powell cited "language difficulties."

With each passing hour the calculations for the presidential trip were shaved finer. He could not leave until the hostages were out, and he had to be back in time for the inauguration.

It was going to be a close thing, but as Powell muttered, "It beats sitting around here waiting for them to pull the plug on the life-support system."

At three o'clock in the morning, the press was sprawled around in Powell's office, watching television clips of the Reagan elegance at the Kennedy Center "Romantic Candlelight Dinner," which made them more aware of their own grubbiness and changes to come.

After the president's announcement, Powell advised the reporters they had two hours to get ready for the dash to Germany.

AND THEN THE SNAG

But dawn came with no word that the hostages were free. And at eleven o'clock, the news came about a snag. Nobody dared say that the ayatollah was giving Carter one last swipe of the scimitar.

But Tehran radio was crowing that Jimmy Carter could not squeeze "propaganda" from the hostages—he could not meet them as president in Germany. At two o'clock, Carter threw in the towel. He would not go.

Reagan invited him to make the trip as his emissary. But it would not be the same. The haplessness which had dogged his presidency was with him all the way. ■

Let Reagan's Friends Buy Him a Missile
—December 6, 1981

Ronald Reagan's rich friends may be wondering what to give him for Christmas. I have a suggestion.

Why don't they give him something for his defense budget?

It's something like $222 billion, and he hates to cut it. He took $2 billion out, but it hurt. And if he won't whack it any more, his whole economic future can be packed into David Stockman's Trojan horse and put out to sea.

Reagan's friends are generous, we know that. The mere mention of the need to redecorate the White House sent them into a spasm of giving. That gives you a clue. They like to be able to see their tax-deductible dollars at work in a conspicuous place.

Imagine the visibility of a gift of weapons—especially if there is a war. *Your* tank, *your* shell, *your* plane would have an audience of thousands.

Reagan is constantly reminding us that if we cut the taxes of the rich, they will repay us. They will invest their money in their businesses, hire more people, end unemployment, and whip inflation. He has also told us that they will patronize the arts and make life richer and better for all of us.

They don't turn on to day care centers, senior citizens' housing projects, or schools. Reagan's rich friends have had their chance to weave a few strands into the safety net, and so far they have spurned it. But just because they won't spring for butter doesn't mean they wouldn't do charity for guns for the Gipper.

Would they not give alms to armaments? How about if they could adopt a tank? The Abrams model costs $3 million. Or what about a pair of matching F-16 fighters? They are expensive enough to be in the Neiman-Marcus catalog. Imagine the thrill of having your name on the fuselage as it streaks aloft.

Maybe Frank Sinatra, the president's favorite minstrel, would like to assume the financial responsibility for the musical side of our defense readiness capability. Military bands come to the tune of $89.7 million. His name could be written on the drums.

It is true that certain items might be a little rich for the blood of the moguls. You take the MX missile. It costs $34 billion, even without its own private subway system. A community effort might be required, but it should not be a problem. The Reagan folks love parties, and a series of MX balls could be held. Let's say it's white tie, glittering with gold braid and brass, and a million dollars a couple.

Large organizations like the National Rifle Association could take tables. I'm just guessing now, but maybe they would want their slogan— "Guns don't kill people; people do"— painted large on the side of one of the new hardened silos being prepared to house the MX.

95

The big defense contractors might be given complimentary tickets on the donation of just one of their famous cost overruns to the kitty. But I should warn you, they may be a bit sulky now. They may say they gave at the office after what happened to them in the Senate last week.

Senator David Pryor (D-AR) got an amendment passed which prohibits them from charging their lobbying costs to us taxpayers. We forked over $11 million to spare them the expense of lobbying Congress for contracts that will enrich them. For instance, Rockwell, which got the B1 business ($22 million), sent us a bill from its Los Angeles division for $653,000, which is what it cost them to influence votes in its favor.

Rockwell may feel put upon if it has to take a congressman to dinner at its own expense. The Pentagon, which agrees with Reagan that fraud and waste are unknown quantities within its walls, is probably embarrassed at this slight to the military-industrial complex.

But let us return to the ballroom. Why not have the weapons systems on display to stir the Republicans' martial blood? Put the B1 next to the orchestra. Maybe Mrs. Reagan's decorator, Ted Graber, could spruce up the interior a bit—say, flowered curtains at the windows, coordinated carpeting, a solid-gold instrument panel. Republicans are bleeding hearts when it comes to decor. Possibly the organizers would want to auction off a cruise in a Trident submarine ($1.2 billion) or a fast ride in an A6E intruder attack plane ($15.5 million).

A display of voluntarism on that order would make it a great Christmas for Ronald Reagan. He hates to see money being frittered away on Medicare, Social Security, trains, training programs, housing, and fripperies of that nature. To those who say the wolf is at the door, he sternly replies that the "window of vulnerability" is open.

If his rich friends don't bail him out, he will have to go in for "revenue enhancement," which is the elegant Reagan term for more taxes, which will make them unhappy. Better they should write checks for the Pentagon for the weapons of their choice. ■

The Reagan Boutique: Designer Lifelines
—January 24, 1982

We have a new class in this country: the deserving rich.

They are the people who, having earned their money, believe they are entitled to more. They know about the poor—many of them grew up poor themselves—but they seem to believe that, by living the good life, they motivate those who shiver in cold tenements, stand in surplus cheese lines, and can't find jobs despite the plethora of want ads in the Sunday paper.

The president is the leader of the deserving rich. He gave huge tax breaks to corporations. He made it possible for them to buy each other's tax liabilities and to buy each other. Congress was so moved by this pageant of greed that it recently voted itself an exemption on its congressional salary of $60,662.50—an amount which presidential assistant Michael K. Deaver recently declared inadequate.

To paraphrase Vince Lombardi's favorite dictum: Money isn't everything with this crowd, it's the only thing. As a *Doonesbury* character—who is leaving government to go back to the private sector to make more money—said the other day, "Mr. President, you've made it fun to be rich again."

The deserving rich do nice things for each other. Comforting the unafflicted is something that comes naturally to them.

They send money to the Reagans to redecorate the White House. Fashion designers send dresses to the First Lady. They are not gifts, it seems. They are loans. When this unusual arrangement came to light, there was talk that when Mrs. Reagan finished wearing the donations, she would donate them to fashion museums, and the word was that Blass, Adolfo, and Galanos could claim tax deductions for their "charitable contributions."

The idea was quickly scotched—as soon as someone realized how tacky it would look if women who patronize the design salons of the Salvation Army and the Goodwill Industries, would be indirectly subsidizing the First Lady's wardrobe.

The arrangement has the marks of altruism, Reagan style, which is to help the helped. Mrs. Reagan's press secretary explained that due to the "inordinate interest taken in everything she wears, the First Lady had been looking at how to take this interest and turn it to the benefit

97

of one of the most important industries in the country."

One of the most important, yes. But hardly, thanks to the opulent standard set by the White House, depressed. Designer Geoffrey Beene sniffed to the *Los Angeles Times* that he hadn't understood that the fashion industry needed rescuing.

The deserving rich like to throw the lifeline to someone standing on the shore.

Our millionaire president has cut the government's allowance to the unfortunate, the old, the cold, the young, the slow. But he cheerily informs us that any big holes in the safety net will be mended by volunteers from the ranks, apparently, of the deserving rich. It is an appealing notion, recalling the frontier, the neighborhood, the covered-dish supper, the church raffle, the hat passed at the club meeting.

Recently he went to New York to make a pitch to the rich to help the poor. The host organization, the New York City Partnership, epitomized the "spirit of shared sacrifice."

"You," the president told the partnership, "are that tough little tug that can pull the ship of state off the shoals and into open water."

The president could have ended the speech with a pledge or a check: "And to keep the ball rolling, I am donating . . ."

He didn't.

When he was asked at his first anniversary press conference if he intended, in the light of his exhortations, to increase his contributions to private charity, the president exhibited a chuckling unease. He realizes "the publicity that has attended upon the tax returns of someone in my position." What he meant was that, in 1980, he gave $3,089 in charitable contributions out of a gross adjusted income of $227,968.

He went on to say that he gives away one-tenth of his income to charity, "but not in ways that are tax-deductible."

Everyone understands the president's warm feelings for individuals, his chilliness toward constituencies and organized groups. Many find tax-deductible giving unrewarding. Better to see the light in the eye of the recipient instead of feeding your gift into the computers of an outfit that will spend half of it on as much red tape and overhead as the dear old federal government.

And for some people, let's face it, making charitable contributions is a form of tax dodging, futile as it may be. Some of us who really don't want to give for poison gas or missiles write checks for Amnesty or St. Ann's Infant Home, not just because we want to endorse what they are doing, but to keep our money out of the clutches of the Pentagon, another well-heeled entity which has Reagan's entire sympathy.

But if the deserving rich are going to save the country, the First Volunteer in the White House maybe should start showing them how. ■

Dr. Reagan's Prescription: Try Not to Think about the Pain—January 28, 1982

Dr. Ronald Reagan paid a House call the other night.

He journeyed to Capitol Hill to have a look at the state of the union, which is a bit sickly due to a form of anemia caused by 9.5 million unemployed.

But Dr. Reagan, who has the best bedside manner in the business, said yes, things are tough, but they would have been worse if he hadn't taken the case.

He knows the patient feels rotten, particularly if the mortgage has been foreclosed and the jobless benefits have run out. And what is he going to do about it? Well, he is going to renovate the government hospital. It will take ten years but, when it's over, the patient will be cured not only of anemia but of an affliction he didn't even know he had—the dread federal bloat.

Everyone knows what renovation means and how long it takes. The patient may find the whole thing—the banging, the hammering, the arguments—extremely aggravating. But the doctor is plainly counting on it to divert the sick. Watching the workmen, inhaling the plaster dust, the patient may have his mind taken off his present pains.

That seems to be what Dr. Reagan is counting on.

He has no intention of changing the medication he prescribed a year ago. So far, the patient has not responded to heavy doses of tax cuts and reduced government spending, and he is still waiting for the private-sector miracle drug, voluntarism.

The patient is somewhat bewildered. He thought he needed a job, not a new federalism. He is being reminded, by one hundredth birthday observances, of Franklin D. Roosevelt, who built the big hospital on the Potomac fifty years ago and thought the way to heal the sick was to treat what ails them.

99

But Dr. Reagan, although he professes greatly to admire FDR, says there's a better way.

The people inside the House chamber listened attentively to the diagnosis but seemed not entirely convinced. Most members of Congress have just been in their home districts hearing the moans of their constituents. None of them was beset by voters panting for the new federalism.

Dr. Reagan got a warm reception. He was cheered into the chamber and clapped out. But the applause was strongest and longest, not for his "new" ideas, which he has been peddling for years, but for the individuals whom the doctor pointed out as proof that the nation, despite its pallor and listlessness, is basically in terrific shape.

When he named Justice Sandra Day O'Connor, the first woman appointed to the Supreme Court, when he named Senator Jeremiah Denton (R-AL), the former prisoner of war who said "God Bless America" upon being repatriated, they responded very well.

They responded best when he named Lenny Skutnik of the Congressional Budget Office, who on the occasion of the Air Florida plane crash jumped into the Potomac and saved a woman from drowning. They rose to their feet and saluted young Skutnik, who sat beside the First Lady.

But hero worship has its limits. California governor Edmund G. "Jerry" Brown Jr. said it was all very well to leave the federal government free, as the president said, to worry about "arms control, not potholes," but the first order of business would be to train and retrain workers who could revive U.S. industry to the point where it could compete with the Japanese. Federal training programs have been slashed in the great drive toward self-reliance.

Brown reminded listeners that Reagan as governor had turned over "responsibilities" to ever smaller entities, from the state to the cities, from cities to towns, an adventure that led to Proposition 13 and reduced services.

Dr. Reagan announced that he is looking forward to turning over his practice to states and local officials who, according to him, have improved wonderfully in the last twenty years. Some citizens, who know them better, wonder if these vitreous folks will spend the money raised from their new taxing powers, along with their allowance from a federal trust fund, on anything other than roads.

On the day after the doctor's visit Democrats took refuge at Dr. Reagan's wonderful performance and his smooth delivery. It was their way of saying they have no alternative.

The unemployed auto worker may have been less impressed by the president's commercial for the new federalism. He is not looking ten years down the road at the abstraction of a remodeled government. He is worried about bread in the morning.

Hearing Dr. Reagan discourse on "a mandatory pass-through of part of these funds to local governments" is not something that comforts a person who is worrying about his credit at the corner grocery. Possibly, listening to Reagan, he got lonesome for FDR.

Roosevelt didn't talk about what he was going to do for government. He talked about what he was going to do for people. ∎

Reader's Digest: A Bland Magazine for "Boors" and Presidents—November 23, 1982

Some people despair of ever stopping the MX missile. There is reason: three presidents have rassled with the critter, and it has made them all say "uncle."

There is a way, though. Have *Reader's Digest* call it a turkey, and the thing is dead as Chelsea.

Reader's Digest, the monthly for people who hate to read, has a circulation of 17,875,545.

The reader who makes the difference is the president of the United States, for whom it is gospel.

You have only to study the transcript of Ronald Reagan's last news conference to see that the staple commodity of the dentist's waiting room is, to him, a bible, even though he's on the airwaves this week pushing hard for the real Bible.

The magazine prunes, clips, compresses, and blands all expression to a brevity and conformity that caused Thornton Wilder, possibly its severest critic, to call it a "magazine for boors, by boors, about boors."

At that last news conference, the president restated categorically that the Soviet Union is pulling the strings on the nuclear freeze, which, he had told us earlier, is being manipulated by "those who want the weakening of America."

Asked for evidence, he replied briskly, "Yes, there is plenty of evidence. It's even been published by some of your fraternity."

He could not quite bring himself to name his favorite publication, perhaps because he senses that not all reporters share his faith in its infallibility. A few sentences later, he slipped in a reference to "intelligence matters," and nobody in the administration seems able to back it up.

But when he has *Reader's Digest*, he doesn't need intelligence reports. The hot item in the October issue, "The KGB's Magical War for 'Peace,'" was enough for him. It's a hard-breathing account about how the KGB is pulling the wool over the eyes of millions of innocent Americans who support the freeze.

It would do no good to cite to the president the multiplicity of the dupes—from the town of Antrim, New Hampshire, to the Santa Cruz, California, Community Credit Union. Nor the distinction of many of its advocates: Harvard's George Kistiakowsky, one of the inventors of the H-bomb, and Nobel laureates Hans Bethe, Owen Chamberlain, and Herbert C. Brown. Geniuses they may be in their field, but do they read *Reader's Digest?* Probably not. They have cut themselves off from information by which their president sets great store.

You understand the depths of the president's belief in the *Digest* when you see how he discounts material from other sources.

At the same news conference, a reporter made so bold as to question the value of certain weapons that have not done well in tests. The Pershing II missile, which after two bad starts was finally fired successfully last week, was cited. So was an antitank weapon that can't quite cut it against Soviet tanks and a missile that can't seem to find its targets.

These failures have been amply recorded by the embarrassed military services that bought them. They have transmitted these reports to newspapers that like to think they have achieved respectability, and even credibility. But not with Ronald Reagan.

"I've read all those same articles also and having access to information close to the source," he said, with scant regard for the quality of military reporting. "I don't believe those things about the weaponry."

Well, he certainly didn't read about them in *Reader's Digest*. The *Digest* has better things to do than dump on U.S. weapons systems. It invites contemplation of "a more picturesque speech," of noble dogs, invincible mothers, and the intellectual challenge of a department called "It Pays to

Enrich Your Word Power." The November issue introduces the folks, for instance, to the word "bland." That scarcely seems necessary.

The *Digest*, like the president, doesn't like people to be negative about nuclear war. Edward Teller has an upbeat piece in the November number in which he lays bare "Dangerous Myths about Nuclear Arms." He admits that such arms could, if used, have a downside but assures us that "our survival can be considered certain."

So, as we remarked earlier, the good news is that if the *Digest* would decide that the MX won't do and then publish an article to that effect. President Reagan would certainly read it and might cancel the program. The bad news is that the *Digest* will never do it.

Nobody knows how much MX—excuse, please, that's "Peacekeeper" —will cost or even if it will work. But these are details that will never infiltrate the pages of *Reader's Digest*, so we're stuck with it. ■

Answers Raise More Questions—January 14, 1988

Dear Mr. Vice President: It was good of you to write. I very much appreciate your answering the questions about the Iran-Contra controversy put to you in this space two days ago. You had asked to be asked, and I was glad to oblige.

I hope you will not think me less grateful when I tell you that I am more obliged than enlightened. Your answers prompt more questions, I regret to say.

For instance, in response to my request to detail the "mistakes" you say were made, you cite the absence of "a formal NSC [National Security Council] meeting on the Iran initiative where all risks and benefits could be aired by all the participants at the same time."

What makes an NSC meeting "formal," and why does it matter if the principals are all there? You say that you were not at the December 7, 1985, meeting—we all know that you were at the Army-Navy game that day. I was talking about January 7, 1986, in the Oval Office, when Secretary of State George P. Shultz says he all but pounded the table in expressing outrage over the idea of sending arms to Iran.

You say your records indicated that you "probably" attended. Surely, if Shultz, who is a pretty composed human being, spoke as forcefully as he says he did, it would stick in your mind.

In a way, it's not important whether you were there or who said what. You had more years of foreign policy experience than anyone in the room. Surely you did not have to hear Shultz—or then secretary of defense Caspar W. Weinberger, who was also opposed—to reach an independent judgment that this was a terrible idea.

You were aware of the grisly reports about Khomeini's mass torture and executions, his silencing of dissent with firing squad and gallows.

As a practicing politician, you knew how the public, not just the crazy left, felt about the ayatollah. Does your acquiescence indicate a feeling that a vice president owes a president loyalty more than common sense?

I understand your inhibitions about revealing your private conversations with the president. That relationship may be in the doctor patient or lawyer client class of confidentiality. But you make a statement that releases you from the bond. You say that "in settings with others present, I expressed the concerns stated above" and you add, "There were apparently others who shared those concerns."

I feel invited to ask you what the "settings" were, who the "others" were, and what concerns you expressed. Were they related to the lack of "formal NSC meetings" or did they go to the heart of the matter—the folly of selling arms to a terrorist nation, for whatever reason?

Did you warn the others about the danger of the secret getting out? Did you express any doubts that there were "moderated" Iranians still walking around with their heads on?

You say in your letter that "there are people in Iran more responsible than Khomeini." This seems a subminimum standard. The government of the United States does not deal with elements who may be marginally less bloodthirsty than the ayatollah. And besides, you knew from Amiram Nir that you were not dealing with "moderates." After the Reverend Lawrence Jenco's release, Nir told you that we were in touch with "radicals" who could "deliver."

In answer to my question about the irresistible connection between arms and hostages, you say, "I have said over and over again that the original proposal was not presented as an arms-for-hostage swap."

Well, you can say it again, and I'm afraid it won't make any difference. The fact that "the president has so stated many times" doesn't change anything either. He once said the opposite. In a speech to the nation after the hearings, he declared that in an argument between his head and his heart over whether it was arms for hostages, his head—which said it was—won.

You were perhaps gratified to see that Senator Robert J. Dole said he doesn't think "the Iran-Contra affair is an issue." You and I know better. Dole doesn't decide for the voters—or the press—what the issues are.

Your role in the Iran-Contra affair tells us a lot about what kind of a vice president you are. Your explanations tell us even more about what kind of a president you would be. That is why your reply to a question about Oliver L. North's document-shredding is striking. I asked whether you thought it was "reprehensible." You say: "The question of whether documents were improperly destroyed is a matter for investigators and ultimately a court to decide."

If you will excuse me, that is another question you should be able to answer without help. If you are going to be that indulgent with subordinates who destroy evidence, people are going to ask why.

As I said, thank you for your response. I look forward to hearing from you again. ■

The Babbling Bush—September 29, 1988

The debate sharpened the choice. Americans now know they can vote for a man who can't express his thoughts or a man who can't express his feelings.

From the first, George Bush has been trying to convey the notion that his arm's-length relationship with the English language is proof of his good heart.

In February, in New Hampshire, he said, in his wonted fractured phrasing, "I have a tendency to avoid on and on and on, eloquent pleas, I don't talk much, but I believe, maybe not articulate much I feel."

The Granite State's surprising reply was, "Poor dear." Another response might be, "Why not?" A man who wishes to lead the Western world should be able to find the right words, string them together in coherent sentences, and steer them to an intelligible conclusion. His sentences have the stuttering start of an old car on a cold morning. They never run smoothly. The only speech part that he has mastered completely is the non sequitur. On the evidence of Sunday night, he invites the accolade one nineteenth-century rabbi bestowed on another: "That man's mind is a howling wilderness."

Here is the beginning of Bush's answer to his previous assertion that most of the nation's homeless are mentally ill: "But—and I—look, mental—that was a little overstated—I'd say about thirty percent."

He had been told, like Michael Dukakis, to stress certain major themes. But Bush took long detours to destinations he never reached. He was lurching toward a discussion of Angola when he was diverted by a target of opportunity, his home turf.

To set the country against Boston—which is seven miles away from Milton, his birthplace—as a source of pride and intellectual, as well as actual, pollution takes much of his time and that of Bush surrogates. Former education secretary William Bennett said, "I know the Brookline and Cambridge crowd. They sneer at patriotism. These people believe they know better."

Bush—perhaps wishing to echo the Barry Goldwater of 1964 who wanted to saw off the Northeast and send it out to sea—lunged at Boston again and ended up on the mat. He spoke of "phony" as "one of those marvelous Boston adjectives." Boston is guilty of a lot of things, but not of coining "phony" which is of English derivation: from "fawny," a word used by thieves to describe gilt rings being passed off as gold.

Fomenting hostility to a city that is a hotbed of good schools is a curious undertaking for a man who wants to be "an education president." He may have been trying to get Harvard in his sights.

Mention Harvard and right-wing blood boils. To Joe McCarthy, it signified treasonous, soft-headed thinking about the Red Menace. Maybe Bush, a Yale graduate, thinks that the guys in the taproom still resent Harvard as an overpriced citadel of elitism and privilege, where students are shamelessly taught to seek excellence. He should never, however, ask them if they would like their kids to go there.

Bush thinks that Dukakis's self-discipline—his obvious command of himself and his facts—is somehow suspect and alienates the Reagan Democrats they are both courting. Maybe he thinks they are in the grip of a preemptive nostalgia for Ronald Reagan and his airy disregard for logic and accuracy. Maybe he thinks he is answering a yearning for mediocrity, the need to feel comfortable with a leader who doesn't talk better than they do.

Reagan at least never blamed his goofs on the Democrats. The "elephant brigade" simply went out and cleaned up the mess. But Bush seems to hint that Dukakis, by doing his homework and having the answers, is playing dirty.

He wants the voters to see the sober little governor, who is really not that verbal himself. Just better organized, as an overeducated, unfeeling robot, a crazed liberal "iceman."

Dukakis is brainy but not intellectual. He doesn't pursue ideas for their own sake, only if they work. To judge from his vocabulary and the absence of literal allusions, he is not a voracious reader.

Bush can do what he wants to Boston and the King's English. But he did something indefensible for a public official and a candidate for the presidency. He announced his intention to make abortion a crime again. That's his right, and many agree with him. But when asked what the penalties would be, he said casually that he hadn't "sorted out the penalties." It was not until the next morning that his campaign chairman, James A. Baker III, came out to tell women who have abortions that they would not face prison. Their doctors would.

Sorting out penalties is the most important thing a president does, even for a man who prides himself on being nice, not ice. ■

Reagan, Rosy to the End—January 15, 1989

If you took the farewell speech and the budget, you got the poetry and the prose of the last eight years and you got the full bouquet of the heritage of Ronald Reagan.

The speech was just talk, of course, as it was expected to be. So was the budget.

But in both spoken and written documents, Reagan was saying the same thing: What problems? Isn't it great to be an American?

Presidential valedictories run heavily to the self-congratulatory, but Reagan's went to the grandiose. "We changed a world," he said to his doting followers. I couldn't have done it without you.

One notable exception to the rule of content-free farewells was a passage in the one delivered by President Dwight D. Eisenhower:

"In the councils of government, we must guard against the acquisition of unwarranted influence, whether sought or unsought, by the military-industrial complex. The potential for the disastrous rise of misplaced power exists and will persist."

Reagan and the Pentagon have constituted a mutual admiration society.

No one anticipated that Reagan of all presidents would touch on any failures of his long spell in office. His style has been to ignore what he could not deny.

But the tone of this speech was more that of the parting remarks of a captain of a cruise ship. Hadn't it been a wonderful ride, he asked his listeners. Hadn't they both done a wonderful job? There were no references to the rest of the hemisphere, where his Central American policy is in shambles. He is entitled to brag about better relations with the Soviets, and about the economic recovery. But some little suggestion that there is more to do would have been appropriate.

As a matter of fact, Reagan sees only one cloud on the horizon. It was a strange one. He fears that the "new patriotism" he has created—the lump-in-the-throat, flag-waving, slightly belligerent brand—may be in danger. He seems to think that there is not sufficient attention paid to American history. He wants "greater emphasis on civic ritual." He can't mean voting. The American voter failed to turn up at the polls in greater numbers than ever this year, but that's not what he was talking about. The low turnout brought victory to his designated successor, George Bush.

He means the lapses at the kitchen tables of the country.

Here is his folk wisdom: "All great change in America begins at the dinner table. So tomorrow night in the kitchen, I hope the talking begins. And, children, if your parents haven't been teaching you what it means to be an American, let 'em know and nail 'em on it. That would be a very American thing to do."

Does this mean that immature minds grasp the new patriotism instinctively and can spot any deviations as fast as the Young Pioneer in Soviet Russia, who is trained to monitor Mom and Dad from earliest years?

What form would the nailing take? Would the kids fire bread at parents who, for instance, opined that the U.S. pilots who shot down the Libyan planes had shot too soon? Would a little patriot announce he was going to the FBI if a parent disagreed with Reagan's view of Vietnam as "a noble cause" or insisted that the invasion of Grenada was a grandstand play?

Reality, not Reagan's strong point, is not an essential feature of a farewell address. But it is supposed to seep into a budget. Reagan's last budget is a view of America as rosy and painless as the immediate past he described on television.

Take one example. The nation's seventeen nuclear-weapons plants are in a state that endangers public health and safety. It is a massive, wraparound failure. The Energy Department failed to set safeguards for their operation, Congress fell down on oversight, and the president led the drive for more and more weapons.

Thousands of citizens have been put at risk. Radioactivity has seeped into the water supplies of cities.

"We can't poison our people," says Senator John Glenn (D-OH) as we build weapons that supposedly will protect us from the Soviets.

Experts estimate that up to $138 billion will be needed to put the plants and related facilities into passable shape.

Reagan's budget calls for less than a billion dollars to start the job.

The public is being told that the real tragedy is that two of the plants which manufacture tritium, a component of the nuclear bomb, have been closed, and we face the awful prospect that we will have to stop production.

What's so awful about that? The Russians have admitted they haven't got the rubles. We now don't have the stuff. Isn't it an opportunity for arms control?

In the Golden Age of Reagan, his world of armored fantasy, such questions never got asked. ■

When the Breeze Dies Down—January 24, 1989

President Bush's Inaugural Address was the statement of a Christian gentleman, who is constrained by his creed and his code to do the right thing. It was a definition of himself, not the president he will be: a sermon on how others should behave rather than on what he should do as their leader.

The tone was humble, prayerful, almost wistful, free of vainglorious rhetoric. He preached on the need to call forth Lincoln's "better angels of our natures"—his guides, he indicated.

He has been the curate so long he can hardly believe he is finally the rector. He succeeds a madly popular, highly unorthodox shepherd, who ministered to the spiritual needs of his flock without setting an example in churchgoing or charity, whose concern for the poor did not extend beyond consigning them to something he soothingly called "the safety net."

Bush's provenance will be different, he promised. The parish has come on hard times, its debts are great. But we will live together in a genteel and high-minded poverty, with the more fortunate looking after the lost souls, the homeless, the teenage mothers, the drug addicts.

He appealed for less crassness. There was an echo of Tennyson's "kind hearts are more than coronets" in his declaration that "deeper successes are made not of gold and silk, but of better hearts and finer souls." It was a timely thought for a $25 million inauguration that moved in mink and ultrastretch blond limousines. In Ronald Reagan's day, it was not good to blush about conspicuous consumption.

It was a speech that was impossible not to like. Bush is believable when he talks about being nice to others. Except when driven by his need for high office, he favors civil public discourse. He does not hate the press—during the transition he exchanged many pleasantries with reporters. He has been tearing around town, exuding good cheer and gratitude. His enthusiasm, which was embarrassing when he was leading the cheers, is appropriate for the leadership of the Western world. Orchestra leader Peter Duchin said the inaugural tempo was "medium bouncy." Actually, with Bush it was maximum ebullient. After eight years of a reclusive, programmed, and scripted presidency, he seems wonderfully spontaneous.

He may well believe that he and Congress can work together. He made a startling, stark mention of Vietnam, the most toxic word in the American political vocabulary. A war he believed in destroyed two presidents, and he thinks that's enough. The Democrats, who were torn apart by Vietnam, have finally come to terms with it. They buried the hatchet in Atlanta last July. But it sticks in the craw of Republican presidents. The day he had won the Republican nomination in 1980, Reagan defiantly called it "a noble cause."

Its legacy is the War Powers Act, an institutional reminder of deceptive presidents. At his confirmation hearings, James A. Baker III called for cooperation in foreign affairs. Senator Joseph R. Biden Jr. (D-DE) hardily told him that the nub of the matter was the War Powers Act. Baker replied that he could say how strongly they feel "down there" (the White House) that it is unconstitutional.

Bush wants a free hand. But there is more to forget on the books than Vietnam. The Reagan administration mined the harbors of Nicaragua and waged a secret war on a congressional ban on aid to the contras. Bush pointedly addressed House Speaker Jim Wright (D-TX), whose resistance fueled the tide against the war, reminding him that "when our fathers were young, Mr. Speaker, our differences ended at the water's edge."

Reagan enjoyed baiting Congress, and would canter up to Capitol Hill to say he could lick any man in the House. Partisanship was the order of the day.

Bush was no slouch in partisanship during the campaign, which he now dismisses as "history." He did not flinch from reputation-assassination. Congress may remember that penchant in an otherwise well-brought-up man to do whatever is necessary to get what he wants. But as long as they do not know what he wants, they will join in the general jubilation at the "new breeze."

He has passed through so many identities—Reagan's obsequious servant, Dan Rather's semihysterical debate opponent. Michael Dukakis's ruthless rival, Dan Quayle's unthinking champion—that the public is still discovering him. His friends say we see now not the "new" Bush but the "real Bush," a free man at last.

Perhaps the most interesting words bespoke came before he began the speech. He looked over at the congressional gallery picked out two familiar faces: "Hi, Jack, Danny." He was speaking to fellow-Texan Jack Brooks (D) and Rep. Dan Rostenkowski (D-IL), chairman of the Ways and Means Committee. It was a nice touch: he knows the players and that the game goes better with a little friendliness. ∎

Two Contrasting Bushes—August 16, 1990

It is increasingly plain that in George Bush, the American people got two presidents for the price of one. Each of the chief executives comes equipped with a totally different personality, so that it is easy to tell them apart.

The foreign policy president is cool, measured, tough, coping. The domestic policy man is strident, petulant, self-pitying—whining that the other boys are not playing by the rules, and he is going to tell their mothers.

Both Bushes were on view at his news conference this week, one which he held to seek full advantage of his masterly handling of the dangerous Mideast situation.

Foreign Policy Bush was edgy, resolute, in charge. He was calling all around the world looking for people who might help, dealing with the self-appointed helpers in a manner that has just the right mix of disdain and appreciation.

He has been like a symphony conductor, coaxing harmonies out of some oversized international egos. He has not heard a boo since he picked up the baton. Even the trustiest violence-deplorers have conceded that Saddam Hussein is not the type to respond to reason. Even those who complain that a national commitment soaked in oil is of a lower order are inclined to agree that Saddam cannot be allowed to hijack Kuwait. Those who usually wince or cry aloud at the sight of massive troop movements accept them this time: With Saddam, you have to pour it on.

The only murmuring the commander in chief hears is of a generic nature: Can Americans stay the course in the sand?

Domestic Policy Bush was clumsily seeking to make the most of the worldwide kudos for his performance in the desert. With no clear strategy in mind, he flew down from Kennebunkport to raid the deserted capital city. What he did, he could have done by the sea, in comfortable clothes. But he apparently wanted to make the point that he was perfectly willing, in the line of duty, to interrupt his vacation to deal with a problem he has ignored since he took office, and where was Congress?

The professional touch that F.P. Bush brings to his international efforts was absent in his assaults on Congress. It is his job to set a budget, to set national priorities. He is not fighting a process, or an ancient committee system that has long since been changed; he is fighting a determined and united congressional majority that knows how hard he campaigned to be president and insists he should remember that his writ does not begin at the water's edge.

Ten days ago, when Congress left town, he made no outcry about unfinished business. Congress only got reprehensible when his rave reviews started coming in about the Mideast. He doesn't keep in touch with Congress the way he does with foreign leaders. He rang up the president of Mexico the other day, he told us in his news conference, and found another friend:

"We've got a good relationship now with Mexico." He had also been on the line with South Africa's Nelson Mandela and Japan's Toshiki Kaifu.

He is confident, masterly. It is plainly his cup of tea. He appears not the least bit rattled, although the potential for disaster is staggering: thousands of Americans being "restricted" in Iraq; the threat of poison gas (Saddam is a user); the prospect that the price of oil will go ever higher, deepening a recession, whose existence would have been front-page news if Saddam had not struck. There is harrowing talk of nuclear retaliation if Iraq goes chemical. And then there is the cost, which blows the budget summit to smithereens.

But not to worry. George Bush is, as Lyndon Johnson learned to say about Jack Kennedy, "the coolest man in the room." The man who could not face the loss of a single conservative vote not so long ago is contemplating these outcomes with equanimity. Did he think there was any hope of a diplomatic solution? "I can't see it right now," he said laconically.

Bush is so genteel that he ended his news conference with a suburban cocktail party exit line: "I hate to rush." But the foreign policy manager keeps royalty waiting. King Hussein of Jordan, who has resisted every opportunity to show his gratitude to the West, has come up with a "peace plan," apparently based on a long weekend chat with Saddam. But he won't unwrap the package until he gets to Kennebunkport.

Bush doesn't want to get hopes up. If King Hussein's package turns out to contain nothing but a plea to let him make the port of Aqaba available to Iraq during the blockade—make that "interdiction," please—the public won't be let down.

F.P. Bush, unlike D.P. Bush, thinks of everything. ■

George Bush, Come Home—January 8, 1991

George Bush has done what Ronald Reagan only dreamed about. He has lopped off the domestic branch of the presidency and made himself responsible only for defense and foreign policy.

In one of his spats with Congress over funding the government and paying federal workers, Reagan announced that as far as he was concerned only the workers at the Pentagon were essential. Bush doesn't know the federal work force exists. He skipped the monthslong row over the federal budget, and he has forgotten everything he promised for education and the environment.

As the countdown for war begins, the president is in another world. He is reliving World War II (Saddam Hussein is Hitler) and refighting Vietnam. Dan Quayle has been drafted to assure us that we do not face another Vietnam.

The commander in chief is resolute and serene, although thousands of lives are at risk. He was born to lead a free world coalition (with a few Arab terrorist nations thrown in) and has no time for domestic drudgery. The Japanese are buying up our national monuments, Yosemite and Hollywood. He doesn't care; he doesn't even mind if Tokyo skips its gulf dues.

Even though the crisis is said to be at least partially about oil—although Bush harps on its high-octane moral content—he has not related it to energy at home. He never speaks of conservation; he spurns alternative sources of energy. His Energy Department has yet to produce a policy. In fact, reports from the department suggest that White House Chief of Staff John H. Sununu, whose proudest boast is that he opened a nuclear plant in his home state, is using the tension in the gulf to promote the future of nuclear power—thus ensuring more strife and acrimony on the home front.

The president is untroubled by word from his military commanders that they may not be ready for all-out war. He could look out the window of the White House and see that a modest snowstorm has brought the capital of the Western world to a halt. He might feel a shade less omnipotent. Everyone here knows that if there were snow instead of sand in the desert, you could forget all about hostilities.

The cost of the enterprise might give pause to a strapped president. The current estimate is $30 billion this year, which would build a lot of bridges, parks, schools, and homes for the homeless.

But politically, it is said, Bush cannot lose. If Saddam backs down, he is a world hero. If he orders an attack, the country closes ranks around him. If Saddam fights back hard, the country is as one awaiting the outcome—although protracted fighting would be bad for the polls. If Bush prevails, and peace is restored, no one seems to have thought of the consequences in the region, beyond the fact that two despotic regimes that richly deserve oblivion, or reform, will be perpetuated. It will all be settled by the 1992 election.

And when it is over, will he come home? Will he contemplate the mundane? The recession, for instance. He finally, grudgingly, marginally acknowledged its existence the other day: "The recession, should it be proved technically that this country is in recession, will be shallow."

On Capitol Hill, a group of eminent economists, who noted that there are seven million unemployed, were analyzing the problem that Bush has no time for. John Kenneth Galbraith of Harvard said that prophets of a "shallow" recession fall into two categories: "Those who do not know and those who do not know that they do not know."

Economist Robert Eisner observed that wars, in a dreadful way, can ease recessions: "If you get a job making coffins, you still get a job."

In another room at the Capitol, senators were considering another aspect of Bush's inheritance from Reagan, the $500 billion S&L mess. The Senate ethics committee is investigating a tiny corner of the problem, the slavish attentions of three senators to Charles H. Keating Jr., a buccaneer of the thrifts. They were slaves because of the deeper problem of campaign financing, which makes mendicants of all but millionaire office-seekers.

On the stand was Senator Donald W. Riegle Jr. (D-MI), chairman of the Banking Committee, who could not remember arranging a crucial meeting for Keating with senators. He said that he always thought that "the notion of the concept of a meeting was a red herring"—an utterance typical of his sentence structure and his thought processes.

Bush pays no attention to the S&L scandal, even though he has a son involved. Nor does he give even lip service to the underlying problem, campaign reform. His concerns—and his obsessions—begin at the water's edge. ■

6

The Clintons

At Last—August 19, 1993

Dear Mr. President:

You must be philosophical about it. A vacation is what you make it. Vacations are not bad things in themselves. Many people spend fifty weeks or more dreaming about them.

You're acting like it's another budget fight or maybe a session with Senators David Boren and Robert Byrd. It doesn't need to be. Martha's Vineyard is not bad at all. It has dunes, white sand, low-growing juniper bushes, high clouds. You can swim in the water without getting hypothermia.

Grit your teeth and think about the millions of your countrymen who are steaming over the highways in cars without air conditioning, with kiddies and pets in the backseat whining and snapping over every inch of space. Remember that a large percentage of them will end up by turgid waters in damp shacks full of mosquitoes and arguing in-laws.

Many are heard to murmur that if you don't want Camp David, they wish you would open it up to them. They would love to try the bowling alley and the trout stream. They don't know what you have against trees and solitude. That most gifted of vacationers, Ronald Reagan, loved it.

You obviously don't know how to go about it.

Give up the portable phone for ten days. You'll be surprised—talking to people face to face is rather fun. You don't have to discuss NAFTA or health care. You don't have to talk at all. If you must chat with someone other than Hillary and Chelsea, make it someone who thinks that NAFTA is a belly dancer.

Remember not to talk about "back east" in derogatory terms while you're there—if you manage to stay a couple of days. The Vineyard *is*

116

"back east," you know. It would be better not to talk about Washington either. In one of the numerous stops in your recent frantic flitting about the country to avoid actually going on vacation, you did the anti-Washington number, the special gig of Republican presidents. You're supposed to be still grateful you got here.

You gave the governors at Tulsa the poor-me, oh-to-be-a-governor-again rap. At another stop—sometime between the pope and the dash to California and the horseback ride in Colorado, and the stopover in Fayetteville, Arkansas—you met with former president Gerald Ford, who used to pretend at campaign stops in the New Hampshire primary that he had nothing to do with what he called "the mess in Washington."

This, in the presence of three hundred reporters, a contingent of Secret Service, an army of local and state police and several thousand voters, is somehow not convincing. Neither was your nostalgia for the good old days before an audience of politicians who would kill for your job and know full well you've been obsessed with getting it all your adult life. Even if the last seven months have not been a rose garden, they would change places with you in a second.

Still the Tulsa lament served a purpose. It made us, if not you, real-ize how ready you were for some time off. Self-pity is the handmaiden of fatigue. That and your outburst at your younger helpers brought it home to us, told us volumes. Although you made one last lunge at bondage by coming back to Washington for an overnighter. We sensed you finally were ready to veg out.

Take a holiday from the press, too. They will not bother you. They will be scattered in the eighteenth-century mansions of whaling cap-tains, and they will be bickering about where to have dinner.

You are missing nothing in Washington. The town has come to a full stop. People are talking about what is happening elsewhere—the killing of Michael Jordan's father, the burial and resurrection of Harvey Weinstein. They are talking about Hollywood, which is acting like an ele-phant frightened by a mouse. Does Hollywood think it is such, a beacon of family values that the country will be shocked to hear its moguls had paid sex—those same moguls who made the scene in *Rising Sun* where a woman is murdered as she is having sex and the camera makes a tour of her body? That's the chatter here.

They are for once not talking about you, except to wonder what your

117

problem is about goofing off. They wonder, but not with their usual urgency, if you will think about Bosnia as you walk the shore. Will history be kind if our whole contribution to resisting savagery is to pull seven children and ninety-six adults from the carnage for hospital treatment here?

Take a peanut butter sandwich to the beach and look at the ocean and think. Take a book of poetry. See how succinctly great things can be put. Mark lines to put in your wordy speeches. Listen to the Yankees around you. They're pithy, too. Happy trails! ■

A Few Words of Advice for a Sister Scribbler
—June 29, 1995

Dear Hillary:

Welcome to the scribblers' corner. I hope you will like being a Washington columnist. I'm not presuming to tell you how to go about it, but you will learn, if you don't already know, that offering unsolicited advice is a columnist's reflex.

You've been on the receiving end of tons of it—your husband, too. Now, on a slow day, you will be telling Congress, the American Medical Association, the American Association of Retired Persons, or even the District of Columbia what to do.

First of all, brace yourself for floods of mail. As a political wife, you've had your share of abusive letters. You give the impression you're still not hardened to it. When you were still smarting after the November defeat, you were complaining about what people said and wrote about you and how they fixated on your hair. Don't give your critics the satisfaction. Remember always how the only previous White House columnist, Eleanor Roosevelt, handled hecklers. She lived Jane Austen's great line. She did not believe they deserved "the compliment of rational opposition."

About the writing, there's no worry: You're used to speaking your mind. But you must, if I may say so, guard against "wonkism." As you said yourself, you have a tendency to "get a little wonky." Suppress it. Enough people in this city are writing unintelligible accounts of recisions in the reconciliation bill. You should concentrate, if you don't mind my saying so, on people, not policies.

Mrs. R was never abstract. Real folks and specific situations were her meat. Once when she asked her husband if she should pipe down, he replied: "Certainly not. You ought to say whatever you want. And I will simply tell people, 'Well, that's my wife . . .'"

It would be grand if you had such an understanding with your Himself and could steal away from the official line, so that people would know you weren't just flakking for him.

Now I come to the tricky part. My conflict of interest is apparent. You could put all your new colleagues out of work. If you were to write what you know, we're history. And you know: You were there. You heard the arguments pro and con on the president's whirlaround on the balanced budget.

We haven't the faintest idea how it all happened. We hope someone at the White House will respond favorably to a full grovel for a few crumbs. We race up to Capitol Hill and grab a senator on his way to a caucus lunch or camp in the Speaker's lobby on the House side, and we buff their vanity by saying we know they know. They give us bits and scraps and fragments, and we construct these little cathedrals of conjecture, speculation, and gossip that would fall into rubble at the first word from you.

So you have the nukes, and we're telling ourselves you won't use them.

You'll be spared the worst indignities of your new calling. You won't have to go to the Roosevelt Room and listen to self-important young men tell you what is behind the latest, faintest nuance of Bosnian policy, or the impact of the balanced budget on the consumer price index. And you won't, as Russell Baker once immortally put it, be "sitting on marble floors waiting for somebody to come out and lie to me." You'll be spared the spinners.

Your real function is to validate the ideas of people who have nobody to speak for them, who can't get to where the action is and need someone to interpret the guff. No one is better qualified to speak for women who are baffled or outraged over some new insurance company medical practice, like the brutal business of kicking new mothers out of the hospital twenty-four hours after they have delivered a baby.

Do a little investigative reporting: It spruces up a column. Check out the District of Columbia schools and solve the mystery of why they cost so much and produce so little.

Don't let anybody tell you writing is easy. Even once a week is a drag. As the deadline approaches, there is always something you would rather

119

do, such as rearrange your glove drawer or estimate your taxes. "Better go down upon your marrow-bones," William Butler Yeats said of writing.

Some weeks you will draw a blank. You simply will have nothing to say. Ask the president; ask Chelsea; ask the cook or the driver. Or just write about Socks. Readers love animals, and cat lovers are more fervent than the Christian right. Socks is a political cat if ever there was one, and you can tell readers how he strains on his leash to greet people he doesn't even know.

Good luck. ∎

Broadway Revival—August 10, 1995

You know how it is in show biz.

You have to keep ahead of the competition. Here is the special Senate Whitewater committee, and you're doing a low-key summer revival of a mystery called "Whitewater." Business is fair, and then all of a sudden a competitor down the street opens up with a Hellzapoppin' extravaganza on the same theme, with a cast of hundreds, and lots of gavel banging and whistle blowing and hallooing and shouting—and lots of press.

One member of the eclipsed committee, Senator Lauch Faircloth (R-NC), had some thoughts for a comeback. He suggested bringing back some of the witnesses and working them over some more. He particularly had in mind the First Lady's chief of staff, Margaret Williams. Senator Paul Simon (D-IL) brought that crashing to earth with a reminder of the toll, financial as well as personal, on hapless White House staffers. Simon said that Williams's legal bills now amounted to $142,000 and it seemed a bit much to add to them. Besides, she is in China.

Faircloth does not look like an impresario, but there's a lot of Sol Hurok in him for a Dixie pig farmer. He had another idea, which just cracked up the hearing room. His real target is Hillary Clinton, and he wants her for a witness. He thought he could get the First Lady through Susan Thomases, her famously shrewd—some say shrewish—pal, a brilliant, abrasive Manhattan lawyer, who was a fabled figure in the campaign, and to Faircloth a regrettably confident feminist just like Hillary.

But she was an unsatisfactory surrogate. She had undergone an almost total personality change. It was one comparable to that of the chairman. Senator Alfonse D'Amato, who used to be as combative as Susan Thomases, but for the hearings has become a diffident, forbearing, heaven-gazing shepherd, who unbelievably begins his sentences with an unctuous "If I may" or "If I might."

Similarly, Thomases had smoothed her hair, lowered her voice, softened her dress, and adopted the soothing manner of a nurse who is prepared to say "there, there" no matter what the provocation from the patient.

Thomases shared the witness table with Bruce Lindsey, a presidential aide who attended a meeting two days after Vince Foster killed himself where funeral arrangements were discussed. He is a black-browed young man with a narrow face and the distracted air which is the mark of the advance man he was for much of the campaign.

Faircloth felt cheated by the meek, demure woman before him. He read to her campaign manager James Carville's professional tribute: "She has the juice." And from another campaign comrade: "She is the juice."

Thomases uncharacteristically demurred from these descriptions of her power and influence. Faircloth was enraged that she denied everything—from taking a message of warning about "unfettered access" from the First Lady to White House counsel Bernard Nussbaum, to telling Nussbaum how to handle the situation and never having had a conversation with either the president or the First Lady about the documents that were moved hither and yon from Foster's office by his mourning friends and associates.

The nonstop telephone calls? It was not guile but grief, said Thomases; she was "reaching out in compassion" to her wounded comrades and also consoling herself for the loss of an old and dear friend. She was not masterminding a cover-up when she had her frequent chats with Bernie Nussbaum, who has been fingered as the bungler-in-chief of the suicide aftermath; she was just listening.

There was some partisan bickering; nothing, of course like the great roaring bawling encounters that make the House hearing room shake. Senator John Kerry (D-MA), a notably polite man, referred sarcastically at one point to the "Bob Packwood standard of hearings." He was calling attention to Packwood's having been spared public hearings about his many advances to women who wished he would get lost. The latest complaint comes from a then-seventeen-year-old; she joins twenty-two other women. Republican Senator Frank Murkowski (AK) bristled, told Kerry his remark was "totally inappropriate."

Faircloth the play-doctor had found a cure. Hillary Clinton talked to Susan Thomases the night of Foster's death from a telephone on Air Force One. Those calls are recorded, he said triumphantly. Tapes, the whole room thought, and broke out in nervous laughter. Finally, a link to Watergate.

"They record them," said Faircloth excitedly, "the air force told me."

"Who?" cried a voice, as even the two witnesses began to smile.

"Elvis," said Kerry, and the room exploded. Maybe the Whitewater committee, having failed as a mystery drama, can go for laughs and beat the House yet. ■

The Spoils—June 18, 1998

The Unseemliness Trophy has changed hands often in the eternity of the Monica Lewinsky matter. There are those who think that the president retired it last January 21, when we first learned he had been carrying on with a twenty-two-year-old intern in the Oval Office.

But almost immediately it became apparent that as reprehensible as he was in lack of judgment and good sense, he was cleanly matched by the independent counsel, Kenneth Starr, who from the first acted like an ambulance chaser. When he was told of Linda Tripp's tapes, he raced to the attorney general crying "Me, me, me" and persuaded her to allow him to let out the seams on the Whitewater investigation to make room for a reviving look at sex in the White House, with a side order of perjury and subornation of perjury. Without waiting for permission to assume jurisdiction, he wired up Tripp and sent her out to interview Monica for yet another recording.

For months it has been a seesaw contest. President Clinton's lame explanations about an inability to talk about the case—he could have cleared it up in a fifteen-minute television special—were balanced by Starr's brutal questioning of Monica's mother, his hounding of Vincent Foster in his grave, and his hauling into court of a shackled Susan McDougal.

The press, terrified of being scooped, poured on poorly sourced or even dead-wrong details to feed the public a story nobody wanted to read, foisting sensational disclosures on a Congress that was cowering under its desk at the thought of having to impeach a popular president during a dicey by-election. *Vanity Fair* published a series of photographs of Monica, for once, miraculously, without her so-called attorney, William Ginsburg. She was with the Stars and Stripes in one shot, a feather boa in another.

Actually only two things have happened in the five months since we learned about Monica. The first is that two weeks ago Monica finally hired two lawyers who have attended law school. Her previous attorney, a celebrity-smitten malpractice specialist, hung out with Diane and Cokie and practically accused his client of adultery. He went down in flames in California. Now, presumably, Plato Cacheris and Jacob Stein will conduct the case in law offices rather than in television studios.

For the few who still care, the big topic is, will Monica make a deal? Will she turn in the man she called "the big creep" and tell us who gave her the incriminating talking points? Or will she be a fresh version of Susan McDougal, keeping mum for her man? If she is indicted, how can her paramour walk around with world leaders and lecture teenage smokers and teenage gunslingers about restraint?

The second thing that happened, just this week, was that Kenneth Starr gave an interview to Steven Brill. Brill is a press reporter, which is bad enough, but he is the publisher of a new magazine, *Brill's Content*, which is grandly subtitled "The Independent Voice of the Information Age." Starr confided to Brill that he and his helpers had leaked information to the press. It did not take Bob Woodward to figure this out.

All sorts of lurid stuff, some of which had to be retracted, flooded the newspapers and the screens of the nation in the first three or four weeks of the scandal. Respectable newspapers published accounts of the president's deposition in the Paula Jones case that in length suggested that something of unspeakable moment to the nation had occurred.

When the winds began to blow in the last few days, Starr, with his genius for missing the point, protested that he had not violated Rule 6E, which relates to disclosure of grand jury testimony. You only have to think back to the magisterial and immeasurably dignified Archibald Cox, the special prosecutor of Watergate, and a stickler for propriety in law and appearance, to see how tacky it was of Starr.

Starr's real problem, and the reason he will get permanent possession of the Unseemliness Trophy, is that he does not understand his case. Despite his legal background, he cannot get through his head the simple truth that has been apparent to the man and the woman in the street from day one: Reprehensible is not impeachable. Americans would prefer a monogamous husband. But with prosperity so entrenched and a reasonable facsimile of peace in effect, they are not going to insist on it. Monkey business in the Oval Office just doesn't make the constitutional standard of "high crimes and misdemeanors."

Two tourists from the South were asked by a reporter in the Senate restaurant what story about the Lewinsky affair would interest them. The woman, a South Carolina schoolteacher, replied promptly: "Only the end of it." Somebody should tell Ken Starr. ■

Impeachment May Be Too Good for Him
—September 20, 1998

I read the Starr report on a rainy afternoon in Ischia, a beautiful island in sight of Mount Vesuvius, which also poured hot ash on the surrounding landscape. I read it in Italian in the *Corriere della Sera*, and it wasn't easy. My dictionary did not have all the words, and I hesitated to ask the bar staff, who were innocently employed in playing baby soccer with a number of young guests.

Sometimes I would look up from the insistently steamy text and wonder what others in the lounge would think about what I was reading. What would they think, for instance, about oral sex in the Oval Office on Easter Sunday after church, while the First Lady was upstairs?

I already knew how passionately they felt about Clinton. The manager of the Hotel Regina Isabella took me aside when I arrived and said gravely, "Signora, I am praying your country will come to its senses and let your president continue to govern for the good of the whole world." At my table, a mild and pleasant man named Pino, a jeweler from Nettuno, grew apoplectic at the mention of Clinton and began shouting at me, "Why? Why? He is a good president, Wall Street likes him, the world loves him. He has reduced unemployment. People are happy."

"Well," I said, "what would you say if you found out that your prime minister was having a disgusting affair?"

"We would say 'bravo,'" he said briefly.

I tried to explain in my halting Italian about Linda Tripp. What would a prosecutor say if a woman came to him with tapes of the prime minister having phone sex with an intern twenty-one years old?

"He would say, 'Go away.'"

I found one dissenter. He was a former Fascist deputy. At a Saturday night gala, he told me how offended he was that a fifty-year-old man would have incomplete sex for three years. He wanted Clinton to resign. "*Non e uomo, e ragazzo* [He's not a man, he's a boy]," he said.

That was certainly the picture that came out of the depressing report. Here were two flighty people, greedy, reckless, and self-centered. He was spewing sophistries, which he was to take to the country and the grand jury, that oral sex is not sex or adultery. She was no provincial maiden led astray by an aging lecher. The first second they were alone, she flashed her underwear at him. The first time they were together, they went at oral sex with no discussion. Again, he did not inhale, so to speak. They couldn't go all the way, he explained, because he didn't know her well enough.

It was all terribly trite and teen. She complained he didn't care about the real her. She said she fell in love with him, but she turned virago, threatened to tell on him and beat on him for a job, a good job. He told her his wife didn't understand him and he might be getting a divorce after his term was up.

There is not a single redeeming moment, not even a sentence when the president sounds kind or wise, or even a day older than his panting paramour.

Now I have come home—I feared that something irretrievable would happen while I was gone—and I have read the Starr report in English. It is just as depressing. No fun, no warmth. But loveless illicit romances are not impeachable, nor is using another human being as an ashtray, as Clinton did during one of the grossest passages in this revolting and grievously overwritten volume. The authors are a little apologetic about being so repetitious and unrelenting. They were dealing with an eel, they tell us. The nature of Clinton's denials was such that every detail had to be nailed down.

They told too much but not enough, it seems, to budge America on the subject of impeachment. America has said no to the Starr report. That doesn't mean the American family approves of adultery. It seems to mean that Starr's charges of perjury, obstruction, witness tampering, and lying—common to people who are cheating on their spouses—are considered part and parcel of the core trouble.

Now the House Judiciary Committee is planning to dump another ton of slime on us. It will release selected portions of the president's testimony before the grand jury. It will tell the people about things they don't want to know any more about. The American people don't want Clinton impeached. In a way, they think impeachment is too good for him. What he did, while reprehensible and disgusting, was not a blot on the Constitution. It never rises to that dignity.

Our boy president is a trifler who risked his great office for some furtive assignations that caused Ken Starr to rage through the White House like a tornado, scooping up every clerk and Secret Service agent, forcing them to inform on their boss. Clinton did not abuse power, as Starr charges. Starr abused his by producing this gigantic account of a silly encounter. Maybe Clinton should resign. It may be the only way out. ■

Enough of Starr's Smut—September 24, 1998

Henry Hyde is a man of good judgment, much respected for his moderation. The chairman of the House Judiciary Committee should tell independent counsel Kenneth Starr to cut it out, to stop flooding this capital with pornography.

Every day there is a new dump of smut. Monday's two-volume delivery ran to 3,183 pages. We are reading ourselves blind for nothing, to read over and over again the details of the president's illicit, admitted lust for Monica Lewinsky. Starr's view of Americans is that we are such donkeys that we cannot understand the simplest facts unless they are pounded into our heads over and over again.

How many times, for instance, did his prosecutors have to ask Lewinsky if the president felt her breasts "either directly or through clothing"? What difference does it make? Do members of the Judiciary Committee, or anyone else for that matter, need to pin down that particular fact in order to make an informed judgment about the impeachment of the president?

Kenneth Starr has succeeded in reviving himself as an issue in the White House sex scandal. After Clinton made his surpassingly stupid, half-baked repentance speech on August 17, Starr's zealotries and excesses faded. Clinton's clumsy pass at an apology infuriated the country, outraged loyalists, and galvanized the forces of impeachment. But this week, with its thousands of pages of prurient and insistent prying, the country slipped back to its original dilemma about the two compulsives, both obsessed by sex, who dominate our political life. Two wrongs don't make a right.

By now everyone over the age of eight knows the unlovely love story of how the trophy-hunting intern and the lifelong cruiser of chicks met in George Stephanopoulos's office and produced a kind of fusion as noxious as the nuclear leak at Three Mile Island. There was the byplay over papers and pizza, the sizzling glances, the voracious, wordless oral sex. The telephone calls from Capitol Hill are part of the sordid legend. The leader of the free world lobbied Congress while Monica was doing her stuff at his direction. Does it sound a little like the emperor and the slave girl? Did W. J. Clinton of Hope, Arkansas, feel more of a man for the girl at his feet? Did he just get a kick out of having his particular brand of sexual satisfaction while pressing for Medicare with a congressman who could not possibly be having that much fun? Who knows? Who cares?

Sixteen more cartons are going to be decanted next Monday, adding hundreds of pages to such detail as: who unzipped Bill, what Monica ate at breakfast with Vernon Jordan and what he ate, and who paid. Afterward, the country may want to go through a national car wash or an eight-day hymn-singing revival. But it won't know any better what should be done with our wayward president or how we can save our impressionable teenagers from following in his footsteps.

We know it all already. We have read the Starr report; we have seen the video of Clinton in his four hours before the grand jury. Starr is doubtless outraged by Clinton's spurt in the polls since the airing of his testimony. This was supposed to finish him off. As usual, his enemies did him an enormous favor, spreading tales of a presidential blowup and walkout, of a distraught, demoralized fallen star. The reality was quite different. Clinton looked a bit bleak at first, as he clung to his weird views about sex that is not sex and ducked questions about kissing breasts and inserting cigars in inappropriate places.

But he has this gift for living in the moment, and there were times when he seemed to forget where he was and to be enjoying the exchange. The invincible sociability of the born politician surfaced. When Starr staff attorney Robert Bittman was asking the president about the fateful stained dress, another man might have expired of shame. But Clinton reminded him that he had given a blood sample. "You came over here and got it. . . . We met that night and talked."

There are better ways of learning about a president's personality. Airing grand jury testimony is expensive to the system. People are appalled at Clinton's reckless pursuit of sex in the Oval Office. But Starr is also guilty of single-minded recklessness. Grand jury confidentiality is central to our system. We offer its protection to gangsters. He threw over our First Citizen's right to privacy.

Plainly, we know enough to decide. There is nothing to be gained from piling on. The president said he was wrong and claims he's sorry. To be impeached, he must have committed a crime against the nation. The House must decide—and can do it without further input from Starr's pornography press. ■

Community Service Could Be Clinton's Penalty and Salvation—December 25, 1998

Maybe I'm getting a little ahead of myself here, but I'd like to get my oar in the water on the penalty for the president in case the Senate decides to censure him as opposed to firing him.

I say, with all the emphasis I can command, no fine. I'm not saying he doesn't deserve one; I'm just saying the country couldn't stand it. The Clinton legal bills must be approximately the size of the Pentagon budget, and growing by the hour. A big fine will galvanize all of Clinton's Hollywood pals, and we all know what that means. Barbra Streisand singing, Whoopi Goldberg whooping, and brilliant film-capital philosophers like Alec Baldwin joking about stoning Henry Hyde to death, driving conservatives up the wall and liberals around the bend.

A fine also could set in motion a new round of White House money scandals. Legal defense funds would spring up and rich Asians would leave million-dollar checks on White House receptionists' desks. New cries for an independent counsel would be heard. Things might be infinitely worse, although it's hard to imagine how they could be.

No, community service, faithfully and visibly performed, is a far better way out. The president should do five hundred hours, which is a little more than an hour for every day he put us through the muck with Monica. He can't sweep the streets, as appropriate as that might be—he would stop traffic. He can't shovel snow, because by the time the Senate passes judgment, the trees will be budding again. No, he should do something that would be a real contribution to society and keep him in touch with reality.

He should tutor poor little boys, twice a week for two hours, and no excuse would be good enough to get him off. If he's bombing, he could direct the fire from a cell phone. He could go to homeless shelters; he could go to St. Ann's Infant Home and sit down with homeless children and read them stories. If they ask him what he does, he could tell them he has a government job.

He would be talking to children who have never known any kindness from men, children whose fathers absconded before their birth or soon thereafter, boys who have experienced abuse at the hands of Mom's boyfriend, or neglect to the point where they simply cannot imagine that anyone could care about them.

No cameras would be allowed, no videotapes, tape recorders, or other devices providing footage that could be watched afterward in the comfort of the White House or leaked to sympathetic journalists. Sessions would be on the children's turf. Poor children don't need to see how much better life can be. They know already. He could take them on field trips. For instance, if they read Beppie Noyes's charming book, *Mosby, the Kennedy Center Cat: A True Story Made Legend*, he might lead them on an expedition to explore Mosby's many hiding places. But after hours, please.

The other day I talked to some young friends of mine at St. Ann's about the possibility of having the president as a tutor, and they were gung ho. I told them that he had done something wrong and might be punished. They nodded knowingly.

Nine-year-old Simon knew just what the president should do. "I would like him to read to me and play with me. I want him to read 'Snow White.'" He knows just what he would say to the president. "I would tell him not to be lying and to be good"—a widely held opinion not always so succinctly stated.

Seven-year-old Delbar would like to read "The Three Bears." He would look forward to talking with the president. What about? He looked at me shrewdly. "Can he keep a secret?" he asked. I said I thought he could. Then Delbar would tell him this: "My father don't like me." I told him I thought maybe he was wrong. "No," he said firmly, "he won't give me a handshake. He say to me, 'You not my son.'"

He's living Clinton's childhood trauma, enduring a hostile stepfather. The president could learn as much as he could teach. He would understand that these brave little souls are walking around with burdens of grief and pain that could shame him out of the self-pity he so often succumbs to as he tries to shift the blame for his troubles.

The third boy I interviewed was six-year-old Sam, who was as searching a questioner as I have come upon in the course of the impeachment row. "What'd he lie about?" About the girl he knew, I explained. "What he done with the lady?" I said he said he hadn't done anything. "What that lady done to him?" he demanded to know. I gulped.

It is the prospect of exchanges like this during a Senate trial that has made censure so desirable to so many.

But Sam is not all prosecutor. He has other plans for his presidential tutor. "I would like him to tickle me," he said. ∎

Joyful Senate Spends Time Praising Its Own
—February 14, 1999

When it was clear that William Jefferson Clinton was walking on both counts of impeachment, jubilation came to the Senate chamber where his trial had unfolded for the last five weeks. What had begun in an icestorm was ending in a burst of spring sunshine.

It was hard to tell winners from losers. Democrats and the president's legal team wore studiously composed deadpans. The Republicans who had voted for both counts seemed of good cheer. If they were disappointed at the outcome, they were not surprised. Besides, the joy that the trial, which had been such a trial for them, was finally over, was joy enough.

In the end, their need was not so much for the sages and prophets the Senate thinks it produces for such crises, but for a Dr. Kevorkian who would put them out of their protracted misery. The galleries packed with history-seekers savored their moment with the decorum enjoined by the chief justice at the outset.

You had to go to the curved table in the well that was occupied by the House managers for emotion and long faces. Their leader, Henry Hyde, sat at the head, staring straight ahead with the expression of a man whose flight has been canceled for the second time. He did not keep a tally of the roll calls. He and his stricken crew knew what was coming. They had tried to move the senators, challenging their brains and their spines. But they could not change minds. They had begged, groveled to be allowed witnesses, but the moderate Republicans, who are so outnumbered in their caucus, put a collective foot down, and Monica Lewinsky was received on the Senate floor only on videotape.

The House managers had done everything to reassure their haughty, nervous hosts, and chose their most nonthreatening member to question the femme fatale. Rep. Ed Bryant of Tennessee looks like the consummate country boy.

But alas for the managers, he was no match for Monica, who has done much time on the witness stand since her fatal fooling around in the Oval Office. She bade Bryant to clean up a question about her first "salacious encounter" with the president. He did, and nobody thought to ask her what she would regard as "salacious" if oral sex doesn't do it for her.

Everyone on the Senate floor was delighted at the prospect of going back to nursing home regulations and troops in Kosovo after weeks of *Playboy* fare. There were dividends to their long-enforced, full-attendance interlude. They knew each other better and think they could work together. They respect each other's endurance, if nothing else.

They pleased themselves, no question. They also pleased the country, although not entirely. The country wanted Bill Clinton to be spanked, censured for his appalling conduct. But Senator Phil Gramm, the gimlet-eyed conservative from Texas, put a stop to all that by threatening a filibuster. Censure would have been the perfect valentine for Democrats. There was, however, a contradiction: Voting to acquit, which all Democrats did, is a statement that whatever Clinton and Lewinsky did in the Oval Office and subsequently to conceal it, was their business; censure says it's everybody's business.

The chamber was too far advanced in jollity and praise-giving to pay much heed. Majority Leader Trent Lott gave Chief Justice Rehnquist a golden gavel as a reward for his services and evoked heavy applause. The House managers were escorted from the chamber to more fervent applause, and with the intruders gone, the Senate settled down to praising its own.

Senators Lott of Mississippi and Tom Daschle of South Dakota had matching problems, one from the right, the other from the left. Lott from the beginning showed unexpected impulses of accommodation of which his caucus was quick to disabuse him. Daschle had the prima donna problem. But they were both patient and self-effacing and got results. Lott spoke nicely of the House managers without giving in to them. He kept caucuses civil. People's motives were not questioned. The right wing was tactfully referred to as "our base." Arms were not twisted or broken.

Daschle had a wayward president and, among notable prima donnas, Senator Robert C. Byrd to contend with. The eight-one-year-old West Virginian fancies himself the conscience of the Senate, and he tried often to seize the steering wheel of the process. In the last televised explosion of pragmatism unbecoming in a conscience, Byrd said the president was impeachable but that he would vote acquittal because the country seemed to want it.

Daschle humored Byrd throughout, showing that a man without an agenda can make things work. Lott is basking in approval. It might be too much to say they covered themselves with glory—there was little glory to be found in such a mass of squalor and tedium—but it is fair to say that they did themselves proud. ■

Dr. Hillary's Diagnosis—August 5, 1999

WASHINGTON—Why did the First Lady give her scandalously stupid interview? The question reverberates through every bar and beauty shop, cloakroom and construction site from here to Cairo. "What got into her?" they ask.

Whenever we are wondering why either Clinton does something exceptionally irrational, it is best to look at a poll. Sure enough, a survey conducted last March by John Zogby, a premier New York pollster, offers a clue. Topmost in New Yorkers' minds about their celebrity carpetbagger was, "Why don't you leave him?"

Hillary's explanation was conveyed, fittingly, in the inaugural pages of *Talk* magazine, the brainchild of the English enfant terrible, Tina Brown, who injected vulgarity and garishness into the stately *New*

Yorker. Both the vehicle and the substance showed a lack of judgment that might disqualify one for the Senate, where good judgment is considered a prime requisite for membership—even though you might not always know it from what goes on there.

You see, it isn't her faithless mate's fault that he can't keep his hands off other women. Oh, yes, he's responsible, as we all are for what we do, she tells Lucinda Franks, but who can blame him? He was "abused" from the age of four, was caught in the cross-fire between two warring women, his mother and his grandmother.

Looking down the road, you can picture the First Lady's campaign turning into a Dr. Hillary traveling show of open-ended advice to the lovelorn, like those tacky late-night TV panels where people tell about how far they went on their first date. You can almost hear the earnest matron from Elmira: "Mrs. Clinton, my husband is carrying on with his bookkeeper. When I tell him to stop, he says he was humiliated in the third grade by an arithmetic teacher and this woman has brought him closure. Should I forgive him?"

In trying to rationalize her husband's conduct and her acceptance of it, Hillary cites two people who, being in their graves, cannot hold press conferences. Why did she talk about these things? Nobody wants to relive the steamy summer when the president of the United States went before a grand jury and admitted an "inappropriate" relationship with a White House intern. But it apparently serves Hillary's purposes to have what she hopes will be one last blast on the subject. "So shrewd to get it out of the way," says one of her few defenders. But Rep. Louise Slaughter (D-NY), with her usual forthrightness, called it "dreadful."

Maybe New York voters will be so focused on crumbling schools and other social problems fifteen months from now that they will not resent the fact that Hillary Clinton is using the Empire State as a couch on which to work out her personal problems. Maybe they will have lost interest in the "sins of weakness" of her husband. Maybe they will forget that she told them in February 1998 that the Lewinsky scandal was the work of a "vast right-wing conspiracy," or sometime later that it came from what Richard Nixon called "sectional prejudice"—anti-Arkansas bigotry. Her most breathtaking claim: Clinton lied to the country for ten months to "protect" her. Don Juan was at heart a Boy Scout.

The First Lady's adoring staff has told us that she felt "comfortable"

133

with Lucinda Franks. It couldn't have been Ms. Franks's syntax. On *The Chris Matthews Show* on CNBC Tuesday night, explaining that the fatal encounter had been set up without benefit of Hillary's aides, she said— and you could hear English teachers gasping from coast to coast—"It was an arrangement between she and I."

On Capitol Hill, Hillary's strategic gaucherie caused a historic first. Senator Charles E. Schumer (D-NY), an ardent Hillary promoter, for the first time in memory said "no comment" about a public matter. "I don't want to talk about that," he said to amazed reporters.

Joseph I. Lieberman of Connecticut, the first Democratic senator to notice that President Clinton's conduct was outrageous, said the interview had caused him his "first bout of Clinton fatigue." Senator Bob Kerrey (D-NE) observed merrily, "Those excuses never worked for me."

On the Republican side, Utah Senator Robert Bennett asked out loud what others murmured. "Why would she want to reopen that wound and pour a bucket of salt in it?"

Actually the wound had been reopened by several hands lately. Monica Lewinsky flipped her car on Highway 101 in California. A judge levied a stiff fine on the president for lying in the smelly Paula Jones case. And Linda Tripp, the self-proclaimed "average American" snitch, was indicted by a Maryland grand jury for taping Monica's babble about the "big creep."

If the weird logic of the Clinton era prevails, neither of the Clintons will suffer for their excesses. The designated casualty will probably be, once again, poor Al Gore. ■

"Can't Help Lovin' Dat Man"—August 12, 1999

She has vowed she won't, but if she discusses her love life for print again, the First Lady would do better to repair to poets and songwriters, not the psychologists she quoted in her infamous interview in *Talk* magazine.

They are much more helpful—and succinct—in explaining the dilemma of a worthy woman who has mated for life to a man who does not emulate her virtues.

William Butler Yeats said it all in a few lines: "Some fine women eat/A crazy salad with their meat."

He was speaking, of course, of his great love, Maude Gonne, the glorious beauty who spurned him to marry "a drunken vainglorious lout," as Yeats described him in one of the greatest poems of the twentieth century, "Easter 1916."

Noel Coward understood the problem, too. Listen to his hit song, "Mad about the Boy": "Although I'm quite aware that here and there/Are traces of the cad about the boy."

The world is full of women who are joined to louts, heels, boors, blowhards, lushes, and leeches, men who smoke smelly cigars and roost in their loungers for ten hours at a stretch watching football, men who sneer at them and put them down in company, who show up five minutes before a dinner party she has slaved over for his boss. Men who belch, bark, and leave wet towels on the floor and have never been known to take a dirty plate to the kitchen or a message for their wives—and never dreamed of changing a baby.

Hillary has long since tied up the worthy wives' vote—the women like herself who put up with outrageous behavior because, when you come right down to it, they don't really want to leave because, well, "I love him, he's I don't know, he's just my Bill." Women say things like: "He's so sweet when nobody else is around" or "He's a good provider" or "He's shy."

There are all sorts of reasons for staying with a man who lies, cheats, steals, or whines. Maybe he does the income taxes. Maybe he can find his way in Virginia after dark and she can't stand going to parties alone.

I remember meeting an Englishwoman on a boat many years ago. She was newly widowed, and as the boat neared its destination, she began a lament about her late husband. I waited for tributes to his kindly nature or sensitive soul. What she said was, "He was so clever with tickets and things."

Or maybe the thumb on the stay-or-go scales was the thought of the alternative, moving from a comfortable house and routine. A friend said once, after detailing the flaws of her spouse, "Do you think I want to live in a furnished room by myself?"

Few like to come right out and say that they are hooked. They are emotionally dependent. Hillary Clinton has traveled the world lecturing women in Outer Mongolia or Beijing about the importance of being independent—while Air Force Two was parked outside to whisk her back to a life of spousal privilege.

135

People won't think less of her if she says, along with Henry Higgins, that she has grown accustomed to "something in the air." It would be so much better than pointing the finger at his mother and his grand-mother. It's no crime to fall for a good-looking guy. *Talk* magazine pub-lisher Tina Brown has testified to the president's sexiness—"tall and absurdly debonair."

Hillary's problem is that she insists on investing everything she does with significance. She demands to be compared to Eleanor Roosevelt, who was also humiliated by her husband. Hillary, however, knows everything but humility. She wants to excuse him because of childhood "abuse," and she wants to excuse herself as much.

Maybe New York will teach her humility and a little humor. Better women than she have been married to worse men than him. Of course, it is of importance to us when he is the leader of the Western world.

He thought he deserved credit for marrying a brain—he had a han-kering for beauty queens —and she thought she was bringing Wellesley enlightenment to the Ozarks. They did very well for themselves. They're still keeping score. He needed her to get to the top and stay there. Now she needs him so she can get to the Senate and away from him.

Hillary has been arguing with herself since she sat up late in Little Rock waiting for the troopers to bring her husband home. She could have quoted *Show Boat* then:

> He can come home as late as can be,
> Home without him ain't no home to me,
> Can't help lovin' dat man of mine.

She could quote it now. ■

Coal Comfort—December 23, 1999

Dear Mr. President:
        Thanks so much for giving me a column idea, which is always what I want most, especially in Christmas week. I hasten to reciprocate—with a stocking stuffer, advice about your Christmas list. I understand it may include a request for legal costs incurred during the long unpleasant-ness with Ken Starr, the eminent fisherman/pornographer.

Here's my answer: You should—and you shouldn't. On Whitewater, by all means get your money back. That was a total waste of time for everybody. There's a phrase in the Independent Counsel Act that applies perfectly to your case. It's "but for"—and it means that if anybody but an obsessed Clinton-hater had been in charge, you would have been off the hook years ago.

Starr acted like a Keystone Kop: pawed at your past in Little Rock; snooped around on stuff on which the statute of limitations had long since run; grilled your state troopers about your nocturnal prowlings; bullied your White House secretaries and staff; and after $47 million and five years, came up clueless.

Starr's leaden-footed Capitol Hill collaborator, former senator Al D'Amato (R-NY), held Capitol Hill hearings to which he repeatedly dragged all your helpers. They ran up legal bills of hundreds of thousands of dollars in mortgage payments and children's college tuitions.

Mind you, I think there should be special compensation for people subjected to D'Amato's clowning and kvetching, but the law does not provide. Your poor underlings weren't "targets" of the independent counsel and not officially part of his investigation, but they are still paying for working at the White House. If you get your legal fees back, you should share them with these Starr victims.

D'Amato's star witness, Jean Lewis, the "whistleblower" from the savings and loan agency whose testimony was supposed to demolish you, was deftly shredded by Richard Ben-Veniste, counsel for the Democrats on the Whitewater Committee. He brought out the fact that she was as possessed by anti-Clinton demons as Starr himself.

The so-called independent counsel was through until Linda Tripp washed up on his doorstep with the electronic equivalent of filthy pictures, tapes of her talks with Monica Lewinsky. As you know, he fired up the Republicans, and the House impeached you just in time for Christmas last year. The Senate agreed with the country and let you go. But you're not a defender of the Constitution, as you now try to present yourself. You're lucky.

You have, if you don't mind my saying so, a tendency toward self-pity. We all do, of course, but you don't fight it much. And you have good reason to feel sorry for yourself—the First Lady walking out on you, your vice president running away. You're not getting credit for what you did so well: Northern Ireland. The men vying for your job never mention your triumph; they're too busy telling us what they will not do in foreign policy to notice that enlightened meddling in another country's business can be a constructive use of a president's time and prestige.

(By the way—and I know I'm getting off the track —have you considered some special Nobel for the chef at Winfield House, the U.S. ambassador's place in London? George Mitchell was the presiding genius, but I'm not sure he could have pulled it off without the cook. He gave the North of Ireland negotiators a succession of meals that must have been ambrosia to the Belfast palate, which is subject to such abominations as something called "an Ulster fry," a breakfast dish that includes black pudding—which is made from pigs' blood. Decent, digestible food—not overcooked Brussels sprouts and mutton—can change hearts.)

But to get back to the subject, yes, you were exonerated in the Monica matter, which makes you eligible for reimbursement, but that doesn't mean anyone wants to go through it all again. You just ask the mothers who had to explain oral sex to eight-year-olds on the drive to the soccer game.

Of course, you get crazy when you read about Newt Gingrich's divorce papers and discover that while he was raving on the House floor like Cotton Mather about sin in the White House, he was engaged in an adulterous affair with a choir singer. And you reflect on what your idol Jack Kennedy got away with, and you think "life is unfair," as Kennedy said. Call in Buddy and tell him about it.

You will not be forgiven if you bring all the squalors back. The taxpayers have suffered enough. And you should keep in mind that your date with Clio, the muse of history, is coming up, and that she is as exacting as a New Hampshire primary voter. She'll tell you to pay the fees for your folly and be glad you can.

Merry Christmas. ■

7

George W. Bush and Dick Cheney

Presidents-Elect Nasty and Nice—December 7, 2000

O f the three men who think they were elected president on November 7, Dick Cheney acts like the real winner. While George W. Bush, modestly asking to be addressed still as "governor," is being nice in Austin, Cheney is being nasty in Washington and demonstrating, by his insults and other activities, that he is in charge.

After Florida Judge N. Sanders Sauls's wipeout verdict on Gore's recount hopes, Governor Bush's press secretary, Karen Hughes, announced that W. would conduct himself in "a humble and gracious" manner. But the day before His Honor swung his ax, vice president-elect Cheney was on *Meet the Press* slinging warnings about a recession and an insult to Al Gore that was your traditional "poke in the eye with a burned stick."

When Cheney was asked, as is everyone in Washington these days, if Gore should pack it in, he replied in a studied and many-layered slur: "I think history would regard him in a better light if he were to bring this to a close in the very near future."

Notice the "better," which is to say that Gore has no hope for posterity unless he tugs his forelock to a member of the ruling class who deserves the job Gore aspired to. Gore was often charged with condescension during his hapless campaign; Cheney may be the champ.

In an interview with *60 Minutes II*, Bush was all compassion for his rival. He said they had both given their all, and that he would not dream of trying to shove Gore out the door. "I think he's doing what he thinks is right." One Republican at least, thinks the nasty-nice two-step with Bush smiling and Cheney snarling will not wear well. Senator Chuck Hagel, a Republican free spirit from Nebraska, said on Tuesday as the Senate reconvened, that Republicans should "tread carefully" and avoid any appearance of hypocrisy. "The situation is tense with a fifty-fifty split, and almost anything could ignite a hell of a bonfire up here."

If Bush is going to try to make good on the civility he promised in the campaign, he will have to do it alone or set up a politeness academy for congressional Republicans that he could run while Cheney is running the country. House Majority Whip Tom DeLay, who, like Cheney, prefers the bludgeon to the scalpel, referred to the Florida recount as "a theft in progress," a charge echoed by fellow Republicans at every turn.

Judge Sauls found the Florida election flawless—saw no evidence of "any illegality, dishonesty, gross negligence, improper influence, coercion, or fraud in the balloting and counting processes."

But Senator Dick Durbin of Illinois came out of the Democratic caucus saying, "If anyone in Chicago tried some of the stuff they pulled in Florida, we'd have had an independent counsel overnight and the Eighty-second Airborne called out."

Cheney will be the most ideological president since Ronald Reagan. In his decade in the House, he voted on the side of the rich and the mighty, western ranchers, the military-industrial complex, and the oil industry; he was for the MX missile and against Head Start. He was for Reagan's war with the contras and against Nelson Mandela. Was he heartless? He says no, we have to judge in the context of the times.

Despite a record of draft-dodging during Vietnam—he got four student deferments and a fifth for expectant fatherhood—he was confirmed as secretary of defense. Like many Republicans, he liked everything about the war except the idea of fighting in it. He dismissed criticism airily: "I had other priorities in the sixties than military service."

Bush liked him because Cheney knows what he is doing and does whatever is necessary to get what he wants. His attack on Gore suggests that his success has gone to his head and that he took a swipe at Gore for the fun of making an enemy a footstool.

Democrats are irritated with Gore for not winning at the peak of a historic boom. He was never one of the gang on the Hill. But they rally to him when the Republicans are kicking him when they don't need to.

Those who yearn for healing and unity in Washington had better look to the National Zoo. A pair of panda bears have arrived from China, and they'll bring people together because they provide amusement and delight, something that is not anticipated from a Cheney-Bush administration. ∎

Hardly a Parsing Score—February 25, 2001

President Bush, in his first White House news conference, proudly observed that he is making progress in encouraging a more "civil discourse." Perhaps, but more grammatical it ain't—not when Bush is doing the talking. It's scandalous, especially for a man who purports to be the "education president." What happened to his own?

The Clinton revelations are so absorbing that they are obscuring other issues deserving of attention and outrage. Because of the daily din from Manhattan, we don't always know what else is going on. Thursday, the day of the president's news conference, Hillary Clinton had one, too. She was emoting about her brother Hugh's "terrible misjudgment" in taking $400,000 from two shady characters who got pardons from her husband. She preempted the State Department briefing on C-SPAN.

Our new president wants the country to be on an even keel, like his White House. He wants to concentrate on servicemen, schools, and tax cuts. But the world has been churning out tragedy and treason and other matters at a rate that shows even Dick Cheney can't manage everything.

An illustration: When Bush was at the height of his exertions for military appreciation week—touring bases and telling our fighting forces how wonderful they are—a navy submarine slammed into a Japanese trawler. Nine people on the boat died. The Japanese demanded an apology from the sub's captain. The navy clammed up, and neglected to tell us that the crew had company at the time. Sixteen civilians were jammed into the USS *Greeneville*'s cramped quarters.

Later, a crewman plotting the whereabouts of nearby vessels said he couldn't do his work for all the tourists in his way. Money was involved. Some of the visitors were being rewarded for big bucks they had given to a battleship restoration.

That's when Bush sent out his first bombers. The media dutifully canvassed his reasons for striking at Saddam. In Mexico with President Vicente Fox, Bush gave a macho response: "Routine."

The sub was bumped from the lead news slot by a major FBI embarrassment. The agency found a mole in its midst—fifteen years after the FBI alleges that he began working for the Russians. Robert Hanssen yearned to be a spy from age fourteen. His role model was Kim Philby, the British traitor.

He put his six children through private schools with the help of dollars and diamonds he allegedly got from the Russians. His co-workers, noting his dark suits and dark moods, dubbed him "the mortician." But when people ask why nobody suspected him, they remember the man for whom FBI headquarters is named—J. Edgar Hoover. The top cop liked to dress in women's clothes, an oddity that was not mentioned at the time.

While all this has been going on, the leader of the Western alliance has been demonstrating his inability to speak English. George W. is the son of a notorious language abuser, but George Herbert Walker Bush was in a different category. The elder Bush was a devil-may-care metaphor mangler, recklessly mixing incompatible images, stepping off rhetorical cliffs into a great void. It was perhaps inevitable for a man bred to filet mignon trying to pass as a pork-rind freak.

George W. on the other hand, is engaged in a losing struggle with pronouns. This might seem a harmless mismatch, except that he proclaims "a passion for education." Last week he offered up a series of howlers that would have earned a fourth-grader a glare from his teacher. Bush said to an elementary school class in Tennessee: "You teach a child to read and he or her will be able to pass a literacy test." Imagine the emotions of teachers—who have heard themselves described so often as "inadequate"—as they look forward to wrangles with eight-year-olds wishing to follow the leader into syntactic chaos: "I don't care what the president said . . ."

Bush's news conference provided more heartburn for language lovers: "Laura and I are looking forward to having a private dinner with he and Mrs. Blair." This was in the Style section's "Reliable Source" column. It was page 1 material.

The news conference also brought an acute moment of what grammarians call "pronoun confusion." Asked what he would tell his family about seeking a pardon from him, he said, "My guidance to them is behave yourself. And they will." In two short sentences, he swung from the plural to the singular and back to the plural.

He also mangled his answer on the FBI spy when he referred to Hanssen's "alleged espionage that took place." Alleged events do not "take place," someone should tell him. People scratching about for nice things to say about the Clintons might note that their sentences parse, at least. ■

Bush Needs to Be an American before a Texan
—August 25, 2002

Don't call George Bush a unilateralist. He'll get sore at you. Don't say he's a chauvinist, either. He's just a Texan, dammit.

His monthlong stay at his ranch—punctuated by meetings of high moment and oodles of fund-raising expeditions—has brought out the Lone Star in him. He says he'll "go it alone" in Iraq if need be, and he sounds plausible on that dusty plain where the lonesome cowboy is a fixture and you don't find authors of hostile op-eds.

And his anti-Eastern, anti-Atlantic Coast bias breaks out, as in that strange outburst the other day about people who unaccountably prefer sea breezes to the dead heat of central Texas.

The president told AP reporter Scott Lindlaw, who was permitted to follow him on his ranch rounds, that he knew not everybody appreciated the local charm, but that more did than you might think: "Most Americans don't sit in Martha's Vineyard swilling white wine."

What was that all about? Was it a reflexive lunge at his permanent piñata, Bill Clinton, who used to vacation at Martha's Vineyard—and forever sullied it for Bush? But islandwide excessive drinking has not been an issue, and so far, at least, Clinton has not been charged with wine-swilling even by Bob Barr. Or was it just his free-floating resentment of the East Coast and his conviction that it is inhabited by whining winos, decadent, supercilious, unpatriotic, elitist liberals, who are now, to their surprise, quoting Dick Armey, the House Republican leader from Texas, who doesn't want to go to war. When Bush was a candidate, *Washington Post* columnist Marjorie Williams took memorable note of his "curious air of resentment, the more puzzling for its place in a life so touched by advantage."

The petulance surfaced in Paris last spring. Who could forget his flare-up at David Gregory, an NBC reporter who asked a question of the French prime minister in perfect French, which he had learned as a child in France. It didn't seem a major offense, but Bush, for some reason, thought he was being challenged and that Gregory was showing off, which he finds unforgivable when it invites comparison to him.

In Texas, it's OK to be a little bit surly; it adds to the aura of a citizen of a large, assertive state that doesn't think much of the rest of the country. And Bush, who is proudly unassimilated, does not just talk

Texan—dropping his *gs* and quoting old wanted posters. He walks Texan, too. He throws out his knees and holds his arms bent and away from his body in the classic pose of the cowboy or sheriff who may have to reach for his pistol at any moment.

He tries in every way he can to live down his long exposure to the East, Andover, Yale, Harvard. Has George W. forgiven his parents for his being born in Connecticut? His father, George H. W. Bush, also a native of New England, longed to be taken for a Texan. It was a bit of a stretch. Although he assiduously dropped his *gs* and professed a passion for pork rinds and truck stops, the prep-school accent and manners gave him away. It is one competition with his father that George W. wins going away. The only question is, does he go too far with it?

We got used to having a Texan in the White House personalize a war—just think back to Vietnam and Lyndon Johnson, a graduate of Southwest Texas State Teachers College, who decided fatefully to take over Harvard grad Jack Kennedy's unfinished business in Vietnam.

Bush surely cannot imagine that he can wise-guy his way into a war with Saddam Hussein. "I'm a patient man," he said this week at a press conference with Defense Secretary Donald H. Rumsfeld that they tried to turn into a soft-shoe routine, feeding each other lines and chuckles. Bush repeated that he was a patient man as if that were all the explanation needed for his intentions.

He will consult our allies, he said breezily, while General Tommy Franks was telling another audience that he had the war plans. Britain's prime minister, Tony Blair, would need a little more to take to his people. Colin Powell would probably like to know what plans Bush has for pacifying the Middle East before he starts another war. The Joint Chiefs of Staff still want to know where the bombers will be based, as country after country in Iraq's neighborhood sends back the NIMBY word.

A show of gravitas is called for, a humble copying of his father's coalition-building when he invaded Iraq. It would be appropriate for a nod and a gesture to the United Nations—an international organization that is held in "minimum high regard" in Texas. Bush could improve his credibility by paying our bill for the UN. As of June 30, we owed over a billion dollars.

There are times to be a Texan. Bush's swagger and defiance met the national mood after 9/11. Now, if he is going to lead the West into war, W. has to be an American. ■

8

Gardening

On Tending One's Own Garden Not Long Enough
—August 29, 1982

The Chinese send ideological deviants to farms for rehabilitation. I do not question their wisdom; but I would like to point out that if agriculture is chastening, horticulture is utterly humiliating and I am suggesting that the garden plot outside my windows is a place to bring low the haughtiest spirit.

Like many would-be Washington gardeners, I storm Johnson's Flower Center in the spring. I have the avid, rapt look we all wear when we are bearing off the ageratum, the dianthus, the blue aster ("blooms all summer"). We see the garden in its glory, the stunning bouquet on the coffee table. We hear the exclamations of the guests, our own modest response—"homegrown."

Now of course, it is August and ashes-in-the-mouth time. The rosebush produced a single bud, which took one look around and apparently committed suicide. The dianthus, after a puny bloom or two, fainted. The marigolds have gone entirely to leaf. I will never know if the asters were blue.

And why, you may ask, do I burden you with this account of defeat and devastation? It is because of the impatiens, which alone has rescued me from floral Dunkirk.

I cannot say enough for this most slanderously misnamed flower. It is the St. Bernard of the doomed gardener. If it were a person, I could not say who it would be. No human I know embodies so many virtues: cheerfulness, endurance, generosity, adaptability, understanding. I look out my window and I see flowers. At the entrance of my apartment house, we have lovely, rioting mounds of red and white. I am—please do

145

not snicker—the chairman of my condo garden committee. The impatiens I credit with saving me from impeachment. People who are spared the sight of my failures in the back, stop me in the hallways to praise my green thumb.

The impatiens is not like the petulant petunia, which demands pinching and gives you sticky fingers in return. The impatiens does like a bit of water, but in the case of lack, it will not like the vindictive ageratum, turn brown. It understands that you forgot, and begins smiling at the first drop.

As if all that were not enough, the impatiens thoughtfully seeds itself, springing up in areas otherwise given over to blight, to the bugs and slugs which make a McDonald's of the marigold bed.

Birds, I regret to say, are different. They have learned nothing from the impatiens.

It all goes back to a time when I wrote about a mockingbird who bullied me into going out in a blizzard to buy raisins. The column brought forth considerable response, from readers who were emotionally involved with mockingbirds, hooked on their charm and cheekiness. One correspondent reported at considerable length about "Casper" and "Bonjour" who had practically gotten credit cards from him. But came also a stern communication from a retired foreign service officer, who adjured me to cut off the raisins during the summer months. He drew an analogy to welfare.

I obeyed, slashing the raisin budget to zero once the ground was soft. The mockingbird was, like other species, not grateful for my attempts to improve his character. He merely patronized another restaurant, the Maxime's, which is run by my neighbor upstairs.

What I get instead of the flutter of wings is the hulls of the sunflower seeds which the male cardinal spits down on my patio as he feasts. I have told my neighbor that he is corrupting the birds, but every Saturday I see him struggling in with armfuls of delicacies for his guests.

I have suggested that he is particularly contributing to the delinquency of the male cardinal, who is rotten anyway. The male cardinal treats his wife in a manner that should make her the symbol of the ERA. Her worthless mate is, I should note, the official bird of seven states, which just goes to show you that the earnest university dons who recently made a study of the effects of beauty, should have started—and ended—their researches in the cardinal's nest.

The male cardinal, in all his gorgeousness, gorges until he is staggering, but let the Mrs. so much as flutter by, and he rounds on her in a flood of abusive squawks. She retreats to the nearest bush, mildly chirping until she has to carry him home.

My neighbor said defensively, "Do you think they're like some parents who never take the same plane, out of consideration for the children?"

I am not sure whether this was male solidarity speaking or simply a reflection of the fact that my neighbor who works for the FAA is soft on anything that flies.

But I renew my invitation to Peking. Their dissidents might not get to compete in the Chelsea Flower Show, but they would learn a lot about the good and bad elements that present themselves daily to people who try to cultivate their gardens. ■

August: The Month When Dreams Are Trampled—August 25, 1991

T. S. Eliot called April "the cruelest month." Obviously, he was no gardener. Had he been, he would have fingered August.

That is when some of us have to abandon, finally, our hopes of having a brave show of blossoms, of garnering bouquets for and from the neighbors, to wonder if we should take up some less humbling recreation like golf or tennis.

My friend George, the neighborhood's premier gardener, looked at the unrelieved green of my plot and said kindly, "They are resting."

Actually, some of the plants have been resting since I put them in the ground last May. They remind me of Congress, which comes back to town with a great clattering of hooves, much hallooing from heralds and retainers, and after shaking hands steadily for a day or two, goes on recess. That's what the alyssum have been doing on the border in front of the boxes. They were meant to provide a lacy white background for the lavender-pink impatiens—yes, we gardeners get carried away by special effects, I admit it. A Victorian valentine was what I had in mind. The alyssum had other plans. It went south.

The impatiens bed is a greater disappointment, but here we're talking casualties, not goof-offs. They are like those innocent bystanders in the ever-popular drive-by shootings. Anyone who thinks me harsh to

147

compare squirrels to homicidal drug dealers has obviously never dealt with the varmints of Macomb Street. They are presently persecuting the wife of the Indian ambassador. They raid her boudoir for the sweets she keeps there, she thought hidden. They paw through her jewelry. Recently they made off with a new toothbrush, with what villainy in mind we hate to think.

In my own long war with them, I have scored one significant victory—and I am still paying for it. Courtesy of Hammacher Schlemmer, I have a squirrel-proof bird feeder, a round one with a conical top that squirrels fly off of, except if ice forms, when they can get purchase on the ridges. But in high summer, I thought, they could only sit on a nearby tree, glare at me, and plot revenge. But they have their kamikaze, too. One morning I came out and one of the squirrels was wound around the base of the feeder like a cobra. I don't know if he got anything to eat. He just wanted to be sure I saw him.

Naturally, when he dropped down, he fell into the impatiens that are planted underneath. That was part of the fun. I didn't think the squirrels could repeat this feat, although I am sure they videotaped it for their young commando trainees, so I got replacements. This is no reflection on the impatiens, the gardeners' friend and, contrary to its name, the most patient plant ever relied upon by people who can't raise cosmos.

The replacements fared no better, I regret to say. I went out two mornings later and they had been uprooted. I suspected the squirrels, naturally, but they were not at fault.

Living on the edge of the forest, I have a resident raccoon. He likes to come up on the deck in the dark of the moon, and he likes to come via the impatiens bed. He is like a tank: Anything in his path must be crushed. So there is a bare patch, and he storms up the slope and steps up to the deck with a "Hi, honey, I'm home" blitheness, which I find maddening.

The gaillardias are not so easily explained. They started out strong. The only thing I can think is that they offended a hummingbird. I heard recently about a hummingbird attacking a full-grown man who had let the bird feeder grow empty. It sounds as unlikely as Russians trying to stop tanks with bare hands, but in the world of nature, I am a believer. A butterfly once jostled me. Are the hungry hummers also nearsighted, like the mourning dove, and did they pummel the nearby gaillardias thinking they were punishing me?

This is speculation. All I know is that the Texaco station on upper Connecticut Avenue has gaillardias that are as radiant and full as stars. Why? Do they like the fumes? Are they talked to? I have never heard a gas station attendant say more than "Cash or credit" and "Look—under—the—hood?" Maybe for flowers they have more.

Perhaps I sound bitter.

The bird life, due to the small size of the perches, is limited to sparrows. People notice it almost at once and go on to tell me about colleges of cardinals in their backyards or about a mockingbird who's been with them for years and who can imitate exactly the squeak on their patio door, or do a note-perfect rendition of the andante passage of Mozart's Flute Concerto.

One caller, noticing the unremitting green on the ground and the unbroken dun on the wing, tried his best to offer comfort.

"Does it help to think of them as English sparrows?" he asked.

"Not much," I said. Nothing does in August, when April's dreams are dead. ■

Flower Power—May 16, 1993

The morning after the storm, I looked outside on a scene that stopped my heart—and made me think of President Clinton. There stood two total strangers, knee-deep in the impatiens bed that had been laboriously planted less than a week ago.

It was the way the president must have felt when he looked out his window and saw Bob Dole digging up his stimulus package. I rapped on the window and demanded to know what they were doing.

"Underground drainage pipe," one of them said laconically.

"The flowers," I screamed.

They indicated a forlorn heap on the ground. "We'll put 'em back."

Oh, sure. My two helpers—not slave labor, please, no matter what you hear—and I had graded and nuanced and rearranged for hours. The lipstick-red shaded to the blush-pink, the white carefully interspersed. Should I offer a chart, like Ross Perot? Instead, I bit my lip and went out to raise some tempest-flattened phlox. Shakespeare was right: "Rough winds do shake the darling buds of May."

We gardeners—you know us by the dirt under our fingernails and the stars in our eyes at this time of year—identify strongly with the president. Like him, we are at the mercy of "sinister forces," as Alexander Haig said of the Watergate tape gap. What the storm was to us, Bosnia is to our home-oriented president—it could ruin everything. He is bedeviled by the Serbs, who are engaged in a gruesome exercise of weeding the human garden and should be stopped, except nobody knows how.

And he has to put up with lobbyists, just the way we endure squirrels. We plant tulip bulbs; they dig them up and carry them off, the way the lobbyists make off with Clinton's tax bills. The squirrels, I assume, head for the river with the bulbs in their mouths. On the far shore, they strike out for the west to present tribute to their great fan, Ronald Reagan, whose most misguided policy, by us, was feeding walnuts to squirrels. That's like putting a soup kitchen in Grosse Pointe. The scourge of the "welfare queens" gave handouts to these shameless moochers and panhandlers because he thought they were "cute."

For pests, who eat holes in leaves and blight blossoms, Clinton has, he feels, the press. He rates us somewhere between aphids and grubs. We have a spray for our tormentors, although much uncertainty. The labels have such fine print only an ant with bifocals could read them. He has no remedy so far, although his "Boys' Town" staff, which works twenty-six-hour days, doing God knows what, may have something in the Bunsen burners.

He has some gardener-friends in the corps, although many journalists these days are given to computerized chess. The president could spot us easily. We are the ones who at Rose Garden events give our attention to the garden and have to be called to account by a brusque reminder from the Secret Service that "the action is over there." How could they think we would steal? Just because we're drooling?

We understand something else that may mystify the general population, or at least people who choose sissy pastimes like golf, tennis, or touch football. He is ambivalent about the economy. He wants it to do well, but if his programs are to take root and flourish, it must not do too well—one of Dole's alibis for killing the stimulus bill was that recovery was about to bloom. It's about the way we feel about the weather. We like sunshine, too, picnics and other summer pleasures. On the other hand. if our visions of horticultural glory are to be realized, rain must fall.

The president complains that he's been "criticized for doing more than one thing at once." We understand. We get that all the time, too. Here's how it happens. We are putting in carnations—I told you we think big—and run out of leaf mold. On our way to the supply, we spot a ragged edge in the grass. Nothing so galvanizes us. We rush for the snippers and fall to our knees. Flowers cannot look their best against scraggly spears. Then we pause by a drooping salvia in our ambitious "Rhapsody in Blue" box, and encourage it to pull up its sox. We know all about detours that look like panic attacks.

He is moved by fantasies of children getting shots, seniors getting home care, and government getting reinvented. We dream of being mistaken for an English country garden. He has so many schemes he's having to use Republican names for them. "Enterprise Zones," right out of Jack Kemp, likewise "Empowerment Communities." We can't talk, we're no laser beam. We buy everything in sight at Johnson's Flower Center.

We wish him well. We know from our experience with difficult dianthus and languid lobelia how hard it must be to raise programs in the unforgiving soil of Washington. And we don't even have Ross Perot cawing from the sidelines, telling us "it's just that simple." ■

Summer Gardens, Like Politics, Are Full of Ragged Blooms—August 27, 1995

S ome of you—OK, it was two, if you must know—have kindly inquired how my garden grows. It's the same old story, but this year not without parallels in the political world. The Democrats, that is the annuals, are losing ground by the day. The perennial Republicans are hanging in, but there is strife and contention among them.

I am not complaining. We gardeners do not. I am not going to lay off on the savage heat of the past few months. Our defeats and disappointments are the kind there should be more of in life: humbling but not embittering. For us, there is always tomorrow.

I look out on my dusty patch and I see astilbe bowing in the breeze, lilies that last a whole week, and ageratum that does not pout and sulk and break into piddling little flowerets, but assembles itself in those plump azure pillows that are shown in the White Flower Farm catalog, source of the most seductive prose in the language.

151

I face certain difficulties in gardening—galloping erosion for instance; our Executive Committee doesn't think much about resodding. I also have a neighbor who has only to look at a plant to make it flower. Her patio box is a lush collection of begonias and geraniums that are tumbling out of the box in gorgeous profusion. Her balsam is blazing with raspberry-colored blooms. Her plants are constantly "spreading" and, as she puts it, "seeding themselves," something that has never occurred to mine.

Marie never gloats. She is far too well bred, a southern lady from New Orleans—except when it is a matter of the Redskins, and a transformation occurs. Call her when the game is on and you take your life in your hands. One Sunday, a visiting friend passed her place and heard shouting: "You idiot, hit him" and, "Fool, grab him." My friend was alarmed. Domestic violence? Should 911 be called? But then he heard a withering "Are you blind?" and realized only zealotry was afoot.

Across the street, it's no better. Alex, alas no longer with us, created a garden that was waiting for Monet's brush. Next to him is Bill, whose studio and grounds are on the bus tour routes.

The plus side is that people take pity on me. This summer it was Jo, from the world of high-tech. She is dear Lizzie's daughter and shares her lamented mother's disbelief of the depths of my incompetence. She drew plans, sent for plants, arrived every other Sunday with a bucket lined with tabs and holders and slots for every conceivable garden tool and a special feeding gadget for the hose. Our only difficulty was in conversation. Jo is as evangelical about cybernetics as Newt Gingrich and given to odes to the Internet, which could be hairspray as far as I am concerned. I am a notorious Luddite and find it hilarious that the guard inspects my reticule as I go home every night, thinking I have a computer part hidden in it. Not bloody likely, I want to tell him.

Jo worked out a symphony in apricot for the big show: dahlias, tuberous begonias, the essence of every sunset I had ever loved. The dahlias did not adjust. They shot up and then fell back in anguished loops. I was reminded of Bob Dole and his contortions to please the right. The begonias bloomed but late and under the cover of leaves that I had to cut back. Washington does not prepare you for such diffidence.

The perennial bed, black-eyed Susans and phlox, was something that not even Jo could find fault with. They started blooming on schedule in

July. There was only one problem, and it is one that plagues the Republican field. It is the phenomenon of the false phlox, a weed masquerading as the real thing—same leaves, same height, and hard to spot. I thought of Pat Buchanan and Phil Gramm, each snarling that he is the genuine article, warning the right that Bob Dole has no place in the garden of the righteous.

The perennial bed reminds me of the U.S. Senate in other ways. It has a rhubarb plant that knows no limits. We know how the Senate is weeding and pruning and clipping away at the ledgers of the poor, while it throws money at the Pentagon for crazy weapons it doesn't need. The rhubarb was brought to me among a dozen other plants by kindly visitors. The others expired, the rhubarb expanded. Its leaves have the wingspread of a B-52. It has overwhelmed the little colony of dianthus that was struggling nearby. Talk about a metaphor.

Some of you may have noticed there's no sniveling about squirrels, tormentors of other years. They have gone, because the bird feeder is. It was stolen, some said by the homeless reportedly sheltering under our parking lot. They, or someone, took the stone angel. The angel's easy—who doesn't need one?—but why would a homeless person want a bird feeder? Who knows? That's part of the charm of gardening. It's all mystery and chance. Like life. ■

This Year's Garden Pest: Deer—July 13, 1997

Faithful readers know that I usually submit my report from the garden at the end of summer when the harvest of failures and successes is in. I'm early this year because the returns came in early. It was all over by the Fourth of July.

Over the years, there have been many Dunkirks; this time, we're talking Dien Bien Phu.

Ordinarily, the triumph of the squirrels, an annual event, would be a major item. It took them awhile, but they cracked the squirrel-proof bird feeder that Jo provided—a beautiful object with wrought-iron scrolls that baffled them. One morning, however, I looked out and saw a gray object wrapped around the seed cylinder like a fur piece. He was hanging by his heels from the top perch, resting his head on the bottom one, gorging.

I thought the squirrels might go light since they broke open the cocoa-mulch bag and feasted around the clock. But squirrels are about food the way politicians are about money: There's never enough.

Then a cat, the most insolent in a long line of cold-stare specialists who make use of my little plot as a thruway to the park, showed up. The other day it put its front paws on the edge of the birdbath and drank deep. When I yelled at it to stop, it threw a look, perfected over the centuries by its kind, the one that says: "Who are you?"

But these are trifles, hardly worth mentioning in the light of the Fourth of July massacre in the perennial garden, which was to have been my summer pride.

I went to Behnke's and splurged on peach-colored phlox to take their place with the black-eyed Susans and the lavender phlox from long ago. They were all gone; slashed at the top. It was Keats's "bare ruin'd choirs," which, of course, is from his "Ode to Autumn."

But who—and why?

Not the raccoons. They like hard stuff. They have chewed off the cover of the birdseed barrel. They got into the basket with the extra house keys, opened the jar in which I kept them, unwrapped the foil, and made off with them. I wondered what they use them for: bookends? toothpicks? The point is that raccoons, who wear leather and ride motorcycles, would not fool around with sissy flowers.

Marie, my knowledgeable neighbor, took one look and said, "Deer."

"Impossible," I said, "two blocks from the Uptown Theater."

She was adamant. "My cousin Sandy had them. They ate all her azaleas."

Matsuko, who lives in our condo, reached the same conclusion and offered me the first of the many solutions I have heard in the past few weeks. "Human hair," she said. "They hate it. Put it in a stocking and hang it from a tree. Go to the barber and the hairdresser and ask them if you can have their sweepings." Yes, I said.

Colum, who had helped plant the eaten garden, concurred with the deer diagnosis. "Rabbits eat from the bottom."

Marie's cousin had used netting to good effect. But the clerk at the hardware store was dubious. "They eat through it," he said gloomily. He was right.

Johnson's plant store was full of suggestions. I could get a dog, build a fence, or buy a bottle of coyote urine for ten dollars.

Coyote urine rang a bell. Mike Wallace had given some to Don Imus on television. I called Imus to ask if he had a deer problem. No. *Sixty Minutes* press man Kevin Tedesco then enlightened me. Wallace did a show last November about dastardly deer. En route to Imus, he snatched one of the leftover props, the coyote urine, as a present.

"I wonder if he thought I would drink it," said Imus.

I record this for those with hard-to-buy-for people on gift lists.

Meanwhile, Bambi had moved to the back of the house and devoured the patio flower box, a beautiful collection of gold pansies and dark-blue lobelia. Stubble now. Kevin warned against high hopes for the coyote urine. "Look at it this way: Do you have many coyotes around the Beltway?" I said we had a few, mostly on Capitol Hill.

A deer-plagued Long Island town had hired archers. Tony Lake, former security adviser to the president, gallantly offered to bring lion dung from the zoo, but security problems came up. *Washington Post* publisher Don Graham thought a lion would be better. Again, though, has in-town Bambi ever met Leo?

I have always been for Bambi and against guns and blood sports. I took Princess Diana's side in her argument with Prince Charles about hunting. Lately, I've slipped some. I wonder if the Potomac Hunt would like to do a little tallyhoing on Macomb Street?

Bambi turns out to be mean. One night she leaves only a few trampled gaillardia behind. The next night she comes back and polishes them off. She passed up on the impatiens until I draped them in black netting, which she laughingly pushed aside.

I cannot pave over the whole disaster with uncomplaining impatiens, always the gardener's last resort. No, now I have only one planting prospect: cactus. ■

Nature's Withering Glance Humbles Even Prolific Gardeners—August 29, 1999

The capital drought has blighted gardens. It has also brought a certain stealthy comfort to gardeners without blooms. We whose gardens always look drought-stricken have loads of company.

Now when I meet a proprietor of a plot usually worthy of Williamsburg, I can look her right in the eye. I no longer cringe at the prospect of hearing her whine about trying to stop the black-eyed Susans from taking over the back yard. "Like weeds," she would simper to me, who is down on her hands and knees just begging them to survive. But when she inquires about my horticultural health these days, I just shrug and sigh and look up. She does the same, my sister at last.

The other night I went to a gathering where a beautifully dressed guest from Maryland held forth on the question of whether she should turn in her neighbor to the water police. No, she had not seen her neighbor's sprinkler running full force, but she knew what was going on. She needed only to look at her neighbor's garden, a vulgar display of abundance and color surrounded by suspiciously green grass, and then back to her own—with its withered stalks and lawn the consistency of shredded wheat—to know the story.

I said nothing, but I was thinking about revenge on her obviously unscrupulous neighbor. I could imagine it would go beyond the poisoned pet or the sabotaged grill to something like Kosovo-style reprisals.

The reason people are so emotional about their lawns and gardens is easy to understand. Yeats, as usual, said it best: "Tread softly because you tread on my dreams." It is not just the time that goes into horticulture, or the sweat and the aching muscles. A vision strikes, and although it should die in early spring, it does not. The blooming bulbs put on a brave show to humor us and keep us hooked. Daffodils and tulips, which have their own little bubbles, can break through ground that more temperamental plants find so inhospitable.

For about three weeks, I can talk about my garden without whimpering. But when the heat comes—not this year's savage, breath-draining kind but Washington's usual dog days—and I have bought enough plants to send the nursery owner's son to Harvard, nature puts me in my place once again.

Defections and disappearances abound. The New Guinea impatiens, all dark leaves and bright flowers, suddenly check out. In my so-called perennial bed, the gaillardia succumb to some mysterious wasting disease. One week, they are thriving; the next, they look as if they have seen *The Blair Witch Project* once too often or are trying out for the *La Traviata* look-alike contest: Their garish and unwholesome petals mock me over the blanched and withered leaves.

My garden blooms in ironies. Right beside the blighted gaillardia are the elephantine leaves of an unwelcome rhubarb that I have tried for years to uproot. You may be sick of the comeback-kid analogy, but it applies.

We gardeners are deeply instructed in the fragility of dreams and the unfairness of life. I watched the decline around me during the recent fuss over the Iowa straw poll—the political equivalent of the preseason game. *Time*'s Margaret Carlson, in a burst of inspiration, called it "a wholesome fraud." She meant, of course, the rural context of the State Fair and its Last Supper sculpture in butter. Lamar Alexander emerged as its designated chump.

I had watched Lamar doing everything a candidate should do in the way of seeding, weeding, feeding. And what was his harvest? It looked like the plot where I have my cousin Brian's gift lion, which I wanted to surround by dark red dianthus so the lion would look as if he were wearing a ruby collar. Brown stalks are all that came about, just like Lamar's sixth-place showing.

I identify with Lamar. My neighbor Marie is the George W. of the back of our condo. Everything comes to her. She buys a sorry little lily plant for thirty-nine cents at the Safeway and the next thing you know it has shot up five feet and put out gorgeous flowers that are the floral equivalent of Handel's Hallelujah chorus.

For the life of me, I cannot figure out why Mother Nature thought we bloom-challenged needed another lesson in humility. But what she did, for this summer, was level the playing field. No one is more grateful than we are for small favors. ■

Who's Sorry Now?—April 15, 2001

Dear Mother Nature:

Excuse me, I am very sorry to be writing so late. Nobody ever told me your rules for planting a garden. I always thought that dirt, water, and sun were all that were needed. It was only last week that I was enlightened by the *Post*'s estimable garden editor, Adrian Higgins, as to what I should have been doing all these years.

In his column Adrian quoted a paragraph from a new book called *Bud, Blossom & Leaf*, by an Englishwoman named Dorothy Morrison. Here are his words:

"Morrison advises new garden areas should be launched by asking the resident Earth Spirits for permission to use them."

For the past two weeks, heaven knows, China has been teaching the whole world about the awful consequences of not getting a go-ahead from the spirits in charge. The pilot of our damaged spy plane had a great deal on his mind at the time, and thought he was following international protocol when he sent a Mayday signal to Hainan airfield, the nearest available airport; but that wasn't enough for China.

Luckily, Colin Powell, our secretary of state, figured out that China is as uptight about its air space as you, Mother N., are about the Earth, and said he was very sorry. He said so in a letter, which he insisted was not an apology. The pilot is happily home and I am grateful to have my horticultural break through reinforced by cosmic crisis.

After years of disaster and fiasco in the small plot outside my condo, I see my faux pas. I may not trust Ms. Morrison and her countrymen on matters of food or fashion, but I revere them on the subject of gardens. Their fanaticism is visible from a train window going anywhere in England, from the gardens at Oxford to the wrong-side-of-the-tracks cottages where some patient gardener trains the hose on a single rosebush.

Every relationship, as the dragon kept telling us, begins with respect. I thought my trouble was that I was working inhospitable soil from the excavation for the condo. I practically bought out Johnson's peat moss supply, and supplemented it with leaf mold from the Indian Embassy next door. But I was clandestine and nothing flourished.

I hope you do not feel, Mother N., that I am comparing you to Beijing in touchiness and implacability. Of course not. It is just that when either of you is displeased, you tend to react rather violently. As the old saying goes, "When Momma ain't happy, ain't nobody happy."

An example: For several years I have had a lovely lavender patch, courtesy of the National Cathedral Greenhouse. It was all silvery and fragrant, but lately you have been carrying on a kind of ethnic cleansing—to remind me, I guess, of my undocumented state. Only four or five stalks remain of the original bevy.

That was nothing compared with the retaliation you took several years ago when I succumbed to visions. I had had a brainstorm about an orange and blue perennial symphony fit for the garden tour. I found orange astilbe and blue larkspur, and I thought I had found glory. You went ballistic. You sent a pack of hungry deer—the nukes in your arsenal. They ate it all, even the roots. I woke up one morning to devastation. If it weren't for impatiens and basil, I would have turned in my trowel.

It isn't as though I needed any instruction in humility. You know my neighbor Marie, who just looks at seeds and makes them grow. I don't know if she made a separate peace with you; all I know is that years ago, she got a scrawny lily at the Safeway for $1.29, and it's now six feet tall, with melon-size rose-and-white blossoms.

Across the street, Bill recreates Wordsworth's poem on daffodils every spring, and Evelyn has primroses. Jo and I planted daffodils on either side of the stairs to my garden. You let only one side come up. You told several of my tulips to do leaves only.

You run the bird concession around my place, and I keep the squirrel-proof feeders filled. Once we had cardinals, mockingbirds, and bluejays. You have replaced them with crows and sparrows. The front of the building gets robins, bluejays, and the mockers, including, I am sure, the one who does the slow movement from Mozart's Flute Concerto. You want us to treasure all your creatures equally, but crows, too?

You're getting raves right now. Washington in spring is your big moment, and I have to say your special effects are spectacular. The city is wrapped in veils of tender green, and the forsythias that bloom on every corner are affirmative action itself. There's a cherry tree on Logan Circle that's a metaphor for resurrection.

Do you ever forgive an illegal trespasser? This is an apology.

Abjectly,

The Sorry Gardener ■

Quite Contrary—August 5, 2001

S everal readers—okay, two, if you must know—kindly wrote to inquire how my garden grows. About the same, I would say, except that this year the squirrels are black—a fact much noted by young visitors, even when I tell them it doesn't make any difference.

They have tails that look like bad dye jobs, henna-streaked ink. They are even more aggressive and vindictive than the old gray crowd. These have been brought up to get even with me for finding, finally, a bird feeder they cannot crack. They shinny halfway up and halt melodramatically at the cylinder that stops them. They sit there and glare at me. I'm afraid there's not a scrap of Saint Francis in me—I glare right back.

I have good reason: The black squirrels scored a huge victory this year. Steve Pearlstein, a colleague with a green thumb, kindly brought me some beautiful daylilies from his vast store to put along the stone wall I had had built to keep my condo from falling into Klingle Road. He put them in for me, too, and as spring advanced they shot up in a most encouraging fashion and even bloomed—something that is never taken for granted in what passes for me as "a lovesome thing, God wot!"

Then one morning I looked out. The beautiful orange blossoms had disappeared. I knew it wasn't deer, who have been known to make a McDonald's of the astilbe bed that I had hoped would get me on the neighborhood garden tour. What had gone wrong? It seems the lilies had picked up stakes and decamped during the night. Eventually I found some on the ground. Had the rapacious raccoon, who goes for grass seed after he has pigged out on the bird food he has clawed out of the bag, suddenly decided he needed beauty in his life—and a big stomach? No, as I was watching the last flower left standing, I saw something black streak through the air. The squirrel blasted out of the low-growing evergreen bush, gripped the long, flexible lily stem, and rode it triumphantly to the ground. I could picture the glee in the squirrels' clubroom. They had committed the perfect crime—and probably sold rides on the "lily trapeze" at exorbitant rates. I put nothing past them.

Other setbacks have occurred that I cannot blame on the squirrels. For instance, an entire lavender patch that had nourished for several years suddenly committed mass suicide. The plant had seemed happy enough. The orange cat who pads through every morning just to give the sparrows cardiac arrest had never bothered it. No trace of Kool-Aid, either.

Did Dr. Kevorkian pass through and drop hints about a swift resolution as preferable to a long, drawn-out indisposition? Or was it more subtle than that? My mind turned to the White House flaw-finders, whose job is to spot imperfections in international treaties. They are summoned every time the rest of the world decides to put its heads together about some little imperfection in the way the world is run.

The treaty scribes haven't scored yet with W.

They've tried the Kyoto treaty, which says there's entirely too much smog around. "Fatally flawed" was the verdict of the perfectionist in the

Oval Office. They tried small arms trade, biological weapons. All close, but no signature. Bush was in sympathy with the goals, of course, but . . .

You can imagine the demoralization of the treaty writers, who, like the unlucky gardener search desperately for the clues to their failures. The wrong parchment? Unappealing calligraphy? Perhaps the grammar failed to pass muster in the Oval Office, although the current occupant makes minimal rhetorical demands upon himself. Or maybe it was worse: The scribes didn't tell the United States that it is No. 1, superior, unique, and not to be confused with other, lesser nations?

After a hard day's fly-specking at the White House, do the flaw-finders moonlight at my place, sidling up to some plant that could go either way and whispering, "Say, I wouldn't get too comfortable if I were you. Dick Cheney was seen in the neighborhood last week and may be casing it as a place to drill." I can find no other explanation for the meltdown of two glorious delphiniums with white, navy, and royal blue flowers that I had found at Johnson's and planted with great expectations. Overnight, they turned droopy and dirty. Like Alexander Haig under difficult circumstances, I suspect a "sinister outside force."

Malaise is in the air, I fear. Once in a great while, a cardinal comes to my feeder. He is gorgeous, especially among the dun-colored, quarreling sparrows that are my regular clientele. On his cameo appearances, the cardinal brings his old lady to keep watch. She chirps away, but he is nervous. I hear her saying, "Go ahead, dear, you had no lunch." But he worries: "It's getting late, I saw a hawk, I felt a raindrop."

Naturally, I am hoping for better times. That's how you know us hapless gardeners—by our dirty fingernails and our absurd, unquenchable optimism about next year. ■

Hope Grows Eternal in the Gardener's Heart
—September 1, 2002

I know my annual garden report is late. Several of you have kindly inquired why, and I hope you will not regret it. Regular readers are familiar with my struggles to reach accord with nature—squirrels, raccoons, chipmunks, and yes, deer. This year it isn't just nature. It's man, too, in the form of a new and implacable board in my condo.

The season started in a familiar way. Of the hundred bulbs my friend

161

Jo and I planted last year, maybe fifteen survived. In past years, the squirrels whimsically planted them elsewhere, such as so far down the hill that only my upstairs neighbors could see them. But this year, they must have had a banquet—an "all the bulbs you can eat" gala.

The spring also brought the news that the board meant to evict me from my little L-shaped Eden at the back of my building and to take it over. The board had every right. It's common property, and the fact that I had brought it from something like a slag heap to a semblance of a garden was no never mind to the board and the new property manager who came with it. My Aunt Kate had combed the hills of New Hampshire for ferns, then wrapped them in damp newspapers and sent them airmail. I had planted them in leaf mold purloined with permission from my next-door neighbors, a succession of Indian ambassadors with whom I got along famously, even during the cold war, when Henry Kissinger was counseling coolness.

Like all gardeners, I am extremely emotional about my bit of ground. Every edict advising "work to begin immediately" made me whimper. I dreaded the bulldozers. Would they flatten the holly I planted while regrouping after a traumatic lunch with Nixon aide John Ehrlichman, who told my antiwar pals—Sam Brown, David Mixner, and John O'Sullivan—that if they went on protesting, the government would build more jails with higher and wider walls? And what about the ever-growing ex-Christmas tree that was set into a steep slope in defiance of gravity by *Washington Post* editor Bill Hamilton and George Stephanopoulos, back when he was a congressional aide taking lip from members and before he became rich and famous?

So I did what any sensible, distraught gardener would do. I called up the crack condo lawyer, Benny Kass. He had a word or two with the authorities, and clemency has been granted: I am allowed a say in what is to be.

But days after détente was reached, nature struck again. The deer came back. Five years ago they staged a series of raids that left me with scorched earth. They ate my orange phlox down to the roots and laid waste to the orange astilbe. I sought and received much advice. Most striking was a gallant offer by Bill Clinton's first national security adviser, Tony Lake, to go by the zoo and pick up lion dung, which deer detest. He found out, unfortunately, that we had signed a global pact to preserve everything about lions, including their excrement, beyond reach. Such a pity George W. Bush was not in charge. He hates international treaties and would definitely have refused to sign such a document—he might have campaigned against it, as he does against the International Criminal Court.

Alas, I'm back to tying deterrent Irish Spring soap bars on every branch.

I have had lots of help over the years in my horticultural efforts, and much social life. People, particularly those with strong backs, would come on Sunday to do a little light farmwork and stay for supper. I have endured criticism for my labor policies—baseless charges of forced labor and cracks about César Chávez. But if you plant the basil and you get to eat the pesto sauce at harvest time, John Sweeney will not take your case.

The tendency to carp was especially notable in a relative, my cousin Brian McGrory of the *Boston Globe*, who, like me, is a professional carper, a newspaper columnist. He brought his complaints and his dog, Harry, who jumped in every hole we dug and napped in what he thought were satin sheets, the impatiens bed.

Impatiens, the last hope of the ungifted gardener. In this summer of drought, they were the only color on the scene. So when the deer came, they hit the impatiens first, nibbling off the blossoms. I caught one of them red-handed on a recent Sunday morning. She was at the Christmas tree, gnawing on a branch. I tapped on the window to get her attention. She raised her head and gave me a doe-eyed gaze. Her look said plainly: "Oh, dear, is this private property? I thought it was still parkland. I'm so sorry."

Am I downhearted after that double whammy? No, I'm a gardener, and we live on hope for better times. Come spring, we'll be in the crowd at the garden center in the stampede for seedlings, certain that a more beautiful and fragrant season is just around the corner. ∎

9

Cars, Laptops,
and Gadgets

Agnes, Meet Mercedes—August 9, 1987

S o now I own a Mercedes-Benz. You want to make something of it? Of course you do. Everybody does.

I was prepared for a certain amount of guilt on my own part, but not, I have to say, for quite so much flak from my immediate circle.

Sure, I flinch when I watch Bob Hope in those "Made in the USA— It Matters to Me" commercials, and I reply defensively, "It matters to me, too."

I had every intention of buying an American car. I drove one for seven years. If they still made Fairmonts, I'd be at the controls today, honest. In 1980, during the Republican convention in Detroit, I met some nice, unemployed autoworkers who hate the Japanese. I promised them I would buy a Ford, and I did.

My Fairmont was not flashy, but it was faithful. It seemed to want only to serve, like some good-hearted old maid named Agnes. Once a year, the mechanics who looked her over before inspection managed to find expensive and exotic ailments and disorders of which she had never complained.

Over the years, Agnes began to embarrass some of my passengers. Her plastic interior, her sagging seats, the dent on the front door caused consternation among people who regard a car as a declaration. I never think of them that way. To me, there was Agnes and there was a Mercedes—with nothing between in the wasteland of my automotive consciousness.

"Getting pretty old, isn't she," said a colleague who had asked for a lift on a stormy night. "Yes," I said, "and so am I. Perhaps you prefer the Metro."

This general malaise about the inadequacy of Agnes peaked during a recent visit of young relatives.

"You think of getting a new car soon?" asked one of my mortified kin on the way to the airport.

Agnes's last encounter with the garage mechanic resulted in an unintelligible bill of $500. Soon after, the windshield wiper paused in mid-stroke and the left-hand turn signal developed a tic.

It was time, I said.

I went dutifully to inspect the latest and best in domestic manufacture. I was doing fine with the recommended model until the salesman said, "Look, a special option, the tilt-wheel," and lifted it up.

I was absolutely horrified. I could see myself in traffic having inadvertently released the mechanism that made it move, clutching an uprooted steering wheel and screaming for help.

It is not my fault, I say, that the dealer also carried the Mercedes. I said I was just looking—and that was the case when I saw the elegant little convertible with a price-tag of $61,000.

On the way back to the domestic showroom, we passed the "previously owned" lot. Even I know there is no such thing as a used Mercedes.

Well, I saw this little beauty, a blue-gray 190E, and I thought there was no harm in trying it. The salesman, a pleasant man named Mr. Azuni, winced when I started the motor. "Don't press down so hard," he said as I put a heavy foot on the gas in the manner to which I had become accustomed over the years.

I rode around the block. You know the rest.

The trouble I had adjusting to my new property was nothing compared to that of my pals.

"You? A Mercedes?" said one fellow-worker, "It's not you."

One editor couldn't believe it. "You, a woman of the people?"

"A limousine liberal," another leered, with technical inaccuracy.

Women friends said, after the first shock. "Well, I think that's wonderful," in a tone that suggested I had finally decided to run off with a thirty-year-old rock singer.

My most persistent tormentor told me, "It means you've joined the psychiatrists and the land developers."

A kindly soul said, "No, it means she appreciates fine engineering."

165

This was so wide of the mark I felt I had to disavow it. I can't divine the mystery of the childproof top on the aspirin bottle.

An old buddy explained his problem: "It's wasted on you."

He is quite right.

Every morning when I turn the key to unlock the door, the latch springs up and the other three clunk authoritatively in sequence. When I start the motor, I get the feeling that I have activated a company of Teutonic knights, with spears atrembling and shields at the ready.

I say, "Hey, guys, cool it. We're just going down to the paper."

I feel the way that Elizabeth Barrett Browning did about her cocker spaniel, Flush, who gave up hunting rabbits to keep her company. This powerful splendor should be on the highway, laughing at the other cars.

Sometimes I wonder if its creators, hearing of the thumbs it has fallen into, will demand I return it. They wouldn't have to have a policy about defective cars; but they might have one about defective owners.

It's something I worry about when I'm not trying to figure out if I could have a sign on one door saying, "I paid my dues to Detroit" and on the other, "It's only new to me." ∎

No Contest: Blenders 3, Columnist 0—August 7, 1988

Usually, I just avoid machines. It's a long, sad story, but what it comes down to is that we have no rapport.

In summer, however, I must deal with them. I grow basil, and I love pesto, that wonderful, edgy sauce which the Italians invented to make us eat more pasta. When you're talking pesto, you're talking blenders, which to me might as well be components of Star Wars.

I have had many blenders, and they have all been instructive on their way to the boneyard. Like most people who instinctively go about anything mechanical the wrong way, I had subscribed to the popular theory that the reason we can't get along with them is that they are impersonal, soulless.

That is wrong. Appliances have idiosyncracies, just like us. Unfortunately they have packed up our less attractive traits—they are proud, spiteful, and unforgiving. I have, for instance, a dishwasher that will not begin when you press the "start" dial. It needs to be jogged to the right. That's just the way it is, like Ronald Reagan.

But the blender has the most temperament I have ever encountered in an inanimate object. It is given to terrible temper tantrums. It literally smokes with rage. I have been through three in the last year.

It is my fault, of course. I was not tactful. I did not understand it. I just put the basil and the pinenuts and the olive oil into the plastic container, pressed the blend button, and strolled away.

I was summoned back to the kitchen by the smell of burning rubber, a shower of fine black particles, and the sound of a moose in distress.

What had I done wrong? I had ignored its power and its pride in performing its stupendous, pulverizing feat. I had forgotten it is an opera star, who must rest between the acts. I had taken it for granted.

I came to understand after Number 2 went up in smoke that the blender does not like to be rushed. I can relate to that. I am very slow in the morning, needing gradual introduction to the fact that "the sun is up and up must I." You must press all the blender's lesser buttons and coax it up to concert pitch. I had asked it to go out without its coffee.

I went back to the appliance store and the gentleman assured me that, with this new model, I would have no trouble. Alas, he knew his wares better than he knew me. I did all I had been taught: filled it only half full, told it to take its time. But I guess I forgot to say please or something, because it suddenly began to rock on its base as if it were going to take off like a rocket. I nervously disassembled it and, sure enough, it was sick. The black rubber ring at the bottom had developed waves in its silhouette, like a sea serpent. It could not be pressed into shape. Nervously, fatally, I operated. I cut it in two, snipped off the slack, and put it back. Could it, would it? People were coming for supper. It gave out an angry roar and expired.

I packed up the makings and went to Joyce's house. She has a kind heart and a Cuisinart. There was another breakthrough. If machines are like people, they are also like dogs. We know that dogs smell fear and become hostile. The great mastiff of blenderdom is the same. As Joyce was presiding over it, I ventured near, feigning interest. It emitted an ominous growl and stopped in midrevolution. I slunk away—and it resumed.

I had recourse to my cousin in the North. She believes there is an explanation for everything: snarled electrical wires, demented Dobermans, failed marriages. She is the most rational person I have

167

ever met, with the possible exception of her governor, who is also her presidential candidate. She carries her reasonableness to extremes. I remember being in utter awe of her when she was driving through Roman traffic at rush hour. A plainly crazed Italian was trying to drive his Fiat over the hood of hers. "Oh, I see," she said pleasantly, "you want to turn left."

She is usually tolerant of me, too. We both understand that people like her need people like me to highlight their gifts. It is a bond.

But for once she had no sympathy. "Maybe you should find a mortar and pestle," she wrote with uncharacteristic sharpness. She enclosed a blender manual. Her next sentence began with the phrase that causes my mind to snap shut: "You just . . ." Those are the words that people use when they are giving me directions about impossible things, like getting to Virginia, squirrel-proofing a bird feeder, filling out an IRS form.

Reader, I purchased a Cuisinart. The nice woman showed me how to prepare for launch. "I have three of these," she said. Three? I was so stunned that anyone would willingly introduce so much technology into her life that I quite lost the thread of the lock-in procedures, vital before takeoff.

The Cuisinart sits on the counter. I am trying to remember what she said after she said, "You just . . ." ■

The Rocky Road to "Loving" a Portable Computer
—May 24, 1992

They handed me a Toshiba, a portable computer (although it weighs a ton) just in from Japan. "You'll fall in love with it," said my coach, Harry, "just like David Broder." If I do, the love will be unrequited.

My nephew, Edward, who actually earns his living teaching people to run computers and tending them when they get sick, gave me an answering machine for Christmas. I learned what buttons to push, and got to find out that while I was gone, someone wanted me to go on a cruise or buy some waterfront property. I was feeling quite contemporary until it turned ugly on me—as machines almost always do. One night I pressed the "message" button and it whirred and cleared its throat in the usual way, and then played back a telephone conversation I had with my neighbor two Sundays ago. I never told it to tape the call;

I wouldn't have known how. And this was not a memorable conversation. I was just telling Lisa that I wouldn't be able to come up and see her because I had company.

I try not to take these things personally, but it is hard. Edward says machines are like dogs—"they can sense when you don't like them."

About the Toshiba, I'm not being irrational. I had an encounter with its ancestor the Radio Shack—which is at least not heavy. Under duress, I took one with me to Budapest, Hungary, because they said I would fall in love with it, and the other things they say when introducing me to some gadget that is about to humiliate me. I wrote out what I wished to say about President Bush's rapturous reception on the Danube and handed it over to David Broder, who not only writes wise and prophetic copy but also transmits it without a hitch on the latest model they hand him in the *Washington Post*'s systems department, which idolizes him.

Broder welcomed me to new-age technology and began confidently the process whereby Washington would be reading me within seconds. He called, it seemed, most of the capitals of the NATO countries, and Toronto, Portland, and New York besides. He plugged everything in and waited. Nothing happened. Only I was not surprised. Once more, he alerted all the way stations. Again, nothing happened.

I silently took the Radio Shack computer from David, went to a telephone, called the *Washington Post* dictation department and dictated nineteen inches to the admirable Olwen, who knows what I mean even when I'm not sure myself.

I am not a Luddite. Some modern inventions strike me as genuine progress. I love TV, for instance, and I have always appreciated the electric light. But I came along in an era when the transmission of one's copy did not require an advance degree from MIT or the schlepping of adaptors, modems, couplers, and other exotic items.

When I started covering presidential campaigns, for instance, all I had to carry was my portable typewriter, and I never really carried that. This was back in the Dark Ages when there were at the most two women on a trip, and we were treated like white goddesses on safari. Yes, dear sisters, we may have been oppressed, but we were spoiled, too. A steady stream of "bearers" tried to anticipate our needs for snacks, speech transcripts, and snappy leads.

169

When it came time to get the copy to the newspaper, there was a charming white-haired man from Western Union, named Lincoln, who moved benevolently through the pressroom murmuring encouragement to slowpokes like me and waited until dawn, if need be, until we all filed.

But somebody had to invent the video display terminal, and inevitably someone thought up a portable model as well. At the *Washington Star*, I held out for a year, but finally even gentle John Cassady, my editor, said I better learn how to use one. A colleague named Robert Pear—I mention his name because you may hear it read in St. Peter's Square at a beatification ceremony—undertook to teach me. For a week he sat beside me and we wrote my column together, amid many curses and fumings on my part and infinite patience on his as he showed me which was the "insert" button and which the "delete."

But the *Star* died and I came to the *Post*, and its machines had the insert and delete buttons exactly transposed. I thought I would have to go into another line of work.

Now the Toshiba is on my desk at home. I have learned to plug it in. It talks to me in gibberish like "ProComm," a term that is unnerving to a survivor of the McCarthy era, and there is a "menu" that has nothing but unappetizing choices like "XyWrite" and "Format 720."

I have a manual. Here is a typical line: "Get to the modem setting by doing a PGDN for the second pop-up screen."

We have not yet bonded, the Toshiba and I. Like Madame Butterfly, I sing, "Un Bel Di"—"One Fine Day." ■

Not the Cellular One—May 9, 1993

Long before I attended a high-tech House hearing on international, in fact, universal wiretapping, I knew the cellular telephone was not for me.

In fact, the decision had been made for me several years before you saw people walking along K Street gabbing away to an oblong in their hands. I sometimes wonder if people who like talking to themselves carry the phone to make themselves look kosher. It is a status booster, I'll say that. You look at someone letting his food and his companion go cold in a restaurant while he chats. Obviously, he is a hotshot, he must be available to other hotshots at all times. John Sununu, of course, needed a military jet instead.

But, as I say, it was not for me, and never was.

A car phone salesman called my office some years ago and started peddling his wares to Liz Acosta, my helper of the time. At a pause in his pitch, she said crisply, "Excuse me, sir, Mary McGrory, as anyone can tell you, can hardly handle the telephone or the car separately. What would happen if she tried to use both at the same time is something I don't want to think about—and neither do you."

That was a fair summary, and besides, I prefer listening to the radio in the car. There's ever the chance you might get Mozart's twenty-fourth Piano Concerto—which, to be sure, poses another hazard, being incapacitatingly lovely.

I'll give the phone something. It is stupendously survivable.

It is because of the car and cellular variety of communication that the future of the British monarchy is in grave doubt. The Prince of Wales and his princess are both victims. He got his first. Some scanner was surfing along and all of a sudden he heard the heir to the British throne talking to his alleged paramour, Camilla Parker-Bowles, in a way that might have caused the queen, his mother, to wonder where she had gone wrong. Sympathy for Diana, beloved by the whole world but not her own husband, surged like an angry sea.

But the cellular phone was evenhanded in this messy quarrel. Some time later, it ensnared *her*. Again, unwariness. When Her Highness, who would never use a pay phone and probably thinks all the palace machines are tapped by MI-5, was nattering into her car phone, she was addressed by an unidentified male as "Squidgie." Some cad, using what I believe is called "an unauthorized alligator clip," tapped in. The papers printed it, and now the pair are at an almost equal level in the regard of the British public.

The British are a long-suffering people, and all they have ever asked their monarchs is to behave nicely in public and be role models for their children. Apparently, at the moment, the people who endured the Battle of Britain are pondering whether they could be happy with a king who says "Tea and strumpet?" to a lady not his wife, and a separated queen who not only tolerated but seems to have encouraged someone to call her "Squidgie."

We have had casualties at home. The character of the race for the U.S. Senate in Virginia has been changed by a politically incorrect tap. Someone sneaked into the car phone of Lieutenant Governor Douglas Wilder, who in the course of a chat with a friend began to trash his brother Democrat, Governor (and soon Senator) Charles S. Robb. Wilder always trashes Robb, and it is not necessary to tap his phone to know it. It turned out that someone from Robb's staff had the tape; it was a monster embarrassment for Robb, who had to go before a grand jury and unnerved Virginia voters to the point Wilder seems to think he can challenge and unseat him.

Add all this to the fact that the word (passionately denied by cellular phone makers) went out that the dandy device could give you brain cancer, and you'd think it would go under. But no. Their phones are in huge circulation although, according to computer ace John Gage, who testified before Ed Markey's House subcommittee, a buff in Moscow can listen in on a Department of Agriculture employee on her way to work from Bethesda who is calling up her son's kindergarten teacher to say he has measles.

All should be grateful I am not on the Internet. My conversations go like this: "Yes, I was sitting at a table near the window. It's a small brown notebook, and . . ." Or: "Where were you? I waited forty-five minutes at the Washington Hilton. Oh, you said the Capitol Hilton. Well, I didn't hear you."

I would be unfair to snoops—sorry, "scanner enthusiasts"—who, I'm sure, are testing the capacity of their gadgets in a spirit of scientific inquiry. ■

Stop the Information Superhighway, I Want to Get Off—March 6, 1994

I am a vagrant on the information superhighway—a loiterer with an attitude. I have had, however, an OK relationship with a word processor called Rayedit. It understands that all I want to do is write 750 words three times a week. Now Ray and I are being forced apart, and I have been introduced to a flashy contraption that wants to run my life.

I don't even know its name. Sometimes it's "Windows," and sometimes "Roadrunner." It is very complicated, but I guess that complication spells progress in the computer world, where change, and particularly difficult change, gets you a big score and big orders. If the instructions are more baffling than your income tax form or the Clinton health-care plan, and they cause the same sinking feeling as your high school geometry midyear exam, then you are a success, apparently, on your block of the superhighway.

We had a five-hour training class in Windows the other day. We were introduced to a mouse—yes, that's high-tech whimsy, a little object with a wire out of the top for a tail; you move it around on a pad and click it, sometimes twice. These presses must be very rapid, says the "quick reference card," or "Windows will interpret the action as Choosing rather than Opening."

It was all downhill from there. I learned how to "maximize" my paintbrush and to play solitaire. I'm not sure why, but this is a wraparound service that for all I know fixes parking tickets.

Not a word was said about signing on, writing a story, and signing off; that's where Roadrunner comes in. Anyway, I was shown how to find "dictionary" and save myself three steps to the Webster's and to avoid going to the library—excuse me, the News Research Center—for a chat with Marylou and the gang.

It was a lot of information, and if we didn't appreciate it, it's because we learned a long time ago that the first step in writing is to clear your mind—forget about the cleaners and the icy sidewalk and keeping your word to a child and finding fresh raspberries and making your way to Virginia. You have to sweep it clean, which is not easy when you're involved with "cascading windows."

In the middle of all this—Roadrunner students warning us about weird placement of quotation marks, signing on twice, and choosing "baskets"—we are moving to another floor. We stumble over cartons. We leaf through old files. It took me an afternoon to do just A and B: "Abortion" isn't over, nor is "adoption," and you can't throw away "Barry, Marion," because our former mayor, whose vicissitudes and romances fill folders, may run again.

Ray came without a mouse. He thought it was OK for me to press the keys without an emissary. He didn't mind my going to the library. He never thought my time was all that valuable, and there was no ominous chat about "floppy disks." Ray knows he is nearly through, and he's testy. When I press "get," he growls, "No such story."

That's when I go and find Diane. She is a redheaded angel masquerading as a systems manager. She loves computers but does not hold it against me that I do not. "Think of it as a friend," she counsels. When Ray acts up, she comes in and gives it a look of questioning concern, the kind a mother directs at a child who is writing on the wall with a crayon. No glares, no curses; she gently taps a key or two and Ray straightens up.

Diane believes in amazing grace. She thinks she can teach me Roadrunner.

While the new machine is teaching me to wind down my human contacts, I have a new office that also discourages them. It is at the end of a short hall and has no windows—not even to other offices without windows. It has the feeling of Dien Bien Phu—or a punishment cell.

I know my sins. I broke publicly with a Toshiba in the Bush pressroom in Budapest. It refused to take copy from a heretic, and stopped sending after one paragraph. I just called up Olwen in the dictation department and read it to her—a practice I continued through the 1992 campaign.

I have also, when being interviewed by aspiring journalists, said foolish things: Latin helps you understand English, and poetry acquaints you with the art of distillation, which used to be a concern for newspapers. From now on, I'm advocating computer manuals and subscriptions to *Popular Mechanics*. Forget composition, concentrate on transmission.

So if the signal from my cave at the end of the road gets as faint as Dien Bien Phu and one fine day there's another name at the top of this space, you'll know what happened. I've lost too many arguments with a mouse and I have gradually lost touch with the human race. ■

Mary's first car. In 1987 Mary stepped up to a Mercedes-Benz after decades of solidarity with Detroit autoworkers. She fretted that Mercedes might recall the car from a "defective owner."

Song, drink, and laughter were part of the newsroom culture at the *Washington Star*. *Left to right:* Dottie Biehlman, Mary McGrory, Ruth Deane, and Fifi Gorska. Crosby Noyes is at the piano.

Mary McGrory in 1950, when she was a book reviewer at the *Washington Star*. Four years later she would come to prominence for her coverage of the Army-McCarthy hearings.

Washington Post cartoonist Herblock presents Mary with the Washington Newspaper Guild Award in 1959.

Robert Kennedy inscribed this photo: "I think you are about to kiss me and that is why I look so excited." Mary was the gold standard when it came to writing on the triumphs and tragedies of the Kennedys.

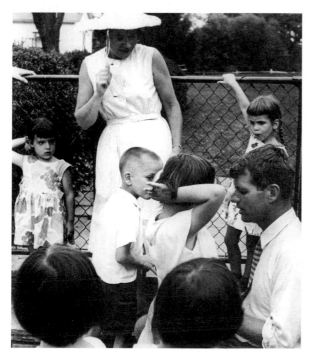

Robert Kennedy greets Mary and children from St. Ann's Infant and Maternity Home, where Mary was a volunteer for more than four decades.

Mary with *Atlanta Constitution* columnist Ralph McGill and Lyndon Johnson. She strongly disagreed with both on the Vietnam War.

Mary and Richard Nixon. Mary said her highest honor was not her Pulitzer Prize but finding her name on Nixon's enemies list.

At the *Star*, Mary celebrates the news that she was the winner of the 1974 Pulitzer Prize for commentary. One of her laments was that the *Post* celebrated such events with cake instead of champagne.

Mary shows Robert Redford around the *Washington Star* newsroom. Redford played the role of *Washington Post* reporter Bob Woodward in the Watergate movie *All the President's Men*.

Robert Redford visiting Mary in her office. He inscribed this photo: "Dear Mary—Boy, can you draw a crowd."

Mary at her typewriter in her *Washington Star* office. Mary's relationship with computers was tenuous and tense. She once called the laptop "a fiendish gadget."

Mary grilling Ronald Reagan, one of her least favorite presidents.

President Reagan came to the *Washington Star* to have lunch with editors on the paper's last day of publication. Edwin Yoder, the *Star*'s pipe-smoking editorial page editor, is to Mary's left.

Mary introduces children from St. Ann's to First Lady Nancy Reagan. Mary rehearsed the children in how to greet the president or First Lady.

Mary greets Prince Charles at the British Embassy in Washington. She once wrote that if the Nobel Committee ever created an award for caddishness, the prince would be a strong contender.

With ABC News anchor Peter Jennings. These good friends died about a year apart.

A portrait of Mary.

MEET THE PRESS WITH
ROUNDTABLE GROUP
JULY 31st, 1994

Mary occasionally appeared on NBC's *Meet the Press* as a panelist. With Mary is Tim Russert, the show's moderator, and Lisa Myers, an NBC correspondent.

Mary and House Speaker Tip O'Neill, an old Boston friend who sang Irish songs at Mary's St. Patrick's Day parties. In the center, Rep. Barney Frank (D-MA).

President Clinton chats with Mary on Air Force One on a return trip from Warm Springs, Georgia, where she received the Franklin and Eleanor Roosevelt Institute's Freedom of Speech Award in 1995.

Mary interviews Mother Teresa during the nun's visit to Washington. Mary was a faithful Catholic who considered Mother Teresa a saint for her work in Calcutta's slums.

Mary chats with First Lady Hillary Clinton. She spared neither the president nor the First Lady in her commentaries on the Monica Lewinsky affair.

Donald Graham, *left*, chairman of the Washington Post Co., and *Post* publisher Bo Jones, *right*, present Mary with the *Washington Post*'s Eugene Meyer Award in 2001.

A portrait.

10

Passings

Dr. King's People Bid Him Farewell—April 10, 1968

Between confrontations and marches, honors and imprisonments, Martin Luther King Jr. always went home to Ebenezer Baptist Church in a poor section of Atlanta.

They brought him back for the last time yesterday, and his people, bade him farewell in a way that explained his life and restored gentleness to his death.

At Ebenezer Baptist Church, which is small and plain, the members had had no trouble accepting the prophet within their midst. They believe in signs and wonders as told by the Bible. Prophecies, dreams, and visions sustain them.

The service was intimate and personal, as befitted a beloved pastor. It was decorous, as befitted a world leader and martyr. His favorite Scripture was read, his favorite hymns were sung by the splendid choir as would have been done for any other member of the flock.

There was one difference. Out of deference to half the cabinet, the vice president, three presidential candidates, high church dignitaries, some of whom had marched with him, and Mrs. John F. Kennedy, the usual lamentations were curbed.

One woman, chafing under the restraint, cried out finally, "Oh Martin, we're not goin' to see you no more," but reproving looks were turned on her and she subsided.

Christian resignation is a powerful theme at Ebenezer Baptist Church. Martin Luther King had prophesied his own death. When his wife heard of it, she simply said it was the will of God.

The congregation was willing to follow this lead, but when the Reverend Ralph D. Abernathy, his friend and successor, read a quotation from Dr. King about the triumph of good over evil, one mustached man standing by the wall shook his head and his shoulders shook with sobs.

The family and congregation, when they could, thanked the celebrities and the representatives of thirty-five foreign countries who were among the thousands who came. But they had strained mightily to make the good-bye their own. Mrs. King, a queenly woman whose strong, piquant face never wavered behind the heavy veiling, had directed all with a careful eye to her husband's spirit. The Negroes, for once, had the best seats, directly in front of the coffin in the center section.

One white man spoke. He was a bald, bespectacled former teacher of Dr. King's, and his name was Dr. L. Harold DeWolfe. His message was the same as that of the others—love and hope.

The absence of rancor, in view of the broken glass and curses of the cities, was striking. The only reproach came from Dr. Abernathy, when he felt the congregation had sung with insufficient feeling Martin's "most favorite hymn." He exhorted them to sing it "as he would have," and the choir led the church through five more stanzas of "Softly and Tenderly, Jesus Is Calling."

It was another hymn, "My Heavenly Father Watches over Me," which Mrs. Mary Gurley had "always sung for Martin" when he came home, that caused the accepting flock to crack.

It said something for Dr. King's taste that he valued Mrs. Gurley's austere, reedy contralto. When she sang "Let the Billows Roar" in tones true as steel, the people began to call out, "Oh, yes, Oh yes, He surely cares, Oh, yes."

The Reverend Andrew Young, Dr. King's bright-eyed shadow on a hundred marches, at a thousand meetings, his clerical robe over his denim suit, put his head back and let the tears roll unchecked.

Dr. Abernathy, following tradition, reported on Martin Luther King's last meal before he was shot, announced he himself was fasting until he felt "ready for the task that is before me."

Then he read from the speeches while the organist softly played "We Shall Overcome," and tears glistened on the cheeks of the choir. Finally a tape was played of King's famous and prophetic last sermon at the church with its blueprint for a eulogy: "Tell I tried to love somebody." ■

The Unconquerable Patriot—December 19, 1989

The stricken faces of the mourners provide his obituary. They have lost a father, with white hair and kind blue eyes. "We are all orphans," said a member of the new Soviet congress. Andrei Sakharov, civic hero, secular saint, was universally recognized as noble.

The expressions of grief in Moscow remind us of a special Russian spirit, a capacity for brooding, for guilt, for poetry.

"Forgive us, Andrei Dmitrievich," said a handwritten note affixed to the entrance of his apartment house, probably an act of contrition from one of many who had remained silent while Sakharov spoke out for so many lost souls. A woman who traveled a thousand miles from the Urals to walk by his open casket told Sakharov's widow, Yelena Bonner, in lapidary terms, "He was a prince of justice."

His death summoned forth the Russian soul, which has been stifled or at least lost sight of during seventy years of iron totalitarianism. The mild, unconquerable, tea-drinking patriot virtually unknown outside the scientific community until the official Soviet press began to vilify him as an enemy of the people, or a lunatic who had been overexposed to radiation while he was creating the Soviet H-bomb, ended as the beloved conscience of his country.

Sakharov's life from the moment be discovered the limits of science was a pouring-out of himself that is matchless in contemporary history. He was prophet and a seer in the Tolstoyan mode, but without Tolstoy's crankiness. He was as gifted scientifically as was Aleksandr Solzhenitsyn in literature, but, unlike Solzhenitsyn, he looked forward.

He gave of himself for everyone with the slightest claim on him. "A tribune of the people," said Alfred Friendly Jr., a former Moscow correspondent. People from all over the Soviet Union sought him out at his cramped apartment: bus drivers who got in trouble for making political remarks, people with relatives in the camps, threatened dissidents, fellow members of the Helsinki Watch, or the Moscow Human Rights Committee. They came "to seek justice." Sakharov was the only possible source.

He became a humanitarian almost in spite of himself. He could have lived out his life as a pampered physicist in the antiseptic confines of the laboratory. He was forty-one, much decorated, and deferred to when he quit the life of the mind for the messy struggle for justice.

In 1962, he put all his learning and his prestige into an attempt to prevent a "useless and criminal" H-bomb test. He failed.

He once wrote, "The feeling of impotence and fright that seized me on that day has remained in my memory ever since and worked much change in me as I moved towards my present attitude."

That "attitude" was much like that of Abraham Lincoln, whose patience and tolerance he also shared: "A government forced to represent the wishes of the governed is likely to be a better government and makes for a much better neighbor."

In 1971, at a political trial, he met Bonner, a World War II nurse and impassioned advocate of human rights. He fell passionately in love and plunged deeper into the exhilarating, dangerous world of dissent. He did not need it, but she urged him on. She shielded him from pests and press; she interrupted him and often strengthened his words. She accepted his Nobel Prize for him in 1975—he was afraid he would not be allowed back if he left Russia.

With reporters, he was forbearing and exacting. He needed them to broadcast his message, but deplored their habit of leaving out or changing words. One Moscow reporter remembers him as gravely cordial— and no more exasperated than any genius would be with silly questions—and always, no matter what the subject, reminding his questioner about people still in camps, calling out lists of political prisoners that he wanted published.

In 1980, when he attacked the Soviet invasion of Afghanistan, official rage boiled over and he was banished to the miserable provincial town of Gorky. He continued to exert his moral authority. He fasted until his stepdaughter was allowed to join her fiancé in the United States, until Bonner was allowed to go west for medical treatment. That grim time ended with one of history's most famous telephone calls, from Mikhail Gorbachev, on December 16, 1986, to invite him back to Moscow—and gaining the world's credibility about genuine change.

More miracles followed: perestroika and glasnost; Sakharov's election to the Soviet Congress of People's Deputies. In his last public appearance, Gorbachev put him down, dismissing his claim that people supported a change from a one-party system. Sakharov did not take it personally. He pressed on. He was sixty-eight. He had proved that the preposterous is possible, even in Soviet Russia, and he had never given up. ■

Thurgood Marshall: The Justice Who Would Not Quit
—January 28, 1993

As the Great Hall of the Supreme Court was being prepared for the lying in state of Thurgood Marshall, his best friend on the bench, retired Justice William Brennan, was brooding that posterity might not give his beloved ally his due.

"He was not valued to the extent that his learning justified," said Brennan, who is eighty-six now and frail. "Because he was so funny they thought he must be stupid—my, were they wrong."

Brennan and Marshall—one a small, twinkling Irishman; the other a huge black man with a hawk's face, a famously gruff manner, and pungent humor—were friends from the day that Marshall joined the court in 1967.

"He was a stickler for the honest truth," Brennan remembered, and then began recalling Marshall's penchant for putting court conferences into an "uproar" by talking jive-talk that came right off streets not frequented by the other justices. "He would have us in stitches," he said.

Brennan remembers Marshall railing against the Founding Fathers— "he didn't think they were such hotshots as people were inclined to regard them"—and he thought the Constitution was full of things that are not true: "Did they really think that men were created equal?" And, said Brennan, Marshall thought the white man did not appreciate what he had in the black man.

But Marshall's celebrated irascibility was "more a pose than a fact," said Brennan, fondly protective. "He could be irascible, but he could also be soft, sweet, and just nice. He was just a decent guy, a very good citizen."

Brennan and Marshall were inveterate, lonely dissenters on death cases. Repeated defeats, as the court grew more conservative by the year, did not embitter either one of them. "We thought it was bound to happen that the court will declare the death sentence unconstitutional. It is inevitable."

Marshall was Brennan's neighbor, and a bracing one. He would greet Brennan with, "You dumb bastard, don't you think you should do something to earn your pay?" Brennan reverted to the theme that "people might make the mistake of thinking he was a bit of a buffoon—they certainly don't know him if they do."

179

The next day, Brennan's worry was swept away in a river of humanity that washed up the steps of the court, under the inscription of the ideal by which Marshall had lived his life, "Equal Justice under Law." From hundreds of people, black and white, old and young, who cheerfully waited in the bright cold for more than an hour, the tributes poured out, unstintingly, unanimously.

They knew exactly why they were there. They were honoring a great man, the real thing.

The praise was often personal. The debt was clear. Because Thurgood Marshall would not quit, because he loved and cherished the law, because he argued successfully before the Supreme Court in *Brown v. Board of Education*, they were in his debt. It wasn't so much the justice they were honoring as the advocate who endured the indignities of a hundred southern towns and sheriffs.

"He made life better for me," said Sandra Wilson, a teacher who was keeping her eye on two grades from the Marie Reed Learning Center. "I am a beneficiary of his concern."

She is a great-niece of civil rights leader Mary McLeod Bethune.

"I don't know what we would have done without him," said Dorothy Chambers, a retired police officer.

Two black naval officers stationed in Washington were saluting an idol. Said Lieutenant Commander Terry Jones, "We gained our freedoms through the court system, thanks to him." Said Commander Taylor: "He was the doorman. He stood there and opened up the door for us and made us set our sights higher."

"The one reason I am out here," said Charles Rhyne, a southerner and a Watergate lawyer, "is because I share his passion for equality."

Bob Davis, an unemployed college graduate who is looking for work in the Clinton administration, said it was easy to say why he was there. "He has done a lot of good for a lot of people."

Inside the Great Hall, they moved quietly past the flag-draped coffin, past a portrait of Marshall, the three law clerks, and Marshall's son John William, who were standing vigil. The line never stopped. Blacks predominated. They had not turned out for Chief Justice Earl Warren, who had written the great decision. Senator Joseph Lieberman (D-CT), said: "They knew Marshall was one of them. I have just read his life, and he ate the dirt."

Brennan's loving assessment of his friend was ratified all day long in the patience and eloquence of ordinary people who, like him, had seen Thurgood Marshall for the giant he was. ■

Tip the Top—January 9, 1994

The last time I saw Tip O'Neill was at a reception for his successor as Speaker of the House, Jim Wright. He was walking with a cane. His great white-thatched head was bent, and his voice, soft as rain in his prime, was almost inaudible. "I'm fallin' apart, darlin'—arthritis, diabetes."

Wright had left town under a cloud—driven out by a bizarre book deal. Not everyone felt compelled to come to the reception. Tip O'Neill had made his way there with great difficulty, but it was his way to show up, to put an arm around a pal with a problem, show his colors.

That was his personal philosophy. and by extension his political creed. Of course he helped the down and out, and fought for a law to help dwarfs grow, no matter how much snickering he heard. He tried to stop Uncle Sam from picking on poor peasants in Southeast Asia—he broke early with Lyndon Johnson on Vietnam—and on ragged revolutionaries in Nicaragua. He spent bitter years resisting Reagan's contra war. That's what it was all about for him.

Rep. George Miller of California, a fellow liberal, spoke O'Neill's epitaph in 1986, when a great, roaring celebration of O'Neill's fifty years in politics was held: "That overwhelming kindness, the comfort he gave to so many poor people. He looked big enough to protect them."

His mandate extended wherever someone needed a friend. In 1981, Sean Donlon, a brilliant and engaging Irish ambassador, was threatened with cashiering because he had offended pro-IRA U.S. congressmen. O'Neill put in a call to the Irish prime minister. It was near midnight in Ireland, but O'Neill did not falter. "Mr. Prime Minister," he said, "Sean is a beautiful fellow." The firing was canceled.

That protectiveness was known. It is why so many people in Washington are feeling bereft and diminished. Tip O'Neill was both a pillow and a rock. For six of his ten years as Speaker, he personified the Democratic Party. He was a rock against Reagan's warmth for the Pentagon and chill for the poor. He was a pillow for disheartened liberals, softening the thankless years.

Says Barney Frank, a Massachusetts representative, "He was the best argument against the bad name that has been given to valuable institutions like liberalism, compassion, politics, Congress."

One of the things that made him unique and beloved was that he gloried in his humble roots. His father, a North Cambridge bricklayer, told him never to forget from whence he came. He never did. One of his contemporaries, Donald Regan, secretary of the treasury and imperial chief of staff in the Reagan White House, who came from the same neighborhood, wanted to put his lower-middle-class Irish origins behind him. Tip had picked this up early on his radar and never missed a chance to twit Regan. He told me with relish, "I'd say, 'Hi, Don, I saw your cousin Agnes on the street the other day. She was asking about you.' "

When Ronald Reagan's handlers realized that their principal antagonist was O'Neill, they could hardly believe their luck. Their horse was sleek and trim, a darling of the camera. Tip O'Neill weighed in at 250, his suits were not made in Rome, and he was known as a passionate partisan and a quintessential Boston Irish pol. He was hostile to cameras and the thirty-second soundbite.

But he caught on, perhaps because he was authentic and had this open-hearth personality and a mastery of the House rules. He was able to beat down occasional Democratic plots and Republican schemes to depose him. And the slicksters in the White House did not notice that he had an infinite capacity for inclusion, for boomers, boll weevils, the blow-dried, and the bewildered.

I was with him in 1982 when he was watching the election returns in his lair in the House. "I always eat beef stew on election night," he said. The waiter, looking pained, said, "This is beef bourguignon." Tip went right on. "I've been eating beef stew on election night since before you were born," he told his son Kip.

He was a party man socially, too, and huge fun. He came to a christening party at my house a long time ago. He took the baby in his arms—little Daniel Gailey looked like a scrap of cotton caught on a big black cliff—and he sang, "If You're Irish, Come into the Parlor." Then he turned to his wife, Millie, and serenaded her with "I'll Be with You in Apple-Blossom Time." He was a stranger to self-importance. His unforgiving Boston constituents would not have permitted it.

The great heart had a streak of malice, or at least mischief. Barney

Frank remembers O'Neill's restoring a large picture of the whole O'Neill tribe—uncles and aunts and cousins—to his office wall and saying, "When he [Reagan] comes up here for the State of the Union, I want to show it to him and say to the so-and-so, 'Mr. President, I *know* my grandchildren.' "

We had a falling out once. I wrote disapprovingly of his career as a pitchman. He cut me dead when we met. But one night at an Irish dinner, I saw him come in and made myself scarce to avoid another scene. I felt an arm around me. "Is that you, Tip?" I asked. "I thought you were mad on me."

"I was," he said suavely, "but now I'm not mad anymore"—and he laughed.

He was the ultimate Himself, the man of the house who looks after his own, a national patriarch disguised as a pol. ∎

Farewell to My Best Friend—May 10, 1994

My best friend, Elizabeth Cleland Acosta, who died on Saturday, was probably the worst enemy ennui ever had.

She did not know how to be boring. She fought boredom wherever she found it. She was party insurance. When she arrived at your house, you could put her in the parlor and go off on other business, knowing your guests would be entirely diverted. She did monologues about life as a suburban housewife and made hilarity from such unpromising subjects as beach vacations or the hopelessness of finding happiness on New Year's Eve: "I've gone to other people's parties, too, including parties . . . where the host and hostess decided to get a divorce; parties where someone's secretary threw a Christmas tree through the window." Sometimes she told stories about her father, a labor man from Chicago with a robust sense of humor.

And she sang. Oh, how she sang in her forty-fathoms-deep contralto. Sometimes she and her pal Gertrude Cleary did a killing duet of "Sonny Boy." She soloed most memorably in "Lucky Charlie Lindbergh." Another showstopper was "Aunt Clara," whose picture was turned to the wall.

Liz was not only my friend—the kind who came right away when there was a death in the family and set out with your cousin for the supermarket to get supplies for the funeral lunch. She was my helper for almost twenty years. We got on well from the moment we met decades ago. We shared much: bad hair and bad feet and a love of poetry. We were uncertain if we could work together. I'm absentminded and she could be touchy, and, like many great comedians, subject to gloom. But she came to the dear, departed *Washington Star* and never looked back.

My forgetfulness was no problem: The mother used to keeping tabs on clothes, toys, and books for five children had me in hand in no time.

She was a treat on the telephone. With irate subscribers, distraught readers, or pushy flacks, she was masterly. She would listen awhile, then slash through the fog and the nattering and bring them to heel with a crisp, "And you wish me to . . ."

The atmosphere at the *Star* suited her. The air was full of encouragement and laughter. Liz flowered. She became a kind of den mother to the young bloods in the back of the newsroom and gave them copious counsel. She was surrounded by jesters and gabbers and others who, like herself, felt they had to make people laugh.

And like everyone else around, she took a hand at writing. She wrote book reviews. An addicted reader, she found books "absolutely essential." Her reviews were like her: blunt, fair, and witty. She also wrote familiar essays, calling herself "a professional housewife and an amateur writer."

She was wrong: She was a natural writer. She sat down at the typewriter, rolled the paper in, and typed without hesitation, stopping only when the page was filled or she was done. I was jealous, being slow myself, and of the product. She used to preach about the necessity of hard-shell realism. But she had a romantic nature, and an eye out for true love and rainbows. She had a total reverence for the English language and those who used it well. Of E. B. White's letters, she wrote, "Your average reviewer—and I am averager than most—must fight the urge to take the typewriter out to the garden and bury it and take up another line of work."

On a blowsy novel called *The Pretenders*, she rendered a succinct verdict: "I am going to pretend I never read it."

Her greatest literary adventure came in 1958 when she wrote a love letter to James Thurber, which, she liked to say, changed her life. She told him: "I am getting old and fat, my last permanent didn't take, my five children have been throwing up for days, singly and in pairs, my husband is at a convention at some posh hotel, and I'M SORRY FOR

MYSELF, SEE?" She told him that she loved him because his latest book had made her laugh.

He wrote back! It turned out that as a child he lived in the house next door to hers in Falls Church, Viginia. They corresponded. Publication of their letters in the *Saturday Evening Post* was a triumph for her. When Maple Avenue was transformed into a double row of townhouses, the new street was called James Thurber Court.

Like many parents in the 1960s, Liz and her husband, Frank, a paragon of patience and kindness, found bringing up children rather taxing. But if she didn't like the process she loved the children, and they loved her. When she was diagnosed with a brain tumor, they flocked to her. Her three sons fetched and carried, and made her laugh. She who had been so morbid did not talk of death; she remarked to daughter Elizabeth, "Heaven is a place with air conditioning where my feet will never hurt again."

She was touched as never before. She told daughter Jo, "I'm a lucky old lady." We were lucky, too. ■

The World Weeps for a Princess—September 4, 1997

The Elizabethan poet Thomas Nashe aptly expressed today's mood four centuries ago:

> Brightness falls from the air;
> Queens have died young and fair.
> Dust hath closed Helen's eye.
> I am sick, I must die,
> Lord, have mercy on us.

The world is taking a princess's death very hard. Lamentation is universal, in capitals and villages. Bouquets are heaped high at palace gates in London. A vase of flowers is placed outside a New Hampshire country inn with a message chalked on a slate: "In loving memory of Princess Diana."

Not since Pope John XXIII and President John Kennedy died a year apart in the 1960s have more stricken people gathered to grieve for someone they never knew, a stranger who lighted up their lives.

Like the pope and the president, who also died too soon, Diana was a luminous presence. Like them, she surprised all by being delightful, a quality not required or expected in high places.

Pope John, leader of an arbitrary institution, had an open-hearth warmth that made atheists weep at his passing. John Kennedy, uniquely graceful and witty among his kind, had an even shorter time. Diana, a bird of paradise among the drab Windsors, combined glamour and kindness in a way that would have made a royalist of Robespierre. At thirty-six, she was still growing.

Circumstances of her death made it more unendurable and laced grief with anger. It was absurd for her to be killed in a car crash in a Paris tunnel, with a drunken driver at the wheel, an Egyptian playboy at her side, and a pack of paparazzi in hot pursuit on motorcycles. She deserved better.

So did her two sons, who are at the worst age to be left without unconditional and extravagant maternal love.

Dodi al Fayed, her latest romance, died with her. He has already been buried while she lies in a royal palace awaiting a grand funeral in Westminster Abbey.

It was easy to dismiss the world's most photographed divorcee as a featherhead, fitness freak, and fashion plate. She may have been all that, but she was much more. She used her blinding celebrity in a truly princely manner, for good purposes. For instance, she exposed herself to others' pain and saw to it that her young sons saw the sadness of life as well. She kissed lepers, helped AIDS patients, and walked through minefields in her doughty campaign against land mines.

Her sketchy, upper-class education had prepared her to be a nursery school teacher, and it was a treat to see her with the tots. She would crouch down beside a small bouquet-giver who was rigid with shyness and concern and coax a smile with her melting eye-level contact.

When she stopped being "Her Royal Highness" after her divorce, she went on being a genius with sick people. Her province was the terminal and chronically ill wards. Her constituency were the defeated, the doomed, the forgotten—old soldiers and young sufferers. She seemed perfectly at home with them. She may have been the woman who had everything, but they all knew she also had a broken heart.

At twenty, she had been programmed to live happily ever after in fairy-tale fashion. She had caught the catch of the century, the heir to the British throne. It was an arranged marriage, but Diana fell in love with Charles.

The British public went mad about his bride. He did not. She became almost immediately a cosmic star, causing near riots of photographers and fans everywhere she went. Inexplicably to millions, Charles carried a torch for an older woman, the love of his youth. She was a country lady who rode to hounds (Diana detested hunting), and to whom he paid clinical compliments that were picked up in a scandalous wiretap of his phone.

In time, palace intimates say, an outraged Diana discovered that her rival had vetted her as the wife for Charles.

The wretched princess tried bulimia, suicide, and looking for love in all the wrong places. Her chilly Windsor in-laws were no help. The public took her side in a bitter quarrel. A child of the confessional '90s, she went on television and confessed to adultery. Charles also told all to the home screen. The disgrace, the tawdriness was complete.

Diana soldiered on, heroine to the jilted and the heartbroken.

Like most of the mourning millions, I never met her. But I did meet her effect on people. In 1985, when she came to Washington, she visited a home for terminally ill cancer patients. I was allowed to come after she had left and talk to the people she had spoken to. She had brought not only comfort but joy. She sat on the edge of beds, she took every patient's hand and inquired gently about their medication and treatment. They told me that the experience was so overwhelming that she had made it seem worthwhile to die for it.

"I would never have met her if I hadn't been sick," said one lung cancer victim.

No wonder the world is weeping. ■

World Looks Less and Less a Place for Genuine Christian—January 31, 1999

The week that Washington was drowning in sanctimony from the impeachment trial, one of sanctimony's fiercest enemies, my dear old friend, Gertrude Cleary, died.

She was the most religious person I know. Daily Mass and communion, good works and Bible study at Blessed Sacrament Church, and yet never a whisper of self-righteousness from her. She lived St. Paul's epistle on charity—"believed everything, endured everything." She was a small person with a great soul.

You probably don't know many eighty-five-year-olds who are laid out in a pine box wearing a pink feather boa. It was totally appropriate for Gertrude. She was what Yeats called Maud Gonne, "a pilgrim soul" who understood the importance of austerity for those who seek God. But she was also a party girl to the soles of her feet.

She was a hospitable hostess and a spectacular guest. She was nice to everyone, respectful and attentive to boors and bores. It wasn't for thinking an angel lurked somewhere within—she was too earthy for Pollyanna piety. I think she felt that if God could love such creatures, she should at least take a stab at it.

It was great sport to watch her with some hot-striver who thought he had been stuck with a little old lady not worth his time and to see what happened. Soon he was guffawing, undone by an apt drollery in her flawless deadpan delivery.

She sang, too. Her biggest number was a duet sung with a sister Chicago Democrat, Liz Acosta, who was also my friend. They did "Sonny Boy." Liz, tall and bespectacled, took Gertrude, a little bigger than a teddy bear, on her knee and raised her rich contralto in a protest of love. Gertrude was the bratty kid, breaking in at every line with "What's my name?" or "Whatcha gonna do for me?" People accustomed to Washington parties where discussions of the Mideast or Star Wars were the entertainment were often fractured.

The high point of her social year was the annual Christmas party for the children of St. Ann's, where she was the hostess. For years she opened her cozy home and then her apartment to some fourteen or fifteen homeless children who needed love and peanut butter sandwiches and batteries for their toys. She loved the invasion, ignored the wear and tear on her furniture.

But she had bad luck. She fell on her face. Daughter Mary came running from St. Louis, and she and I made what we thought were powerful arguments that we should party elsewhere. Gertrude fixed her large dark brown eyes on us in an unblinking stare and said no. She could scarcely walk at that point—various infirmities and vicissitudes had struck her;

she had trouble talking, a new affliction, a paralyzed vocal cord, had struck her; and she was having trouble breathing. But she hung in. She beamed on them through her bruises, which had turned purple and green. The only story she told about herself was during an encounter with a nine-year-old boy, who was so startled at seeing his hostess at eye level when she opened the door that he blurted out, "Is you an elf?"

Gertrude accepted adversity and she knew much of it, beginning with the death of her adored husband, Dan, at age forty-three. She was left to raise three children on her own in the angst of the '60s. She did not rail. And she embraced contradictions that tear other people apart. In Chicago in 1968, she had traveled in the train of Senator Eugene McCarthy, a politician she served with blazing loyalty; she saw his followers being clubbed in the streets. She kept in touch with relatives who served Mayor Richard J. Daley and were cheering the billy clubs on. She accepted it all. It was just part of life that doesn't make much sense. There was always heaven to look forward to.

The last time I saw her, I knew that I might not see her again. For the first time since I have known her, she gave me a true account of how she felt. "Terrible," she said when I asked her. But as always, she quickly changed the subject to me. I mustn't come again. I would get lost as I had looking for the Washington Adventist Hospital, which gave her fine care for her lung problems but had failed to understand her basic needs. She informed the doctor in the emergency room that she was accustomed to a Scotch at the end of the day. It was essential to her recovery. He said there was none. Surely, she said to son-in-law Tuck, there is a tavern nearby. But there wasn't.

Her three children kept watch over her in relays. A compromise was reached—she got half a beer. But the struggle to breathe was too much. She loved the world and almost everybody in it, but it looked less and less like a place for a genuine Christian who never did complain and never for a second thought she was better than anyone else. ■

Evolution of a Newspaperwoman—July 19, 2001

Katharine Graham died as she lived, doing what only she would have seen as her duty, attending a business conference in Idaho. The preeminent personage in American journalism spared herself nothing. The

English poet Gerard Manley Hopkins described her well: "Strung by duty. . . . Strained to beauty."

I first met Katharine Graham when she was the doting wife of Philip Graham, a brilliant, volatile Florida lawyer, whom her father chose to be publisher of the *Post*. I was working for the *Star* at the time. Phil thought I should come over to the *Post*. I didn't think so, but she had me to dinner anyway, to those fabled, dazzling affairs where I sat next to notables whom I had no other chance of meeting, especially if I had written rude things about them.

By the early '60s, her marriage was collapsing. Phil Graham, diagnosed with manic depression, had noisily taken up with another woman. Publicly humiliated, Kay was heartbroken, but she held her head high, kept giving dinners, as was expected of her. One night is etched in memory. John Walker, the late director of the National Gallery, was seated opposite me and I was recounting my difficulties in bringing an elderly, art-loving nun from Baltimore to see the *Mona Lisa*—I have no sense of direction. John was laughing and Kay appeared to be laughing, too, but her eyes were brimming with tears and she had to tilt her head back to keep them from spilling.

After Phil died, Kay, with her usual conscientiousness, set about training herself to run the paper, even though the men in charge advised her just to sign the documents they brought her. That was not her way. As part of her self-education, she came out on the campaign trail with Barry Goldwater. We sat together, and she was an endearing companion. She was humble about "the professional writers" around her—she was later to write them into the ground with the stunning autobiography—and readily joined in the foolishness that is always aboard campaign planes. At one stop, we sat on railroad ties—there was no place else—and she confided her dread of having to speak at the *Post* Christmas party. Couldn't she just greet them at the door? I asked. No, she said sadly, she had to do what Phil would have done, even though the thought of speaking in public made her ill.

From across town, I watched the evolution of the "doormat wife"— her phrase—into the daring, resolute newspaperwoman. At the *Star*, we heard tales of her unsuspected business acumen; we knew the hiring of Ben Bradlee, a WASP with pizzazz, meant trouble for us—we had no idea how much.

Watergate whipped us at the *Star*. We couldn't catch up with the fleet-footed Woodward and Bernstein. Kay was the miracle to me. Was Katharine Graham really taking on Richard Nixon and his cutthroats? She was no bomb-thrower, not even a rebel. She was conventional, close to the establishment. But she endured anatomic threats from the attorney general. She had power and money, but she was a woman alone. She had her hair done in New York, she bought her clothes in Paris, but she was vulnerable. She expected to be on civil terms with every president. But there she was, betting her newspaper and her family fortunes on two twenty-eight-year-old reporters. The bet paid off and she and Bradlee brought down a president. The doormat had become an ornament to the newspaper business, a journalistic immortal, the most elegant one in the pantheon.

But her trials were not over. A strike of pressmen tested her as never before. Violence broke out. She took on the unions for 139 days. She agonized endlessly at night, after long days taking classified ads and doing other chores. Meg Greenfield told me. "I told her once, 'you don't have to do this, you know,'" words that always fell on deaf ears in her case.

In 1981, the *Star* died, and finally I came to the *Post*. Kay told me she thought that Phil, "wherever he is, is pleased." For me, it was a different world. At the *Star*, we did no end of laughing—perhaps more than consonant with survival. At the *Post* people took themselves seriously.

Kay and I never talked about it, but at a dinner given for me at the Press Club, she made a speech that was funny and sharp and gave the evening a splendid edge. She recounted my several refusals to join her paper; she reproached me for failing to love the *Post* as I loved the *Star*. I was delighted, if only because she had taken it all in and had paid us all the high compliment of speaking her mind. Back came a long letter I could barely manage to read, full of apologies and explanations. Self-doubt was back. It was, as ever, out of place. Katharine Graham was a valiant woman. It was an honor to be on her newspaper. ■

Our Leaders Could Take a Lesson from the Queen Mum—April 11, 2002

God bless the Queen Mother of England. She served us in death as she did in life. The funeral of the woman who behaved so well gave us an hour's respite from a wraparound spectacle of violence, cruelty, and witlessness. Just seeing soldiers holding guns they didn't fire was a treat. And it was nice to see CNN's Christianne Amanpour in Westminster Abbey instead of a box seat at the Middle East carnage.

I am totally in agreement with the London trader who told an Associated Press interviewer he thought it was right "to give the old girl a proper sendoff."

The Queen Mother learned long ago in an earlier war on terrorism, the Battle of Britain. She understood that the first law of politics is to be there. When the Luftwaffe was raining bombs on the Thames, it was suggested that she take her two daughters to a safe haven across the water. She scoffed at the notion. Her girls, she said, would not leave without her, she would not leave without the king, and "he will never leave."

She and George VI toughed it out with the people of London. In her pastel crepe, marabou-trimmed ensembles—with matching pumps—Her Majesty picked her way through the rubble, murmuring pity and encouragement to the bombed-out. She was credited with one immortal line. After Buckingham Palace was hit, she said—cynics claim it was fed to her by some public relations whiz—"Now I feel I can look the East End in the face."

She bonded decisively with the British people, and all over the world people who were saying, without total conviction, that "there'll always be an England" had her in mind. Winston Churchill, Britain's peerless wartime leader, came to regard the king and queen as friends and most valuable allies in the fight against "the guttersnipe"—his name for Hitler.

When her husband died, waves of sympathy washed over her and the House of Windsor. He never wanted or expected to be king, but his glamorous older brother, Edward VIII, left him and the country in the lurch to run away with Wallis Simpson. Bertie, as he was known in the family, was appalled. He was as shy as his Scots wife was outgoing, and he had a stammer, which made public speaking an agony. At his death in 1952 the incomparable Rebecca West toured the line waiting to file by his coffin. In a poignant dispatch, she reported about Britons who had been moved and inspired to overcome stuttering.

The Queen Mother continued her royal duties. She required no "humanizing" from palace publicists: She went to the racetrack; she was extravagant; she imparted warmth to family gatherings, a knack her elder daughter did not inherit.

Her funeral service was strangely impersonal. The eulogy was given by George Carey, archbishop of Canterbury, who obviously knew her and loved her, and spoke of her "strength, dignity, and laughter."

CNN had promised that Princess Anne would speak, but she didn't. She was, it was noted, the first royal to march with the men in the family at a royal funeral, and she certainly was the first to wear a pantsuit—she was in her Royal Navy uniform—to enter Westminster Abbey. No one from the family spoke.

The television audience had to content itself with trying to spot Prince Charles's mistress, Camilla Parker-Bowles, who was an invited guest. But no camera caught her. It dwelt on Charles's two sons, Prince William and Prince Harry.

It was as if the queen wanted to avoid any scenes of public emotion. She was badly burned five years ago when her charismatic daughter-in-law, Princess Diana, died tragically at thirty-six. The British public was outraged at the queen's remoteness from the universal grief. Prime Minister Tony Blair rushed forward with a heaving salute to Diana as "the people's princess." The death of the Queen Mum was hardly a shock; she was 101. But the queen was taking no chances.

It was a wonderful show of the kind only Britain knows how to do, with trumpets and drums and boy sopranos. The crowd was exemplary—large, reverent, and singing and praying with the congregation inside.

Only the context was jarring: In a news break, Secretary of State Colin Powell was shown in Morocco, whose king understandably greeted him by asking why he was not in Jerusalem. Ariel Sharon kept saying, yeah, yeah, he's withdrawing, but kept the tanks rolling on the West Bank. Yasser Arafat didn't say anything against suicide bombing in any language, and from Boston came new evidence of perfidious prelates who lied and sent a pedophile to an unsuspecting California parish.

No one in authority seemed to be behaving well. The Queen Mother, in a century on Earth, showed people how to act: See what needs to be done and do it. That was her way. It seems to have gone out of style. ∎

Boston Fans Mourn Their Touchy Baseball King
—July 14, 2002

When asked about the freezing of Ted Williams, Senate Democratic leader Tom Daschle said only that he could "think of a lot of people he would rather see frozen." He spoke for all of us.

In a week of outstandingly bad ideas—Daschle spoke during a break in the debate over the Yucca Mountain nuclear waste dump, and the House was voting for guns in cockpits—the idea of delivering the remains of Ted Williams to an Arizona businessman who runs something called the Alcor Life Extension Foundation was indisputably the worst. The ballplayer of the century, who carried himself like a king as he went to bat for the Red Sox in Fenway Park, is now reportedly turned upside down in an iced tube.

Williams's son, John Henry, arranged to have the body snatched from the Florida hospital where his father died. He has not explained his grotesque decision. Is Ted Williams considered a candidate for resurrection in this new hall of infamy, or is his body destined to be a merchandise mart for a parasitical offspring planning to peddle his father's DNA—or sell off his remains inch by inch?

Boston's Red Sox fans, which means everybody, are beside themselves. Williams's death at eighty-three was long expected, but when it happened, the *Boston Globe* put out an extra. Williams wore the Red Sox uniform for twenty years, with time out for service in two wars. He brought glory to his team and his town with his .406 batting average; but the relationship between him and the fanatics in the stands was stormy. Williams thought the only thing the fans should ask of him was that he play the game well.

He did that superbly. But Boston fans, who are of a special order of fanaticism in sports as in politics, thought he should share in his triumphs—specifically that he should tip his cap after he hit a home run. Williams thought he had done all that could be expected of him, and that taking bows was pandering. No one expected the poet Yeats to join the PTA.

Loyalty to the Red Sox is something pervasive and enduring. I know because I was born a Sox fan, and in spite of myself, I have primal reactions to their fate. I could not give you a statistic if my life depended on it, but I am always glad to hear they have won; on the dark side, I am ashamed to say that I cannot scrape up a flicker of compassion for Darryl Strawberry when he gets into new trouble. I have not forgotten that he was involved in the 1986 World Series, which we should have won.

I wish that touchy Ted had been a little more amiable, but I admire singlemindedness in the pursuit of excellence, although I cannot condone spitting at hecklers in the stands, as he did, or throwing a baseball bat into a crowd. Once, when Williams was manager of the Washington Senators, a sportswriter asked him if he could get along with a player as temperamental as Ted Williams, and he answered dead-on: "If he could hit like me I could."

For the ultimate explanation we are indebted to author John Updike, who was in Fenway Park when Williams played his last game, on September 28, 1960. His last time up, Williams hit a homer—and went straight to the dugout. Prolonged cheers could not summon him back. Updike: "Gods don't answer letters."

But Williams, irascible god, had a human side. Unlike many stars, he was a dream teammate, kind and generous. When the Sox finally hired their first black player, Pumpsie Green, Williams took the trouble to play catch with him—to let people know he wanted no sauce. And he melted at the plight of sick children—just ask *Boston Globe* sports columnist Dan Shaughnessy: Williams befriended his ten-year-old daughter Kate when she was stricken with leukemia and sent her autographs and cheer. Without publicity, he raised millions for the Jimmy Fund, which benefits child cancer victims.

Boston tipped its cap to Williams when it named its new Logan Airport tunnel after him. Williams accepted the announcement of the honor with his usual cool. The hero of a defiantly Democratic town, he let his benefactors know he was an in-your-face Republican, for George Bush against the state's governor, Michael Dukakis. Rep. Richie Neal (D-MA), remembers that Tip O'Neill and Joe Moakley were pretty sore about it but of course said nothing.

Baseball has a special place in our hearts. It is the game that shows us as we would like to be. But baseball disgraced itself while we were mourning Ted Williams and his frigid fate. The All-Star Game, which was supposed to confer a Most Valuable Player Award named for Williams, was called off after eleven innings. The pitchers were saving their million-dollar arms, maybe for the picket line they threaten. The award was not given.

It's just as well. Williams played his heart out at every game. Declaring a game over when it wasn't finished would have outraged this most valuable player. ∎

11

Dogs

A Hot, Nonpolitical Story—December 2, 1984

Post television critic Tom Shales has brilliantly described the post-election letdown. Endless as it was, and meaningless as it turned out to be, the campaign, he pointed out, had addictive properties.

I underwent withdrawal in a rather acute form. I went to Boston to close out my aunt's apartment. In a burst of humor, she, who in her ninety years had become intimately acquainted with my fabled incompetence, had made me executor of her estate.

I went from chasing candidates and scribbling about Star Wars, secret wars, taxes, and trends to making dates with the Salvation Army and reading Christmas letters of the '30s from my aunt's boss. Kate was a "saver."

I had a curious feeling that the rest of the world had stopped, too. The newspapers I bought every day at the White Hen in an effort to keep in touch with it had reduced the universe of public concern to two baby girls: Baby Fae in California and five-month-old Jerri Ann Richards, who had mysteriously disappeared from her humble home in Providence.

One morning at the White Hen, the policeman from the station house next door told the cashier he was going to Providence to look for Jerri Ann. Baby Fae, he said, was being given too many drugs. "She'll be up around the chandelier."

At home, with my heroic helpers, Mary, my sister-in-law, and Mary, my cousin—it only seems as if all the women in Boston are named Mary—we talked about the babies. The baboon heart—would it break? Would Baby Fae, with her endearing topknot and her bright eyes, live? Would Jerri Ann be found?

I began to sound like someone in a television commercial. I heard myself saying. "Yes, Lestoil cuts the grease."

One night, hungry for diversion, I went to a church supper. At my table, we talked some about Geraldine Ferraro, but it was as if she had died—as she might well have done, having vanished entirely from the scene. I enjoyed a flash of celebrity: I was "the girl whose niece married Tom Beatty." I should explain that females in Boston are "girls" up to and including the time they enter the nursing home.

The two babies died within twenty-four hours of each other. First the little pioneer Baby Fae. Jerri Ann's body was found in an alley behind her house.

On television, we saw more stricken babies in Ethiopia. My aunt's friend, Monica Sullivan, came by to pick up some things and she observed, "Why can't they get the food there? If there was a war, they'd get the planes and guns in fast enough, you can be sure."

I cleaned the cellar and thought of Welsh miners. I made mistakes. I gave heirloom champagne glasses to a young relative setting up a bachelor's home, who would have been glad of jelly glasses. I had to retrieve from my nephew a painting that I had clearly labeled for a friend in Washington.

After the beds had been taken away and I became a homeless person, my cousin Mary took me in. Every day, we commuted from Norwell.

There, the one noteworthy event of my stay occurred. When we got home one night, Cody, the eldest of the three animals Cousin Mary has taken in—she has a weakness for strays of all species—was not at home. As we went about getting her husband's supper, she would sigh, and with reason.

Cody, a mix of Irish setter, collie, and whatever, is ancient and infirm. His back legs don't work very well, and I am told he had a hip replacement. Once I took him for a walk, and he staggered so badly over every stick and stone in his path that I thought I might have to carry him home. The anxiety level in the kitchen rose.

Finally the phone rang. It was a neighbor. He had Cody in custody. The rap? Breaking into the neighbor's garage and making off with a cooked Thanksgiving turkey.

We set off down the road, and sure enough, there was Cody. Tied up and looking pleased. And there was the neighbor with the goods, a large, ravaged box of unrecognizable remains. Cody had been caught galloping down the street dragging it by the string. He had eaten the white meat and the stuffing.

Cody? If I had been told that a decrepit seventy-five-year-old athlete had stormed down from the stands and onto the field in the last quarter of the Harvard-Yale game, grabbed the ball, and scored a touchdown, I could not have been more amazed. But pride was not in us. The cock began to crow. My cousin delicately distanced herself from the criminal. She got him when he was a year old from someone who had neglected him. I said that I was related to him only by marriage, which is true. Mary is my cousin's wife.

"Will this be in the paper?" the neighbor asked me after the damage had been paid.

I temporized. But I knew even then it would be. That turkey trot is by far the biggest story I've come across since November 6. ■

A Kinder, Gentler Watchdog—December 25, 1988

At Christmastime, I think of the usual things: carols, wrapping paper, mangers, the post office. But I also—and it's not because I'm morbid—think of break-ins and of my cousin's unusual burglar-alarm system.

Break-ins come to mind because one occurred at my premises a few Christmases ago. While I was out of town, an uninvited guest or two went through my premises with a lighted candle and inspected my closet very thoroughly, leaving wax on all my clothes and me with a fear of standing close because I might stick to someone.

After that, I got a burglar alarm. I couldn't wait to tell my cousin about it, thinking that for once I would come out as the more prudent and coping of the two of us.

"You know," I said in a superior manner, "you really should have a burglar alarm. The country can be as dangerous as the city."

"I already have one," she replied smartly.

"What do you mean?" I asked.

"I have Chino," she said smugly.

"*CHINO?*" I cried, and burst out laughing.

Chino is a Doberman who would not dream of interrupting a burglar at his work, "I've seen her whimper when a kitten lifted a paw to her," I said.

199

"The burglar doesn't know that," my cousin replied, as usual, having the last word.

I knew she had a point—but never quite how much of a one until I read a gripping story about a mild-mannered retriever named Brownie, who foiled a robbery with a single bark. On the night in question, Brownie, roused from her sleep in the master bedroom, went down the stairs and barked once, driving the burglar into a closet, where he fell asleep and was discovered the next morning.

The thief's account gives the key. "Big brown dog. Yeah, kind of quiet, but he's able to maybe bite."

Of course. Perception, in burglary as in politics, is everything.

But I still have trouble with the idea of Chino inspiring fear. No, if you knew her, you might have a sliver of sympathy for the robber.

What if she backed up to him and presented her rear end to be patted, as is her wont? Most people find this unnerving.

And what if she greeted him in blankets?

Summer and winter, Chino sleeps by the kitchen stove under two blankets, one of which is an ancient steamer rug. The first time I met her she came to the door, with both of them cascading off her back. She had a distracted air, and I was put in mind of a four-legged Lady Macbeth.

What if she went to the door in her Yasser Arafat headgear? How many burglars have seen a Doberman with fringe over her eyes?

Chino, who is tremendously insistent about little things, has to be completely covered. A great deal of keening and yelping goes on if a centimeter of her body is exposed. If she gets to her feet suddenly she peers at you through the fringe in a manner that many people find irresistibly comic. A crook with a sense of humor would have a problem.

If he's brusque and says sharply to her, "Take a walk," I assure you there would be hell to pay. "Walk" makes Chino ballistic, as our president-elect might say. It is avoided in my cousin's household. Hearing it sends Chino into a fandango of delight. She leaps in the air, she sobs with joy, she dances, hurls herself against the speaker of the W-word.

She could well knock the intruder down.

I wonder what would happen should she be unwell. Chino indisposed is a pretty awesome thing. There's no end of sighing and staring, particularly at my cousin, whom she unaccountably dislikes, although my cousin is heroically patient with her. We think that Chino has heard her mistress remark that she is the dumbest dog ever born and that the slur somehow penetrated Chino's tiny brain.

Anyway, she glares at my cousin a lot, and she gets even with her in the immemorial way of neurotic females. She has frequent, melodramatic illnesses and is forever being hauled off to the veterinarian. She loves the vet and, characteristically, displays her passion by trying to take over the steering wheel or throwing herself out of the car as it nears his office.

The last time she had a seizure was when my cousin went out of town to a wedding. Chino threw a scene that so frightened her sitters that they called my cousin long distance at seven o'clock in the morning to report it.

"She knew what she was doing," says my cousin grimly. "She was punishing me. She may not like me, but she doesn't want me to go away, either."

I guess what I'm saying is that any thief who knew Chino would be even less inclined to invade her home. She may not bite but, on the other hand, she is totally ungluing—which, I guess, is what a burglar alarm is supposed to be. ■

White House Shenanigans Don't Extend to Buddy
—March 22, 1998

At last I have found something I can agree with columnist Bill Safire about. Our disagreements go back a ways, to when Richard Nixon was president and had Safire on his payroll and me on his enemies list—twice and with an asterisk. But now I must hail him for a splendid piece of prose he wrote recently: an open letter from Buddy to his master, Bill Clinton. It is an appeal for a stay of sentence to be neutered.

You must not think I have broken my published pledge of three weeks ago to give up sex-scandal mongering until something new actually occurs. I am not stealing back into the swamp via the kennel entrance. This is a freestanding outrage. It's not about adultery, affidavits, perjury, passes, impeachment, book deals, talking points, or lewd advances in the Oval Office. It has nothing to do with Kenneth Starr, the budget-busting Savonarola who sent to Japan for a witness who went to school with Monica Lewinsky. It's about how a man treats his best friend.

In his short life, Buddy has been a model of constancy and fidelity, which is more than is said about his master. He gives unconditional love. He doesn't ask for anything except to doze under the desk and retrieve tennis balls. He doesn't cry or ask for work, or go running to the grand jury, or tape, or leak. Buddy is housebroken.

Like all dogs, he understands his job. He must reassure his master, lick his hand, and make him feel like the most important person in the world.

Buddy seems to have been born knowing that his master is emotionally needy. When others come and go, Buddy gives them a raised eyelid. When Himself shows up, Buddy springs to his feet, saluting. When this godlike creature unaccountably puts him out of the Oval Office when a meeting is being convened, Buddy barks to remind him of the mistake he makes so often: not knowing who his true friends are.

And what is the reward? He's going to be whacked. Why now? Certainly the full-time spinners on the White House payroll could have noticed the grotesque timing and the obscene cartoons and one-liners that would ensue. Certain background dissonances cannot be controlled. For instance, *Don Giovanni*, Mozart's masterwork about a wolf, is closing a brilliant run at the Washington Opera Society. The captions played over the stage could have come out of the day's paper, and audiences did a lot of nervous twittering. What a grand jury witness the Don would have made. He kept meticulous records of his conquests. He is done in eventually by a statue, gray and stony-faced, who looks a lot like Starr, as some in the audience noted.

Poor, sweet, skinny Buddy has brought out the side of Clinton that is worse than what has been alleged about his job-counseling activities: his habit of turning his back on those to whom he has made promises. Buddy now joins the gays, the Haitians, the Chinese dissidents, Lani Guinier, the Democratic Party, and others whom he has callously exploited—doing the politically correct thing to exhibit civic virtue.

He maybe never told Buddy specifically that he would not take him to the vet's for neutering, but the dog may have taken it for granted. He will do no carousing, fathering litters better unborn. Buddy lives behind an iron gate under armed guard. As Safire had Buddy say in the letter he had him write for the president, "If I get lost, twenty guys lose their jobs."

Again I ask. If Clinton gets caught, why should Buddy pay? Don't worry; I'm not going to get into comparisons with some of the humans who have been biting Clinton in the ankle lately. The only thing Buddy could have done to save Clinton from himself was to screen female visitors for book deals. Dogs are so intelligent, they can learn almost anything. They answer the telephone, tell time, keep children from falling downstairs. Buddy could have been trained to sniff out manuscripts that were either in or on people. Had he checked out the latest lady—a handsome, bankrupt widow with halting voice and high cheekbones, much in the tradition of Barbara Stanwyck, the last generation's diva of "women's pictures"—things would have been different. She was many cuts above the other job-seekers, and made an impression on consequential commentators—although not on the perverse public, which gave him yet another boost in the polls. They registered even before they found out that the unhappy author was peddling a book.

I long ago lost my papers as a Clinton soothsayer. In 1992, I was sure he would not survive the New Hampshire primary. All I can say now is that any other politician would long since have gone under in all this lascivious second-term slapstick. But with this Dogpatch Don Giovanni, you just never know.

Do I have a dog in this fight? I sure do. It's Buddy, the only true heart around. ■

Lesson for the New Year: Look to the Dogs!
—January 2, 2000

Would you excuse me if I hang back in the old century for just a few minutes? I feel that with all the treachery going on both with technology and humans, I would mention a few dogs I saw over the holidays who embody the loyalty, concern, goodwill to men, and other qualities that are not vastly on display elsewhere in the world.

I speak first of Harry, my cousin Brian's golden retriever, an elegant and amiable creature, with just a dash of con man and pol in his nature to give it spice. He, of course, came with his master to meet me at the airport. My cousin had kindly invited me to a holiday lunch at Boston's incomparable Ritz Café. The only hitch was that Brian had to shop for his entire gift list before we could sit down to scrod prepared by a band of angels. This involved my waiting outside with Harry, while Brian raced up and down the aisles grabbing gifts with a bandit's speed.

The entry to Lord and Taylor was unheated and the temperature was twenty-five, and people scurried in not just desperate but frozen. Harry had a miraculous effect on them. Everyone spoke to him. The most clouded countenance lifted and broke into a smile at the sight of him. People who obviously did not have time to breathe stopped to scratch his ears and whisper endearments. They wished him a Merry Christmas, often graciously including me in the greeting.

One young woman who seemed especially stricken by the stress of the season came out of the store empty handed, and sank to one knee to kiss him on the forehead. Harry, of course, responded in kind and licked her face. She thanked us both.

Others asked his name, age, and sex. An older couple came toiling into view. The man asked, "Boy or girl?" I said, "His name is Harry."

"We have a girl," he said, "her name is Rosie. Would you like to see her pictures?" He whipped out his wallet and proudly showed a dog like Harry.

"She's very smart," he said.

"Harry," I replied boldly, "sits down without being told the minute he gets to a curbstone and doesn't move until his master tells him to."

I felt we could go on indefinitely extolling our pets' champion qualities. The man's wife, pale in the jaws of the Christmas crunch, towed him away.

Harry had given us all an excuse to be nice to each other; he had brought out the best in everyone, as dogs so often do. I was chilled to the bone by the time Brian reappeared, but my heart was warm.

The next day it was my feet.

We went to Christmas dinner at Jud and Maryann's stately new mansion. It was garlanded and festooned, and everything was what it ought to be except that I was still cold. People were very kind. They gave me a seat by the fire, a lap robe, a brandy. Happily, the household includes two blond Labradors, and one of them, Murphy, is a humanitarian. He cased the situation, then came over and lay down on my feet—not at them, on them. Instant Palm Beach was the result.

And he stayed there. Samantha, the other Lab, started at the sound of cars or sudden sallies by the children. Murphy the Merciful never budged. I told his mistress that it was remarkable that he had sensed a need and filled it with no fuss. "He's that way," she said with understandable pride.

Danny, Tom and Anne's dog, is also a golden, but not yet into social work. He is young. He sits by your chair when you are eating your breakfast, and sometimes he puts his head in your lap. He beams on you a melting gaze that would make a saint feel guilty. He is all but saying, "It's entirely up to you, but I want you to remember that if you cannot finish that cranberry bread but don't want to hurt Anne's feelings by leaving any, I am here for you. I want to help."

Coming back on the plane, I read a riveting *New York Times* story about a furor in England over a Yuletide television special, part of a series, called "One Man and His Dog." It was about shepherds steering their sheep into pens with the indispensable help of their sheepdogs.

The English keep a tight rein on their emotions, but when it comes to dogs, they just let 'em rip. According to *Times* reporter Sarah Lyall, the English are riled that some of their countrymen might seek more piquant TV fare. I am with the dog-lovers. Marveling at dogs who cope with silly sheep is an excellent corrective for Internet heads who think they know it all.

I also hope somebody makes a documentary about a group called Therapy Dog Training that certifies some breeds—Rottweilers among them—as caseworkers in nursing homes and mental hospitals. Seems they're born shrinks. People pour out their hearts to dogs. I think every now and then it's good to remember that while we train dogs, they can teach us a whole lot about love and devotion as well as being nice. ■

The Saddest Loss—January 10, 2002

Even Bill Clinton's most curdled critics can summon up a little sympathy for him. He has lost his beautiful, beloved dog, Buddy. Life holds few bleaker moments. Wisecracks about Buddy's being his only true friend are out of order. Buddy was a credit to his master and the White House.

Buddy had a gleaming chocolate coat, a glad heart, and an acute understanding of Clinton's bottomless need for unconditional love. He did his White House job superbly as a mood-altering and ice-breaking presence. The self-indulgent Clinton was an indulgent dog-parent, giving the animal the run of the Oval Office without a care in the world about priceless furniture coverings. Buddy followed the sun around the room.

He was like Clinton, too, in not wanting to be left out of any gathering. Many an international parley or down-and-dirty session on domestic politics was suspended while the chief executive went to admit a whimpering Buddy for a high-level ear scratching under the eye of his beaming boss.

I had an opportunity to observe this White House relationship during the post-Christmas season of 1998, the year the House of Representatives impeached Buddy's master. The Clintons had kindly invited the older children (ages four to nine) of St. Ann's Infant and Maternity Home to view the lavish White House Christmas decorations. I tagged along as a volunteer. The children, I am sorry to say, expressed minimum interest in the decked halls. What caught all eyes was the helicopter parked in the backyard. As a preternaturally patient Secret Service man herded the children through the historic rooms, they dashed to the windows, checking the recurrent miracle of the helicopter.

We fetched up in the Diplomatic Reception Room, where we found a little collection of sightseeing families. We were told that we might, just might, see the president and the First Lady as they headed for the helicopter. The children and I spent the time rehearsing for a possible encounter, except for Tiffany, who was having a bad hair day and refused to come out from under a table where she had taken refuge from the world. Buddy caused a stir when he entered the room led on a leash by a Secret Service agent. The children broke through the light rope lines to greet him. They embraced him and he bore their caresses negligently, his attention plainly elsewhere—he was waiting for his main man. As soon as Clinton appeared, Buddy went into a dance of delight.

The president plunged into the little crowd with his wonted zest. We of St. Ann's rejoiced when Stephen darted out of line to greet an astonished Clinton with a perfectly rehearsed "How do you do, Mr. President? I'm glad to see you." Clinton seemed gratified at the ardor of Stephen's greeting.

Buddy was unhappy. He set up a yelping with a clear message that started everyone laughing: "I am here, your pet, your pal. Why are you wasting time on these nobodies?" Clinton called, "Hold on, Buddy, I'm comin'." And when he did, Buddy jumped up and planted his paws on the president's shoulders, and covered his face with kisses. Clinton inhaled. Buddy and he had bonded during impeachment. Alex Munthe, author of a book about the Villa San Michele, has studied monarchs' dogs and writes about the role of a Buddy during a sad and troubled moment: "He creeps up and lays his head on his lap. . . . Never mind if all abandon you. I am here to replace all your friends and fight all your enemies."

Now Clinton is condemned to relive Buddy's last hours, when inattentive caretakers failed to thwart his dash for freedom that led to a rendezvous with death on the highway. When he goes home he sees Buddy everywhere, and for weeks, he will make wide arcs around Buddy's favorite flopping places, still trying to avoid stepping on paws. He waits in vain for the delicious sensation of the cold snout in the palm of the hand that signals the arrival of the number one fan, the ecstatic welcome at any hour of day or night.

Clinton has lately been discovered whining that his successor had the supreme luck of a galvanizing world crisis. Recently, according to Richard L. Berke of the *New York Times*, he rallied White House alumni to consider how they would revive his legacy of good times and centrist politics. He cannot leave it to heaven or history, to thank his stars that the Senate did not judge sex in the Oval Office.

Whatever he did, dog-lovers can tell you, he is paying for it now. ■

12

Botox, Dieting, Elizabeth Arden

Farewell, Garden of Arden—August 12, 1990

My subject today is Maurice, a magician who works at Elizabeth Arden on Connecticut Avenue, an establishment I prize because it is a place where I can do no wrong. Naturally, a corporation has now come along to close it down.

I never met Elizabeth Arden, but I honor her. She figured out that people who go to beauty parlors know they are not beautiful and need to be put together, not put down. Nor do they need to be hassled or hustled to have a perm or buy expensive products. She asked only that her clients permit themselves to be spoiled.

There is no Muzak at Elizabeth Arden. And no arguments. So a moon-faced woman wants a modified whiffle, with the hair snarled or standing on end. Maurice might suppress a sigh, but he would go to work and produce an approximation, which made her think she had gotten her own way, and comb out the worst consequences. I call him a magician because for seven years he has produced an illusion that I have hair. With women who do have hair, he wrought miracles by the hour.

Yelle, Maurice's acolyte and shampoo-giver, is a gentle, quiet soul from Indonesia. She brings you springwater and coffee and pays your bill for you if to do it yourself might mean you would smudge your manicure. She is there to steady the pedicure customers who are shuffling about in paper shoes.

The manicurists all come from exotic places—Cuba, Iran, Ecuador. Someone is always going off to "my country." When Yelle went home to Indonesia to get married, a huge farewell party was held. Maurice, who is Lebanese and a demon cook, roasted a farewell lamb.

A proud and loyal veteran of seventeen years, Maurice said Arden provided "a complete beauty service." But what it really provided was ministrations. I have seen women straggle in with an inch of dark roots showing, their whole attitude suggesting defeat and low self-esteem. After a couple of hours of kindness and a lot of tinfoil, they march up to the desk where the stupendously well-groomed Mrs. Schaefer presides over the cash register and the appointments sheets, and they are transformed. They are blond, triumphant.

A corporation called Unilever, which owns Elizabeth Arden, wishes to close this temple of restoration. They will sell the building. Legions of satisfied customers will grind their teeth at the mention of Unilever's name.

Corporations spend billions building up good will, improving their public relations. And then they raise their prices as soon as Saddam Hussein gives the order for the tanks to roll. It was a terrific encore to Exxon's gross handling of the Alaska oil spill. I heard an unctuous oil executive explain that this was "an anticipatory increase." It's also called "gouging."

A few of the big guys have understood that in order to be beloved, you must do nice things. StarKist, for instance, announced it would not buy tuna that came from nets that killed dolphins. StarKist made a million friends among dolphin lovers. And 7-Eleven is sponsoring a literacy program. I am not surprised. 7-Eleven is itself a wonderful idea. Like the United Parcel Service, it makes life easier. My local 7-Eleven is manned by Cambodians. who are quick, quiet, and ever smiling, sort of in the Arden mode.

The Arden spirit does not, alas, pervade all corners of the beauty business. Elsewhere, people feel obliged to tell you what you already know, that your hair is thin, your skin is greasy, and your hands would not be tolerated in the Bolshoi Ballet. And they have high-tech gadgets to study your defects, so that a simple attempt to purchase an item can be as punitive as an encounter with a prison matron.

The other day I went to a Clinique counter to buy a jar of cleansing cream. The woman, a blonde with severely plucked eyebrows, asked me suspiciously, "Have you used the cream before?" I said yes. It was not enough. She whipped out a chart with a sliding light and informed me she would have to see if the cream was suitable for me. She checked the color of my eyes, although I didn't see the relevance of it, and my skin tones. She asked me what moisturizer I use. I said I didn't use any.

There was a sharp intake of breath.

"Why don't you use a moisturizer?"

I couldn't think of a reason. I felt the silence of fellow shoppers. I felt guilty, inadequate, as if I were about to be turned over to the FBI. "Forget it," I said, and crept away.

That woman wouldn't have lasted "A Morning of Beauty" at Arden. I will miss Maurice and Olga and Nora and Connie and Marcella and all the others who helped me face life. Arden's prices are high, but the attitude is worth anything you have to pay for it. ∎

Italian Spa Food Isn't for the Weak—November 27, 1996

SATURNIA, ITALY—Of course I know that the words "Italy" and "diet" provide the perfect ingredients for an oxymoron. I just thought that at a spa a certain measure of the austerity that is so blessedly lacking in most aspects of Italian life might be operative.

I was wrong.

The first clue was the breakfast tray: five rolls straight from the oven, about a quarter of a pound of butter, and a croissant dusted with powdered sugar. The second, I met at lunch. It was Mirco, my waiter, a delightful person with cloudless blue eyes and an unlimited desire to please.

I had been told that if I ordered from the "light" side of the menu, I would be in splendid shape—there was no point in seeing a dietitian unless I would be staying at least two weeks.

I watched with interest as Mirco whirled by with trays of mashed potatoes, strawberry shortcake, mounded pastas, and éclairs in the shape of the onion domes in Red Square. In my limited Italian, I explained to Mirco that I would not like to gain weight. He looked a bit puzzled. Obviously his culture was at war with his professional instincts. His family had been in Tuscany for many generations, and all his genes told him that visitors should be fed copiously with the succulent dishes his countrymen had prepared for them. And it should be properly seasoned: He came flying over with the olive oil cruet cocked at every turn. The soup would taste much better, as would the salad, as would the pasta.

The one claim that the Terme di Saturnia (Baths of Saturn) did not make for the magical waters in the pool beside the dining room was that they would make you thin. Otherwise, the other guests assured me, they would improve your skin, your lungs, your bones. They had been doing so for centuries. Julius Caesar's legions had splashed in them. Generals who had bolted down too many small countries without the benefit of Maalox repaired their ravaged nerve ends amid the rich sulfur fumes.

To me, it was a marvel that the Romans, a notoriously suspicious lot, had ever tried the waters. The Olympic-size pool, which decanted its waters into various showers and waterfalls, smells bad, and the sulfur can make your eyes red. The fact that the Romans' predecessors, the Etruscans, who were the native Italians and who had a high degree of civilization, had discovered the baths and enjoyed them did not influence the know-it-all Romans. Besides, at dark, when finally everybody is out of the pool, curls of mist rise over the water, giving it a faintly sinister look. How could the Romans have taken the plunge?

My theory is that one legionary pushed another legionary, and the slam-dunked one came up smelling bad but feeling good. Ever since, people have come to Saturnia, named for the Roman god of abundance, in all seasons. Neither rain nor snow disturbs the cozy temperature. Over the years they have added such refinements as mud baths, Jacuzzis, massages, and facials. They have built a large luxury hotel, and people who partake much too liberally of the dining room's delicious excesses can make amends by joining the morning hike through the Tuscan hills, doing "abs" every day at five o'clock and waddling to the gym for the postdinner instruction in the macarena.

The historical mix in the neighborhood was as rich as the cuisine. You could float in the pool and gaze up at the unbearably picturesque hill town of Saturnia, with a bell tower and crenellated walls. Nearby is Sovrano, which has Etruscan tombs and a fortress that Charlemagne himself once stormed.

Mirco and I locked horns over the pasta item on the "light" side the first night. He assured me it was "verra light," his only English phrase. It turned out to have a rich cream sauce and a pastry crust half an inch thick. He was crushed that I was not pleased with it.

The next night, the feature was "risotto alla Parmigiana." I demanded to know what was in it. He was triumphant. "Only butter," he said proudly. His face fell when I tried to explain that "only butter"

211

is a contradiction in terms and that butter is about as bad as it gets. "Verra light," he murmured disconsolately, and "just a little cheese."

Piero from Florence, who sat at the next table, explained the Tuscan attitude, which translates roughly into "Every day is Thanksgiving." He had heard someone—thankfully not me—asking for a half-portion or some other dietary heresy. "Why they come here?" he fumed. "This beautiful place, this wonderful restaurant, a marvelous chef. They want to diet. They can diet at home."

I could see the logic of his position.

At my last supper there, Mirco ceremonially asked if he could bring me my first *dolce* (sweet) of the week. "No fruit, signora, tiramisu." That is a savory, calorie-laden custard-type dessert. For once he did not say "verra light." I was grateful. ■

Mirthless Laughter Perfectly Suited to Washington
—July 21, 2002

I haven't yet been invited to a Botox party, and I don't know if I ever will be. Should I be glad or sad?

Peter Jennings told us Wednesday night about the craze sweeping the West Coast, which is a hotbed of hospitality to new and loony ideas. But even for La-La-land, this is a bit much—going to a party for an injection of a poison that is supposed to erase wrinkles, especially laugh lines.

My problem is that I have never thought an injection—even if I get champagne afterward—is "something fun," as a thirty-one-year-old Golden State belle burbled into an ABC microphone. Obviously, she was not following the advice of the English poet Robert Herrick to "gather ye rosebuds while ye may." She is following the dour counsel of the New England poet Robert Frost, who preached, "Provide, provide."

Looking at her lineless face, we recognize instantly her gambit—it is a preemptive strike, like what the administration plans for Saddam Hussein.

Will the Botox party come to Washington? We like to be with-it here, although you would not always think so from what we do. We don't create trends—that's what we have California for—but we like to follow them. And if we do decide that we want to be needled, I ask myself if I would make the list. While the in crowd is booking its doctor for the mass needling, can I hope that something more than wrinkles may be needed for admission? I am painfully aware that I do not talk the talk that would immediately identify me as someone in the loop.

I have only lately learned not to reference a couple as "going steady," a phrase of my youth. By the way, I hope you will notice my slick use of a noun that has recently become a verb, the kind of new grammatical wrinkle I try to keep up with. "Reference" joins "impact" and "nuance" in the Cinderella division. Nouns who used to droop by the fire, hoping for notice, are out there now with the big-boy muscular verbs that are often used by high officials who really don't have much to say, like Colin Powell on Israel.

Forgive the digression. I just thought it would juice up my credentials as someone who keeps up. Now I resume the catalog of my shortcomings. I have not entirely kicked the lamentably bourgeois habit of inquiring about the marriage plans of the boy and the girl in the relationship that I call "going steady." I still think that if they have a joint checking account and are living in a house they bought together, a merger might be an option.

I am much obliged to "Vows," the *New York Times*'s Sunday feature about how people meet and marry. It's Jane Austen updated, although strikingly different in some particulars. In Jane Austen's novels, when the man is being reeled in, he immediately asks the heroine, "Will you be mine?" whereas at a comparable moment, today Fitzwilliam Darcy asks Elizabeth Bennett, "Your place or mine?" The M-word comes up much later, often in some exotic setting and with the diamond hidden in an artichoke, and the word "commitment" is preferenced.

The kind of a person who can expect a bid to a Botox party must be up to the minute with the changing terminology of today. For instance, in Washington, you have to be sure to know the difference between a press secretary and a communications director. Our caste system is as rigid as India's. I spend a good part of my life spelling my name for press secretaries who don't read the papers and sometimes condescend to tell me to call back at precisely 3:14 for three minutes of the Great One's time.

The other day I committed a major faux pas. I respectfully inquired in the absence of the press secretary about the availability of the communications director. The frosty answer: "The communications director does not take reporters' questions."

I wanted to know what he does do, but how could I communicate with him? Without his permission, I am not even allowed to speak to the staff expert who doubtless wrote the senator's speech that took twenty pages in the *Congressional Record*. We talk endlessly about the tyranny of Saddam Hussein. What about the tyrants in our midst?

Botox is particularly efficacious for deleting laugh lines, but who, may I ask, is laughing here? The biggest joke in town is George W. Bush's Middle East peace plan. Or, if it's sardonic mirth you crave, you have the spectacle of our most self-righteous citizen, Vice President Dick Cheney, under investigation by the SEC on the currently fashionable subject of accounting practices.

Attorney General John Ashcroft, that reliable source of merriment, has come through again with his plan to recruit mail carriers and meter-readers to spy on us. It is always good for him to be distracted from his abiding worry about the shortfall in guns and death sentences, but if that's the best we can do for laughs, maybe we should go back to Tupperware parties. ∎

13

TV–Pop Culture

Cheers **and Trembling**—May 23, 1993

How did I love them? Yes, this is another dirge for *Cheers* offered without apology by someone who, at last call, is standing in need of the ministrations of the in-house psychiatrist of Boston's most famous bar, Dr. Frasier Crane.

Let me count the ways in no particular order and with some omissions because they are all wonderful: Sam the stallion with the Cro-Magnon brow and the big hair; hapless Norm, the world's worst husband—uncertain if his father-in-law is dead or alive, he calls poor Vera and asks: "Do I have a dark suit?"; Cliff, the boring stiff; his mother, the only one who even approximates the Boston accent, although she sounds more down Maine than Beacon Hill.

I am crazy about Frasier. Naturally, I adore Sam, while dutifully deploring him. But Frasier is special because he comes on so strong and comes apart so quickly, like so many Washington politicians. His ego has the strength of an eggshell. His pals have no respect for him; when a medical emergency arises, they say dismissively, "We need a *real* doctor." He gives unsolicited advice. In one of my favorite passages, he is dispensing grief counsel to a regular. Suddenly, he hears what he is saying and his face crumples, "Mommy," he sobs.

In a singular act of self-destruction, Frasier married Lilith, a fellow shrink with a Chas Addams pallor, a steely deadpan, and a demeanor alternately withering and smoldering. She is a woman of a passion that poor Frasier cannot slake. She tries to seduce Sam at an evening's frolic at a resort hotel, and easy as that should be, given Sam's shamelessness, Frasier ruins it by showing up.

Why were we hooked? *Cheers* never let us down. It presented no role models, not the slightest social significance. Unlike their striving Thursday night brothers and sisters of *L.A. Law*, who push our faces in cutting-edge legal problems and exotic personal conduct, *Cheers* only wanted to make us laugh. And it did for eleven years, bless it.

Some had an anxious period, when Shelley Long, the incomparable Diane Chambers, decided to leave. I trusted the creators of *Cheers*—let me name them, James Burrows and the brothers Charles—to come up with something wonderful, and they did. Kirstie Alley, as Rebecca Howe, a confused careerist who really wanted a rich husband, fit in just fine after she had been cut down to size by the regulars and sexually harrassed by Sam.

At one point, she and the show got bogged down in a soggy, clinical sequence about her having Sam's baby. It ended finally, and it wasn't her fault. They soon found their way back to farce, where they belonged.

The Diane vs. Rebecca debate has been revived, but hard-core buffs take no part. Diane embodied the essential quality of a *Cheers* character. She was a maddening person from whom you would flee if you met her in real life: a nattery, chattery, high-strung, high-flown bundle of pretensions with a lot of Ancient Mariner in her. But on the screen, a delight. Diane hated herself for falling for Sam—and he knew he was out of his intellectual league. But after he threw out her stuffed animals, their arguments ended blissfully in bed. More proof of Sam's deep belief that sex solves everything.

Carla, the resident bad fairy, hated Diane with a great passion. But she hated everybody except Sam. Her putdowns of Cliff Clavin, the postman with the empty heart and the brain stuffed with facts nobody wanted to hear, were poisonous. "I'm the first Clavin without a beard," he brags. Carla sneaks up behind him, drink in hand. "You're the first Clavin without a tail."

Cliff's redeeming feature was his mother, brilliantly played by Frances Sternhagen. She, like Lilith, always made fans' hearts beat faster, because we were never sure what she would do. One splendid segment had her in a nursing home, winning the tango contest.

Only one thing we the bereaved cannot forgive. *Cheers* got even funnier as they prepared to turn out the lights and lock the doors. In one of the late episodes, Carla made a drink of her own invention called "I know that my Redeemer liveth." It flattened all consumers, including herself. The next day she can't remember who she slept with, and is horrified to discover it was Paul, an odious regular. Sam tries to comfort her by showing her that he, too, has a terrible secret. He takes off his toupee. Carla, is, of course, merciless. "A rug," she cackles. Sam, who resists modernity in all other aspects, especially feminism, bristles at her brutality. "Please," he says huffily, "it's a hair-extension system."

All we can look forward to is the reruns. We have to hope they don't conflict with *MASH* reruns—the reason so many of us never see *Nightline* or Jay Leno. ■

Surviving Reality—July 23, 2000

Last Wednesday night, for the first time, I watched *Survivor*, just because so many other people do. I couldn't see why it is the summer's smash. It looked to me like office politics in wet bathing suits. Tom Shales called it "a game show for sadists and voyeurs."

There was much sniveling and groveling, as I guess there is bound to be when one of sixteen castaways is cast out every week. Banishment is a severe punishment for those wanting in interpersonal relationships skills, but you don't have to go to a tropical island to encounter it. Why would so many Americans find it relaxing to experience rejection vicariously? They don't get enough of it in their daily lives?

I was a little apprehensive at first that the pariah was going to be sent into the jungle to die. I was relieved that the recipient of the ace of spades would not lose a life, only the million-dollar prize offered to the ultimate survivor. I realize that in today's culture, one is as bad as the other.

I will admit to not sharing the current craze for "real people" on the screen, which I am told is what draws young viewers to *Survivor*. It's so hard to see it as a diversion.

The same night I was glumly watching that show, the Roman Coliseum was reopened for a presentation of *Oedipus Rex*. The ancients sought diversion in invented sorrow and in the real thing as well. Poor Oedipus had major bad luck—married his mother, killed his father, and ended up banished. The Coliseum also plays a big part in the boffo digital epic *Gladiator*, which, of course, is based on actual happenings. Romans liked to unwind in a packed stadium watching men chop each other up with spears and short swords, and liked voting with their thumbs for either life or death in the arena. Hollywood must consider its brand of mayhem—blowing off people's faces and the like—fairly reasonable in comparison.

Daytime soap opera is full of tears, and treachery of illicit love, and unplanned pregnancies and confrontations between women who hurl disemboweling accusations at each other. Why harassed young mothers and other stay-at-homes would seek to lift their spirits with exposure to manufactured misery is just another mystery.

The Jerry Springer Show has a following. Its fare is gladly gross: Foulmouthed hags brag about sleeping with their daughters' boyfriends; cheating wives parade their paramours before hideous husbands. An audience that is, directly descended from the mobs in the Coliseum howls its verdicts about their merits.

I realize my problem is generational. I come from an era when entertainment was supposed to be fun—and romantic. With Tracy and Hepburn, the sparks and the badinage flew; Cary Grant and Ingrid Bergman sighed and plotted in the unforgettable *Notorious*. You may not be surprised to hear that *Frasier*, which is about as far from a documentary as you can get, is my favorite television program. Frasier and his brother, Niles, are psychiatrists. Their father, Martin, an ex-cop, regards them as impossible. They are—snobs, name-droppers, status-seekers, ditherers, and natterers. But they are nice, and unfortunately in my case, addictive. They are Thursday night regulars in season, but channel 12 plays an hour of reruns nightly when I should be watching the news. It takes great character not to sneak over for a good guffaw or two.

Frasier is divorced from the indescribable Lilith, a creature of fire and ice played brilliantly by Bebe Neuwirth, whom we don't see often enough. At the start, Niles is getting a divorce from a monster named Maris, whom we never see. Frasier nervously plays the field, fussing and fuming every step of the way. He has a radio show that nobody listens to and a producer named Roz, a philosophical nymphomaniac of hilarious presence. And then there is dishy Daphne, Dad's physical therapist, a lusty Manchester lass on whom Niles has a consuming crush—he quivers like a Chihuahua when she comes into a room. Naturally, after he splits with Maris, he immediately falls into the clutches of another man-eater, a plastic surgeon named Mel. Daphne is set to marry an oafish lawyer.

The season's closer was so blatantly romantic it's a wonder it got on the air. After years of crossed wires and lost nerve, Daphne and Niles admit they love each other. Niles, finally divorced, has impulsively married Mel, and it's the eve of Daphne's wedding, but they end up on a balcony. Niles, the wimp, his blood flowing in the right direction for once, turns crisp and witty. The next day, the bride knocks on the door of his Winnebago.

It was terrific. I know no good will come of it. Daphne and Niles will be destitute—rapacious Mel will sue him for his teeth—and have to move home with Frasier and Dad. They're not real. But they are realer to me than the real people on *Survivor*. And I like them better because they make me laugh. ■

14

Squirrel Wars

Blasted Squirrels!—June 2, 1985

I feel about squirrels the way Ronald Reagan feels about communists. They lie, cheat, and steal. I had my strongest fellow-feeling with him when I looked out my window and watched them scurrying about on missions of sabotage, subversion, and other evil.

Alas, this current of understanding was fatally jammed when I read a *New York Times* account of springtime at the White House. The president, Maureen Dowd reported, gets walnuts from the Park Service to feed to the squirrels.

It was information I could not handle.

Why, I have asked myself a hundred times since, would he do it? Who would seek out squirrels, give them handouts, encourage them to hang around?

To me, it was as astonishing as if he had announced he was having the Sandinistas in for supper.

Obviously, the president does not understand the squirrel menace. Today it's walnuts; tomorrow it's the Oval Office. When his back is turned they will dart in and start pawing through his papers, running up the curtains, hiding in the fireplace. Does he not understand that squirrels are the Brezhnev doctrine in fur? Once they take over, they never leave.

I speak as one with bitter firsthand experience.

Take the bird feeder war, which I lost. I like to feed birds. I like to see how long the gorgeous, spoiled male cardinal will eat before he allows his mate a crack at the table. I like to watch the nearsighted mourning doves groping and stumbling their way to the seed.

But squirrels, who are as singleminded as Soviets and just as much opposed to enjoyment, would not have it. They climbed into the little feedboxes, which were attached to the window by suction cups, and gorged themselves, while the birds sat on nearby trees looking on glumly.

Every morning started with a scene, me banging on the window with a bottle opener and yelling at them. They would give me a blank stare or jump off the ledge a few seconds, then leap back. Sometimes I would dash out in the snow to chase them away. This greatly amused them and made me late for work.

I took steps. I put the feeders so high up I could hardly reach them. The next morning, the squirrels were furiously flinging themselves against the window trying to bat down the boxes.

They glared at me between leaps. Serves you right, I said smugly. The birds were frightened away by the gymnastics. Nobody got anything. That's the way squirrels like it.

Finally, of course, they won. I came out one morning and saw that the feeders had been knocked down and were nowhere in sight. I found them later; the squirrels had hidden them in the ivy.

Dwight Eisenhower was much more my kind of president in his relations with squirrels. He liked to practice putting on the White House lawn, and the squirrels knew that, so they dug up the turf and ruined the green. He, too, took steps. He had them trapped and transported to the Maryland countryside. There was an outcry from the nature lovers; the squirrels, as ever, had the last laugh.

Let me tell you what the squirrels did to my garden. They do vindictive landscaping, you know.

My garden isn't much, but they see me spending a good deal of time over it, and they made it their Afghanistan.

I plant daffodils. They do not require a green thumb, they do not droop and pine like other plants I know. They have their own support system and do not go to pieces if you forget to water. This year, their ranks looked thin. A friend who frequents the apartment one floor above finally explained to me why.

"There's a wonderful clump of daffodils halfway down the hill," she said. "Why did you put them there?"

I didn't I said, and instantly I knew. It was the squirrels.

They had dug up the bulbs from my plot and replanted them halfway down the slope, where I could not see them.

They also dug up the hyacinth bulbs from one of the two beds in front of the building. They know I am chairman of the garden committee of my condominium, and they knew how embarrassed I would be. They only did one bed so that on one side we had a good show, and on the other, a few bedraggled tulips. I am sure they were snickering in the shrubbery as people sniffed about slackness in the garden committee.

And our president, the expert on evil empires, gives them walnuts.

I have a friend who owns a large, overwrought springer spaniel, who feels about squirrels as I do, and keeps his property free of them. I want to hire Prince the way Reagan hired the contras to do in the Sandinistas. Proxy war. I know. But that's what you're driven to.

I do not despair that the president will one day sit down with the Soviets. Anyone who likes squirrels will deal with anyone, I tell myself. ■

How I Lost My War with the Squirrels—August 11, 1985

I am losing the war against the squirrels. I had hoped since I last reported from the front, in June, to report total victory. In fact, I was on the point of announcing that we were all about to enter a new age where the birds would feed in peace, and we could all turn our energy and emotion to tax reform or the future of the whale.

Alas, instead, I am at Dien Bien Phu.

My recent dispatch brought forth considerable response from other people who feel about squirrels as Ronald Reagan feels about the Sandinistas. Retaliatory options poured in. Some of them were of a technical complexity beyond my grasp and one of them was literally shocking.

A woman from Chevy Chase wrote that she and her husband had gone nuclear. They had rigged up copper tubing on the roof of their bird feeder and wired it into the house current.

The bird can sit on the perches with impunity, but the squirrels "sit only once," she writes. "The zap they get sends them flying into the air."

Of course, it was just a prescription for wimpy Liberal angst. You know how we blanch at the thought of capital punishment. Besides, if anybody is going to be electrocuted by any charged copper tubing I might be involved in, it wouldn't be a squirrel.

My cousin Katherine wrote from North Carolina. She is a deeply believing woman, but she hinted that God had taxed her patience somewhat by creating the squirrel. Her husband, Ray, a graduate engineer, had come up with a contraption that involves a Christmas tree stand, a lamp standard, and an inverted wastebasket. They sent a sketch, showing spooked squirrels and grinning birds.

A gentleman in Washington hurls old tennis balls at the critters. A woman from New Hampshire, who had suffered the loss of endless bulbs and flowers, fires potatoes at them—she isn't sure why, since she always misses.

All but one of my readers exuded wholesome hatred, but from Dearborn, Michigan, came a reproach from a terminally smarmy woman, who said she felt sorry for me because I am not, like her, "a lover of all creatures, not just some."

She is of the tribe of Ronald Reagan, who feeds them. She gushed about "furry brown lovable little guys" for whom she leaves goodies on her apartment grounds. One thing completely destroyed her credibility. Some of the squirrels, she said are "a little shy." I never saw one that was any more shy than a state trooper about to deliver a speeding ticket.

Early in July, it was breakthrough time. My friend Frank, who has a strain of St. Francis of Assisi in him and takes pity on the oppressed, presented me with the ultimate state-of-the-art squirrel-proof bird feeder. He had won it in a raffle. It was the last of its kind to come from the hands of a master craftsman in New Hampshire, who had to quit because of the high cost of production.

With great ceremony and many witnesses, he installed it on a tree outside the dining room window. I have never seen a handsomer object. It is rectangular in shape, with redwood at the top. It has a glass panel, behind which is stored the bird food. In profile, it looks like a wayside shrine. But its technology is most cunning.

When anything heavier than a bird lands on the perch below the glass panel, a little chute falls down, cutting off access to the eats.

I settled down for the day of reckoning. I dreamed of advising all victims of squirrel aggression and terrorism that liberation was at hand, of giving the Yankee inventor such volume that he could afford to stay in business.

So much for my dreams. The first patron was a particularly obnoxious black squirrel. He sat on the end of the redwood top, bent over in the attitude of Rodin's *Thinker*, and glared angrily around. Various of his shy siblings made desultory leaps at the tree trunk. I enjoyed it.

But after a day or two, I noticed that the marvelous contraption was attracting only sparrows. Oh yes, I hear the lady from Dearborn telling me, I'm a snob. It's true. I like a bit of color.

I consulted my neighbor, Jim, who lives above, and works for the Federal Aviation Administration. He likes anything that flies and feeds birds winter and summer. His usual clientele is still with him; he dropped a few names—chickadees, cardinals, crested titmice. Maybe, he said darkly, there was a colony of cats under the parking lot.

My next-door neighbor, Marie, said cardinals prefer sunflower seeds, and kindly gave me some. I carefully put them at the front of the trough. I tied the bag up and left it out. The next morning there were no cardinals and the squirrels had untied the bag and strewn the seed all over the grass.

The squirrels chewed up the redwood board in their fury. They left deep toothmarks. Now they've left town. But so have the birds. Were they kidnapped, threatened, brainwashed?

I don't know. I've put up the white flag. ■

Our President Is Soft on Squirrels—May 22, 1988

To me, the most shocking revelation in Donald Regan's book has nothing to do with who runs the schedule by the light of the moon or who knew what about the Iran-Contra business. It is that President Reagan keeps a bag of acorns in the bottom drawer of his desk and feeds them to squirrels outside the Oval Office every day.

I have known for some time that he is a squirrel-feeder. As reported, he got a couple of acorns from a park policeman and every now and then, and for reasons incomprehensible to me, handed them out to squirrels. But I assumed it was a random weakness, well in hand.

For those of us who spend much money and emotion, trying to keep the varmints at bay, to hear that the chief executive seeks out their company is the most damaging charge that the vengeance-mad Regan has made. Feeding them is like giving a course in assertiveness-training to Morton Downey Jr.

Here is a president who believes in means-testing for all other forms of charity. Ronald Reagan has spent his political career bewailing the fact that the government gives handouts to the undeserving. He has preached self-reliance, individual initiative, self-help.

The squirrels must be snickering. The White House grounds have seven splendid oak trees. The squirrels have only to wait for the acorns to fall on their heads.

Let us pass over the fact that the president likes squirrels—there is no accounting for tastes. I understand also that giving to those who have is a Republican trait, deeply ingrained; the vice president wants to reduce capital-gains taxes. But so is, I had thought, an aversion to waste motion and duplication. The acorns, Regan tells us, are gathered at Camp David and brought back to the acorn-rich White House, so the president can give them to avaricious rodents who would, with half a chance, storm the Oval Office and clean him out of jellybeans before he could buzz for the Secret Service.

I realize there is a theory that if you feed squirrels they will be nice and not eat your bird food or dig up your bulbs. Oh, sure, and General Noriega will give his drug money to the poor and turn himself in to the United States attorney in Miami.

In the condo where I live, and where I, as the chairman of the garden committee, planted tulips and hyacinths on either side of the entrance, the squirrels dug up all the bulbs on one side only, making sure that when spring comes, we look absentminded or unbalanced.

Of course the president is not running again, so he has nothing to fear from the large antisquirrel constituency that I know is out there. I wrote a dispatch from the front about my losing battle and got more mail than about anything I ever wrote except for Jane Austen and sullen postal clerks.

I was taken aback by the ferocity of this group. One woman reported that she had strung electrified copper wire between her house and her bird feeder, and zapped the raiders as they came. Another zinged them with potatoes which she kept in a bag by the backdoor.

This year, I thought I might be gaining on the squirrels. I found a squirrel-proof feeder in the Hammacher Schlemmer catalogue, a large plastic affair with a cone-shaped hat that I could see the squirrels sliding off of. I could also picture them standing on each others' shoulders until they got to the tiny troughs, but I had faith and had it installed.

225

My clientele from the first day has been sparrows only. I have been lectured on bird-snobbery (by a cousin who does a brisk trade with cardinals, finches, and other glamorous types) and I am fighting it, but I'm not there yet.

Last Sunday, my heart leaped up. A cardinal came. He sat on a branch about a foot from the cafeteria. My neighbor said cardinals never feed at feeders. I rushed to get sunflower seeds and put them where he might get them before the squirrels struck. But he flew away—whether put off by the clientele or the cuisine, I have no way of knowing.

Finally, in desperation I cut up crusts, fried them in bacon, and put them in the feeder. Alas, they were too big to ooze down to the proper place. It may be the same old story. Pencil-size perches small enough to foil squirrels are not big enough for anything heavier than sparrows.

The squirrels are off in the bushes, I know, killing themselves laughing. Or—and I hate to say this, having been warned by the attorney general about leaping to conclusions about guilt in the absence of indictment—they may be zonked out. Here's why. I had a large bag of heady cocoa-mulch lying around. One morning I found it slit open and beans in the grass. I am sure the squirrels thought that's what cocaine comes from and had snorted their fill. I put nothing past them.

Ronald Reagan is stubborn in his devotion to unsuitable friends. I hope this will make him think. ■

Ingrate Flowers and Drunken Squirrels—July 9, 1989

Once again, I have had confirmation of my theory that if man doesn't put you in your place, nature will. I have been the subject of two major open-air putdowns this summer. In one case, I got above myself. In the other, as usual, I was confounded by squirrels.

I started off the planting season in my small spread with delusions of grandeur. It happens to everyone who puts things in the ground. Study the faces of people leaving Johnson's parking lot on Saturday morning, bearing a cardboard box as if it were the Holy Grail, their faces alight with dreams of glory. You may see a couple of spindly plants. They are looking at tomatoes the color of Krakatoa's fire; they can taste the tomato sauce, their neighbor's envy. You think they are carrying petunias, larkspur, the gaudy zinnia. You are wrong. They are holding in their hands a garden of the type Percy Grainger wrote music to. They see a riot of blossoms, they smell the perfumed air.

This year I had a fateful encounter with the dianthus, the flower that looks and smells like a small carnation and is also called a pink. They go to my head. I don't know how many I had bought before I came out of my trance at Johnson's. It was a new life, horticulturally speaking, for me.

No more the humble, long-suffering impatiens, the uncomplaining, ever-blooming, sun-or-shade, if-you-forget-to-water-me-it's-OK plant that has saved so many gardeners from a blossomless summer. The pink, the cerise, the delicate flame-color, the fringed, the exquisite dianthus would take its place.

They looked lovely in June. I was miffed when a neighbor came by and said in a tone that suggested that I had forgotten my roots. "No impatiens?" "No," I said, I suppose a mite smugly, "not this year."

I admired her loyalty of course, but I pitied her for not seeing the little Versailles that was unfolding at her feet.

But now it is July, and the dianthus, having done their stuff, are resting. They have gone to green stalks. The only blooming in sight is being done by—who else?—an impatiens. I put out, strictly for auld lang syne, a last year's relic that had obligingly wintered over inside. It is foaming with orange blossoms. It has even put out a few striped blooms. It is a reproach to the exhausted dianthus, a reproach to me.

Meanwhile, there is high drama in the basil patch. It is my one reliable crop. It makes me feel like a farmer. I am insufferable about my pesto.

One morning I went out, and there were cutouts on the leaves. They were not exactly shredded, but I was put in mind of Fawn and Ollie.

"Slugs," said the organic gardener, who gave me the plants. "Put a saucer of beer in the middle of the patch. The slugs will climb in and drown. They will die blissfully happy."

How humane, I thought. How environmentally sound.

I poured out the Coors in two foil tins and placed them in the ground.

The next morning, the tins were flung on the grass, one of them upside down. They were empty. I suspected a late-night orgy.

Obviously, lightweight containers that could be carried off by the customers would not do. I got hold of a heavy terra-cotta saucer, filled it to the brim, dug a little space for it, and waited.

By this time I knew who I was dealing with: the squirrels who are still trying to get even for the bird feeder they can't crack. They can do everything else, like the urban guerrillas they are. They transplant bulbs. They moved all my daffodils down the hill so I can't see them. A reader wrote that a squirrel tried to gnaw down his house in Chicago when he stopped putting peanuts on the windowsill.

But I hadn't known they drank. How could I not have known? They have all our vices. Avarice, greed—take over, eat everything in sight. Where do you think Michael Milken learned about getting it all?

Next morning, the saucer was still in place, but empty. So was a box of raisins I had dumbly left out. But there were no slugs in sight, dead or alive. No squirrels with big heads and unsteady feet, either. They had gone underground, which is what they do after a big job.

A friend from Georgia offered a rural recipe. Eat the contents of half a cantaloupe. Line the rind with salt. Place in garden. I did all that. The next morning the melon was gone.

The squirrels may have sold the husk to a susceptible raccoon as a quonset hut. Who knows?

My guess is that the slugs hired the squirrels as consultants, and that I now am like so many people in Washington—fighting an unseen enemy that has unlimited resources and no conscience. I can go on putting out melons and beer until the squirrels get so fat they can't function. Or else I can face the fact that the only thing I can grow is impatiens and learn to love Franco-American spaghetti. ∎

15

Birds

To Foil a Mockingbird—August 14, 1983

I won't say I feel about the mockingbird just the way Ronald Reagan feels about Fidel Castro, but it's close.

I hasten to add, out of respect for the birds' fans a formidable and fervent flock I happen to know, that my hostility is mixed with sincere admiration for my adversary's gall and talent— where did he learn the first three notes of the Mozart Flute Concerto which is his musical signature?

I know how many people feel about feathered mockers from the mail that poured in some years back when I wrote about going eyeball to eyeball with Fidel, as I may well call him.

In brief, he hounded me out into the cold and icy streets the day after a blizzard.

For hours, he hopped up and down the windowsill of the kitchen, where I was trying to hide from him, and banged on the window until I gave in and went to the Safeway to buy him raisins.

I thought I was making a point about giving in to bullies, but it was plain from the response that I had wasted my breath. My correspondents were obviously besotted. One man wrote pages about "Casper" and "Bonjour," the mockingbird couple who had conned him into building them a kind of Taj Mahal birdhouse—I believe it had several baths— and, I believe, into serving them filet mignon.

Lately, I met another cultist at a party, who raved on about his mockingbird, who had divebombed him that morning on his way to work. This man was a good liberal, and I wondered at his applause for such aggressive behavior.

"You know," he said, "the mockingbird is the only bird that will attack human beings in defense of its young."

A couple of springs ago, Fidel had forbidden me to read on my patio. He would buzz my nose and savage the newspaper. I had not associated this particular campaign of terror with parental solicitude. I assumed it was a part of his plan to conquer the world—all the other birds scattered at his approach, except the mourning doves, who weren't standing up for their rights, by the way. They just couldn't see him.

After the raisin showdown, he transferred his patronage to my neighbor upstairs, who, and I have said this to his face, is Fidel's pigeon. There is no wait at my neighbor's groaning board. My neighbor, I believe, would rise up out of his deathbed to put out Fidel's raisins.

So he passes by with a great flirt of his wings, pausing only to sneer at my poor garden, a pitiful collection of neurosis, blight, and malaise. Fidel knows how much time I have spent there and to what little avail.

I knew, of course, that he was casing the one exception. A kind friend brought me a blueberry bush from New Hampshire. Uprooted from a lovely forest home, it put on an astonishing display of New England character and adaptability. Early in the spring for instance, it put forth delicate mauve pink buds, which turned to beautiful white blossoms. As I watched in wonder, the blossoms became small, but unmistakable, blueberries.

Fidel disappeared. I knew where he was. He was plotting the heist, lining up a fence, perfecting his alibi. I began to brood. I asked around, and was told that I had to get a shroud for my treasure. The idea of veiling my one success seemed a little cruel—and a victory for Fidel and his kind.

But I went to a hardware store. I was shown a length of netting so coarse that it would have made Fidel, with his surgical beak, laugh aloud. "It works very well on tomatoes," said the clerk. I sadly went away.

I didn't venture to a fabric shop. The one I know best is staffed with hard-bitten types who take a firm line with customers who are seasonally obsessed with transforming their young into clowns, angels, witches, and fairies and, eventually, brides. I could not face asking one of these Nurse Ratchets for veiling—I could hear the dripping irony of "For yourself, darling?" To say, "No, for a mockingbird" was beyond contemplation. They would have called the cops.

The berries turned as blue as the New Hampshire sky. And they were sweet. My neighbor and I each tasted one on the Fourth of July. I told her I would pick the next day.

There was no tomorrow. Fidel, naturally, had bugged the bush, and he struck during the night. Every ripe berry had been stripped clean. I found one he overlooked, defiantly ate it, and he struck again. Next day, the red berries were gone, too. He wanted it all.

What will I do next year? Well, I'm thinking of resuming the raisin tribute. Appeasement? No—abject surrender. And what's wrong with it? Make him so fat he'll know he can't make it to the getaway car. Make him think I like him. Take the fun out of harassing me.

I'm not saying it's an example to Ronald Reagan, but maybe it's a thought. ■

Charity for the Birds—January 22, 1984

Ed Meese, with whom I rarely agree, has a point. There are ringers in food lines.

I don't know about the human kind, and I have a feeling he doesn't either. I suspect that when he told us in December about those freeloaders in the food lines which so embarrass his boss, the president, he was speaking from his biases, not from experience.

But I run a soup kitchen myself—for the birds—and I have seen daily, maddening evidence of creatures who have other resources wolfing down the provender intended for deserving others. I am speaking of squirrels.

To watch them hogging the bird feeder is to have a fellow feeling with Ed Meese.

The squirrels who hang around my building are black, which makes them think they are irresistible. In my case, they are dead wrong. I don't even like them in the summer when they crouch outside the patio door, under the delusion that I want to let them in and make housepets of them.

Besides being pushy and obnoxious, they are not, as far as I know, deserving of winter welfare. They could, if they would dip into capital, dig up all that stuff they have buried for just such an emergency.

Every morning, they take over the dish of bird food. They sit in it and eat their fill, while the deserving poor shiver and cheep piteously from a fearful distance.

Please don't tell me I should have a squirrel-proof bird feeder. I know. I once had two, but the suction cups that hold them to the window got lost. I bang on the window; I yell at the squirrels. They dive off the window ledge, but they leap back up within seconds.

The birds are terrified by the racket and fly away before I can explain to them that I am really just trying to help them. By the time they are back, the squirrels are, too. I think sometimes I will have to give up my job to devote myself to bringing "fairness" to the dining area.

I even thought of closing it down just to get even with the varmints.

I consulted my superbenign friend Ernie Miller, who, as a colonel in the Salvation Army, has seen his share of impostors in soup kitchens. He said, "It is better to err on the side of compassion and concern than on the side of giving nothing." He was right, as usual.

I soldier on. The cardinals, the chickadees, the crested titmice seem to have wised up some and time their flights better. But I worry about the mourning doves.

They fascinate me. They are obviously unequal to the demands of daily life, and equal to the demands of daily life, and I identify with that. They are fearfully nearsighted. How they get around is beyond me. I see them lurching about on the wrong ledge looking for lunch. I see them, finally, in the vicinity of the food, but with their backs to it.

I like having them around. They are handsome and dignified and they make a lovely sound. But how do they cope? I know all about ineptitude. My mechanical skills do not extend beyond tuning in a radio. My joy in our Metro is shadowed by my terror of the farecard machine. I have never mastered an essential tool of my trade, the tape recorder. I might say that my distress at discovering that I had joined the new elite, those taped by USIA [United States Information Agency] Director Charles Wick, was tempered by a wonder at how he had mastered the machinery.

The mourning doves, who like me, cannot follow directions, make me think there must be some kind of winged "safety net" at work. From the flying wedge, we know that birds are brilliant organizers. Do they have heavy duty social workers for mourning doves, those beguiling, feathered Magoos who can see neither small objects like sparrows over whom they are constantly stumbling, nor large ones, like cars bearing down on them. Their survival makes you believe in Divine Providence.

My soup kitchen has other usurpers. Pigeons. They belong in parks. Everybody knows that. They give bag ladies a reason for living. The ladies carry feed for pigeons in the shopping bags they trudge around with, along with all their earthly possessions. They don't need to come to my place and confuse the regulars, offering yet another hazard to the mourning doves.

And lately we have had grackles, who cause another kind of irritation. They are ugly. I once had a neighbor, a dedicated nature-lover, who took me aside and confessed that she simply could not like the grackle. I know. They have beady yellow eyes and greasy feathers. I tell myself it isn't their fault, and they get hungry, too.

Poor people are also sometimes unattractive. Sometimes I feel that at the White House they feel about poor people the way I feel about grackles. They wish they would go away. ■

16

Jane Austen

Spirited Away by Jane Austen—July 12, 1981

You will have to excuse me. I've been away. Not out of Washington in person, but in spirit. I can't tell you anything about the shakeup in the Polish Communist Party, the tax cut or the revisionist Marxist theory about Mao Tse-Tung, if that's how you still spell his name.

B-l, Gramm-Latta II, the brouhaha in the city council over lowering the age for sex, the tantrums of John McEnroe, the suit of Alexander Haig—these things swirled around me. I observed them out of the corner of my eye. I was unavoidably detained in Highbury. I was, in short, out to lunch with Jane Austen.

It was not my fault. I have gone as much as a year without taking down the big book with all her novels in it. I save her for big crises, death, war, and the failure of the disposal. What triggered the attack was a letter from an old friend. I will name him: Ned Kenworthy of the *New York Times*. Musing on the mixed blessings of retirement, he said, "At least you have time to weed and read Jane Austen."

It was as if the pusher had sidled up and offered some really great stuff just in from Colombia. I knew a page or two would do me no harm. I picked up the book and opened it at random. I was in the middle of *Emma*. Four hours later, the Sunday papers unread. I had gone back to the beginning and was spending a "quiet, and conversible" evening at Hartfield.

Emma's father is nattering about the madness of marriage. "Ah, my dear," said he, "poor Miss Taylor. It is a grievous business."

Mr. Woodhouse is referring to his daughter's erstwhile governess, who has married very well and is living nearby. Miss Taylor's removal from Hartfield is to him both tragedy and betrayal, even though he sees her every day. He admits "she does come and see us pretty often; but then she is always obliged to go away again."

Emma was just as I had remembered her: officious, fat-headed, high-handed, and a matchmaker of actionable obtuseness. Also a raving snob. She can be cruel, as to poor Miss Bates, the babbling old maid with the elderly mother, who never shuts up. But Jane Austen wants me to like Emma, and so I do. How she accomplishes this I am never quite sure. She slyly puts in nice things about her. Emma is a mimic and she has a sense of humor, although not always about herself. She has a good heart. She is kind to her father and good with her sister's children. She was just coming to about her real feelings for Mr. Knightley, when I turned out the light at four A.M.

Don't ask me the secret of Miss Austen's awesome power to blot out the world for her readers. She is, of course, a marvelous writer, word for word, but that hardly explains it. Her characters—apart from being mainly marriageable with the eternal fascination of their kind—are not people you would especially want to spend time with, except for Mr. Knightley, who, like all Miss Austen's heroes, is a darling. From Mr. Woodhouse, with his open-ended alarms about people catching cold, tiring the horses, or getting married, you would probably flee.

But it's no use arguing. The heat was one hundred, the District City Council was being pelted with criticism about "encouraging sex," and I was free of it all.

I was off to Box Hill for the disastrous picnic, where Frank Churchill and Emma flirted so outrageously and Emma was mean to Miss Bates and Mr. Knightley berates her.

By the time the city council was backing off its sex plan, I was lost in the shock and horror of discovering that Miss Jane Fairfax and Mr. Frank Churchill have been *secretly engaged* for months. The enormity of this transgression is something the contemporary reader cannot appreciate. Since, in Miss Austen's pages, passion finds its ultimate expression in the pressing of an arm, we can assume that nothing irretrievably shameful occurred during their guilty clandestine romance. But the gravity of the thing is attested by all, and the only hope held out is that the love of Miss Fairfax will redeem the depravity of Frank Churchill.

Miss Austen is such a hand with snobs, frauds, climbers, and name droppers, that I cannot help wishing that she could have been turned loose in the Washington social scene. David Stockman, who with his sharp features and graying thatch, somehow suggests the young clergymen she so often accompanies on their search for a living or a wife, would he be someone to intrigue her. The chief justice, Warren Burger, a man of many opinions and florid expression might be a fit subject. But she is concerned only with the fine-grained politics of the drawing room. The "big bow-wow stuff" as Sir Walter Scott deprecatingly described his own writing in comparison to hers, was outside her interest.

I finally finished *Emma*. I am back to matchmaking in the corporate world—mergers instead of marriages. I am with tax cuts instead of cutting remarks. I am with mammoth federal follies instead of the gripping inanities of the morning calls at Highbury.

I am almost resigned. ■

I Prefer Jane Austen's—July 11, 1982

I cannot write about sex and drugs on Capitol Hill, although it is probably my duty. I know nothing, for one thing. For another, I resent the intrusion of scandal on our summertime calm in Washington, which is, except for the weather, delightful.

The mighty and consequential have fled, often mercifully taking their press secretaries with them. It is a time for eating raspberries and watching fireflies—many evening parties move outdoors, and it is possible to tune out the babble about the space shuttle and the flat tax and go undetected.

But there is another reason, and I must be honest about it. I fell in with Jane Austen, the great enemy of incivility and squalor. A friend bequeathed me her collection of books by and about my favorite author. I fought down temptation for a while, thereby, I think, winning Miss Austen's approbation. I turned my attention to the pages and the cocaine addicts. I tried to figure out whether it was seven or seventeen and what was firsthand and what was not. But I thought a few pages of *Mansfield Park* might refresh my mind and sharpen my perceptions of these disgraceful events.

You who love her, too, can guess the rest. Miss Austen took me by the throat in the first sentence. Here it is, and why it hooked me I leave you to judge:

About thirty years ago, Miss Maria Ward of Huntingdon, with only seven thousand pounds, had the good luck to captivate Sir Thomas Bertram of Mansfield Park in the county of Northampton, and to be thereby raised to the rank of a baronet's lady, with all the comforts and consequences of an handsome house and large income.

Six hours later, I turned out the light. I had reluctantly left Fanny Price at her father's wretched house in Portamouth, uncertain of the progress of her beloved cousin Edmund's courtship of Mary Crawford, awaiting with her wonted flutters and nerves the arrival of the post from Mansfield Park, where all were in grievous turmoil caused by the elopement of Henry Crawford and Maria Bertram Rushworth. My interest had not flagged. My eyes had given out.

Early on—I say this without any pretense of rationalizing, a practice of which Miss Austen disapproves—there had been the odd flicker of relevance. For instance, the odious Mrs. Norris, a penny-pinching busybody, who torments the terminally tormentable Fanny, lives in a modest dwelling called the "White House." Fanny herself takes refuge from her frequent alarms, headaches, and shrinking spells in an old schoolroom called the East Room.

Thin, I know. But in the larger sense, I told myself as I galloped along, much applied to what is so murkily unfolding. Miss Austen speaks insistently of the necessity of proper education—and did not Rep. Paul Smith (D-IL) point out long ago the importance of reforming the page school? And Miss Austen reminds us that the most promising characters can be blemished by the wrong associations.

Mary Crawford is a bewitching girl, and as the besotted Edmund says, of a true sweetness of disposition. But early commerce with mercenary and vain people has warped her view.

The scales finally fall from Edmund's eyes when—as he recounts in horror to Fanny—Mary bemoans not so much the evil of what his sister and Henry Crawford have done as the folly of being caught.

"No harsher name than folly given! So voluntarily, so freely, so coolly to canvass it. No reluctance, no horror, no feminine, shall I say, no modest loathing. This is what the world does."

Mary Crawford is a modern character. I can imagine her in

Washington. She is pretty, witty, elegant, and musical—Edmund is enthralled when she plays the harp. She is opinionated and outspoken. She means to marry money, she has no use for clergymen, she tells Edmund, due for the living at Thornton Lacey, to his face.

Edmund is sweet, but a little stuffy. He and Fanny are a pair of prigs clucking over Mary Crawford's cutting, although unassailably accurate remarks about her scoundrel uncle. ("Very wrong, very indecorous," Edmund says.) And Fanny, an early Elsie Dinsmore, can be a trial. I guiltily rejoiced when her cousin Tom called her a "creep-mouse." But Miss Austen stands by her heroines, and when I got up early the next morning to follow Fanny back to Mansfield Park, I decided, as was the author's wish, that she is a dear girl. Edmund's obtuseness is almost canceled by his kindness. I sigh for the lost Crawfords. Fanny, married to Henry, might have become merry. Edmund, with Mary, might have laughed more.

But I do not quarrel with Miss Austen, who, despite her high irony, is unrelenting in her celebration of virtue and right-mindedness. Two properly formed characters deserve each other.

I realize that she would censure me for devouring *Mansfield Park* in one gulp. She deplored unrestrained indulgence. But you can see that this week I am not in a position to judge undetailed excesses on Capitol Hill. How can I, at this time, pass judgment on addicts of any kind? ■

Wisdom, Not Heaving Bosoms—December 16, 1984

Today is her birthday, and it offers an alibi—any will serve—to talk about Jane Austen and her mystery. Why does this novelist, who was born 209 years ago, and who wrote about the English gentry on, as she said, "two inches of ivory," continue to hold readers in thrall?

I can tell you that one account of a Jane Austen Society meeting brought more mail than any other topic discussed in this space.

The Jane Austen cult was the subject of a recent front-page story in the *Wall Street Journal*. Five hundred and sixty thousand copies of her novels have been printed since 1981. This might well amuse the daughter of the rector of Steventon, who offered her first novel, *Sense and Sensibility*, to a publisher with such diffidence that a refusal came back by return of post.

She had a few contemporary admirers. The prince regent of England, for instance, kept a complete set of her novels at all his estates. He never knew when he would require a quick fix of wit or principle. Today, my friend Linda Wertheimer has three sets of Jane Austen, one bound in leather, a second more pedestrian hardback, and a third in pocket books, of a size suitable for being slipped under a notebook at a press conference dealing with say, "revenue-enhancement" or possibly the choice of a new Democratic Party chairman.

Sir Walter Scott was smitten by her. So is Nora Ephron, an utterly contemporary young woman, who reads *Pride and Prejudice* at least once a year, because she is entranced, as any sensible person would be, by Elizabeth Bennett.

Volumes have been written about Jane Austen since she succumbed to an unknown illness in 1817 at the age of forty-one. I have gone through some of them, enjoying them most when she is quoted. Her critics point out that she dodged the hurly-burly of life, averting her eyes from passion, never writing about childbirth, death, poverty, war, or any of life's more wrenching moments. Louis Kronenberger observes that some people find her "tea-tablish." Charlotte Brontë laments the want of the "heaving bosom" in any of her novels.

And yet, new Jane Austen societies are formed every day, and once a year they meet in convention to devote two days to impassioned discussion of one of her six novels. Emma and Anne Elliot and Fanny Price seemed to be in the room.

Maybe it is because she deals with one subject, what is called today "interpersonal relationships," and the eternal theme of young women in search of husbands. Jane Austen recorded the pursuit with fidelity and clarity that has never been matched. The young woman in the singles bar recognizes the truth, if not the circumstances, of her account.

She also describes loneliness, mostly through her delineations of old maids (she was one herself) who must be ingratiating, obliging, never revealing their own feelings in order to be tolerated. Miss Bates of *Emma* is her masterpiece in this line. Miss Bates is forever praising, doing, offering, hoping to be included. Emma makes fun of her, in one of the most memorable scenes of that much-praised novel, and when Mr. Knightley, her mentor—and her future husband—takes her to task, she gives way to bitter tears and turns a corner in her life. The thing about Jane Austen is that she is as decent as she is perceptive.

That's a stab at the "why?" The "how" remains.

She never left the south of England for any length of time, never traveled abroad, never met a writer or even corresponded with one. She had no friends outside her warm family circle, to whom her novels were read aloud with great delight and pride. She had no other sources of encouragement, except the prince regent's librarian, who suggested she write a romance about Saxe-Coburg, and some readers who marveled that she had taken them into another world.

She created those compelling characters and wrote those incomparably fine-grained books on a portable writing desk in the parlor, subject to frequent interruptions from family members, servants, visiting nieces and nephews wanting counsel on courtships and later on novels they were writing. She was warned of their coming by a squeaky door that she forbade to be fixed, and simply thrust the pages out of sight as she rose to greet them.

By today's standard, she had nothing: no word processor, no creative-writing courses, no workshops on the novel, no prospects, if successful, of being sent on publicity tours, autographing parties, and appearances on late-night television shows with Joan Rivers.

All she had was her sharp eye. Her true pen and her sense of what men and women are—and what they ought to be. ■

17

Washington Star

A Paper Worth Saving—July 26, 1981

Don't worry. I'm not going to weep all over you.

I've just lost a newspaper—and so, people of Washington, have you.

But obviously you're not to blame if you're reading this. You've bought the paper, you may even subscribe, for which all of us here thank you.

Don't get me wrong. We're sad. But we're mad, too.

We've lived with uncertainty and the fear of death for several years now. But we could give our anxieties only a certain amount of time.

The great thing about working for a newspaper is that there is always a deadline coming up, and someone else's trouble to check out, It is a most exacting, and diverting, trade.

Colleagues on other papers have treated us like the wives or husbands of a mate who is terminally ill. We couldn't go to a press conference or the congressional galleries without someone drawing us aside and saying, "How is the *Star?*" My answer was a bit sharp, I fear.

"We're alive," I would say before they offered to do the funeral lunch. "It's all we ask."

Now the life-support system has been pulled.

Our most reliable newsroom rumor-monger failed us in the end. Lance Gay, our labor and environmental reporter, who kept a close eye on corporate fauna, this week chronicled only the prolonged absence of the editor at the headquarters of Time Inc., where people we did not know made mysterious decisions about our fate.

If we didn't understand them, they didn't understand us. The gulf between the weekly and the daily, between structure and free form, between reverence and cheekiness, had never been bridged. To us, they were Roman generals, who came to the provinces and found natives who had their own ideas and not the slightest hesitation in expressing them. We acted as if we thought we owned the paper.

That's because, in a way, we did. In 1974, when the angel of death hovered close, we were faced with a choice, take a 20 percent pay cut—euphemistically called a "four-day week"—or let it die.

I remember that black day in December. Young faces, with little children and big mortgages, came to my door. I remember I had to write a story about the Watergate jury, which had offered to sit over Christmas. "Do you think the paper is worth saving?" I would ask to end the lugubrious exchanges.

The answer was always yes.

We tried. We knew about the circulation and the advertising, we certainly knew about the mechanical failures which lengthened our days and shortened our nights. A fiendishly expensive monster called the Logicon, a technological marvel that ate our stories and "went down" on deadline, seemed more of a threat to our survival.

We soldiered on. We had to spell our names to Capitol Hill press aides. We found that people hadn't even read stories about themselves. But we thought somehow we would make it. We were going on the pledge of Time Inc. at the time the empire bought us from Joe Allbritton, the Texas tycoon who bought us from the families which had owned the paper for a hundred years—and who hadn't understood us too well either, although he tried. As we understood it, Time would stand by us, ragged and poor as we were, for five years.

Wednesday night, I went home, planning to write a Sunday column about a small victory for the underdog that had been won in a congressional conference committee on food stamps. Senator John Melcher (D-MT), an unpretentious and dogged man, had been fighting to keep them for people in alcohol and drug abuse programs. The Senate had said no on the floor, but unexpectedly "receded." Naturally, with my background, I am especially interested in rescue stories, and I was all set to write something upbeat.

Thursday morning just before eight, the phone rang. It was Harry Kelly, the national editor. "I want to tell you something. Time is closing the *Star* in two weeks."

Well, there was no time to repine. The Sunday copy has to be in by noon on Thursday. No cosmic thoughts intervened. The space must be filled. I arrived at the building, to see the usual crowd of reporters who have gathered periodically over the years when the ace of spades was supposed to be the next card up.

I told my lucky colleagues, with notebooks and microphones and solvent institutions behind them, that death had come when I had it least in mind. We had not, I might say, at that moment, been officially informed. They asked me why the paper had failed. I said I didn't know. I told them I was proud to work for the *Star* and hadn't wanted to work anyplace else for going on thirty-four years.

People here are asking each other what they're going to do. We all know. Until August 7, we're going to be telling you what goes on in this city and hoping to make you think about the scandal and the outrage of it—the capital of the Western world a one-paper town. ■

It Was Home, and the Luck of My Life—August 7, 1981

W hen I stepped over the threshold of the Sunday department of the *Washington Star* on August 4, 1947, the book editor, Hudson Grunewald, said to me, "God bless you." I knew I was home.

I also acquired a family, a wonderful company of titans and eccentrics—among the latter a nature columnist who was as skittish as the woodland creatures he reported, and an editorial writer who fancied himself a new Lewis Carroll and sent out spidery, faintly sinister Christmas cards of his own creation.

The *Evening Star*, as it was then known, was owned by two families, the Kauffmanns and the Noyeses, who sent their employees to college, helped them buy homes, and sent city kids to summer camp. It was the most successful evening paper in the country.

We were part of a large, untidy, noisy operation that resulted every day in the production of five editions, ending with a splendid Night Final. Chuck Egan was the news editor, a rock-jawed giant who knew everyone's middle initial, as well as knowing who won the Kentucky Derby (and with what time) in 1906. At edition time, his shouts for "copy!" could shake the pillars.

In those golden years, Benjamin M. McKelway was the editor. He presided in a corner office that looked over 11th Street and Pennsylvania Avenue. He was revered for his probity, his dignity, his fairness, and for the whimsy that glinted through his shy sternness.

Once, Newbold Noyes, who was to become editor himself, recounted a conversation he had had with Mr. McKelway, that even now disconcerts me. He had said, "Well, as Mary says, 'What the hell does Ben know about it, anyway?'" It wasn't that I disagreed with this august figure—freedom of expression was rampant—it was that he would think that I ever, under any circumstances, in my private thoughts, call him anything but "Mr. McKelway."

Thorough reporting was demanded, good writing encouraged. Mr. McKelway sent handwritten notes to young strivers.

Unbelievably, we had a strike in 1958. For four icy days, we picketed our beloved home. It ended *Star*-style. Newby Noyes came hurrying up to the entrance, where Fifi Gorska, the teen editor, and I, erstwhile pickets, were standing. He threw his arms around us and said, with a magnanimity that I still marvel at, "Oh, my, you're cold."

The removal to a grim modern building in southeast Washington was a wrench. The new neighbors were hostile and we missed our downtown haunts. But we carried our spirit with us, and we had one of our finest hours there. When John Kennedy died, we gathered together and, with broken hearts, put out papers that showed we had no equals in reporting breaking news.

In the newsroom, people spoke quietly and kindly to each other and worked around the clock. We were professional, we were civil. We were the *Star*.

The mysterious malaise of evening papers began to creep over us. In 1974, the families who had owned the paper for 132 years sold it. The buyer was Joe L. Allbritton, a small and stormy financial genius from Texas, whose background in banks and mortuaries had not quite prepared him for the sloppy, gabby, cheeky people who gave him so freely of their opinions and chatted and gossiped all day long—except when they were hunched over their newfangled writing machines and growled at anyone who interrupted them.

Allbritton brought us Jim Bellows as editor. Bellows was an edgy, gray-eyed wizard who communicated largely in serpentine hand-motions and had total flair. "Fawn not upon the great," the motto of the legendary Ed Lahey, was his. He shook up the town and the "OP," as he always called it.

It was an era of great liveliness—and apprehension. The staff watched nervously the emnity between Allbritton and Bellows. We became accustomed to seeing ourselves referred to as "the financially troubled *Washington Star*." We had one reporter to the OP's six. No matter. We could be the Viet Cong.

Bellows resigned on a cheerless November day in 1977. Would we then die? No, Time Inc. came to save us. We were grateful for a five-year stay of execution. A clash of traditions occurred—between a magazine that speaks with one voice and a daily paper that speaks with many. It was not a happy time.

When the end came on July 23, the people of the newsroom were shocked, orphaned, homeless, bereft. Editors began calling from all over the country, offering openings. People studied cards from Calgary, Cleveland. The awful void appeared. What if they had to leave the business? What if they were banished forever from the newsroom, from the grubby sustaining paradise of camaraderie, cracks, mutual aid, and common effort in a worthy enterprise? The place was swept by successive angers—at Time for closing us down, at the Newspaper Guild for trying to raise us up. Some final, collective judgment had been made in the minds of people who had lived on the brink of extinction for so long. It was over.

People said it was like a death in the family, and it was: telephone calls, telegrams, flowers. But it was worse. It was the death of a family. I consider it the luck of my life that I belonged to it. ■

Light from a Dead Star—August 4, 1991

Last Wednesday, the *Washington Post* said good-bye to its lionhearted editor of twenty-six years, Ben Bradlee. Foreign correspondent Nora Boustany put it best. In a cable from Beirut, she called him "a grand and brave man of the news."

Ten years ago this Wednesday, we said good-bye to the *Washington Star*, a grand and brave newspaper that lost out to the *Post*, among other factors menacing evening papers, and closed its doors after more than 128 years of publication.

Bradlee's departure left many *Post* people feeling vaguely orphaned. The death of the *Star* meant for those who loved it—those for whom it was the newspaper of the heart—exile from a happy valley of kindness and fun.

Bobby Hornig, who covered energy—sometimes under a hair-dryer, her editor complained—is now an NBC producer. She says, "The *Star* was my home; the people were my family."

Since 1981, much has been written about its unique flavor. The late-comers think its incomparable camaraderie and warmth came out of a lifeboat mentality, or something akin to *MASH*, where outnumbered, out-gunned, and eventually doomed people accomplish impossible things.

But for those of us who went there decades earlier, when the *Evening Star* owned the town, it was just as lovely a place to work, a garden of eccentrics, wits, and strong wills, where copy boys read the *Iliad* in the original Greek and others were not allowed to take themselves seriously.

There was a pervasive benevolence, not the slightest corporate overlay and—wonderfully, considering it was owned and often edited by members of three families—no caste system. The generosity of finan-cial plans for the employees and sponsorship of summer camps for poor District children carried over into the newsroom. Hard-pressed editors—and with five editions a day, they always were—assumed that they must teach the young. Patiently, or sometimes profanely, they took them in hand. There was no end of encouragement or of freedom of speech. Anyone who could speak voiced opinions about how the paper was being run; anyone who could write could get a byline.

Those who did it well could expect a handwritten note from Benjamin M. McKelway, the editor.

He was an immensely dignified man, with a delightful, covert sense of humor, and democratic to the bone. He gave a stupendous Christmas party every year, and everyone in the newsroom—copy aides, tele-phone operators, secretaries—was included. We sang a lot. In his quiet way, Mr. McKelway liked to harmonize. All the Noyes boys of the own-ing family had voices, and Newby played the piano by ear.

In the old days in the picturesque building on the corner of 11th Street and Pennsylvania Avenue, we partied at the Chicken Hut across the street. These were heroic, hilarious affairs, held on the slightest pretext. The high point for me was a bullfight pas de deux performed by Dottie

Biehlman, the managing editor's secretary, and John Horan, one of our finest photographers. It was the funniest thing I ever saw until Rex Harrison and Julie Andrews did it in *My Fair Lady* to "The Rain in Spain."

We worked hard, too. You bet we did. When Newby Noyes was national editor, something strenuous and demanding was afoot. It was during the horrendous McCarthy years. One day, early, he got a tip that McCarthy's chief counsel had been a socialist in his youth—stop-the-press stuff in those days. He deployed his staff of fourteen across the city. They got the story—not just the fact of the counsel's radical past but his resignation—in time for the Night Final.

Underneath the noisy, frantic activity, through the shouting matches about leads and heads that raged between Chuck Egan, the burly, erudite news editor, and slot editor Earl "Tiger Ass" Heap, ran a river of risibility. The quips and gibes never stopped. Every fatuous headline or pompous lead was seized upon and nailed to the bulletin board with appropriate commentary.

Self-importance was regarded as the enemy within. One editor, William Hill, who tried to swim against the tide, issued edicts from time to time. Hardly had they been posted, when someone carefully changed the period after his "I." to a comma.

We had a strike once. About money, I think. Our hearts were not in it. At our Chicken Hut strike headquarters, our preposterously mild-mannered national editor, John Cassady, presided over the cold cuts, and John Stepp, a quizzical metro reporter, massaged the frozen feet of lady pickets.

When it was over, Newby Noyes, who by now was executive editor, came to greet us. Fifi Gorska and I threw our arms around him. "My, but you're cold," he exclaimed. Considering what we had cost him in revenue and trouble, it was totally unwarranted solicitude. There was a lot of that at the *Star*. ■

18

Kissinger

White House Cowboy—November 26, 1972

We are all deeply in the debt of Oriana Fallaci, the brilliant and formidable Italian journalist who interviewed Henry Kissinger on November 4 for *L'Europeo*.

Through Miss Fallaci, we have learned that deep in the heart of the president's national security adviser, there lives a secret cowboy.

Nobody ever thought if you scratched Henry Kissinger, you would get John Wayne, but it's there in black and white, and the State Department, which has been waiting for just such a moment, has circulated the transcript around the world.

Miss Fallaci is an ornament to her trade, and the text of the encounter should be required reading in all journalism courses. She ran the show from start to finish.

He said he did not want to talk about Vietnam. She did and asked him five questions. She taxed him about not signing the peace treaty, informed him he was a cold mathematician, and finished up by telling him he was the worst subject she ever met.

Still, all pales beside her discovery that Kissinger does not model himself after James Bond, the cinematic parallel her innocent American colleagues had always cited, but after John Wayne and other riders of the trail.

She disdained the Metternich-Machiavelli axis, too. She smelled the smoke of campfires. Abruptly in midcourse, she changed direction. Having failed to bait him about war and peace, she asked the question no man can resist: How come you're so wonderful?

Kissinger was coy at the beginning: I'm not going to tell you. But he was hooked, and you could see him thrashing: "What do you think?" he asked.

Miss Fallaci replied rather dryly that she supposed it was his successes—China and all that.

Kissinger could hold out no longer. China had gone well, yes, but that was not the principal reason.

"Yes, I'll tell you," he said. "The main point comes from the fact that I have always acted alone. The Americans love this immensely. The Americans love the cowboy who leads the wagon train alone on his horse, the cowboy who comes into the town all alone with his horse, and nothing else, not even a gun . . ."

Hi-yo, Silver.

If a middle-aged Harvard professor who wears a vest and glasses, speaks with a German accent, has a double chin, a staff of a hundred, a chauffeured limousine, a jet always at the ready, two Secret Servicemen, and no horse, wants to think of himself as a lonesome cowboy, it's a free country, isn't it?

In due course, the pollsters will fan out around the nation and bring back a poll telling us of the percentage of Americans who do think of him as a cowboy, do not think of him as a cowboy, or have no opinion.

Where did the idea begin? Did people come up to him at Georgetown dinner parties and say, "Say, pardner, shall we rustle up a little grub"? Or maybe he said to them, "I think I've got me a deal with them varmints."

One of the impediments to the view of him loping into the sunset humming "Home on the Range" is, of course, his reputation as a lady's man. Cowboys kiss their horses. Your more sociable, ordinary lonesome cowboy—Henry Fonda, James Stewart, even John Wayne—is usually fiddling with his hat and scratching his boot in the dust, saying, "Aw, shucks, Ma'am, I cain't talk purty, but I shore do wish . . ."

Miss Fallaci comes to the rescue here. She confronts Kissinger with his "playboy" fame and Kissinger tells her women are just a "hobby" with him—the equivalent of whittling in the corral, let's say. Big ranchers like Chou En-lai and Mao Tse-tung were reassured that he was no wooden Indian. He was just doing it for the country.

It's doubtful that any of the Orientals he's been hanging around with lately put the ten-gallon hat into his head.

No, the trail leads to the Oval Room. The leader of the Western world is also the No. 1 Western movie fan in the nation. The president told us how he feels about John Wayne and the horse opera generally in August

1970, after he had seen *Chisum*, which he loved. He went on about it at some length.

Kissinger, who has read Machiavelli and knows about pleasing the prince, doubtless registered this fondness. The president also gave a revealing interview himself recently, in which he spoke of the average American as "a child in the family."

Maybe it all began one morning when the president said, "Say, Henry, did you know I'm a secret father figure?"

Kissinger probably replied, "Oh, that's nothing. I'm a secret cowboy." ■

What's Good for Kissinger Is Good—April 22, 1975

It is too late to save Saigon, but not too late to save Henry Kissinger. General Frederick Weyand, who has been there, told the House Appropriations Committee that the South Vietnamese capital is "indefensible." The secretary of state followed him to the stand, however, and explained how his reputation can still be evacuated from the doomed city.

All that is required is for Congress to vote some money—any amount will do—and Henry Kissinger can again walk tall in the world, having proved once again that when he makes a promise, the United States keeps it.

Chairman George Mahon rather quizzically noted that there was "some question" of whether we could get the money over there in time. Also there is some question, now that Nguyen Van Thieu has gone, as to who would be at the presidential palace to sign for it. Possibly it would be the first check in history made out to "To Whom It May Concern."

Kissinger's thesis requires vast numbers of people to enter the Disney World of U.S. policy in Indochina. The North Vietnamese are supposed to stop in their tracks at this new manifestation of White House-congressional unity and presumably plead for negotiations.

The South Vietnamese army, buoyed by new evidence of America's concern, will assume "control" of the situation; the Americans will be safely evacuated, and history will say according to Henry Kissinger, that "we at least will have done our best."

The secretary of state came as a beggar to Congress. But the glint of a dagger showed through his rags. If they reject his calls for alms, he will turn on them and stab them for the loss of his credibility.

The members were, for the most part, willing to go along with him. It is their habit. The $150 billion we have sent over the years, passed through them, and now, when all is lost, they are willing to kick in a little bit more. Better to be accused of having lost their reason and Vietnam than to be charged with being beastly to Kissinger.

The secretary's arrival caused the usual commotion. He was surrounded by Secret Service men, briefcase-bearers, folder-holders and a small army of frenzied photographers. General Weyand was hastily excused, and Chairman Mahon left his seat to escort Kissinger to the witness chair.

The members, always cowed and wistful in the presence of authentic celebrity, listened to him respectfully as he explained his determination "to avoid the impression the U.S. is not capable of mastering events."

Even the hawks and domino-players, however, occasionally strayed into the suburbs of reality during the presentation of his scenario. The secretary pushed them back with unintelligible answers.

One of them said, "I would really like to help you, but I don't know what these words mean."

Another, having perceived unassisted that the evacuation of Americans by the entire U.S. Air Force was not that vast a maneuver, asked finally in bewilderment, "You are saying the number of people evacuated would be dependent on the amount of money we voted?"

Kissinger rejoined, "No one has blackmailed us."

Nobody asked Kissinger if he was trying to blackmail Congress. But the fear of being blamed is uppermost in many minds.

If Henry Kissinger still wants to play with mirrors, they can at least provide an audience. They are not illusion-destroyers. He has pulled the wool over their eyes on Vietnam for six years now, and if they abandon him now, it would be a reflection on them.

What is money after all? Some $338 million, which in all likelihood never will be dispatched, is a small amount to make Henry Kissinger feel better. They can go home and tell their people they were trying to avert a battle over Saigon, another of the murky objectives he offered them, and where's the harm?

They went into executive session and voted the trifling sum that may convince the world we are still standing with our allies but will certainly show that one committee of Congress is not going to betray Henry Kissinger in his hour of what he called "maximum travail."

The principle of foreign policy has been reaffirmed. What's good for Henry Kissinger is good for the United States. The two are still, as he says about American credibility, "indivisible" for the time being any way. ■

Kissinger: Incredible Shrinking Cabinet Man
—August 24, 1976

The days of wine and roses are over for Henry Kissinger.

His job is safe until after the election, but the thrill is gone. After a long run as the most lionized foreign policy figure in history, he is about to have the star taken off his dressing room door. He has become just another problem cabinet officer, one of the many embarrassments Gerald Ford is taking into a difficult campaign.

Aleksandr Solzhenitsyn is the official new foreign policy idol of the Republican Party. In its "morality in foreign policy" plank—which was uncontested by the president—Solzhenitsyn is acclaimed as "that great beacon of human courage and morality." Kissinger is not mentioned.

Nor did he figure in the president's acceptance speech. Kissinger was almost as much a forgotten man as his first patron, Richard Nixon. Solzhenitsyn was the stick used to beat him. The right-wingers will never forget that it was Kissinger who prevailed upon the president to snub the bearded Russian genius during his capital visit last year.

Kissinger can thank Ronald Reagan's perfervid followers for a period of grace as secretary of state. His dismissal now would signal abject surrender to the right. The foreign policy plank, which says in effect that the Republicans have done nothing right in the past two years, was read as appeasement on the president's part and will doubtless be thrown up to him by Jimmy Carter in the debates to come.

Kissinger's response was "Nya, nya, they didn't hurt me."

But when Ronald Reagan went down, he intended to take Kissinger with him. In his brief and highly effective valedictory, he took note of the difference between the Republican and Democratic platforms, and the lost legions cheered his warnings about "freedom," of which Kissinger, author of détente, agent of the Helsinki Pact, is the enemy.

On his entrance into the hall on the last night—some Ford men frankly hoped he wouldn't show up at all—Kissinger was booed. Four years ago, in Miami, he had been onstage throughout, taking curtain calls in President Nixon's box.

Two years ago, life without the doctor was unthinkable. When he had his tantrum in Salzburg—he was being closely questioned about wire-tapping—and threatened to take his ball and bat and go home, the Senate in an agony of remorse, fell to his knees and begged him to stay.

Today, if he would so much as hint at resignation, he would be taken up before he could complete the sentence.

He has been campaigning for the past six months, touring the provinces with his enormous entourage, hoping, apparently, to convince the White House of his continued box-office appeal.

A few in the president's inner circle profess to believe that Kissinger might still be an asset in the general election. But Ronald Reagan, on his way back to California last Friday, let it be known that the unity he pledged on the last night of the convention was conditional. If there is a return to what he called "foreign policy as usual," he will sound the alarm for his followers.

Henry Kissinger without a high profile is Cyrano de Bergerac without his nose. What will he do during the campaign? He cannot bear to be out of the limelight, and has already shown a powerful inclination to take a hand in political affairs—as when just before the Democratic convention he announced that Jimmy Carter's views on foreign policy were "compatible" with Gerald Ford's, which was to say, of course, Henry Kissinger's.

It was his dovishness on Panama that did Kissinger in with the right. He wants to negotiate. Ronald Reagan was ready to fight. Kissinger for years presented himself as an authority on conservatives. When he first came to town he spent much time warning war critics that they must not press Richard Nixon too hard to put an end to Vietnam, because a premature conclusion would inflame the conservatives and set them to tearing the country apart. As it happened, his theory was never tested, because the war was continued through the 1972 election.

He did not begin to lose the left until the Cyprus crisis when congressmen with Greek constituencies began to question his infallibility. And he failed to anticipate the rage of the right on Helsinki, détente, and Panama. It was Reagan's gentlemanly personal decision not to mention Kissinger by name in the foreign policy plank that rejected the Kissinger foreign policy.

If Kissinger had been named, Gerald Ford would have had no choice but to fight. And he might have won. But he was afraid the right wing would resign from the party if it lost another round so soon after its defeat on Rule 16c, Reagan's attempt to make him cough up his vice-presidential choice ahead of schedule.

So, in the face of anguished cries from moderate Republicans, the president decided to pretend that someone else had been responsible for the grievances detailed in the plank. His people are saying that platforms don't matter. But what happened in Kansas City says quite clearly that Henry Kissinger doesn't matter, either. ■

Kissinger for Christmas—December 5, 2002

You probably thought you'd never see the day when George I's record for bizarre personnel picks might be challenged, but Pater Bush has been outdone by his own son. George W.'s choice of Henry Kissinger to lead the probe into what went on before 9/11 is right up there with Dad's big-time howlers: Vice President Dan Quayle and Supreme Court Justice Clarence Thomas. In both cases, George I thought he had pulled a fast one. Quayle would melt female voters and show youth how cool Bush really was. Thomas was irresistible: Democrats, no matter how repelled by his views, would not dare vote against a black nominee.

With Kissinger, we have again the Grand Canyon–size discrepancy between man and job. Kissinger is a brilliant diplomat devoted to asserting his country's power—and his own. He helped write some of the darkest chapters in American history: The prolonging of the Vietnam War included the shameless exploitation of U.S. POWs as the alibi for covering a retreat that had been inevitable for four years. The subversion of Chile's elected Socialist government led to more rage, tears, and deaths that are not yet counted. In Central America, of course, Kissinger was on the wrong side.

From George W. Bush's point of view, he's ideal. It's not just that Kissinger the power-lover guarantees exoneration for the powerful. He shares Bush's view that 9/11 was all Bill Clinton's fault. He loves secrets;

he loves bombs—he was proud of the "secret" bombing of Cambodia. He thinks leakers should be crushed. Like the president, he thinks it's unpatriotic to question the government.

Bush resisted the creation of a commission that would go poking around into what he knew and when about the worst domestic disaster since the Civil War. The victims' families insisted on trying to find out why more than three thousand Americans were killed that bright September morning. Bush thought to silence them with a celebrity. Some who would have preferred truth spoke longingly of Warren Rudman or Rudolph Giuliani as top sleuths. Bush knew Kissinger would outrage the left, which regards him as a war criminal—but with his constituency, that's fun. He feared no Democratic backlash; their mantra is the beatitude "Blessed are the meek, for they shall inherit the Earth."

Optimists point out that no one knows the back alleys of bureaucracy better or is more able to sniff out, from long practice thereof, skulduggery at government agencies. Others take comfort in the thought of "balance" being achieved by the righteous presence of former senator George Mitchell. But Mitchell is vice chairman, not cochairman, and in any competition for the spotlight, Kissinger has to be the favorite.

Before it's over, Mitchell may come to think of his long negotiations with the obdurate Northern Irish as a walk in the park by comparison. Kissinger will effortlessly elbow him aside. This was a man who, while the Vietnam War raged on, conned Harvard and Hollywood with tales of how lucky they were that he was in the Oval Office holding back the paranoid incumbent.

In 1974, when a rookie reporter at a State Department briefing had the temerity to ask Kissinger whether he would get a lawyer to represent him in legal difficulties arising from his indiscriminate White House wiretapping, Kissinger threw a fit and had to be calmed down by passage of a Senate resolution declaring him to be wonderful. It's an old tale, but cautionary for anyone dreaming of Dr. K as a humble teammate.

Kissinger has always had a doting press corps to call on. It will be interesting to see whether he has lost his touch during his long sojourn among the corporations that pay him fortunes to front for them. In Washington, they gushed about him and faithfully reported his conquests of starlets and tycoons and his midnight dashes from Georgetown dinner parties to Beijing. The doctor will be spared the tedium of listing his clients. It's only a part-time job, the White House says.

Kissinger has never been called to account for duplicitous activities. Other Republican policymakers have, and Bush appreciates them. Robert E. White, former ambassador to El Salvador, writes in a recent issue of *Commonweal* of a pattern of hiring people, some of them lawbreakers, for high posts in the administration. Elliott "Better Dead than Red" Abrams in the National Security Council is an example. John Poindexter of Iran-Contra infamy probably is wiretapping us all legally in his Pentagon Information Awareness Program. The administration is laced with human rights violators. There's nothing of the reeducation camp about it. The Bushies approve of what they did. Kissinger will fit right in.

We mustn't scratch our heads as to why Bush chose him. There is a natural affinity between a president who wants a war for Christmas and an appointee who was the coauthor of the Christmas bombing of Hanoi. ∎

19

John Adams

Dear John, This Will Never Reach You.
—Abigail

—April 25, 1976

It is entirely possible that some American wife will write to her husband as stirring and vivid an account of the Bicentennial as Abigail Adams wrote to John Adams of the first Fourth of July—and be as uncertain that he will receive her letter.

The letters of John and Abigail Adams are national treasures, particularly as assembled in a new Bicentennial edition with homely details and Abigail's atrocious spelling restored. For today's reader, the recurring expressions of concern about their arrival constitute a poignant bond.

"I generally endeavor to write you once a week, if my letters do not reach you, 'tis owing to the neglect of the post," wrote John to Abigail during one of their frequent, painful separations in the cause of liberty.

"I am very sorry I did not know of Mr. Carey's going," wrote Abigail from Braintree to John in Philadelphia, where he was attending the Continental Congress. "It would have been so good an opportunity to have sent this as I lament of."

Modern letter writers are not yet reduced to finding friends to carry their letters, but the official attitude seems to be, they better consider it.

The Adamses, who sacrificed so much and dreamed great dreams of the future, must have envisioned a day of prompt and ungrudging delivery of the mail. It seems further off than ever. National policy appears to be that postal service is a luxury, not a right. Letter writing is subtly discouraged. Good citizens will use the telephone.

If it had been invented in their day, the Adamses, who were enduringly in love, might have used long distance. "Next to conversation with you, correspondence is the greatest Pleasure in the world," John Adams wrote, and "Your letters are a Cordial to the Heart."

Abigail received his with tears of gratitude, and in low moments was wont to retire, and read over the whole file, weeping.

It was unlucky for them and lucky for us that they were so often apart. They were a remarkable pair, their passion for each other matched by their passionate patriotism.

"'Tis vain to repine," wrote Abigail. "I hope the publick will reap what I sacrifice."

She was a spectacular woman, high minded, warmhearted, practical, witty, a mother, manager, feminist, war correspondent and, as her husband remarked, "a statesman." She was also a born writer.

Her qualities are most affectingly displayed in a letter she wrote on the birth of a stillborn daughter. She tells him about the beauty of the child and the inevitability of its death—all that he must know, but no more than he can bear— "in a letter which may possibly fall into the Hands of some unfealing Ruffian." She assures him of her own good condition.

John Adams prized his wife. "You are really brave, my dear," he wrote, "You are an Heroine." He acknowledged her superior gifts: "I really think that your Letters are much better worth preserving than mine."

He had great descriptive powers, if not her totally animating pen. A more inhibited Yankee, he had the embarrassment of having one of his letters from Philadelphia with critical comments about his congressional colleagues intercepted and published. He was thereafter more guarded. When he was sent to Paris as aide to Benjamin Franklin, the vagaries of the domestic post were aggravated by the peril of shipwreck, piracy, and spies. His formal communication evoked an impassioned reproach from his wife:

"By Heaven if you could you would have changed Hearts with some frozen Laplander or made a voyage to a region that has chilld [sic] every Drop of your Blood."

She went on writing, of course. "I apprehend that this will never reach you yet this apprehension shall not prevent my writing by every opportunity."

It isn't just "apprehension" that keeps people from taking pen in hand these days. Letter writing has gone out of style, and you can't entirely blame the postal service for that. The telephone did to letter

writing what television has done to reading. It's sad for future generations of historians, who will not have the kind of thing that the Adamses
wrote down for each other—and us. ■

Adams Family Values—July 4, 1993

John Adams, our second president, looked to be a rather dour sort,
but he was a great believer in "publick happiness."

Hear how he thought we should celebrate the anniversary of the
Declaration of Independence: "It ought to be commemorated, as the
Day of Deliverance by solemn Acts of Devotion to God Almighty. It
ought to be solemnized with Pomp and Parade, with Shews [sic],
Games, Sports, Guns, Bells, Bonfires, and illumination from one End of
this Continent to the other from this Time forward forever more."

Adams, who was then a member of the Continental Congress,
wrote these instructions to future generations in a letter to his wife,
Abigail, his "Portia," his "Diana," his "dearest friend."

Their copious exchanges have been gathered up and published in
The Book of Abigail and John, which should be obligatory reading for
this holiday weekend. This colonial pair are Mr. and Mrs. Fourth of
July. They were two high-minded Yankees who were passionately in
love with each other and who endured cruel separations for the country that was struggling to be born. His most vivid impressions and
most intimate thoughts had to be evasively couched. There was
always the fear that his letters would fall into British hands and be
published for the world's ridicule. She was in agony for fifteen years
of her life trying to find a conveyance for her outpourings of loneliness and longing. When he was sent to France and Holland to win
recognition for the tremulous new United States, the problem was
exacerbated by the fear that the vessels chosen for transport would
be seized or sunk.

When he was still in the same country—mostly in Philadelphia,
where the Congress met—she bore up quite well. She was sustained
by her duty, by her feelings for posterity. In 1782, after years of
absence and many letterless months, she was asked if she would
have consented to her husband's going had she known the extent of
the privations.

Like a Roman matron, she replied: "I feel a pleasure in being able to sacrifice my selfish passions to the general good and in imitating the example which has taught me to consider myself and family but as the small dust of the balance when compaired [sic] with the great community."

She complained only when he failed to assure her of his love in sufficiently warm terms. In a letter from Braintree, in 1778, she railed at him. "By Heaven, if you could you would have changed Hearts with some frozen Laplander or made a voyage to a region that has chilld [sic] every Drop of your Blood."

He replied in exasperation: "For Heavens Sake, my dear, dont [sic] indulge a Thought that it is possible for me to neglect, or forget all that is dear to me in this World."

And later: "If you write me in this style I shall leave off writing intirely [sic], it kills me. Can Professions of Esteem be Wanting from me to you? Can protestations of affection be necessary?"

What saved the Adamses was patriotism. For him, it overcame ill health, a capricious Congress, the backbiting of his contemporaries, and the sight of lesser men passing him by in wealth and fame. For the sake of their country, she held fort in Braintree, coping with balky help, baffling accounts, refugees from Boston fleeing the redcoats, and being a single parent to their four children. (John provided a stream of exhortations to instill Virtue and Industry in them and teach them French.)

How well she performed is history. Her son John Quincy Adams not only followed his father as the sixth president; after he left the White House, he humbly entered the House of Representatives and served nobly. Generations of overachieving Adamses followed.

For those demanding readers who cannot be satisfied by either a chronicle of enduring married love, Puritan style, or colonial history close up, there are some charmingly relevant references from the high-flown pair.

John's description of the Continental Congress would apply equally to the contemporary spectacle of congressional budget "reconciliation": "The Fidgets, the Whims, the Caprice, the Vanity."

Abigail records the complaints of tax-averse citizens in terms right off today's talk shows. She is most renowned as a feminist before her time. She abjures "him whom my Heart esteems above all earthly things" to "remember the ladies." She bewails the absence of female education; she has never been to school. She is, however, learned in her way, if not in spelling and punctuation. She is a born writer, and she has yards of poetry for each crisis.

You can observe the Fourth no better than by reading about her and her love. ■

20

Christmas

Merry MXmas
—December 19, 1982

If you think about the MX—and how could you not?—think about it as a Christmas missile.

It isn't just its seasonal name—"Peacekeeper"—or even that it's what the president wants most from Santa.

Start with its plight. We all know that the basing mode was a terrific problem with the Nativity. Joseph and Mary were turned away from dense-packed hotels in Bethlehem, and had to improvise. The Pentagon planners could be humming "Away in a Manger" as, back at the drawing board, they try to find a crib for MX's bed.

When you are talking homelessness—and many people who live in their cars were doing that on Capitol Hill this week—you are talking Peacekeeper. It's been evicted from thirty-four proposed dwellings already.

I wonder if the Joint Chiefs have applied to the Salvation Army. It has an excellent shelter program.

I first knew that MX had Noel written all over it the day I listened to the president's science adviser, Dr. George A. Keyworth, at the Senate Armed Services Committee. He was talking, I think, about the timers Soviet missiles have. He mentioned "terminal homing."

Isn't that a lovely phrase? Isn't it just another way of saying, "I'll be home for Christmas?"

I don't know exactly what "terminal homing" means on a Soviet ICBM as it speeds toward its rendezvous with our warheads in Wyoming. But "terminal homing" is what is going on all around us now—people jamming terminals, eagerly undertaking fatiguing travel just to be present in the family circle around the fireside.

Another beautiful, pastoral phrase comes up in Peacekeeper terminology. George Wilson, who has mastered its special vocabulary, wrote the other day about "low-grazing Soviet missiles."

Makes them sound like sheep, doesn't it? Puts you in mind of the manger, the shepherds—"the cattle are lowing"—the whole scene.

The nice thing is that the sheep missiles may skip off the target like flat stones skittering across a pond. That means that our MX, tucked deep in its coffin, would be secure. The low-grazers wouldn't hit Wyoming, although they might blow up California when they stop skittering. But Christmas is a time to forget workaday details of that nature.

The air force talks about a "pathfinder missile" which makes you want to go right out and deck the halls.

The context, in Pentagon testimony, may be a bit grisly, but don't go away.

"The detonation [of the Soviet missile] raises ejecta, which consists of large boulders, some of them larger than a Volkswagen, that are thrown up and ejected out of the crater for some significant distances."

The Pathfinder acts as an escort for the Peacekeeper, as it sets out on its retaliatory strike at Moscow. It will go first "to determine if a safe dust and debris environment existed after the MX field has been attacked."

The Pathfinder is a pretty parallel to the Star of Bethlehem, which guided the wise men. The wise men, the first Christmas shoppers, are admirable in many ways. On hearing of the birth of the Prince of Peace, they saddled up and set forth. Some of us wish they had mislaid the gifts, as us addled types do so often at this time of year, but that is another matter.

I hope the president is not too chagrined that the MX will not, after all, be under his tree. Christmas, for all its joys, can be a time of disappointments. He should think of the woman, dreaming of a diamond drop, who is gifted with a selection of imported cheese; of the man who wants a video game, who finds a snow shovel in his stocking.

Yes, it is a time of wassailing, homing, and giggling under the mistletoe. But it is also a time when the "window of vulnerability" in human affairs is wide open. Christmas cards bring greetings, but how often, too, tidings of death, divorce, or the defection of a child to a cult requiring temple-charring in Sri Lanka. Such news inevitably arrives just as you have mailed off your certitude of the recipient's well deserved earthly joys. Composing the message of condolence cuts seriously into resting merry, gentlemen.

Come to think of it, maybe the Pentagon planners should abandon their search for a new basing mode and go to work on some kind of Christmas card synchronization scheme: people in the first half of the alphabet to mail on a certain date, while M to Z holds off until later. That way, 50 percent of the population could reply rationally to its cards. Next year, the order could be reversed. OK, it's not perfect, but haven't we been saying what is?

Betimes, I wish you an MX. That's short for "Merry Xmas," which is, the president tells us, all that Peacekeeper was trying to say. ∎

A Christmas Card from Prince Bandar
—December 16, 1990

What may be the season's most bizarre Christmas card comes from Prince Bandar, the ambassador of Saudi Arabia. On the outside there is a depiction of two crossed scimitars and a palm tree. Inside, in Arabic and English, is a description of the birth of Christ from the Koran.

It begins, "Behold, the angels said 'O Mary, God giveth thee glad tidings of a Word from him; His name will be Christ Jesus, the son of Mary.'"

Very nice, you say, a Muslim, getting into the spirit of things, proving the tolerance of Islam, which acknowledges another religion.

Trouble is, though, that while in principle, Islam accepts Christianity—and Judaism, too—you better not try to practice either inside the Saudi borders.

And our American soldiers, who are waiting in the sand to defend Prince Bandar's country and who want to celebrate the central event on the Christian calendar, are required to do so "discreetly." We mustn't upset the Saudis, you see, while we are saving them.

In a recent edition of the *Boston Globe*, Cohn Nickerson reports that a twenty-two-year-old Jewish medic was discouraged from observing Hanukkah by lighting a candle. It wasn't a good idea, she was told, from the fire-protection point of view. Then Muslim "sensitivities" were cited.

Oh, come on. And what's this about service chaplains having to hide their crosses or Stars of David? And being called "morale officers?" Are the Saudis really all that sensitive? They hang, stone, and behead law-breakers, which suggests a certain hardness of spirit. They regard apostasy as a capital offense.

Does anyone think the Saudis, if they found out that Hanukkah services were being held or mass being said out in the open, would call us in and expel us from their country? And start shopping around for some other nation to rescue them from the jaws of Saddam Hussein?

It is good, in a way, that we have taken so much time and trouble to learn Saudi ways and to honor them, right down to striking the Stars and Stripes at local request. It's the opposite of what we did in Vietnam, which was to ride roughshod over local customs and to know apparently as little as possible about the Vietnamese culture and economy.

North Vietnamese talk sadly about GIs who—for sport—shot water buffalo, the sole support of many peasant families, or destroyed centuries-old Buddhist temples because statues of Buddha with a reverse swastika medallion on his chest suggested Nazi sympathies.

Now we seem to have gone too far the other way. If Muslims have such hair-trigger religious sensitivity, we should tell them about our own religious sensitivity—especially our supersensitivity to freedom of worship, a pillar of our Constitution and our Republic.

Our poor servicemen and women are bearing the brunt of the involvement with these touchy people. They can't have beer, a deprivation that admittedly has a positive side: The authorities report a sharp decline in accidents and fights since mandatory temperance went into effect. They can't have a traditional Bob Hope show or troupes with dancers in them. Even the quieter consolations of religion seem to be questioned. No one else has been asked to sacrifice much of anything.

Nor has anyone yet given an entirely satisfactory answer to the question of why our troops are there, either. They know they will not be fighting for democratic values. Saudi Arabia is a feudal monarchy and Kuwait, which George Bush has vowed to liberate, is an emirate and no better. They have to settle on possibly fighting, and possibly dying, to deter aggression—while understanding they might not be doing it if it weren't for oil.

The subject of who is on our side in this confrontation does not bear close examination. Syria, a conspicuous Arab ally, is a terrorist nation that is widely, suspected of blowing up 241 marines in Lebanon. George Bush recently received a Chinese official at the White House because the Beijing government, which has begun a new crackdown on dissidents, voted for our war resolution in the United Nations.

Nobody wants to say that petroleum is the reason that hundreds of thousands of Americans will spend Christmas far from families, far from children. Let us hope, by the way, for a more humane policy regarding babies who have both parents in uniform and in the desert. We see soldier-couples turning over infants to grandparents. Is it a function of feminism that the woman insists on absolute equality of treatment? But if she can't stay home, shouldn't he? America has enough problems with parentless children.

Nobody at home has been asked to give up anything, not so much as a teaspoon of gas for their cars. The word "conservation" is never heard. Senator Jay Rockefeller (D-WV) is pushing hard for a federal subsidy of alternate fuels, but people are still asking if he should. We would rather fight than switch on oil. ■

Swamped by the Yuletide—December 19, 1993

Christmas has long been the festival for the competent here on earth. Recently, our pitiless government put on a demonstration of how it's the same in the stratosphere. The crew sent up to fit the Hubble telescope with a new pair of glasses was doing home repair in outer space, making us manually hampered feel more inadequate than ever.

I am talking about people who cannot open a package of Fig Newtons or an umbrella without help, and who can have trouble just tuning in the radio. In other words, people like myself. When I heard on the radio astronauts telling mission control that they couldn't get the door closed, I was sure that all was lost. But they kicked it and jimmied it, and sure enough, it closed, as it never would for me.

I went back to writing Christmas cards that I am sure will not arrive in time. Not only do I not know how much it costs to get a card to India, I don't know even where the stamps are.

I have friends (and you do, too, I bet) who sail through it all in triumph. They tell you, if you're crazy enough to ask, that they "picked up" their presents during the summer while on vacation, had wrapped them all by Labor Day, and mailed them on Thanksgiving. As for cards, they ordered them months ago. They are engraved, stamped, and sealed. Smug, are they? You bet.

They soak up the stress of the season. The holidays give them further opportunity to show off their organizational skills, their control of their environment and their blood pressure. Not for them the panic, the dash, the unlimited opportunities for losing, dropping, and forgetting that the lifelong klutz experiences in the mall—leaving the charge card at the cash desk, picking up the wrong package, or buying again the selfsame wool scarf you ended up not sending last year.

The holiday belongs to people who set out to Christmas parties in Virginia and cross the river without a tremor and actually get where they want to go. They do not end up whimpering by a white picket fence in the middle of hunt country, having traversed the highway three times in hopeless pursuit of "the sharp left you can't miss" that would carry you home.

The Christmas tree holds no terror for them. They whittle the trunk as if it were a carrot, pop it into the stand, juggle strings of lights, know everything about switches, transformers, and balky bulbs. We, the deftness-disadvantaged, cower at the edges, fingering ornaments we will inevitably hang in unsuitable locations.

For the rest of us, thanks to the way the Christmas present and card complex has grown and solidified in our lives, there is little hope of resting merry, or, for that matter resting at all. We who are unequal to life and sink during the Yuletide find that what counts at Christmas is the ability to tie a bow, and to stand in line at the post office without giving way to the gloom and resignation that hangs so heavy in the air, especially when the woman in front of you is trying to send a registered letter to Bangladesh.

What makes it worse is knowing we're supposed to be having a good time. We feel gypped.

Excuse me. I have just committed a political incorrectness. As life becomes more violent in the United States we are under heavy pressure to make our language as pallid as possible. "Gypped" is a no-no, according to the *Los Angeles Times* correctness guide. Gypsies would be offended. How do they know? Was a poll conducted? Is there a National

267

Association of Gypsies—could there be a finer acronym than NAG?—in the swelling ranks of professional umbrage-takers?

In the holiday gloom, I must report a bright spot. The Clintons turn out to be committed but not confrontational Christmas people. Herself is baking cookies instead of policy, and she has transformed the White House into a place of radiant light and warmth. She and her husband have people in to see the place every night—the glorious Blue Room tree with ornaments from every state. East Room with red velvet, gold-edge bows, and garlands and beads and greens everywhere. It is a show that leaves the beholder free of guilt and envy. The Clintons have so much help, we don't have to mourn the travail that made the magic. It's so far beyond anything else, you'd have to be daft to think of trying to emulate it.

There's more. The president prides himself on his imitation of a "partridge in a pear tree." In the receiving line for the press party the other night, he gave a performance. Shoulders hunched, hands crossed for the partridge, a rigid stiffening for the tree.

It's an act within the grasp of just about anybody, and it is heartening for us who can't seem to do anything else. ∎

21

Postal Service

Out of Touch—March 24, 1988

Of course, the postal service raised the rates for letters. It always does when I've just been to the post office and laid in a big supply of the latest commemoratives. I just got a sheet of Australia's birthday and William Faulkners, and I might have known it would go for the twenty-five-centers and send me back for a batch of three-centers.

I will admit to a certain paranoia about the mail I have thought for some time that the postal service was trying to stamp out letter writing. It began when I heard those Christmas time radio commercials that made me feel guilty about not mailing early enough and imposing on overworked postal clerks.

The postal service is not alone, of course, in trying to discourage correspondence. The telephone is to the letter what television is to reading. But some of us are addicted to writing and receiving mail, and I don't see it, in the scheme of current addictions, as a particularly harmful one.

I remember the first time I went to England and being smitten with how much the authorities encouraged writing. There were then four mail deliveries a day, which is just about right for the country that produced the immortal love letters of Elizabeth Barrett and Robert Browning. They had many worries, those two, but the zip code wasn't one of them, and they knew that their letters would not be returned if, in the distraction of high emotion, he put the wrong number on her Wimpole Street address.

Each took pen in hand with perfect confidence that the letter would be promptly received and read.

It's not like here, when a letter produced in the Northwest and intended for someone only blocks away can, even in the absence of the storied obstacles of rain, sleet, or "gloom of night," take a week to get there.

You have only to read the letters of John and Abigail Adams—which you should do anyway—to understand what a difference the post office could make in a relationship. Abigail was a splendid woman, but while she had much to complain about—he was eternally out of town—the one thing she fretted most about was whether John would read what she was writing. She was on the lookout for someone who could carry her letters, ever hoping that coach or a packet would be leaving at the right time. That high-minded pair had dreams for their country; one of her ones was that the nation they were helping to create would have a regular and reliable postal service.

Well, we got one. Due, however, to the volume of mail, some of it maddeningly addressed to "Occupant," the postal service began to feel sorry for itself, and tried to put a damper on the noble promise carved in stone over the main post office: "Messenger of Sympathy and Love, Servant of Parted Friends."

Changing the Post Office Department to a corporation called the U.S. Postal Service didn't change anything except that we heard about plush headquarters offices and we saw a lot of television ads about express mail, which has nothing to do with getting the regular stuff through, which is all we ask.

I think, though, that incurable letter writers would accept the rate raise if we could look for a comparable decline in surliness at post offices. Why are they the way they are? Why are they so angry at us?

Post offices have ropes to keep us in line. The clerk's faces tell us they wish we hadn't come. I wish they could realize that we have not come to cause them harm. All we want to do is send packages and buy commemoratives, which I enjoy—apparently more than I am supposed to. Once, maybe in the fifteen-cent days, they had lovely butterflies, and they've done Abigail Adams and Scott Joplin and other fine folks.

It's not the waiting I mind, when I go to buy them. It's when I finally get to the window and the clerk says, "I don't have any in my drawer. Maybe one of the others . . ." It's back to the end of another line.

It doesn't have to be that way. I know. My father was a postal clerk, and a more gracious man never lived. He could have had a more glorious destiny. He was the finest Latin scholar his high school ever had, and won a scholarship. But his father died and he had to go to work. He wasn't bitter, he never took it out on the public—or anyone else. He believed he was engaged in a worthwhile enterprise, helping people keep in touch.

I don't see much of that spirit in my post office.

I hope that some of the new revenues will be diverted to trying to discover the grievances of post office clerks. Do they hate their jobs, or just us? Do they think being polite is, as a New Yorker once said, "a sign of weakness."

I may know more when I go back to buy one hundred three-cent stamps. ■

The Day the Mail Stopped—July 2, 1989

When I called the zone delivery supervisor at the Friendship Heights branch of the U.S. Postal Service to report that I had received no mail at all for three days, he put my letter carrier on the line.

"You get too much mail," she said by way of explanation.

"Oh, no," I thought. "I don't get nearly enough. Mary Gunn owes me a letter, and so does Edward, and . . ."

But I said nothing. I was trying to cope with the revolutionary message: If I get too much mail, I won't get any. It was far too cosmic a question for me and my letter carrier to resolve on the telephone. We agreed to rendezvous in the lobby of my condo when she was making her appointed rounds that day.

I found her gloomily putting envelopes into boxes, a process which I had no wish to disrupt. I tried to think of ways to open the conversation without sounding hysterical, I am emotional about the post office. I am the daughter of a postal clerk, and I am addicted to the writing and receiving of letters.

"Whatever you do," said a friend from New York, who had called that morning while I was trying to figure out an agenda for the meeting, "don't antagonize her. You'll never get another piece of mail as long as you live."

The letter carrier said in a tone that had a certain finality, "Mail is lighter in the summer."

Was she suggesting that I was out of seasonal sync, expecting more when the norm was less? In what I hoped was an acceptably neutral tone, I said that I would like very much to get my mail every day.

We in zip code 20008 have known for a while that the tradition of "the mail must go through" is a sometime thing.

In my building, for instance, we have had mail deliveries as late as 7:30 P.M. One Saturday, my neighbor was sitting in the lobby waiting for a check that had been mailed from Silver Spring seven days before. It was 5:00 P.M. when the mailman entered with his gray tub. He put down his burden and announced, "I'm too tired to put this up. I'll come back Monday." A call to the post office brought him back, but it was enough to make us realize that we must not take this "Messenger of Sympathy and Love," as it says on the main post office, for granted.

In the beautiful old days, Danny Simmons was on our route. When anyone got too much mail, he would bundle it up and leave it at the door. He died some time ago, and things have never been the same.

I didn't think reminiscence was in order with Ms. Letter Carrier. Perhaps I could make my case on economic grounds, which sometimes is better than a straight-out appeal to the sense of duty or, for that matter, to the post office's reason for being.

"If I don't get my bills . . ." I started out, thinking I would point out that if the delivery of my bills was delayed, I would pay a penalty.

Ms. Letter Carrier cut crisply through my maunderings: "You'll get your bills."

I couldn't tell whether this was ominous or reassuring. Did it mean that she would sort my mail, give me the bills, and take the rest back to the post office? Or was she saying that henceforth I will get all my mail?

I started to say, "Look, if it's a choice between bills and letters, I would like to get the letters. I really would rather hear from Mary Gunn and Edward. They're both supposed to come, and I don't know when, and . . ."

Ms. Letter Carrier had been on the route for some three weeks. If she didn't like it, she could bid for another route. I inquired diffidently whether she was happy on Macomb Street. Her answer was brief: "So far."

She left me in a quandary. Do I write to Mary Gunn and Edward to ask them if they have in fact answered my letters? If not, must I assign them days to mail their replies, so they will not overcrowd my mailbox, vex my carrier, and kick me back into the "over and out" mode again?

I dread Christmas. Should I start now writing to my list, suggesting staggered mailings, beginning, say, on Columbus Day? But I might unknowingly write to people who were planning to delete me from their lists, and cause guilt and consternation, which, of course, is not the real reason for sending Christmas cards.

I have other courses open to me. I can communicate entirely by telephone, pulling people up from naps, out of showers, away from the bridge table, or from the moment when Colombo explains who did it. Express mail, which is the only kind I'm sure the post office approves of, because it advertises it all the time, could be, at $8.75 a letter, impoverishing. Carrier pigeons?

I finally decided to ask the question that I fear the answer to. What would have happened if I had not called up and asked about my empty mailbox three days in a row? But I can't get through. My zone delivery supervisor's line is always busy. I can understand why. ■

22

Many Subjects

On the Matter of Red Smith and His Editors
—January 15, 1980

Of course, I have no idea—and neither do you—what *New York Times* sports columnist Red Smith wrote in favor of an Olympics boycott. The *New York Times* killed the column.

None of us knows why, either.

Smith, who in thirty-five years never had it happen to him before, said, "It's a little difficult to figure out."

As usual, he is right. Statements from *Times* editors compound the mystery. Sports editor Le Anne Schreiber apparently thought that Smith had gone too far when he said that "sentiment would grow" for a boycott as the Soviets continued their "bloody work" in Afghanistan.

Is Schreiber against the spread of such sentiment, or did she find Smith's description of the invasion excessive?

In the slain column, Smith made reference to the grisly preparations the Soviet hosts were making against the world's arrival. This information was gleaned from the *Washington Post*. The mighty *New York Times*, which does not like to take anyone else's word for anything, attempted to verify the sweeps of "undesirables " through its own correspondent, who averred that they were only "rumors."

Arthur Gelb, a deputy managing editor, lamely tried to justify the censorship on the grounds that the column being the second on the subject by Red Smith, "sounded like a crusade."

Oh, come on.

Isn't that what columnists are for? Columnists, or so everyone but the *Times* hierarchy thinks, are supposed to burn, nag, and rage. Wasn't H. L. Mencken, another Olympic-class newspaper writer, known as the

"Disturber of the Peace?" And if crusading is a no-no, how come the *Times* prints William Safire, who writes many columns designed to redeem the name of his one-time employer, a man by the name of Richard M. Nixon?

Smith, we hear, took a swipe at the editorial writers of his lofty paper. He noted that they probably weren't around when the free world went to the Olympics in 1936 and gave Hitler a chance to flaunt his loathsome "master-race" theories.

In many newspaper offices, editorial writers are considered fair game. A natural, wholesome hostility exists. Editorial writers think that the likes of Red Smith, who does his own reporting, are shallow, sweaty fellows who race around missing the significance of everything. I would not presume to speak for Red Smith, but I think there's a fair chance he thinks the Ivory Tower chaps are name-dropping, tea-drinking, tennis-playing dilettantes who rarely come in contact with the real world and wouldn't know news if they fell over it.

And since when has agreement with the editorial policies of a newspaper been the standard for being printed? It is not so on the *Washington Star*, I am happy to say. If it were, some of us would be looking for work.

The *Times*'s own most recent editorial utterance suggested U.S. participation on condition of a pledge for "reform" of the games. What is envisaged by the boycott is something more ambitious—the reform of Soviet manners, a sharp blow on the side of Ivan's thick head to convey to him that a tank is not a calling card.

I happen to agree wholly with Red Smith that the United States should take the lead in saying we won't play. I didn't need Afghanistan. I was saying that we ought to tell them to go ahead without us when Shcharansky and Ginzberg were sentenced. I haven't begun to get over what they did to Hungary and Czechoslovakia.

A Russian dissident, Edward Kuznetsov, told me he wanted the games in Moscow in the hope that some athletes might claim their medals in the names of dissidents. But after hearing the pompous statements of the Olympic bureaucracy about the threatened boycott, I cannot share his fantasies. People who fatuously insist that "sports is above politics" would surely warn their athletes against any kind of protest.

Offhand, I can't think of anyone who is better qualified to say what I think he said than Red Smith. Who loves sports more? Or people? He knows all about young athletes who, fired by dreams of glory, have trained for four years. He knows about coaches who make champions out of farm boys. He would take those things into account. But he may have noticed that farmers, who also put in long hours, are being asked to give up something in order to make an important point.

Let us put aside the merits. Let us pass over the freedom of the press and First Amendment considerations. Let us even turn away from the sad spectacle of editors who were willing to face jail to bring their readers the Pentagon papers suddenly choking over a legitimate expression of opinion by their best writer.

What it comes down to is that the *New York Times* has no right to deprive its readers of anything Red Smith has to say.

Here is how his column in last Sunday's *Times* began: "Eddie Gottlieb was a wonderful little guy about the size and shape of a half-keg of beer."

Who was Eddie Gottlieb? I have no idea. But if Red Smith sees fit to write about him, I want to read about him. You don't have to like sports to like Red Smith. You only have to like the English language.

I know the *Times* is a stickler for usage. But maybe just this one time, they might loosen up. How about printing a headline like WE WUZ WRONG over the Red Smith column they shouldn't have killed. ∎

Gene Pickers Should Seek Mr. Niceguy—March 9, 1980

We perhaps should not be too hasty in judging California, which is once again poised on the frontier of social experiments which make the rest of the country nervous.

The state, which is beautiful and overwrought, has given us the hot tub and the sensitivity encounter. It is now grappling with the idea of producing a superrace.

A wealthy Golden State businessman named Robert K. Graham is collecting sperm from Nobel Prize-winning scientists and making it available to young women with high IQs. He wants to improve "the genetic stock." The experiment seems well advanced.

Some people think that Mr. Graham's thesis is racist. It is true that genetic theories can be repulsive, and one Nobel Prize-winner, William

Shockley, a contributor to the Graham Bank, has already given it as his opinion that whites are superior to blacks. So while the Shockley baby might turn out to give us in time something spectacular on the subject of the "electronic structure and geometry of molecules," it might also turn out to be a bigot.

But perhaps Mr. Graham, who, like many Californians is very rich and alarmingly literal minded, might be induced to steer his enterprise along more constructive lines.

Somebody might tell him that while the human race can always be smarter, it needs even more to be nicer. It is always good to have men in white coats who crash through barriers of knowledge, but it is even more essential to produce people who can get us through the day.

Why doesn't Mr. Graham hunt down some kindly bus drivers? There must be somewhere drivers who do not slam the door in the face of a passenger who has braved three lines of traffic in order to get to the stop. The kindly bus driver, properly mated, could give us the hope that millions of people would start the day without aggravated heart action and a grievance toward the human race which could take violent expression before the sun sets.

Another strain that obviously needs breeding up is the obliging gas-station attendant. Perhaps the one who used to clean your windshield without being asked and offered to check under the hood has vanished from the face of the earth since the days of the gas line. But what a challenge for Mr. Graham that he might track down someone who would father a child who would grow up to insure that many Americans would know where they were going—and have a chance of actually getting there.

Another major contribution to the quality of life would be an effort to encourage a super-race of permanent bank tellers. Banks have a habit of shuffling their help around, according to some intricate system which guarantees that the customer is treated as half of the "Bonnie and Clyde" team on going to the local branch. It is extremely disconcerting for a customer of thirty years' standing to get the blank stare from the teller and to hear the call to Central to make sure that he is not a forger, embezzler, or an imposter.

Mr. Graham might then look to future generations of ad-copy writers. It is entirely possible that he could find someone who would be willing to admit in print that oil companies are in business for a profit. People who are seeing the price of gasoline and home heating oil double and triple have the added burden of reading in the paper or seeing on television that the oil companies which are impoverishing them just never look at the ledgers. According to the ads, big oil is entirely wrapped up in improving the environment, finding more energy, and doing everything it can for the bankrupt consumer.

Perhaps Mr. Graham, with his tremendous resources, could find someone who would simply say to the public, "Hey, we're making out like bandits. We just put these ads on because they are deductible."

Finally, of course, there is the impossible dream of the reliable workman. He could benefit more of mankind more surely than someone looking into the function of the enzyme.

Anyone who has undergone home repair lately knows that your everyday artisan uses language so loosely and makes false promises so glibly as to make your politician, even the presidential candidate, seem like a model of accuracy and rectitude.

"Be there Wednesday at nine." The workman will tell you. It is a lie. He is humoring you. He says it to silence you, the way you will tell a child you will take it to Disneyland if it will stop crying.

Workmen do not hear unless you scream at them, like police dogs who only respond to a certain high piercing whistle. It is only when a certain level of frustration has been reached that he is able to judge the sincerity of the consumer and the persistence of his notion that the work may be done. He may oblige if he is persuaded that apoplexy or a lawsuit are not far away.

So you see, Mr. Graham has endless possibilities if he really wants to help the human race. He should not be discouraged, merely redirected. ■

Exit Walter, as Good as Ever—March 8, 1981

Okay, so I fell down on the job. I watched Walter Cronkite interview Ronald Reagan, and I paid more attention to him than to the president. I have a weakness for Walter Cronkite, and I was experiencing severe anticipatory withdrawal pains as I saw him gently leading his eighth and last president across my screen.

They were both misty-eyed at the end. Reagan because he is at last stepping into the presidency of the United States, and Cronkite because he is stepping out of the presidency of the airwaves. The logic of it escaped me. Here's Cronkite, not sixty-five until next November, being sidelined, while a seventy-year-old comes to bat as leader of the Western world.

Why, I wonder. He's as good as ever. He bore in in a totally civil and amiable way. He watched with out a twitch of his moustache while the president, who was equally civil and amiable, went into his number about Soviet godlessness.

"You don't think," he observed mildly, "that name-calling, if you could call it that, makes it more difficult when you do finally . . . sit down across the table from Mr. Brezhnev?"

He brought up the modern equivalent of the slap on the cheek with the glove—the denial of a special parking place to the Soviet ambassador.

"Don't you think the Russians kind of think we're childish when we pull one like that?" he asked with perfect good humor.

He didn't move in like a Green Beret, or press like a prosecutor or put words in the president's mouth—like Barbara Walters, with her insistent "what-you-mean-is." And he didn't presume to advise the president—remember Ms. Walters counseling President Carter to "be wise and be good to us?"

Cronkite never presumed, never postured, never got in the way of the news. I just don't know how we can face the '80s without him.

He's taken us through some bad times. You remember him choking up when he sat there, the most reassuring figure on the unbearable scene, reporting the death of John Kennedy. You remember him, rock-steady, at the Chicago convention of 1968, recounting the mayhem, showing us film of Dan Rather, who is to be his successor, being decked by a local goon.

For me, his finest hour was the Jerusalem summit. Naturally, Sadat and Begin said yes when Walter suggested the get-together. He made the decent thing seem natural and inevitable—a gift mere statesmen, envy him.

The one place I couldn't follow him was outer space—I think we have enough to cope with down here. On his way to the moon, Walter lost his cool. There is a gadgeteer in every man, and with Walter it came out in unabashed boosterism for boosters and launching pads.

Campaigning with him was an experience. He really loved to be out there, even though he knew his presence turned the process on its ear. I recall a marvelous occasion in a union bar in Wisconsin in 1976, when poor Henry Jackson was almost trampled in the mob that turned and broke as one at the sight of Cronkite.

Several times, on presidential primary days in New Hampshire, he and I went to Antrim, a little town I know well. He shook off the clustering executives and technicians and headed for the town hall to watch the citizenry make that all-important first cut. We walked in, and the scene froze: Pencils upraised, jaws agape, Yankee voters stunned out of their proud reserve at the appearance of the one person they could not pretend did not impress them.

He enjoyed celebrity. It was part of the fun of being in the news business. which never palled for him.

Who will take his place? Dan Rather has a jackhammer delivery, his manner suggests viewers must understand not only what he is saying but how he feels about it. Walter trusted the public as much as it trusted him.

Phil Donahue? I must confess to bias here. I was a fan of Barnaby Jones, the detective of late-night television, who in so many ways resembles Walter, being gray-haired, dignified, and good at his job. Jones used to come on at eleven thirty every night, and for me it was a cup of hot cocoa that led to sleep. The plots were not taxing, and I could trust Barnaby never to shoot to kill.

One night, without warning, at the usual hour, Phil Donahue showed up, surrounded by an audience of blue-haired, tittering women. What was worse, his guest was a woman who was telling me that she was a victim of incest. I was awfully sorry, but I didn't really want to hear about it. Donahue never replaced Barnaby Jones for me, and he has no chance to take Walter's place.

Life will go on, I guess. But without Walter to tell us about it, it won't be the same.

And that's the way it is with me on the eve of the first day that Walter Cronkite won't be telling me how it was. ∎

Take a Left at the Crater—May 30, 1982

Have you made your Doomsday plans yet? I ask because my own are bogged down. I have just discovered that when the SS18s start flying, I am, under the Crisis Relocation Plan, supposed to head for Fort Defiance, Virginia.

It is, I am told by the principal of the high school where we of Washington's Ward 3 are to assemble, an unincorporated township of two thousand.

"They are good people," Charles Huffman told me on the phone. "I think they would accept the people from Washington pretty well as they came down Route 81. But when they saw them taking over their homes and their food supplies and their gas, I am not really sure."

I would take my chances with Fort Defiance except that I know I could never find it. I have never been able to find any place in Virginia. It goes back to my early days in Washington, when both major highways in the Old Dominion were named for "Marse Robert," Lee Highway and Lee Boulevard. I have spent many hours in police stations, in my dinner dress, screaming at a policeman, "Stop saying east and west, say left and right."

The last time I crossed the river unattended, I ended up in an old people's home. As usual, my host had said, "It's easy, you can't miss it." But four highways later, I took the first right available in search of signs of human life. I flung myself into the first lighted building I saw. "Where am I?" I asked in the stillness of the lobby.

The gentleman who came out from behind the desk had a speech impediment. I caught the words "retirement village." But as I raced down the hill in the direction of the telephone, he followed me in great agitation. He managed to convey the fact that if I left my car in the driveway, it would be towed away. Marvelous, I told him. If the police came, one of them might know how to get to Hummingbird Lane, and might even tow me there.

While I was dialing, my eye fell on a poster asking for volunteers for the variety show. Could I qualify? I know the words to lots of old songs; I don't waltz badly. If accepted, I might be allowed to spend the night.

My host on the phone chirped, "You're only three blocks away." Then, picking up the Virginia panic in my voice, he added, "I'll come and get you."

281

I don't know anybody in Fort Defiance well enough to call up and ask for escort service. It's 3½ hours away from Washington, and rich in possibilities for missing the turn at the aqueduct. Don't tell me I could simply follow the other cars down 81. What if I blundered into the line destined for Elkins College and got turned away?

Bus transportation will be provided, I hear. I have considered it. Maybe I could make it to the proper stop with my shovel, my lunch, my documents, my change-of-address notice for the post office. But what about the door for my fallout shelter? I feel I would get a much warmer welcome in Fort Defiance if I brought my own. Mr. T. K. Jones of the Defense Department says if you dig a hole, place a door over it, and pile dirt on top, you won't get to glow. But assuming I could get a door off the hinges, it certainly wouldn't fit in the overhead rack of the bus. Do I really want to go to my grave with a door on my lap?

So I don't think Fort Defiance, although I love the name, is for me.

I recently checked out the facilities near the *Post* on a tour with Women's Strike for Peace, and I had to agree with the review of the Lafayette Building accommodations given by one of the marshals. "It has a lot of electrical equipment and exposed steampipes, and you could have 11 floors fall on you."

In the course of my reading, I have discovered another option for survival. I read about it in *Science* magazine—a Pentagon plan to bury missiles and missile crews inside mountains, for extrication after a nuclear attack and one last blast at the Soviets. It's called Deep Underground Missile Basing (DUMB). If you don't mind being buried alive for as long as a year, it might be for you. It's not perfect yet, mind you. For instance, how can you get the missiles and their sitters up to the surface when the all-clear is sounded, presuming you could hear it at five thousand feet below?

The solution put forward by one of the DUMB planners, a Mr. Eugene Sevin of the Defense Nuclear Agency, gives me pause about volunteering. "A good demonstration would probably consist of locking up a crew and letting them dig their way out."

It's the being locked up that has kept me from inquiring if the military takes people whose favorite television show is *MASH*.

It would be my luck to end up entombed with a bunch of cigar-smoking, bridge-playing, punk-rock fans who talk professional football statistics and support the war above. Or even an ex-policeman from Virginia who says north and south instead of right and left. ■

Whatever Happened to English?—September 1, 1985

The other day, I gave my name to the secretary of a man who almost surely would not call me back, and she asked, "Can you spell it?"

Silently, I replied, "Of course I can. Do you think that I am, in addition to being the kind of person whose calls your boss does not return, illiterate—or retarded?"

I like the way the airlines do it. "How are you spelling that?" they ask.

The use of the present participle gives me the feeling that I am a creature of infinite whim, likely to spell my name one way one day, another the next.

I want to say, "Let's see, this is Tuesday, I guess today it will be . . ."

The airlines have other forms of speech that catch my ear.

For instance, they will tell you when the departure is delayed that "we are waiting for other equipment." That means that the plane you hoped to board in Washington in fifteen minutes has conked out and that they have to send in a substitute from Dallas or Seattle.

Until I knew this, I spent many anxious hours wondering what "equipment" we were waiting for—a wing, an engine, a tail?

The syrupy sendoff by the stewardess—excuse me, flight attendant—is another favorite. "On behalf of Captain Muldoon and the entire flight crew, we would like to thank you for flying Sincere Airlines this afternoon."

The "entire" always reminds me of a famous cartoon by Carl Rose. It shows a pack of hounds being blessed by a clergyman, while one glowering beagle sits apart. It is called "The Atheist."

I wonder if there is an atheist on the crew, some Jenni or Bobbi who is at that moment cursing under her breath and ramming things into those little metal drawers in the galley, not thanking anyone, wishing she were back in Bloomington, Indiana.

This is not a good time for phrase-seekers. The federal government, which can be a mother lode of evasive, deceptive verbiage, is not producing much. Ronald Reagan is one who quotes other people's one-liners: "Make my day" or "You ain't seen nuthin' yet." It says a great deal about the state of the language that the most quoted set of words from the recent campaign, "Where's the beef?" which were spoken by the loser, came out of a hamburger commercial.

Since the departure of Alexander "Let-me-caveat-that" Haig, no one in the cabinet has shown any linguistic distinction. The formulations have run to the defiantly preposterous, as in "peacekeeper" for the MX missiles and "freedom fighter" for an ex-Somocista guardsman who is burning down peasant villages. The only phrase that may make it to the mainstream is "constructive engagement," a term of aggressive vacuity that means smiling while you watch someone playing with fire.

OMB Director David Stockman, who recently left the government, has received an advance of $2 million for his memoirs, although nothing indicates he is a wordsmith. He has given us "in-house," a phrase that so infuriates one of the editors of this paper that he has forbidden its use in his jurisdiction. Stockman must also answer for "out years," a term that adds murk to budget discussions. It means "future years," but the use of "out" suggests the speaker is in, and even "in-house."

I regret to report that the noun is losing its war with the verb. Such odious assaults as "It will impact my kitchen floor" and "You access the alley by the delicatessen" have resulted in the taking of much ground. The transformers' greatest victory, however is the capture of "parent," a straightforward term for a mother or a father which has been verbalized as "parenting," a maddeningly mushy word which redefines the whole dicey, interminable business of bringing up children as some kind of a process, for which you can take courses. A parent is what you are, not what you do.

Surrender is also imminent in the struggle against the use of "I" when "me" is mandatory. The rout of the objective case was completed on *Dynasty*. I heard Ali MacGraw explaining why she is so crazy about Blake Carrington. "People like he are hard to find," she simpered, to what dismay of her English professors at Wellesley I can only imagine.

The most discouraging trend of all is the substitution of "OK" for "thank you." I first ran into it at my People's Drugstore, where I stood for a long time behind a sulky adolescent who had a picture order worthy of a *Life* photographer three enlargements: two complete prints of a whole roll, one in black and white and one in color. The clerk was a patient and fatherly man who took it all down with unbelievable kindness and finally said, "It will be ready on Thursday."

"OK," said the lout, and not another word. His habit has impacted a lot of people, and others will probably access it in the "out years." ■

The View from the Sofa—November 30, 1986

Some people of consequence in this city have started a campaign to get folks to sit down at cocktail parties. One of the leaders, National Gallery of Art director J. Carter Brown, says he seeks out sitters because "they're confident people who don't feel the need of contact-polishing."

I welcome the creation of a new curve I have ever been ahead of but I must quarrel with that characterization of seated people. I am not confident, particularly when enduring the slings and arrows of standees, who inevitably accuse me of being "antisocial" or "holding court." Actually, I am neither, but I find it hard to explain why I sit. Fallen arches are regarded by those who do not have them as a comic affliction, utterly lacking the chic of the bad back.

Just for the record, if I stood for the entire length of a two-hour cocktail party, I would be on my knees for days after. So I put up as best I can with being misunderstood. The alternative is to wear a sign: "Weak Metatarsals—Be Kind."

Militant stand-ups are a special bane. These superior souls come over to your chair or sofa and literally look down on you. You find yourself shouting inanities at a belt buckle, causing severe strain to neck and shoulder muscles. If you are in a chair, of course, and they decide that you are worth talking to, they must crouch or sit at your feet, and someone inevitably comes along to administer the "royalty" needle.

I prefer a sofa, which can be patted to encourage a winded passerby to rest a spell. Many people cannot bear to be out of it for more than a minute. A nervous inquiry about my health, and they plunge back into the pool.

I do not feel I miss much by remaining on the bench.

I meet charming creatures that others may overlook. Dogs, I see a lot of. They wander about with reproachful looks at favorite places on the rug preempted by sling-back pumps or the Guccis of the great. They will come by and lay a head on your lap, which is a lovely variation on the often insincere, "It's so nice to see you."

I also meet a great many children. They are always seeking someone with whom they can communicate at eye level, and a seated adult is the most they can hope for in a crowded room. They are pleasant companions. For one thing, they are not perpetually peering over your shoulder in search of someone more important to talk to. They give you undivided attention, particularly if you take them on a guided tour of the contents of your pocketbook.

I once eased into a corner of a sofa that was occupied by a ten-year-old with a broken leg. In a grave and wondering way, he told me how it had happened. It was many cuts above the usual cocktail-party exchange.

Sometimes when there is no dog or child to chat with, I look out at the heaving vortex of the party and try to guess what people are talking about. I have spent so much time on the bank of the mainstream that I don't really know, although I sometimes pick up a clue or two en route to my roost.

For instance. I saw early on in Nic-Iran scandal-time how easy it was to spot a Reagan loyalist without a program. During the babble over the money and the arms and the missile-carrying capacity of "a single cargo plane," as the president likes to say, I heard the call of the true blue: "I find the Boesky case much more fascinating, don't you?"

Since the roof fell in last Tuesday, it is possible to be polite and still say no.

I wonder if people are considering things I might take up were I on my feet and in the thick of it. How would they feel about officially designating the Ayatollah Khomeini as the great boa constrictor of American politics? He devoured Jimmy Carter for lunch; he may dine on Ronald Reagan. Has anyone given thought to the idea of writing into both party platforms a pledge by the nominee to forswear any dealings whatever with Iran?

I also wonder if anyone worries as I do about the possibility of war in the Middle East. Will the Iranians stand still for the blow to their national pride? The world's premier bazaar hagglers were taken to the cleaners by the Israelis, who marked up the weapons' price by three times. Am I the only one thinking about this explosive issue?

The chances are, though, that people are talking about boats. There is more talk about boats than people realize. Being in a line of work that makes eavesdropping not only respectable but mandatory, I know this. When the spectators are filing out of a great event—a close Senate vote, a hard-fought nomination—I lurk about, hoping for the ultimate quote. Once, after a particularly vicious debate, I tuned in on a pair who were talking with great emotion.

One was saying, "I bought, I sold, but now I rent. It's better on the river." Maybe people just talk about boats when I'm around. But I disagree with the spectator who let me down. It's better on the shore. ■

Bork's Justice—September 17, 1987

Robert H. Bork looks vaguely like a man out of a Rembrandt canvas. He has a fleshy face, a distinguished nose, an aureole of kinky graying hair, a stubbly beard, startling eyes that speak of intelligence, anger, and a kind of melancholy.

The members of the Senate Judiciary Committee have done their homework. They spent the recess reading his voluminous printed work. They have heard from constituents who see Bork's nomination to the Supreme Court as President Reagan's boldest assault on legal questions answered and social advances made. They have heard from the White House that they have no right to turn down a man who could be mistaken for the man he succeeds, centrist Lewis F. Powell Jr.

Liberal fears that he would "North" the committee vanished early. His vaunted wit and warmth were under wraps. Hopes that he might come on as a cerebral right-wing kook were soon dispelled. The swagger and bluster of his enormous literary output—only Joyce Carol Oates writes more—is absent from his spoken text.

He was guarded, although not defensive, in explaining his cranky views of the Constitution. No one on the committee is a match for him. He is used to argument, at home with nuances. He was temperate and civil. The old Yale law professor treated the senators without the contempt for Congress with which his work is so liberally laced. He seemed to be participating in a seminar. He didn't lecture or patronize them; he seemed to assume that his quotations from other justices, from fellow academicians, would quiet all doubts about his "mainstream" quality.

Those daytime viewers trying to follow the long journeys down the dry and dusty paths of *Roe v. Wade* and *Skinner v. Oklahoma* and Bork's gratuitous and demeaning commentary about the constitutional flaws in the Court's decisions may have turned back in bewilderment and boredom. There was no drama to keep them. Are they asking themselves, as the Democrats hope, if their lives will be different with him on the Court? Do they believe, as the White House is instructing them, that only "extremists" and noisy special interests could oppose this erudite fellow, who claimed in his opening statement that his philosophy of judging is "neither liberal nor conservative."

The country first met Bork under grossly inauspicious circumstances—during the massacre of October 1973, when President Richard M. Nixon demanded the head of special prosecutor Archibald Cox, Senator Howard M. Metzenbaum (D-OH), the scrappiest member of the panel, took Bork back to what some Republicans insist is his "finest hour."

Bork told how Attorney General Elliot L. Richardson refused. So did his deputy, William D. Ruckelshaus. Bork, after pacing the floor in their company, decided to do the deed.

Chairman Joseph R. Biden Jr. (D-DE) asked why he had hesitated.

"I did not want to be regarded as an apparatchik," Bork replied.

But Nixon's apparatchik he became to the left that day—and, of course, a hero to the right. His reasons were as narrow as his arguments in the civil rights cases: he had not promised the Senate, as had Richardson and Ruckelshaus, not to fire the special prosecutor except for "extraordinary impropriety."

It was, according to his detractors, the first step in the long march to the Supreme Court nomination. The writings were calculated to keep the right reassured that if they wanted a high-gloss version of their wildest dreams of "strict interpretation" he was their man.

Surely the firing established him as a true believer in a conservative tenet: the supremacy of the president and his unlimited power. His vigorous, copious prose output further identified him as suitably doctrinaire, admirably hostile to whining minorities, devoted to the "original intent" of the Constitution.

In 1963, he attacked the public accommodations section of the Civil Rights Act as a "principle of unsurpassed ugliness." Ten years later up for confirmation as a federal judge, he took it back.

Bork explained that he was in a "libertarian" phase and objected to all "coercion" in commercial transactions.

Senator Edward M. Kennedy (D-MA) asked Bork if he had thought about the suffering of blacks who in their travels could not sleep at hotels or eat at restaurants. Plainly, Bork had not.

His writings are devoid of humanity. People should pull up their socks, or pull up stakes, if they are not happy where they are and cannot prevail upon state legislatures to change laws they find oppressive. The function of the Court is to fulfill the original intent of the framers of the Constitution. That's justice, Bork style. ∎

A Liberal and Proud of It—October 30, 1988

Unlike Michael Dukakis, I don't mind if you call me a liberal.

I know George Bush has succeeded in making the word so vile that I wouldn't be surprised to see some urchin with the "L-word" branded on the sheet show up along with the Halloween hobgoblins, witches, and Draculas.

I still think it's a respectable word. Its root is *liber*, the Latin word for "free." and isn't that what we are all about? I've heard Bush list "freedom" as number one in his value trinity—before even "family" and "faith."

I personally think Bush calls Dukakis a liberal because if he calls him a Democrat he might wake the sleeping giant of the Democratic Party, and he doesn't want to do that. Most liberals are Democrats, it is true; but many Democrats are not liberals, and Bush wants to scare them away from the polls.

I can't quite figure out why Dukakis is so defensive about the "L-word." Maybe he thinks it is a mislabeling. A reader from Washington, one of many correspondents who seem better able to interpret Dukakis than Dukakis, says that what "Dukakis really means is that he will accept from the conservatives what worked—and that he will accept from the liberals what worked—that what works is what he is after rather than ideology of any kind."

That may be the case. We can only surmise, since Dukakis refuses to speak for himself on the matter.

Liberals are hard to count and hard to define, but certain rough standards can be used. Dukakis was opposed to the Vietnam War and is opposed to the contra war. He qualifies on that minimal standard. On the domestic side, liberals can handle the idea of the welfare cheat having a swig of vodka on them better than the defense contractor slurping at the public trough. That apparently makes liberals "soft on defense" in the minds of conservatives, who think that extremism in the cause of the defense buildup is no crime.

On the whole, liberals have done more than conservatives to make ours "the kinder, gentler nation" that Bush babbles about when he's not busy hurling the "L-word" at Dukakis's battered head. When you are talking about "a thousand points of light" as he does, you are talking about programs like Head Start, Medicare, and Social Security, which are the handiwork of liberals. In the main, liberals hope that people can be free—free of worry over old age, over doctor bills, and over their children's education. The defeat of Robert Bork, liberalism's only recent triumph, showed also regard for civil rights and the right of privacy.

But Bush has made the "L-word" the equivalent of the A-word in seventeenth-century Massachusetts and the C-word in the Washington of the '50s, when Joseph McCarthy was branding anyone who didn't agree with him a pinko.

Bush has brought liberalism and all its works down to one ghastly case of a prison furlough gone wrong—Willie Horton, the killer who was given a weekend pass from a Massachusetts prison and wrought havoc on a Maryland couple. By extension, Dukakis is depicted as soft on crime. Even liberals think it is a bad idea to let out first-degree murderers. Dukakis's refusal to explain why he thought otherwise at one time has cost him a lot.

But it is strange, nonetheless, that an honest, earnest Democrat, who has governed his state well, could lose a national election to a murderer. A historic first, Richard Nixon would call it.

The conservatives are rejoicing at the prospect. They were derided and ridiculed in the '60s, and now they are getting their own back. From the tone of the letters they write these days, to me anyway, they are badly out of sync with their candidate in his "kinder, gentler" phase. There is a good deal of preemptive cackling and gloating.

A reader writes that one reason she is so delighted about the prospect of a Republican victory is "your gloom for four more years—gloom because your perfectly vicious articles had no effect on the reading-voting public."

Another Washington woman accuses me of "the sneering, patronizing attitude adopted almost uniformly by liberals toward non-elites."

I understand how they feel. We thought the John Birch Society was pretty funny. As a matter of fact, the Right's whole attitude toward government strikes us as weird. Conservative Republicans—and Reagan has made every other kind obsolete—regard government on one hand as a monster, sapping the lifeblood of hard-working businessmen, and on the other as a delicate flower that must be protected against Americans who want to tell on government when it does wrong. Liberals think of government as a servant that occasionally needs a swift kick.

It will be over soon. ■

The Dough Boys—October 12, 1989

The two old adversaries are locked in a new battle: Which of them will make more dough; who will be the more crass?

Former president Ronald Reagan is taking $2 million to make a trip to Japan. Former House Speaker Thomas P. "Tip" O'Neill Jr. (D-MA) has become one of television's most ubiquitous and well-paid pitchmen.

O'Neill says he is going to give his fees ($100,000 a day when he's shooting) to his grandchildren, so they won't have to scramble for money the way he did—as a teenager he mowed the lawns at Harvard.

Reagan, who does not justify his money-grubbing and has always been loath to spend his own money as he has the government's, also grew up poor. But he's made up for it. Friends tend to buy him houses to spare him the fatigue of raising mortgage money like other mortals. His wife shamelessly cadged designer dresses when she was First Lady.

Money was always a burning concern in his administration. The first thing the public learned about Michael K. Deaver, the president's media wizard, was that he could not possibly make ends meet on his $60,662 White House salary. It was news to a lot of people who work in steam laundries.

For eight years, Reagan and O'Neill went to the mat over such rich-poor issues as Social Security and corporate taxes. The worst thing O'Neill could say about his tormentor in the White House, after Reagan had made a speech about corporate income taxes, was: "He showed

291

that his heart was still in the corporate boardroom." Now, however, O'Neill is huckstering for supertycoons like Donald Trump. In one of his latest ads, he is seen with a chortling ("Let me caveat that") Haig, pitching for the Trump shuttle.

The irony is that Ronald Reagan made Tip O'Neill a star. When they were arguing over the shape and fate of the nation, Reagan tried to make O'Neill the bulky emblem of what was wrong with Democrats. The White House masterminded a New York congressman's campaign that made O'Neill—said to be overweight and out of control, like his party—the issue. The congressman lost, and O'Neill became a household word.

O'Neill was dreadfully self-conscious about his girth, tote nose, and his bon vivant's complexion, and he cowered away from the television cameras. He humbly accepted the Reagan sneers that he was no match for the Gipper on the screen.

Now, however, it is impossible to turn on your set without seeing his madly telegenic presence; he comes writhing up out of a suitcase, to extol the virtues of a hotel chain. He is such a celebrity that he does not have to be identified.

The idea of O'Neill as a model is unnerving to some viewers. They were used to him pitching for the homeless, the hungry, the little guy—he was definitely proud of introducing the country's first legislation to assist dwarfs. He is so popular with Democrats that they won't breathe a word of criticism about what some of them call the "tackiness" of seeing him rear up out of a suitcase like some elderly, white-thatched cobra. They wish he'd do a couple of public service commercials for his old constituency, the down and out. Surely his battered party could use a spokesman for its causes.

Similarly, Reagan is so beloved by his party that no Republican wants to comment on the screaming unseemliness of his being paid $2 million for a two-day trip to Japan. The trip is being cosponsored by a media communications giant, Fujisankei, and the Japanese government. The ex-president will be called on to make two speeches, each about twenty minutes long. His take will be $50,000 a minute, which is pretty rich even by Reagan standards.

The *Washington Post*'s Fred Hiatt reports from Tokyo that the government is complaining that Reagan is doing little for them during his visit, which required a newly fitted 747 plane and the $140,000 refurbishing of a guest house.

The real question is why a corporation and a government are so intent on doing an ex-president so much expensive honor. The answer seems to be that the Japanese are eager to convey to Reagan their intense gratitude for his trade policies toward them, his failure to impose restrictions on their merchants.

Is it a payback? We don't know. But it has that faint odor about it, and Reagan ought to explain. He'll probably try to alibi that it was to transport on his luxury craft relatives of servicemen in Japan so they could see their dear ones. But if that was his aim, he could have passed the hat and raised the fares himself.

He looks worse than O'Neill. He had the higher office to degrade.

Both of these old boys ought to do something for nothing, so they won't leave the young with the impression that money is the only thing that matters. ■

What Cards Those Trumps Are—February 18, 1990

Let us be grateful to Donald and Ivana Trump. They have given us a public issue in which we do not have to take sides. This is infinitely relaxing for the people of Washington who are forever trying to formulate positions on knotty current events like Ronald Reagan's videotaped testimony in the Iran-Contra case, George Bush's sleeping in a hangar before taking off for Colombia, and the evaporating peace dividend.

The Trump divorce is different from our scandals, which require the expertise of a CPA, a law degree, and, in the matter of Iran-Contra, a computerized compendium of presidential professions of total ignorance, interspersed with claims of close supervision of forbidden aid to the contras.

By contrast, the Trumps offer us an easy-to-follow spectacle which all can enjoy—except of course, when we think of the three small children involved—and endless opportunity to titter and cluck.

The defense budget is the closest we come to the sums being talked of in the divorce settlement between Ivana and Donald. She has asked for the Plaza Hotel—which she manages, although he denies it—a jet and $150 million. He has opened with a counterbid of a house in

Connecticut roughly the size of the Pentagon, $20 million, and, oh, yes, the three children. The dispute has eclipsed the fall of Drexel Burnham Lambert, the junk-bond house.

It is excess, which is New York's signature vice. We in the capital are into greed, of course, but not on this grand scale, and we do a lot of lying, which, as the verdicts in the Iran-Contra case indicate, is not all that bad. Viewing Wall Street, watching the Trumps, Washington thinks of itself as wholesome.

The heavy lifting in the recriminations department is being done by their respective publicists. Most people have to do their own in these breakups and spend hours telling potential partisans how he never picked up a sock in his life or how she nagged him into bankruptcy with her demands for a Jacuzzi. Donald has given an interview in which he avows his love for his wife, despite tabloid trumpetings about the Other Woman. But he sometimes complains that his wife is getting too much like Leona Helmsley, and he seems not to be referring to her tax returns.

What makes it so satisfying to read about it is that all the minor characters—lawyers, friends of the Trumps and the Other Woman—have understood their obligation to the public and come through with delicious quotes.

For instance, who could ask for more than this defense of Marla Maples, the lissome Georgia peach who is the third corner of the triangle. Says her former beauty pageant coach, also a Georgian: "Heavens to Betsy, she's no home-wrecker. She's one of the sweetest persons you've ever seen."

The New York Post tells us that Donald and Marla met in church—the Marble Collegiate Church, by the way, where Donald and Ivana were married—and set us to wondering, although we really shouldn't, what each of them was praying for. Was Donald trying to make a deal with the Almighty for his own continent? Was she asking for a rich husband?

But back to the quotes. The New York Times has been trying to cover this rich stew with some sort of dignity and has hit a vein of lawyerly talk in which we learn about love among the rich and famous: They spend inordinate amounts of time with lawyers and accountants haggling over community property and signing things, both prenuptial and postnuptial.

The Times quotes a lawyer who said, with a worldliness which takes "family-values" Washington's breath away, that postnuptial agreements sometimes evolve after a wife has discovered a husband's affair.

"What a postnuptial does," he went on, "is eliminate jeopardy for the wife. Sometimes that puts romance and relationship back in the marriage."

Will that sophisticated wisdom travel down here, where the innocent belief in chocolates and roses as romance-restorers prevails? Will a hangdog husband bring his accountant to the candlelit dinners that used to melt a sulking mate? Will they skip dessert while they go over the accounts receivable and settle the custody of the dog?

Ivana scored a coup on Valentine's Day by having lunch with Donald's mother and sister in a celebrity-packed restaurant. How will he respond? Give his mother an airline, his sister a railroad?

We have to wait. Meanwhile, nothing Reagan says could possibly compete with this drama of sex and power among the skyscrapers. Reagan had to testify because Judge Harold Greene said he was "the most logical and consistent witness" in the Poindexter trial. On both adjectives, His Honor was wrong. Reagan has been neither, and he won't change now. ■

Conviction of Their Courage—June 28, 1990

In the last seven months, three ex-convicts have paraded through Congress to give the members lessons in leadership. They presented no formulas, no answers. They provoked huzzahs—and uncomfortable questions in our officials: "How much am I willing to sacrifice?" and "Is it worth it?"

What Lech Walesa, Václav Havel, and Nelson Mandela have in common, beyond conscience and conviction, is time spent in jail. That and the fact that they were caught up in causes larger than themselves.

"They are willing to die for what they believe," mused Senator David L. Boren (D-OK), a supercautious conservative and unlikely Mandela fan. "We're not willing to risk one bad poll."

Walesa and Havel spent shorter terms, but the circumstances were comparable. Walesa could have stopped organizing Solidarity. He chose not to. Havel, a playwright, could have gone along with the commissars in Czechoslovakia—and a majority of his countrymen—on human rights. He didn't.

And Mandela, because he held the antiapartheid cause more dear than personal freedom, stayed in prison for twenty-seven years, coming out, finally, on his own terms. He is, with his straight back and his straight talk, something of a miracle, and an argument for long incarceration. His incandescent quality was such that he got standing ovations all over. Even people who deplored his taste in allies, his anachronistic bent toward violence, were impressed.

All three forswore that most crippling of emotions, self-pity. None of them, in madly acclaimed joint session speeches, mentioned their suffering. A Democrat who voted against the flag-burning amendment or a Republican who swallowed George Bush's taxes, carries on more. Mayor Marion Barry, on trial for drug possession and perjury, sees himself as a martyr.

Walesa baited his captors. Havel said prison was the only place he could get any writing done. Mandela does not talk about his days on Robben Island; the man, at seventy-one, is all tomorrow.

But members of his entourage who had talked with Mandela's fellow prisoners say that he led a structured, highly disciplined life, totally engaged as a college president and political organizer. A fitness fanatic, he got up at 3:00 A.M. to do calisthenics in his cell; relaying messages through the people who brought the food, he presided over unending seminars for fellow ANC inmates; drew up a curriculum for those, like so many blacks, deprived of education, and organized each cellblock under an ANC captain.

It isn't appearance that determines esteem. To be sure, Mandela, scion of a royal family, walks like a king, but Walesa is stocky and Havel is slight. Moral stature comes in all sizes.

Friends of the South African government have tried to rally the right to indignation over Mandela's singular preference in allies. "Yasser Arafat, Colonel Gadhafi, Fidel Castro, support our struggle to the hilt," he forthrightly replied.

"I wish he hadn't said that," says Boren, "but I can understand it—you never turn your back on the people who were for you when nobody else was."

Boren, an ardent defender of the CIA, the agency said to have fingered Mandela for the South African police, made a trip to South Africa in 1989 and is the first to say he hasn't been the same since.

It is one thing to see red-necked southern sheriffs in their inefficient way practicing discrimination, but in South Africa it is efficient and official. Meeting Albertina Sisulu [wife of then-jailed ANC leader Walter Sisulu] was "the single most radicalizing experience of my life."

Boren went to New York to greet Mandela and was struck by his "inner peace—so rare in our system, especially in politics."

Is oratory the key? Probably not. Walesa, who came last November, had the House chamber rocking with enthusiasm for a real, live profile in courage, addressed the assemblage in a man-to-man manner, saying bluntly that Poland appreciated kind words but really needed money. Havel treated them to a literary masterpiece, an exquisite exposition of moral responsibility and Europe's determination to be a civilizing force again.

Mandela's luminous face set off a storm; the place was packed with people just palpitating to applaud. His accented English was somewhat hard to follow, and his speech was more conventional than, say, his beguiling rebuke to President Bush on the subject of ANC armed struggle the day before.

He spoke of the Constitution. It's what we have that our imported heroes don't. We have a peerless system of government that forbids the kind of oppression that they suffered. It may be why we don't really need heroes. ■

Barry Putting His Trial on Trial—July 3, 1990

Almost any other man, especially a mayor, would, after the worldwide airing of a videotape showing him smoking crack, be walking around with his coat collar up and his head down.

Not Marion Barry, the unregenerate, unapologetic mayor of Washington. He swaggered into his trial wearing a Kente cloth, the woven scarf that came into vogue during Nelson Mandela's conquest of America, and two yellow rosebuds in his lapel.

"Yellow," he explained to one of the several crowds he has been addressing after Hazel Diane "Rasheeda" Moore told the court about their long, and, according to her, drug-taking relationship, "is for canaries."

Barry is busy outside the courtroom conducting a trial of his trial. He goes to churches and temples. He has become the darling of Nation of Islam leader Louis Farrakhan, the separatist anti-Semite, and George Augustus Stallings Jr., an excommunicated Catholic priest who made himself a bishop.

U.S. District Judge Thomas Penfield Jackson excluded Farrakhan and Stallings from the proceedings. The mayor is shocked. He complained on the courthouse steps, after Moore testified about how he knocked her down and how they took drugs together all over the city, including his house and office, "more than a hundred times." The ban reminded the mayor of Nazi Germany.

Jesse L. Jackson, who despite his "Down with Dope" slogan has recklessly flung himself into defending the mayor, was reminded of Soviet surveillance.

Inconsistency is one of the hallmarks of the Barry case. The rivals for his job, except for Sharon Pratt Dixon, never criticize him or ask for his resignation. Instead, they are lusting for his endorsement. By their silence, they are by implication joining in the mayor's characterization of the case as an exercise in unbridled racist persecution.

The mayor fans the flames at every opportunity. During the noon break, he went to a Marion Barry Appreciation Day rally in the park across the street from the District Building. About three hundred city workers poured out to hear Judge Jackson referred to as "Bull Connor Jackson"; the trial called "a lynching," and rabble-rousing oratory about slaves being brought over here and "whipped and chained and tortured and burned to death."

The mayor explained one thing: why his wife, Effi, has been acting out a parody of wifeliness by sitting in the front row of the courtroom listening intently as other women tell of having sex with her husband.

"People," said the mayor, when it was his turn to speak, "want to know why Effi does this and why she does that. She told me, 'Marion, God has forgiven, you, and I have too.' "

The crowd yelled and cheered and cried "hold on" with the fervor that comes with a weekly city paycheck.

Then His Honor returned to the trial to a jury which hears the unremittingly tawdry details of the life of a man who can't say no to drugs or sex—to a world where "Rasheeda" is queen. Barry's able lawyer, R. Kenneth Mundy, tried, over and over, to get her to admit that she forced Barry into taking drugs.

Moore is a handsome woman with considerable presence. She has put on weight since her scrawny model days. For yesterday's appearance she wore a gray scarf tied around her forehead, a gray suit with a black tank top, and a gold chain. In a full voice, she delivered her answers with a matriarchal calm.

What she had to admit, she admitted. Yes, she had forgotten that Barry referred to a night when she and a friend of Barry's had stayed up drinking all night. Mundy seemed to think it was an indictment of her credibility.

"The memory does slip sometimes like that," she said imperturbably.

Barry said no to drugs nine times, Mundy pointed out to her.

"He gave me the money for the drugs," she said.

Moore is desperate. She cooperated with the FBI in the sting in hope of earning a better deal on charges pending against her in California. She has three children, and a husband in jail. Her prospects, once brilliant—she was a college graduate with a promising modeling career—have dwindled to a hope of survival.

Barry went to the hotel to have sex with her, not drugs. He was a virtuous, would-be adulterer, his followers claim, not an addict. The clergy supporting him apparently have no more trouble with a broken commandment than they do with his videotaped drug-smoking.

Why does Barry race around the city in search of easy ovations? It may be good for his ego, but not for his case. Nurturing racial hatreds is a wretched business that will not help in the courtroom. Does he think that by whipping up black solidarity he will ensure some kind of outbreak if a guilty verdict is returned? It's just one more indication in a depressing anthology that shows that Barry thinks he can get away with anything. ■

The Politics of Peter Pan—May 26, 1991

Now that he has time to read—the doctors have forced leisure on him—President Bush might want to take in some ancient wisdom, such as is found in Cicero's "De Senectute," or "About Old Age."

The president is not old—only sixty-six—but sometimes it seems he is fleeing from the advancing years the way he once fled his "wimp" image. No one would think less of him if he were to dash about less—he doesn't need to go to Minnesota to see a school—or seek less strenuous recreation. In fact, he would calm the nerves of the republic.

Cicero, who was also a public man on the fast track of Roman politics, is firm about accepting limits: "Practice moderation in exercise. Nor indeed are we to give attention solely to the body; much greater care is due to the mind and soul; for they, too, like lamps, grow dim with time, unless we keep them supplied with oil."

If the president were to discover the quieter pleasures of gardening over golf and walking over running, he might lengthen his days— and ours. The White House gardeners don't leave him much to do, but he could have his own small plot and would soon become its slave. He would love pulling weeds if he thought of them as Democrats.

Pruning is another kick, giving the pruner the idea that he is imposing a new order on at least one small part of the world. If he were to think of a scraggly bush as the Middle East, he could snip his way to peace of mind.

"Moderation" is Cicero's key word. It is not conspicuously on view in our public men. Take the astonishing case of Clark Clifford, the personification of Washington wisdom and influence, the theatrically handsome embodiment of suavity and probity. At the age of eighty-four, he has been caught in the kind of fix he has rescued clients from.

After sixty-two unblemished years in the practice of law and a dazzling record of counseling presidents, he finds himself, in the words of a best friend, looking like "a failure in ethical reasoning."

When he was seventy-five, for the fun of it, he took over a Washington bank. He was misled, he says by unscrupulous foreign investors, who bought a majority of stock in the bank. He is under investigation. It does not seem possible. His survival rests on his ability to convince the authorities that the savviest man in Washington had the wool pulled over his eyes.

Why did he do it? He surely did not need the money. Men are funny about money—they honestly believe it's a measure of their worth.

Look at another Democratic icon, Justice William J. Brennan Jr., who is also eighty-four. He accepted a total of $140,000 in cash and forgiven loans from a good friend, developer Charles E. Smith. What an example to set grasping politicians—and other judges who think their efforts are insufficiently rewarded.

Clifford has explained that acquiring the bank was a "challenge"—that it was either that or going for the mail every day like some of his retired contemporaries. But were those his only choices? Could he have stepped out from behind the scenes and gotten involved in some public cause? It would have kept him out of trouble, and with his name and muscle he could have done no end of good. He could have taught a course in law or tutored poor students. He is an unparalleled explainer, as a generation of journalists can attest. What if he had tried to get Washington a ball team or a lower homicide rate?

And there is Senator Edward M. Kennedy, who at fifty-nine most definitely does not want to grow old, or even to grow up. Most recently he awakened two sleeping young men—in itself an act of aggressive self-indulgence—in the dead of night to go bar-hopping with him. Now one of the young men, his nephew, a fourth-year medical student, has been charged with rape, and his son Patrick, a state legislator, is hounded by questions about the squalid details of the evening.

Cicero says he likes a little age in young men and a little youthfulness in the old. But Teddy hasn't got the right mix. He was the baby, never meant to be a paterfamilias. But upon the violent deaths of his three older brothers, the women of his family made him, in spite of himself, Himself, as the dominant Irish male is called. They were used to that form of domestic government: Joseph P. Kennedy was the absolute ruler in his time.

So Uncle Teddy, kindly, boisterous, affectionate, became willy-nilly, a role model. And nobody is around, except perhaps Senator Orrin Hatch, to tell him that it's time to quit being "the wild rover" of the Irish song, and to quit drinking—and that if destroying himself is a bad idea, wrecking the lives of young relatives is beyond the pale.

A little stock-taking all around is in order. Reading. Thinking. ∎

Fast Times at Trend Central—June 9, 1991

The other day my niece told me she was going "food shopping." It had always been "grocery shopping" before. The next day, my cousin called and said she was going "food shopping." Not for the first time. I had missed a trend.

Who told them to say "food" instead of "grocery?" When were they told that food was in and grocery was out? Not for the first time, I felt out of the loop.

Did they call a number? Do they subscribe to a service that puts out the word, like the one that made everybody say "hopefully"? I figure they are behind the widespread use of "no problem," which is replacing "yes" as an answer to a question about whether something could be done or given. It's a kind of putdown, as if the questioner had been neurotically summoning up a difficulty where none existed.

Is it possible that the same authority has told young women they must wear crimped hair? So many in life and on television wear their hair crinkly now. It is tightly waved in a style that suggests a sort of overwrought home perm that former generations paid large sums to have straightened. Recently, they began dying their crinkles a kind of Strom Thurmond orange. Does Trend Central give out brand names too?

But just as arresting is the new wave in men's hair fashions. Young men have gone back to wearing ponytails. Who told them to? Didn't we have that argument back in the '60s, when political young men had their locks shorn so they could go out and prove to voters that they didn't hate them, as long hair was supposed to suggest. Then, hair was a political message. You saw long hair, you saw a critic of society. You saw a mop and you said, system-burner.

Today's ponytails, however, are difficult to read. Truck drivers wear them. Maybe you have the courage to ask them what they are protesting, or saying. Maybe they just want to be challenged and know that nobody will have the courage to ask. It's unsettling. These were the people who in the '60s protected us against "the effete corps of impudent snobs" who wanted to end the Vietnam War. Who can you trust?

I had a talk with a parent of a ponytail wearer—he'll soon be able to sit on it—and she said that he said that it was "European." Who in

Europe said it was "European" and sent the idea across the sea in a note in a bottle?

Men are also wearing suspenders—in response, I can only think, to some dictate from Trend Central. I think suspenders are ugly, and they look hot, but men are becoming fashion's slaves as surely as women. Men doff their jackets on television so you can see their suspenders and know them to be hip.

Verbally, trendwise, things are at a standstill. The Gulf War produced no new lingo except for Saddam Hussein's reference to "the mother of all battles." "Mother of" has made its way into the language to indicate something of a humongous nature.

But Saddam stole it—wouldn't you know? In Dublin, people have always talked about "the mother and father of a traffic jam."

The war has, however, revived Republican speechwriters. They were floundering around with leaden concepts like "new paradigm" and "empowerment." Now they have taken off on a bold campaign of claiming that social programs should be run the way the military ran the war. The Pentagon, which not so long ago was ducking incoming because of $700 coffeepots is held up as a paragon of efficient performance to U.S. businessmen.

Trend Central has also been active on behalf of Dan Quayle. People speak of how "unfair" it would be to deprive him of the vice presidency in 1992, since he has done "a good job" at filling the job so far. Reporters and columnists have been doing interviews in which they urge their readers to pull up their socks and remember that Quayle speaks English, knows about the deficit, and is passionate about the space station. The hint: "What more do you want?"

President Bush, who as a candidate was so rich a source of quotables (remember "deep doodoo" and "read my lips"?), is a disappointment in office.

But we must be fair. Who could compete with Richard Nixon? The former president, who has been inching his way back to respectability on the op-ed pages and opinion sections of our newspapers, has given us a new set of unforgettable Oval Room utterances, via a fresh release of tapes. The world statesman so sought after by editors with an insatiable appetite for the geopolitical claptrap that he and Henry Kissinger turn out by the yard, is his old self. There he goes again, fingering Jews

303

in the antiwar movement—"Aren't the Chicago Seven All Jews?"—and contemplating hiring Teamsters thugs to beat up peace demonstrators— "Just ask them to dig up those, their eight thugs."

Just wait, though. Trend Central will think of something. It always does. ∎

Patriotism Is in the Eye of the Beholder—July 4, 1991

A reader from Gaithersburg, Maryland, writes: "To be a patriot, in my view, you have to have at least one time in your life actually supported your country in its actions without reservation or desire for political advantage."

He wasn't, as it happened, talking about me, but he might as well have been. The last military action I supported without reservation was World War II.

"Without at least one documented case of unequivocal support of their country . . . no one has the right to call themselves a patriot," he writes.

There is a man who has no doubt about the fact that he is a patriot and that those who disagree with him are not. This Fourth of July there are millions like him. They are waving flags and cheering "Desert Storm." I hope they won't be chanting, "We're number one!" but they may well be. And they should if they want to, because if the Constitution says anything, it says different strokes for different folks. At least it did, until the present crowd at the Supreme Court got hold of it.

There's another kind of patriotism, too: less visible, less vocal, and Judge Learned Hand, one of the great jurists of our time—why wasn't HE on the Supreme Court?—is the spokesman. He put the case to thousands of people who gathered in Central Park for "I Am an American Day" on May 21, 1944.

"The spirit of liberty is the spirit which is not too sure that it is right; the spirit of liberty seeks to understand the minds of other men and women, a spirit which weighs their interests alongside its own without bias; the spirit of liberty remembers that not even a sparrow falls to earth unheeded; the spirit of liberty is the spirit of him, who, near two thousand years ago, taught mankind that lesson it has never learned, but has never quite forgotten: that there may be a kingdom where the least shall be heard and considered side by side with the greatest.

"And now in that spirit, that spirit of an America which has never been and which may never be, nay, which never will be except as the conscience and courage of Americans create it; yet in the spirit of that America which lies hidden in some form in the aspirations of us all; in the spirit for which our young men are at this moment fighting and dying; in that spirit of liberty and of America I ask you to rise and with me pledge our faith in the glorious destiny of our beloved country."

How similar to the thoughts of our quiet general, Major General Jay Garner, who commands Joint Task Force Bravo in northern Iraq, which has taken the Kurds under its wing. Garner wrote about the work in a letter that "the sons and daughters of freedom" are doing in "Operation Provide Comfort," an enterprise that made some Americans much prouder than the bombing of Baghdad. He writes of a vision that is worthy of the Fourth of July.

"We may have chanced upon a new formula for world tragedy; the use of the free world's professional military, trained for war but so effective in crisis, could truly be the merciful instrument in shaping future humanitarian operations. If all of us, military, government, private organizations, pull together toward a common goal, maybe—just maybe—we can begin to place the final tiles in the mosaic of human rights."

Garner's style is strikingly different from that of General Norman Schwarzkopf, who, says Ralph Nader, "has become a war god." He is collecting some $5 million for his memoirs, something like $60,000 apiece for his lectures.

Cashing in? Yes, he is, and why not? That's the American way. What isn't is that the general bundled "flag-burners" with "dissenters" in a speech to Congress. Just because you don't have a yellow ribbon tied to your car's antenna or didn't "support the troops"—whatever that means—doesn't mean you're going to abuse Old Glory.

Dissent is, after all, what our country was founded on. Read that hotheaded, rip-roaring, pounding political document, the Declaration of Independence, and imagine it being passed by Congress today without a hundred cautionary amendments.

Part of the problem is that our presidents keep telling their fellow citizens how wonderful they are just as they are. George Bush laid it on thick in his post–Desert Storm triumph before Congress. We are "good," "generous," and "caring." Yes, some days, we are. So are the Swedes, the Irish, the Italians, and the Kurds.

What makes us different is our luck, not our virtue —having a country stretching from sea to shining sea, with everything we need in between, and a form of government that we can criticize without being unpatriotic. We've done bad in our day, too—to Indians, to African-Americans—and haven't entirely stopped.

The thing is, as Learned Hand said, we can always be better. ■

Bad Guesses during the Thomas Hearings
—October 20, 1991

It figured that I would be in Sorrento—that's Maine, not Italy—on the second and third days of the most sensational hearings in the history of the republic.

I have an unbroken record of bad guesses on cataclysmic events: During the October Massacre, I was in Rome (Italy, not Georgia); the day Richard Nixon resigned, I had to be fished out of a New Hampshire lake hours before he appeared in the Oval Office to complain that the Republicans had deserted him.

I had long planned to spend the October 12 weekend visiting my editor from the *Washington Star*, Newbold Noyes, who, in 1954, sent me to my first hearings, the Army-McCarthy set-to. This is the tenth anniversary of the death of the dear *Star*, and a reunion was indicated. He was a great editor, the kind who just doesn't check out the first paragraph before going home. He wanted to see the second graph, where it can all fly apart. I had written a Sunday piece on the Thursday before, making the point that if the Senate Judiciary Committee had been on the ball, the hearings would not be necessary.

On Friday, I went to the Caucus Room, where so many years before I had seen Joseph McCarthy—who was to be much invoked again—for the first time. In those days, the press tables were drawn right up beside the witnesses, and we could see the whites of their eyes and almost their tonsils. Through the years, we of what is called redundantly the "writing press" have been gradually moved back so that we see only the backs of their heads.

It was the way it always has been when someone is about to lose or gain a reputation, and some tale of betrayal, chicanery, larceny, or dirty pool was about to be revealed—if only partially. The photographers were crawling about on the floor, aides were bringing coffee, and the public was straining against the velvet ropes outside. On the way I saw a sign that said, "Anita is making a mountain out of a molehill."

That was prophetic.

I don't know what I expected, but certainly not what I got. What Anita Hill said I could not believe. Words streamed out of her mouth that suggested a smoker. At any moment someone would bring in a huge cake and a girl wearing a few pinfeathers would rise out of it. What Clarence Thomas had said to Anita Hill on taxpayers' time in government offices was unbelievable, or would have been from a less credible witness. They tell us now she should have cried.

Plainly, I had to rewrite my Sunday story. Could I still go to Maine? Surely, I thought, they won't go on with this. It will be called off. Clarence Thomas will ask to have his name withdrawn. Somebody will say we must not have this poison in our souls.

I thought I would be safe to leave. On the plane north, I rewrote for Sunday—it was a time for the explicit, not the abstract.

When I arrived in Bangor, Maine, Newby said, "I didn't think you'd come." The hearings had got there before me. At Bangor, a transfer point for soldiers returning from Saudi Arabia, the television was going full blast in the lounge.

A GI watched Anita Hill for a few minutes, then turned to Newby's son Terry, and asked, "Who's the chick?"

"It's a long story," said Terry.

After dinner, we watched Clarence Thomas. We heard him turn his deep bass on Senator Howard Metzenbaum (D-OH). "And God is my judge, not you, Senator Metzenbaum."

We thought it was a good hit. Congress-haters would cheer. We heard Thomas say it was "a high-tech lynching." We thought that might thrill blacks. Whatever kind of justice he would make, Thomas was clearly a good politician.

Saturday, before showtime, we took a walk along Frenchman's Bay, where the mountain islands rise steeply out of the water. The trees were cerise and gold. The air was crystal—no pollution of any kind.

Beppie, Newby's wife, had a rule that she would not listen to Senator Orrin Hatch (R-UT). Leaving meant that she had to tip the cat out of her lap and pick her way over three dogs, but she stuck to her principles. In the evening, we drove to Ellsworth, twenty miles away. The parking lot rang with car radios—Senator Alan Simpson's (R-WY), leering references to Anita Hill's "pro-cliv-i-ties." Little children strapped in car seats were bombarded with words they would get their mouths washed out with soap for repeating. Senator Howell Heflin (D-AL) unintelligible most of the time, came on loud and clear with jolting talk of date rape. Senator Joseph Biden (D-DE), groped for a proper verb to replace old-fashioned "date." He chose "going out," right out of the '20s.

Saturday night I made another wrong guess. From thinking the hearings would be called off, I decided they would never end. At vast cost, I changed my reservation. The trashing of Anita Hill ended early and we sang old songs.

On Sunday, friends, old Washington hands, came to lunch. There were bare greetings, and no talk. We watched Anita Hill's four estimable, corroborating friends. "Bush should choose one of them for the court," said Newby.

By Sunday night, the polls had spoken. Thomas had won in a walk.

When I got home, the hearings were over. So was the suspense. He would be confirmed. My guilt was for naught. The hearings had changed nothing. As Senator Herbert Kohl (D-WI), said, "I don't know as there is anyone in our country who has been helped by this unhappy situation." ∎

Children Caught in Bureaucrats' Legal Battle
—September 22, 1994

When I arrived at St. Ann's the other day, I found the place in turmoil. People were running around collecting clothes and records, trying to soothe children who were about to be snatched from a place they called home.

St. Ann's Infant and Maternity Home is an institution for homeless children, which was founded in Abraham Lincoln's day and continues to exist as a refuge for unlucky children. Various groups and experts—most of whom never trouble to go and see it—condemn it out of hand as a relic of Victorian unenlightenment.

Since the advent of crack, brave souls like Dr. Joyce Ladner, interim president of Howard University, have written that an orphanage is not the worst place for a homeless child. We volunteers see it as a place where children can get their breath before going on to the next chapter of their lives. It is licensed as a child-care institution, but because it takes in children in emergencies, it is called, in the case under consideration, "an emergency shelter." It survives because it is needed.

On the day in question it seemed more like a Mexican restaurant that was being raided by the Immigration and Naturalization Service on the hunt for illegal aliens. The Child and Family Services Division of the D.C. Department of Human Services [DHS] had suddenly realized that a deadline had come. District Judge Thomas F. Hogan had ruled that every child placed in its care had to be relocated in foster care within ninety days.

The urgency was extreme for the adults: They would be in violation of a court order. It was a different story for the children.

The conflict of interests was graphically on display. Two sisters—I will call them Clarissa and Caroline—had been told hours before that they were about to go and live someplace else with someone they had never seen before.

Clarissa and Caroline are seven and five years old, and had come to St. Ann's in March. They were wary and not given to much conversation. I heard that they had never been to school. Gradually over the summer, with swimming and picnics and other pleasures, they settled down, warmed up, and began to act like giggly little girls.

Clarissa has black hair and an imperious manner and was given to bopping people on the head as she passed by. Caroline, with hazel eyes and hair to match, smiled all the time. They came apart at the idea of leaving. They didn't say why, or whether they like the child-care workers, the other children, the sisters, or the soothing routine that made daily life so predictable. For some children, having three meals a day at set hours is a wonderful novelty.

Clarissa threw herself on the floor and sobbed that she would not go. Caroline wept quietly.

They met their prospective foster mother in the art room, where they did their finger painting and their coloring. After the interview, Clarissa, whose heart was hammering so hard I was surprised she could talk, told Sister Maureen that she thought it would be all right. But Caroline just shook her head when I asked her. They were to leave the next day at 4:30 P.M.

None of the ritual of departure had been observed: the doctor's visit, the gradually escalated home visits (overnight, weekend). What was under way looked more like legalized kidnapping.

The next day I went to court to hear Judge Hogan's further rulings on the fate of Child and Family Services, whose work on foster care and adoption he called "outrageously deficient" in his famous 1991 court order. The spectators' benches were filled with DHS representatives. Maybe they were trying to convince the judge that they loved their work and could do it.

In his 1991 ruling on the suit brought by the American Civil Liberties Union against DHS, Hogan wrote, "The District's dereliction of its responsibilities . . . is a travesty."

He said he didn't think things had gotten much better. He didn't think District bureaucracies paid much attention to court orders—he might have to send somebody to jail. He put Child and Family Services into receivership.

The mayor who was the founding father of the mess, Marion Barry, who promised more social workers but never delivered and failed to take advantage of federal funds that would have provided for them, is headed for reelection.

I asked some of the officials how come so many foster mothers had miraculously turned up at the last minute. They didn't know. I asked how many foster mothers they had in reserve. They couldn't say.

Later, one of them called me to report a reprieve for Clarissa and Caroline. They weren't leaving until Monday. But the foster mother told St. Ann's she couldn't take them until she got day care.

Finally, the little sisters left on Wednesday. Quite cheerfully, I am told, as most do when they have been properly introduced to the idea of "going home for good," ending a trauma that never needed to be. ■

Charles and Di as Apple Pie—October 23, 1994

If the Nobel Committee ever decides to give a prize for caddishness, England will have two strong contenders. The first of course would be Major James Hewitt, the swine who wrote a book about his alleged five-year affair with the Princess of Wales. But a strong runner-up would be, alas, the Prince of Wales, who has collaborated on a book himself, in which he says he never loved the Lady Diana.

The bonny pair are locked in a dance of death, convinced as they are that one more book will settle the score and make the world see that it was the other one's fault that their marriage collapsed in a heap of recriminations. They are children of the '90s, deep into victimhood, awash in self-pity, intent on the last word—and trapped by technology. Both have had intimate telephone calls taped, and the princess allegedly was videotaped doing it with the perfidious major in his mother's garden.

People are trying to make a solemn constitutional crisis out of all this bedroom farce. Learned questions are asked about the survival of the monarchy. How much more will the British people take from the Windsors? The queen is in Moscow, smiling at Yeltsin while fuming that the heir to the throne has gone and spilled the beans about her over-bearing husband and her chilly treatment of her son.

Is this the end? Probably not. The cost of the monarchy is stagger-ing. Maintenance of their castles, yacht, planes, trains, and cars runs to more than $100 million a year. The British had hoped to purchase role models for that price; instead they got the cast of a daytime soap opera.

But to each his own. We get our scandals, romances, embarrass-ments, and scenes from Oprah and Phil. People willingly humiliate themselves for money or glory, telling of stupendous rejections, insults, misunderstandings, lover-swappings, aberrations, suicide attempts, and vengeance. The British get all that and more—and with castle back-drops. They merely have to look to Buckingham Palace for humiliations so many-layered and vibrating that you might think the objects would never be able to face their subjects again. The prince was recorded telling his horsey mistress, Camilla Parker-Bowles, that he wished to come back to life as her tampon. Her Royal Highness had crank tele-phone calls traced to her private line.

Yet the princess is visiting Washington, and the prince is off soon for a jaunt to Los Angeles.

U.S. royalists have been rocked by the book that Charles authorized Jonathan Dimbleby to write. It is not quite the thing to tell how Dad is a fascist right out of the Barretts of Wimpole Street, or that Mum never had time for him. Why he imagined that he would put himself in a better light by protesting that his father bullied him into marrying the delicious Diana when he was thirty-two years old is one of those mysteries—like why Brits overcook their food and don't heat their houses.

But fans of royalty in the United States want the show to go on. They argue that Charles and Diana are, individually, nice people and have something to give. He is thoughtful; she is lovely with sick people. He could come here and show potential vice presidents how to act: show an interest in architecture, music, art, and urban living; comment now and then. Dan Quayle should have followed his lead and stayed away from spelling bees.

Diana could conduct classes for nurses, medical secretaries, and other personnel involved in the care of the sick. She should be asked to impart her magic sympathy to people who have been trained to greet sufferers with a brisk, "How will you be paying for this?"

If they are inclined to stay in the colonies while things chill out at home, they should settle—separately if they wish—in Washington. This is Resurrection City. We forgive everything. Our former mayor, Marion Barry, was caught on FBI tape doing dope and he is a cinch to become His Honor again. Across the river, Oliver North, the famous felon, is thought to be washed in the blood of the Lamb.

What we have here is redemption without contrition. Senator Charles Robb, who is being challenged by North, has been using the Clinton approach—"my wife has forgiven me." Political consultant Ed Rollins, whose career was thought to be over, convinced people he was a liar who never said what he said he said. Now he has more clients than he can handle. Former congressman Tony Coelho quit the House over a financial deal and has come back as Clinton's top campaign consultant.

So Washington is ready for the Windsors. They are forgiven in advance. Let them hum a few bars of "Amazing Grace"—and get the words right as Barry never does. Infidelity, in politics anyway, is common here. We can handle it. ■

FDR's Zest Could Energize Clinton the Victim

—April 16, 1995

It took President Clinton a long time to make up his mind about going to Warm Springs, Georgia, for the fiftieth anniversary of the death of Franklin Delano Roosevelt.

Roosevelt's greatness is beyond dispute, and his memory is burned into many hearts who even today think of him as "the president." But he is also the father of the welfare state, the author of federal programs that are now being clamorously shredded by Republicans. FDR was an unabashed tax-and-spend Democrat, a label his party now is desperately fleeing. Today's Democrats disavow his core belief that government can do everything.

The paradox is that Republicans, despite their abhorrence of his philosophy, have tried to kidnap the incomparable spirit of the man. Ronald Reagan, a man without shame, gratingly invited comparisons. House Speaker Newt Gingrich, who is busy dismantling Roosevelt's legacy, is shamelessly clutching his mantle. In his pretentious State of the Union speech, Gingrich compared his hundred days to the hundred days of Roosevelt. Finally, last Saturday, some eight months after he was invited, Clinton decided to contest custody.

He went to Roosevelt's Little White House, a simple cottage with bare wooden walls and a few ship models scattered about. Inside the door, he could see the no-tech, no-arms wheelchair, a narrow seat backed with wooden slats and no arms. How FDR could revive a country from the Depression and mobilize it for that war from that penitential perch is beyond imagining.

From the White House, Roosevelt went to Warm Springs to regroup. He went originally to learn to walk. He came away, everyone said, having learned to live, to be grateful for every breath he took. He convinced Americans that he "felt their pain," as Clinton so often said during the campaign.

Former president Jimmy Carter told a ceremony commemorating Roosevelt's Four Freedoms organized by the Franklin and Eleanor Roosevelt Institute that his father, a poor farmer, was sure that Franklin Roosevelt cared about him personally.

FDR's triumph as a man was that he simply refused to accept the limitations of polio, a disease that strips a sufferer down to the bones,

313

burns away pride, dignity, and independence. That was the great leveler. Hungry, jobless Americans knew that, like them, he had seen the bottom of life.

But as Governor Zell Miller said in the afternoon's most telling line, "Franklin Delano Roosevelt was never the 'victim' of anything."

In one way, that is a difference between Clinton and Roosevelt. In the fashion of the new age, Clinton lets it all hang out. In his speech to the Democratic convention, accepting the nomination, Clinton told the world of his painful childhood, his brutal stepfather, his victory over fear. This is in keeping with the contemporary cult of victimhood. Roosevelt never spoke of his personal difficulties. He did not, miraculously, feel sorry for himself.

Unlike presidents who came after him, Roosevelt did not represent himself as an icon of virtue. He smoked, he drank, he played poker, and he flirted with pretty women. He did not make heavy weather of his working habits. Nothing interfered with the cocktail hour—he mixed the martinis himself. He also took vacations without making any bones about it. He went off to Hyde Park, he went fishing, he went to Warm Springs.

He liked to sleep late. In this he could be most instructive to the present occupant of the White House, who in his youth trained himself to sleep only four or five hours a night. Roosevelt boasted about sleeping until ten o'clock in the morning when out of Washington. Nor did his staff make a fetish of the sixteen-hour working day that has gripped this White House since its inception. Decisions made on junk food and sleeplessness can sound that way.

Because he was often well rested, Roosevelt could fluff off things that would drive a careful politician like Clinton to seeking oracles, focus groups, and polls.

Doris Kearns Goodwin, in her incandescent biography of the Roosevelt White House in wartime, *No Ordinary Time*, tells of the dilemma that Eleanor Roosevelt posed for her husband. She disagreed with him sometimes, about the pace of progress for women, blacks, Jewish refugees. As a journalist—she wrote a column called *My Day* six times a week—she sometimes carried her dissent into print.

She asked him once if he minded if she said what she thought. "Certainly not," he replied, "you can say anything you want. I can always say, 'Well, that is my wife; I can't do anything about her.'"

He laughed it off, in short.

In the leafy glades of Warm Springs, Clinton may have picked up a few tips from the old master about a zest for life and the light touch. And maybe he learned to embrace a heroic idol, who is still his party's greatest pride. After all, what's he got to lose? ■

Diana's BBC Interview a Case of Indecent Exposure
—November 26, 1995

The Princess of Wales, the Mount St. Helens of the British royal family, has erupted again, leaving hot ashes all over the queen, Prince Charles, her separated husband, and herself. This time she was on the BBC, confessing to adultery and ambition for her older son to inherit the throne.

She sounded like an elegant, updated version of Alec Guinness in *Kind Hearts and Coronets*, a killing comedy from the 1950s about climbing over the dead bodies of nine contenders to claim a dukedom. She just has to off the Prince of Wales to get a crown for her son. But Diana has to be careful about the monarchy, because the succession is the only excuse she has for indecent exposure.

The princess is a child of her times, no question about it. The 1990s is a confessional age. There has been so much self-revelation on both sides of the Atlantic that many people long for Victorian hypocrisy or a deftly executed royal cover-up.

It is all so un-British, the unreserve, the whining. The British are famous for enduring in large matters, such as bombing, and in small, such as missing the bus by a few seconds. I remember a middle-aged woman who puffed up to her London stop just as her bus for Islington was wheezing out. She watched it go and stoically observed there wouldn't be another for thirty-five minutes. She reached down into her innermost being: "We mustn't grumble, must we?" she said brightly.

But Charles and Diana have not hesitated for a moment to bewail the irretrievable disaster of their marriage, to seek allies and partisans, and to encourage hatchet jobs on each other, in print or on air.

The British public is eating it up. It beats Whitewater, the long-running scandal that is our regular fare.

There is some complaint that the material is more soap opera than

315

operatic, but those sniffing about standards have only to think of Henry VIII to be reminded that England's royals have never been expected to act like other people.

Charles continues to date the horsy lady he finds so inexplicably alluring, and Diana goes on looking for love in all the wrong places. It's diverting—except for its supposed beneficiaries, Prince William, thirteen, and his brother, Prince Harry, eleven.

The princes go to school at Eton. Even with top hats, teenage boys are not celebrated for tact and kindness. What do you suppose they say to the royal brothers, the only boys in school whose parents have done matching videos about adultery?

Can you picture the scene in Kensington Palace when the boys are admitted to their mother's boudoir for their daily chat.

"Mummy," asks William, "what is adultery?"

Diana suggests it is not a subject of concern to her sons.

"But," says Harry, "Beastly Minor, who's in my form, says you've done it."

"Darling, you're in my light. Move over a bit. And William, put down that tiara. And stop fidgeting."

William explains that he is studying the Ten Commandments in his "roots" course. "It says you mustn't, that's what 'thou shalt not' means."

"Well, Papa has. I suggest you ask him when you next see him."

"So when Papa is king, it will be all right for everybody, even Beastly Minor's mum and dad? And you'll be queen, right, Mummy?"

"Harry, I didn't say that. Don't you have some French to study?"

"Oui, Maman, but I was wondering, even if Papa let them, would God mind?"

"Papa may not be king, you know. It's not certain."

"Oh, yes, Mummy, the minute anything happens to Granny, he gets the crown. It says in my history book."

"Well, what if someone else did?"

"What would happen to you, Mummy?"

"Darling, I would be the Queen Mother, and I should be queen of hearts, too."

"And William would be king? What about Papa? Would he be in the Tower? Mummy, why are you smiling that way? Mummy?"

No, it's not funny for everyone. We can well understand Diana's rage.

It's crushing to lose out to Camilla Parker-Bowles. She must also find it hard to forgive herself for falling for the caddish cavalryman who turned their affair into a best seller or for being called "Squidgy" on a recorded telephone conversation. And Charles is a bounder.

But Diana mustn't tell herself she's doing anybody any good by her periodic bouts of vituperation, least of all her sons. The young princes are the casualties in this war that so desperately needs a cease-fire.

We are always intrigued by the sight of people who have everything making themselves absolutely miserable. Diana has a palace, two fine boys, and plenty of money. She should be counting her blessings and keeping her mouth shut. ■

New Memorial Doesn't Reflect Roosevelt's Greatness—May 1, 1997

The Franklin D. Roosevelt Memorial, 7½ acres of brown granite and aching political correctness, is opening this weekend for the ages. Why brown for our least drab president? Maybe the creators wanted to show the grimness of his times—depression and world war. FDR is depicted sitting down wearing a cape the size of a compact car. He, too, looks grim, and even a little puzzled. His signature cigarette holder has been taken from him in deference to tobacco haters.

His wife, Eleanor, the first First Lady to make a presidential memorial, has been diminished, too, in the light of latter-day sensibilities. Her bronze likeness not only looks nothing like her, but she also has been divested of her trademark fox fur piece—the animal-rights activists have struck again.

Of course, FDR shouldn't have smoked. But he did. He also drank— excellent martinis of his own making. At the time, his countrymen did not begrudge him his small if dangerous pleasures. He was trying to revive his country; later he had to save the world.

As for Mrs. R, she did not have great style; she was, in fact, dowdy. It hardly mattered. Like her husband, she was on permanent 911 duty. She tugged at his sleeve about people in trouble, children, soldiers, refugees. She was indomitable.

Granite is no good for showing gallantry. Granite is for grandeur, which as a historical figure was Roosevelt's long suit. But the source of his greatness is not shown.

Roosevelt was a force of nature—so ebullient, resilient, optimistic because he survived polio. He lost the use of his legs. He dragged himself across the floor on his stomach when he began to recover. He knew helplessness, indignity. Polio gave him patience and hope.

He went to Warm Springs, Georgia, hoping to learn to walk again. He never could. But at Warm Springs, he learned how to live each day to the fullest.

The wheelchair was the great leveler for this handsome, high-handed, privileged aristocrat. The Dust Bowl farmer or the apple seller had nothing to teach him about loss.

The only sign of a wheelchair in the vast reaches of the memorial is the castors on the bottom of the chair in which he is sitting in his massive statue. They can be seen by peering under the folds of his enormous cape.

There is another reference carved into a stairway in the Fourth Term Room—there is a roofless room for each term. It says he was stricken with polio in 1921 and "never walked again unaided."

The disabled community, led by Michael Deland, has been agitating for a depiction of a wheelchair. The memorial commission, led by Senator Dan Inouye (D-HI), insisted quite rightly that FDR did not want to be shown in his wheelchair. FDR and his press entourage conspired never to show him in his wheelchair. He feared that the metaphor of a cripple leading a nation crippled by depression would be too much.

But now it seems little less than imperative that people see where Roosevelt sat to galvanize government to resurrect an expiring economy and to mobilize the free world.

It is important in a generation of politicians who are stricken with self-pity and given to sniveling. Last week President Clinton, who often feels put upon, stepped into the deadlock between the commissioners and the disabled and ordered the secretary of the interior to arrange that a statue of FDR in his wheelchair be added among the fountains. Congress must approve, and Inouye has graciously offered to lead.

The matter can be easily resolved, with full consideration of FDR's wishes and those who need him so desperately as an icon (that isn't only the disabled, either, we should note): Show the wheelchair without him in it.

Simply take Roosevelt's Warm Springs wheelchair, one of the most moving artifacts of the age, cast it in bronze, life size, and place it in the opening, or First Term, room. There is plenty of space under an inscription from FDR's early writing: "No country however rich can afford the waste of its human resources." No man more exemplified that wisdom.

Interior Secretary Bruce Babbitt is a sensible man, and he will seek an expeditious solution to the problem of letting future generations know how great Roosevelt really was.

A fan of the memorial and one of its largest benefactors, philanthropist Peter Kovler, says his children relate to FDR when he tells them that "Roosevelt beat Adolf Hitler out of a wheelchair."

If the memorial does not give us the personality of FDR, it has better luck showing his times. The statues of a gaunt farm couple and desperate men in a bread line can help Americans get some idea of why Roosevelt has subsumed so many Americans' idea of what a president ought to be.

His park will find its place. As Kovler says, "Maybe children will splash in the fountains."

Americans will flock to Roosevelt; they always did. He may not have been correct, by today's standards, but he was a giant. ■

Pizazz in the Piazza—September 9, 2001

SIENA, ITALY—This Tuscan town not far from Florence is known for its graceful oval square, the Piazza del Campo, which is the site of an insane horse race—a twice-yearly event that draws hysterical horseplayers from all over the world. The square is covered with straw, *paglia*, for the fabulously unfair contest, which is named the Palio. The occasion is the antithesis of Ascot. The whole cast of jockeys, trainers, and flag-throwers wears medieval garb. The jockeys come from ten of the seventeen wards, *contrade*, of the city and have all been blessed at Mass in their parish churches before they go out to display outrageously bad sportsmanship: They whip rival horses and jockeys. I remember the shrieking approval of these tactics from experiencing it long ago. There's none of the English sentimentality about horses and riders. They meet for the first time the frenzied day of the race, a cab driver told me.

When I went back to Siena last month, I found the piazza in the grip of a totally different kind of excitement. For three nights in a row—a run-through in mufti, a dress rehearsal, and, finally, the Sunday night performance itself—the square rang with the melodies of Verdi's *Nabucco*. We heard solos, duets, trios, and a magnificent chorus from the Arturo Toscanini Foundation.

My friend Elizabeth Shannon and I found that opera-going in Siena is not like elsewhere, in that, here, the opera comes to you. We were staying in an apartment overlooking the square—which commanded a wonderful view of everything but the action, which was, in any case, unintelligible: It was about Nabucco, the king of Babylon, who was engaged in hostilities with the Jews as well as with his own daughters, one of whom was really the child of a slave. Italian opera's staple—unsuitable attachments—was much in evidence, with the royal sisters fixed on the same man. A scorecard is useless; it's the music that matters.

The first night, we sat in the square and ate ice cream as Verdi wrapped us in beautiful sounds. A full, bright-orange moon was rising over the crenellated walls of the fourteenth-century bell tower. Stars shone in the dark blue velvet sky; the chorus sang its heart out. The soprano's voice floated like a banner over the choral harmonies, and the baritone's obbligato was like a bell tolling.

A tableful of American men sat next to us. They talked of taxes and surpluses and private vs. public schools. Like some fanatical focus group, they never strayed off message. Liz wondered if they had Verdi with their beer every night back at home. The cast members were wearing shorts and slacks as they portrayed ancient monarchs and traitors. Our neighbors noted nothing. The opera was a distraction they could overcome.

Others were paying fervent attention. Local opera lovers sat on the unforgiving cobblestones, with nothing between them and the ground except a newspaper page or two. They hunched over their librettos. Some stood by the hour at rapt attention a few feet from the orchestra.

Nabucco's haunting chorus, "Va, Pensiero," began. The lament of the Hebrew slaves is Italy's favorite song; many have long felt it should be Italy's national anthem. The rendition provoked a thunder of applause.

The music finally stopped, but the crowd did not. It was hard to tell if exiting members of the orchestra were hijacked for further service, but soon we were hearing the familiar strains of "Avalon." Then, hilariously (Siena was suffering its worst heat in fifty years), a two-saxophone riff on "Jingle Bells." A trumpet turned up and accompanied an enthusiastic, heavily accented "Ain't She Sweet?" (*"Ent Shi Swit?"*). Shucking and jiving broke out as a small but resolute group of English speakers did "Bye, Bye, Blackbird."

I felt sympathy for the mothers of Siena's babies. Verdi's choruses have splendid, rocking, lullaby-like rhythms, but this was a jam session. It was getting on for two in the morning, but there was no sign of Siena's finest. Genoa was under fire at that moment for its G-8 excesses, but Siena saw no reason to stop the fun.

Sunday night was the real thing. The crowd—the daily *Corriere di Siena* put it at twenty thousand—gathered early, and proud Sienese placed torches on the roofs of the medieval buildings that ring the square. The orchestra and the singers were at the top of their game. The conductor radiated verve and mastery. The audience was as still as if in church. The maestro turned ceremoniously to the audience, then back, and gave the downbeat. It was the moment the piazza had been waiting for. The chorus began, a little tentatively, but gathered strength and soon the square was awash in tears and glory.

This was opera, Italian style—not just opera but an experience overflowing with emotion and the feeling of sharing the beauty that makes the world such a fine place. ∎

Beyond Recognition—September 16, 2001

It was not just the New York skyline and the Pentagon that were altered by the hijacked planes. All is changed, "changed utterly" as Yeats said. Nowhere is this more evident than in politics.

Even before the calamity of a lovely September morning, the country was demonstrating its feelings for President Bush in a variety of polls. The two major strains were somewhat contradictory: A high percentage (45 percent) weren't entirely sure that he was up to the job, but said they liked him and wanted him to succeed.

Since the terrorists rammed into our symbols of financial and military might, the country has rallied to the president's side. Even those who wished for a little more initial eloquence from him did not want to hear a word against him. Ask any journalist who raised questions about his early handling of the crisis: They have been inundated with furious calls calling them a disgrace to their profession and even traitors. If Bush lacked eloquence on Tuesday, he more than made up for it with his fine speech at Friday's National Cathedral service.

Congress is well aware that George Bush has become a colossus, surpassing his father's 90 percent approval rating after the Persian Gulf War. Congress has been more than satisfied with a supporting role in the wake of the horror. On Tuesday night members convened and sang "God Bless America" and pledged allegiance to Bush.

Democratic consternation and misgivings have been expressed behind the scenes. When Bush requested blanket authority for retaliation, some remembered the Gulf of Tonkin Resolution, which they unwarily gave to Lyndon Johnson during Vietnam and came to regret. They said the president's current powers give him all the authority he needs to punish the authors of the obscene attacks. But, as one Democrat said disconsolately, "No one wants to say no to Bush now."

The Senate Armed Services Committee could take up the defense bill next week. The inclusion of Bush's request for funds for a national missile defense has prompted extensive debate. Some members hoped to put off such a hot potato.

Although the reverberating calamity had exposed the futility of missile defense in stopping suicidal terrorists, the reluctance of critics to argue with the White House makes it a major opportunity for Bush.

The lock box for the Social Security surplus, the future of the education bill, and similar domestic considerations are for the moment crushed by the graver questions about our future in a world with so many maniacs at large.

Bush was pursuing with obsessive concentration his goal of a protective shield against missiles that would make us even more secure. The protests of our allies dubious about antagonizing Russia and China by ignoring or shredding the Anti-Ballistic Missile Treaty, with its prohibition on deployment, made no difference to Bush.

We were the omnipotent superpower. We didn't mind being thought arrogant and overbearing. We were Number One.

See us now. We are victims. We are covered with dust. We closed our airports and Wall Street, canceled our entertainments. We cry a lot. Hour by hour we sit by the television, transfixed by impossibly brave men who refuse to stop going into shaky, smoldering buildings to search for their comrades and other victims. Our heroes are firefighters, police officers, and rescue workers. The Winston Churchill of the ashes is a scandal-splattered politician named Rudy Giuliani, who presides over city services that are no less than awesome. The terrorists were well-organized, but they were no match for New York. Our most sophisticated city, which thinks it knows it all and has a name for brusqueness, demonstrated a depth of humanity that tells terrorists that they are wasting their time blasting our cities. We are a great nation ready to join the world against evil.

We now stand hat in hand, asking for help. We are vulnerable. But look at our volunteers, our blood donors, the bucket brigades, the outpouring of offers to bombed-out businesses of a hand in relocating. Look at the endless kindness of strangers.

We may be heartbroken, we are playing hurt, but we know we're going to win. ■

Loved Letters Lost—October 28, 2001

The post office crisis, I am taking personally. My father was a post office clerk for forty years in the South Boston branch, and "The mail must go through" was holy writ around my house.

I can still see him on Christmas Eve, exhausted to the point of collapse by the holiday rush. He worked overtime for weeks. The idea of a single card going undelivered by Christmas Day was simply unthinkable to him.

Today, when I look at deserted post offices, at pictures of ceiling-high piles of intercepted letters, I wonder what we have come to. When I read about the anthrax deaths of two employees at the Brentwood Road mail facility, where the bacteria-packed letter addressed to Senate Majority Leader Tom Daschle was sorted, I mourn and protest. Thomas Morris Jr. and Joseph P. Curseen Jr. were both admirable civil servants and model citizens. They were let down by other civil servants—the U.S. surgeon general admitted making a mistake about the need for testing—and inattentive local doctors. Curseen was sent home once from the emergency room.

The anthrax crisis, which many people think was manufactured by home-grown creeps, has brought out the worst in both Washingtons—

the federal city and the town. No class, alas, not like New York, which stood up to the September 11 attacks and revived national spirits. The House of Representatives set the tone by shutting down, a move that can't be justified if you keep certain standards in mind—the New York firefighters, for example, who shouldered their way up the steps of the burning trade towers against a human tide coming down—or ask yourself what Hitler would have said if Parliament had closed up shop during the Battle of Britain.

Constituents told members that they understood the concern for the young people who handle the mail, but they think it would have been a far better thing to send the kids home and find another place to meet—just to show the flag. One lack was sharply felt—a federal shoulder to cry on. Homeland Security czar Tom Ridge, speaking to mayors, inexplicably praised Washington's "rapid identification and treatment." He may be more of an administration cheerleader than comforter in chief. Health and Human Services chief Tommy "We Are Prepared" Thompson is too embroiled in his own controversies to put an informed arm around the victims. The president, after he came back from the Far East, reassured us that he did not have anthrax, but he could offer no other reassurance.

I don't know about public reaction because I haven't seen any office mail since October 17. I don't miss it that much. Recently, I almost drowned in a flood of molten reader response to what I wrote about President Bush's September 11 peregrinations. A right-wing radio talkshow harpy sicked the dogs on me, and I got a great deal of abusive, sometimes unprintable communications questioning my patriotism and my sanity. I composed a form letter of laborious civility pointing out that we still lived in America the Beautiful. One reader answered: "You may have lost your marbles, but you have kept your manners."

But even that cannot cure me of my fondness for letters. I like to write them. I also love reading other people's mail. The letters of Elizabeth Barrett and Robert Browning, who lived in a London of four daily mail deliveries, are among the loveliest ever written. The letters of Abigail and John Adams, who were passionate about their country and each other, are a treasure of American history and literature. What makes those letters unbearably poignant now is that they speak so longingly of a postal system in the country that they were helping to bring into being. Poor Abigail was ever on the watch for someone who could take a letter to her beloved when patriotic duty took John to Philadelphia and later to Paris and London. And here we are now with a system, and it is being ground to powder before our eyes.

That is not the end of my sorrow. Letter writing was already in decline long before September 11. E-mail is irresistible to a generation that is in such a hurry that it would rather have wrong election returns than wait a few hours for the right ones.

Now, nonwriting relatives—particularly young people who find the writing of thank you notes an indescribable imposition—have an excuse. They're sparing you anthrax.

The lesson of the anthrax crisis is the same as the more violent and irretrievable events of September 11: Take nothing for granted. Disruption is your new routine. Don't put your faith in the authorities or in daily trips to your mailbox.

There's no way to go back to my father's time in the post office, when your greatest health hazard was conscientiousness during the holiday season. ■

I, Patient—December 9, 2001

The patients' bill of rights is dead stuck on Capitol Hill, but not dead, according to one of its chief sponsors, Rep. Greg Ganske (R-IA), who thinks it may recover as terrorist-related urgencies recede. Since a blessedly brief stay in a local hospital of the finest reputation, I have become interested in the subject. I thought some basic human rights got short shrift, like the right to sleep and the right to eat.

I also got awfully sick of people asking me to do things "for me." "Hold your arm out for me," they would all say as a preliminary to needling me for more blood. Are they taught that in their training? Is it meant as a bonding device? They all do it ickily. I wanted to say, "I will hold out my arm, but not for you. We don't know each other, and you are going to do something unpleasant to me, and I don't want you to think I am doing anything for you—although I might want to if I knew you better."

I learned on my arrival about the food issue. It was about 3:30 P.M. and I had had an early breakfast and no lunch. I mentioned being hungry to the nurse, who said, "We have nothing to eat on this floor." I wondered aloud if someone might go to the kitchen and rustle up a peanut butter sandwich. She was not amused at my presumption. "The cart has already left," she said. Could we intercept it and maybe steal a roll? She said "I'll put your name in the computer for a early dinner." An hour went by, and I bleated again. She said, "I have put your name in the computer." I gathered this was her generation's idea of chicken soup. When another hour passed and I raised the subject yet again, she took umbrage. "I am a nurse," she said. "I don't have anything to do with the food service." I wanted to ask why she didn't, but forbore.

The night brought out the attitude toward sleep. My blood pressure was jumping around, so they shook me awake every four hours to measure it or take blood. When they weren't there, there was a terrifying surrogate I called the Cobra. It was a harmless-looking cuff on my arm. Every hour, it rattled a bit and then took a powerful grip on my upper arm. When the big chief of the section, followed by an adoring retinue of students, came by the next morning to make cheerful inquiries as to how I was feeling, I answered sullenly, "Exhausted." I quoted my favorite line from Shakespeare—"Sleep that knits up the ravell'd sleave of care." The entourage looked worried. Later, the chief relented and let me sleep six hours at a shot.

In the meantime, I discovered two nurses who were nothing less than ministering angels. One of them was from Thailand, and during her night watches, she told me her story. Her family, caught up in global trade, decreed she should become a bookkeeper. The money was good, she said, but the satisfactions were nil. She wanted to make a difference. Her dream is to go back to her native country and teach nursing students about being kind to patients. The other angel was an infinitely benign Peace Corps returnee, just back from Mongolia, which she loved. I asked her why she thought my blood pressure readings were so variable, and she said, "Maybe because you're in the hospital." I found it very healing.

When I got home, I found a friend had sent me a book that a friend of his had written. It was ideal for the moment. I started it and couldn't stop. It was called *Across the Red Line: Stories from the Surgical Life.* Author Richard C. Karl, chairman of the surgery department at the University of South Florida College of Medicine, was born into the profession—his father was a surgeon. He is also a natural storyteller and writer. Two chapters, one about a patient of his who died after a successful operation, and the other about Dr. Karl's time as a patient, give the flavor of the unusual double perspective. He writes short, pithy sentences and gives a description of an MRI that should speak for everyone who has survived that procedure.

Dr. Karl has an acute sense of patients' rights, and members of Congress would do well to read his book before voting on the matter. I called him to ask if he thought doctors had more trouble admitting their mistakes than other people, and he said that might be the case. The work they do is so intense they develop strong defense mechanisms, and some have never gotten beyond the "doctor is king" concept. I mentioned doctors I have known who got mad at me when I didn't react as predicted to medicines they have prescribed. They cited the American Medical Association and never tried to conceal their impatience with me for bucking the statistics. Some are insecure, he explained; others genuinely arrogant.

Like the rest of us, he hopes that the patients' bill of rights gets out of the chronic care ward and onto the law books, so everyone can understand that patients are very important people. ■

Catholic Church Still in Its Defensive Mode
—April 25, 2002

The age-old formula for a sinner seeking absolution in a Catholic confessional—"Forgive me, Father, for I have sinned"—has been revised during the current scandal.

On the eve of the twelve U.S. cardinals' summit in Rome, Cardinal Edward Egan of New York issued a letter to the faithful in which he changed the formulation to "Forgive me, Father, I may have sinned."

His Eminence went into the passive voice and the subjunctive mood often favored by people in high office who would rather not be discussing the subject at hand. In Egan's case, it was his record as a bishop in Connecticut and New York, where, it is reported, he consistently reassigned pedophiles to various parishes. It was the same shuffle-and-cover-up method used by Cardinal Bernard Law of Boston, whose resignation has been clamorously urged in his home diocese, and, according to the *Los Angeles Times*, has been surreptitiously discussed by his brother cardinals.

Egan's conditional apology would not be accepted in most confessionals and fell far short of the candor and contrition that many Catholics hoped for. "If in hindsight, we also discover that mistakes may have been made as regards prompt removal of priests and assistance to victims, I am deeply sorry."

The "modified, limited hangout" route made famous in Watergate seems to be operative in Rome. The pope, in a weak and halting voice, told the assembled red hats things they already knew, such as that pedophilia is not only a crime but also "an appalling sin in the eyes of God." He offered them ambiguous advice as to the remedy, counseling "zero tolerance" and at the same time an unshaken belief in redemption. Law's presence at the table implied an approval of the methods that so outraged Boston Catholics that their cardinal can go nowhere without being picketed.

The degree of regret and remorse among the red capes is trifling when measured against one of history's most celebrated penitents, Henry II of England, who in 1163 fell into a bitter dispute over the jurisdictions of ecclesiastical and royal courts. He had—inadvertently, he said—condemned Thomas, the archbishop of Canterbury. He cried out, "Who will rid me of this troublesome priest?" Four knights-at-arms immediately saw it as their duty to do the troublesome priest in, and rode to Canterbury to kill Thomas à Becket as he said mass at the high altar.

Henry II didn't use any ifs, ands, or buts in undertaking to seek forgiveness. He did not claim that a lament had been misinterpreted as an order, or that overzealous underlings were to blame. He said that he had done wrong and that he would make amends.

And he did. He walked barefoot to Thomas à Becket's church, the cathedral at Canterbury. He submitted to being scourged by the monks. He changed his way of doing business, restoring independence to church courts.

In Rome, in the papal palace, the mood was defensive rather than penitential. The faithful who were waiting for justice and enlightenment must accept the fact of the meeting as more important than what was said or done.

The greatest pity is that no victims were there to hear the pope's apology for the unspeakable wrongs that had been done to them by men whom they had been brought up to respect. The victims tend to get lost while their clerical elders discuss the tragedy in political terms. The speculation about Law is that the pope keeps him because his resignation might start a domino effect. The three or four lieutenants who carried out the cardinal's orders might have to go, too, producing major Vatican embarrassment.

A seething laity would like to know a few things, for instance: Why did the hierarchy cling to the perfidious priests whom one cardinal called "moral monsters"? Was it because there are so few priests that they felt they had to hang on to the perverts and protect them, even though it meant risking what they feared most, "giving scandal to the church"? Or was it because they did not regard molestation of children as that serious, referring to it as "a dumb thing" or a "lapse"?

No one, at least in public, quoted Christ's view of the matter as reported in Luke 17:1–3: "It were better for him that a millstone were hanged about his neck, and he cast into the sea, than that he should offend one of these little ones." ■

Amateur Sleuths Have Lost Their Chance to Snoop
—July 28, 2002

I can't help thinking what might have been if the House Homeland Security Committee hadn't deleted Attorney General John Ashcroft's plan for an officially amateur version of the CIA. We have been hiring so many baggage scanners we may soon be a nation equally divided between snoopers and snitches. Up to now we had thought Ashcroft saw as our most critical shortages guns and death sentences. We were wrong.

His vision is of a Terrorist Information and Prevention System (TIPS). It was based on the sound premise that there is a James Bond in everyone, and we should out him. You may look at a plumber and see someone who might or might not come when he says he will and charges you seventy-five dollars just to look down the kitchen drain. John Ashcroft looks at that same plumber and sees a terrorist-spotter, gleaning information while he puts his drill down on the delicate table your Aunt Sarah left you.

Similarly, Ashcroft looks at a letter carrier, who also might not come when you expect him to, and he sees 007 with a key to the front door of every apartment building on the block. He can ferret out such information as that a neighbor has removed a "Proud to be an American" sticker from her bumper without a word of explanation.

The postmaster general is against having his people be Ashcroft asterisks. He wrote a letter telling him so. The general seemed to feel that letter carriers have enough to do delivering the mail.

I am partial to post offices because my father worked his heart out in one for forty years, and I am of the dying breed of letter writers. I think letter carriers may be demoralized because they keep hearing that cool people keep in touch via e-mail without the bother of pen, paper, envelope, and stamp.

But to them I say help is on the way. "Infectious greed" has infected cyberspace, and I'm not talking about WorldCom. Just today, when I tapped into the magic box, I had to fight my way through 296 unwanted messages, offering unsought advice on everything from bargain rates on burial plots to getting a free stay in Las Vegas. The postmaster general is right, and Rep. Michael Capuano (D-MA), wrote him a letter—not an e-mail—to commend him.

I have to confess I was most intrigued by the possibility that our principal law enforcement officer would take a hands-on approach to his pet project. That is, I pictured him in an unmarked van, wearing a headset wired for trouble, and rolling around to crisis spots to check on his rookie spooks, Ashcroft's Asterisks. The chances are that he might be summoned to the site of a hot dispute between a householder and a painter about the right shade for the guest room. The painter says she ordered oyster white, but she is sobbing that she distinctly said eggshell.

The attorney general would be equal to the task of mediator; his credentials as an interior designer are well established. Remember that bold girl, the topless aluminum statue in the Great Hall of the Justice Department. Fearing the onset of lewd thoughts among the reporters who were scribbling down his wisdom about detaining suspicious-looking strangers, he draped her in blue. (*Sex and the City*, in its opening show, took up the subject of breast-baring from a different point of view.)

I would have liked to see how Ashcroft adjudicated in the multiple-grandmother deaths that seem to plague some of our no-show artisans.

I would have liked his take on a tiler who was doing his stuff on my small bathroom. He carefully placed some carefully chosen decorative tiles in spots where they could not be seen. I asked if he could relocate them. I was told that was impossible because he was in North Carolina attending his grandmother's funeral. This was her second death to my certain knowledge.

I have not even brought up the subject of the arming of the Asterisks. Knowing Ashcroft's views on the Second Amendment, which he interprets as a call for arms, that may be a silly question. Uniforms? Or a pin that says piously, "I spy for you"?

My air conditioner is kicking up, and I am too busy planning my strategy for the repairman, if I can get him. This torrid summer has him hopping. I'm going to play it as if he is an Ashcroft recruit. He must be very rich, being so busy, and may be into the stock market in a big way and think that Kenneth Lay is misunderstood. I plan to leave in plain sight a copy of the *Weekly Standard*, which I read not because it is right—it is very right-wing—but because it is well written. It has a wonderful, savage parody every week and long discussions about such issues as Ginger Rogers's worthiness to be Fred Astaire's partner. The big thing is this week's cover with its headline, THE COMING WAR WITH SADDAM. That should certify my patriotism.

I am not complaining, but, thank you very much, Mr. Ashcroft, I honestly thought life was complicated enough without your TIPSters. ∎

Blossoms and Bombs—March 16, 2003

Note: This was the last column that Mary wrote.

The hounds of spring are on winter's traces and so, of course, are the dogs of war. Who will win the race?

The signs of spring are everywhere. Snowdrops bloom where snow was banked just yesterday. City workers have turned in their shovels for flats of pansies to plant around our trees.

The sounds of war grow louder every day.

The winter made the natives a little leery of Mother Nature. She was a harridan and a shrew this year, throwing snowstorms like tantrums, one after another. She divided a city already divided between war and peace even more. We split into two subdivisions, the plowed and the unplowed.

Finally, last week, after making sure the mornings were piercingly cold, Mother Nature had a change of heart. The sun came out, and a faint dusting of tender green was seen on bare branches. But George W. Bush and Colin Powell and Condoleezza Rice and Donald Rumsfeld warned us every day that time was running out.

Just when life was becoming more livable, we saw on our home screens the war's progress. We saw troops practicing desert warfare and fighting sandstorms. Administration officials tried to maintain the fiction that war or peace was still an open question. "If the president decides to use force" was the genteel phrase used before the official launched into new details about the "shock and awe" that awaits the Iraqi people.

Spring has a little shock and awe up her sleeve, too. Always does. The slopes off Rock Creek Parkway will soon be carpeted with daffodils. The crocuses and hyacinths will perfume the air. Wait until the stands of azaleas start blazing. Spring really is inevitable.

Mother Nature has her calendar. Rainy season, dry—it's all the same to her. She has everything lined up, ready to go in sequence. Forsythias first, showering gold on every street corner, dandelions fiercely pushing up through cracks in the sidewalk, violets shyly venturing forward.

Mother Nature is like the Pentagon in one respect: She likes everything in profusion. We have 245,000 troops in Kuwait for the invasion offensive; she's got an abundance of beauty in reserve. When the floral show starts to ease off in late May, she opens another front. Unlike Generalissimo Tommy Frank, she does not have to rely on Turkey. She unfurls the redbud, a spectacular burst of lavender that transforms the landscape.

Although you can depend on her to produce her lovely weapons, Mother Nature cannot be programmed. Already, the authorities are conceding that the cherry blossoms will not be in their prime for the festival here, an annual event that draws thousands of visitors. That is, if they're not afraid of retaliatory acts of terrorism once the laser-guided bombs start dropping on Baghdad—with specific instructions, as we understand it, not to kill those children who are on so many minds.

The prime minister of Canada made a sensible suggestion to George Stephanopoulos: The United States should declare victory over Iraq. The strategy of a huge force on the border, inspection teams at work and world pressure bearing down is working—war is not necessary.

He was brushed aside as the troops fought sandstorms, correspondents were "embedded," the United Nations went into overdrive and panic, and Tony Blair contemplated the ruins of his political career.

At this bleak moment, the Irish prime minister, Bertie Ahern, stepped into the picture. He came to the Oval Office bearing shamrocks for the president—and bad news: The United States could not use any Irish air bases unless there was a second Security Council resolution. Talk about shock and awe—and from doting, dependable Ireland.

The Irish people had demonstrated eighty thousand strong in the recent worldwide protest. And the taoiseach was giving the president a timely reminder about friendship in all seasons. Ireland loves America, but Ireland is grateful for Tony Blair's crucial intervention in the Northern Ireland problem and his perseverance. Ahern paid him back by offering what Coleridge called "the sheltering tree of friendship."

The next morning, the president, who a week ago had declared "it's time for people to show their cards," came out into the Rose Garden to say he was shuffling the deck. He was talking about Middle East peace.

For the hounds of spring, it was a great leap forward. We can celebrate St. Patrick's Day toasting Ahern—in French wine, of course. We can rejoice in the coming of spring. ■

Acknowledgments

I t didn't take a village to do this book, but it helped immensely to have the support and encouragement of so many of Mary McGrory's friends and colleagues. There would have been no book without the full cooperation of the *Washington Post*, where Mary was a treasured columnist for more than two decades. The *Post* gave us reprint permission and opened its news library and archives when I needed to locate columns and photos missing from Mary's own files. Donald Graham, chairman of the Washington Post Company, and Leonard Downie Jr., the paper's executive editor, did everything asked of them. So did Tina Toll, Mary's longtime assistant.

I'm also grateful to Robert Pear, a veteran reporter in the *New York Times* Washington bureau, for providing me with copies of Mary's commentaries on the Army-McCarthy hearings from the 1950s. Robert, a devoted friend and former colleague of Mary's at the late *Washington Star,* also was instrumental in finding a permanent home for Mary's papers—the Library of Congress.

Even Mary's estate lawyers, Ruth Flynn and Charles O'Connor, did their part and more. They handled the legal work for the book, stored more than two dozen cardboard boxes containing Mary's columns and papers at their law firm, and provided me with an office from which to work during the weeks I spent in Washington going through those treasure chests.

Mary requested that I give Andrews McMeel Publishing the first refusal on the book because of her loyalty to Universal Press Syndicate, part of the same Kansas City company. Andrews McMeel didn't hesitate, and Dorothy O'Brien, my editor, made the project easier than I had expected.

My greatest source of support and encouragement was my wife, Joyce, who misses Mary as much as I do. ■